Hike
AMERICA™

NORTHERN
CALIFORNIA

Contact

Dear Readers:

Every effort was made to make this the most accurate, informative, and easy-to-use guide-book on the planet. Any comments, suggestions, and corrections regarding this guide are welcome and should be sent to:

Outside America™
c/o Editorial Dept.
300 West Main St., Ste. A
Charlottesville, VA 22903
editorial@outside-america.com
www.outside-america.com

We'd love to hear from you so we can make future editions and future guides even better.

Thanks and happy trails!

NORTHERN CALIFORNIA

An Atlas of Northern California's
Greatest Hiking Adventures

by Dan Brett

The Globe Pequot Press

Guilford, Connecticut

Published by
The Globe Pequot Press
P.O. Box 480
Guilford, CT 06437
www.globe-pequot.com

Produced by
Beachway Press Publishing, Inc.
300 West Main St., Ste A
Charlottesville, VA 22903
www.beachway.com

Cover Design   Beachway Press

Photographer   Dan Brett

Maps designed and produced by Beachway Press

Cover Photo   Index Stock Imagery

Find Outside America™ at **www.outside-america.com**

**Library of Congress Cataloging-in-Publication Data
is available**

ISBN 0-7627-0923-5

Printed in the United States of America
First Edition/First Printing

Acknowledgments

There are many people whose help in various areas is very much appreciated. Advice on which trails to include was given by Susan Tebbe, Dave Atwood, Brenda and Errin Odell, Jen Westenberg, John Mayer, and numerous total strangers whose ranks include the rangers, interpreters, and trail personnel of Northern California's public lands. Thanks to family and friends who offered support and encouragement. Thanks also to those who accompanied me on hikes over the past year and a half: Susan, Brenda, Jen, Daniel Mettke, Peter and Sara Starr, and last but not least Margarete Mettke—who at 85 years young hiked the Fisk Mill to Stump Beach Trail with us. For all of the above reasons and much, much more, I would like to thank my wife and best friend, Mirjam.

A toast to the unsung heroes of the hiking world—those hardy souls who put the "grunt" in grunt work: trail crews. They remove rocks and logs from the path, move dirt, build waterbars and rock walls—often with nothing but hand tools—so that hikers can stroll through the wilderness unimpeded. For all that hard work: Cheers.

Unending gratitude for all those who with open hearts and unbending will have fought, sometimes risking—and sometimes losing—their lives to save what is left of Northern California's natural heritage. They have been arrested, threatened, beaten, and ignored. One was car-bombed, one was crushed—by the falling body of the redwood he was trying to save. Several names come to mind here: Judi Barri, David

"Gypsy" Chain, Darryl Cherney, Josh Brown, and Julia "Butterfly" Hill. To the hundreds more who deserve recognition but are unknown to me, thank you.

Thanks to the very patient souls who edited and guided this work to its final form: Scott Adams, Ryan Croxton, and Marcy Fine. Special applause to Brandon Ray for putting up with the many rounds of hike cues and maps, and remaining cool throughout.

And finally, a tribute to the torn, battered, abused, misused, and damn near indestructible boots that bore me over most of the ground covered in these pages. They have seen rain, snow, saltwater, and nine kinds of hell on adventures in Europe, Africa, and North America. They have now reached the ripe old age of six (that's 72 in people years) and are herewith, officially, retired.

Table of

Contents

Coastal Mountains

Lava Land

Sierra Nevada & Gold Country

The Art of Hiking

HIKES AT A GLANCE

1. Berry Falls Loop
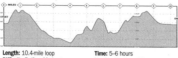
Length: 10.4-mile loop   **Time:** 5–6 hours
Difficulty Rating: Moderate   **Nearby:** Saratoga, CA

2. Old Railroad Grade Trail
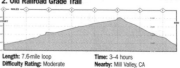
Length: 7.6-mile loop   **Time:** 3–4 hours
Difficulty Rating: Moderate   **Nearby:** Mill Valley, CA

3. Shoreline/Ridge Fire Loop
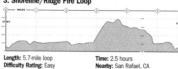
Length: 5.7-mile loop   **Time:** 2.5 hours
Difficulty Rating: Easy   **Nearby:** San Rafael, CA

4. Olompali Trail
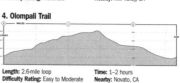
Length: 2.6-mile loop   **Time:** 1–2 hours
Difficulty Rating: Easy to Moderate   **Nearby:** Novato, CA

5. Sky Trail/Laguna Loop
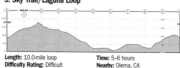
Length: 10.0-mile loop   **Time:** 5–6 hours
Difficulty Rating: Difficult   **Nearby:** Olema, CA

6. Bodega Head Loop
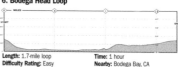
Length: 1.7-mile loop   **Time:** 1 hour
Difficulty Rating: Easy   **Nearby:** Bodega Bay, CA

7. Wolf House Trail
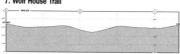
Length: 1.2-mile out-and-back   **Time:** 1 hour
Difficulty Rating: Easy   **Nearby:** Glen Ellen, CA

8. Juniper/Summit Loop
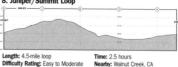
Length: 4.5-mile loop   **Time:** 2.5 hours
Difficulty Rating: Easy to Moderate   **Nearby:** Walnut Creek, CA

9. Willow Slough Trail
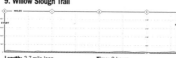
Length: 3.7-mile loop   **Time:** 2 hours
Difficulty Rating: Easy   **Nearby:** Galt, CA

10. Coastal Trail: Fisk Mill to Stump Beach
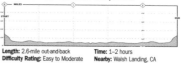
Length: 2.6-mile out-and-back   **Time:** 1–2 hours
Difficulty Rating: Easy to Moderate   **Nearby:** Walsh Landing, CA

11. Russian Gulch Trail
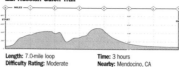
Length: 7.0-mile loop   **Time:** 3 hours
Difficulty Rating: Moderate   **Nearby:** Mendocino, CA

12. Ten Mile Beach Trail
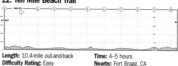
Length: 10.4-mile out-and-back   **Time:** 4–5 hours
Difficulty Rating: Easy   **Nearby:** Fort Bragg, CA

13. Lost Coast Trail
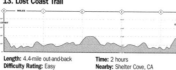
Length: 4.4-mile out-and-back   **Time:** 2 hours
Difficulty Rating: Easy   **Nearby:** Shelter Cove, CA

14. King Peak Trail
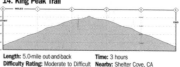
Length: 5.0-mile out-and-back   **Time:** 3 hours
Difficulty Rating: Moderate to Difficult   **Nearby:** Shelter Cove, CA

15. Mattole Beach Trail
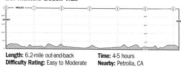
Length: 6.2-mile out-and-back   **Time:** 4–5 hours
Difficulty Rating: Easy to Moderate   **Nearby:** Petrolia, CA

16. Bull Creek Flats Loop
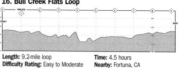
Length: 9.2-mile loop   **Time:** 4.5 hours
Difficulty Rating: Easy to Moderate   **Nearby:** Fortuna, CA

17. Drury-Chaney Loop

Length: 2.5-mile loop
Difficulty Rating: Easy
Time: 1–2 hours
Nearby: Scotia, CA

19. Tall Trees Grove Loop

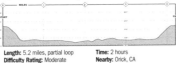

Length: 5.2 miles, partial loop
Difficulty Rating: Moderate
Time: 2 hours
Nearby: Orick, CA

21. Fern Canyon/James Irvine Double Loop

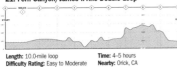

Length: 10.0-mile loop
Difficulty Rating: Easy to Moderate
Time: 4–5 hours
Nearby: Orick, CA

23. Anderson Marsh Loop

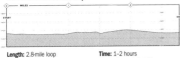

Length: 2.8-mile loop
Difficulty Rating: Easy
Time: 1–2 hours
Nearby: Lower Lake, CA

25. Stuart Fork Trail to Emerald and Sapphire Lakes

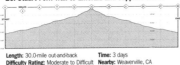

Length: 30.0-mile out-and-back
Difficulty Rating: Moderate to Difficult
Time: 3 days
Nearby: Weaverville, CA

27. Haypress-McCash Loop

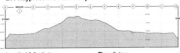

Length: 12.2-mile loop
Difficulty Rating: Moderate to Difficult
Time: 2 days
Nearby: Orleans, CA

29. Devil's Punchbowl Trail

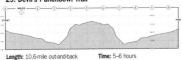

Length: 10.6-mile out-and-back
Difficulty Rating: Difficult
Time: 5–6 hours
Nearby: Hiouchi, CA

31. Horse Camp

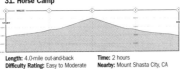

Length: 4.0-mile out-and-back
Difficulty Rating: Easy to Moderate
Time: 2 hours
Nearby: Mount Shasta City, CA

18. Headwaters Trail

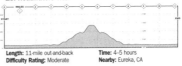

Length: 11-mile out-and-back
Difficulty Rating: Moderate
Time: 4–5 hours
Nearby: Eureka, CA

20. Skunk Cabbage Section of the Coastal Trail

Length: 10.5-mile out-and-back
Difficulty Rating: Moderate
Time: 5-6 hours
Nearby: Orick, CA

22. Damnation Creek Trail

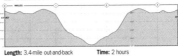

Length: 3.4-mile out-and-back
Difficulty Rating: Moderate to Difficult
Time: 2 hours
Nearby: Crescent City, CA

24. North Yolla Bolly Loop

Length: 12.6-mile loop
Difficulty Rating: Moderate to Difficult
Time: 7–8 hours
Nearby: Wildwood, CA

26. Water Dog Lakes Loop

Length: 14.7-mile loop
Difficulty Rating: Moderate to Difficult
Time: 10 hours
Nearby: Willow Creek, CA

28. Kelsey Trail

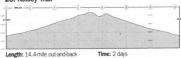

Length: 14.4-mile out-and-back
Difficulty Rating: Moderate to Difficult
Time: 2 days
Nearby: Fort Jones, CA

30. Crags Trail

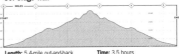

Length: 5.4-mile out-and-back
Difficulty Rating: Moderate to Difficult
Time: 3.5 hours
Nearby: Dunsmuier, CA

32. McCloud River Trail

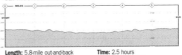

Length: 5.8-mile out-and-back
Difficulty Rating: Easy to Moderate
Time: 2.5 hours
Nearby: McCloud, CA

HIKES AT A GLANCE

33. Burney Falls Trail

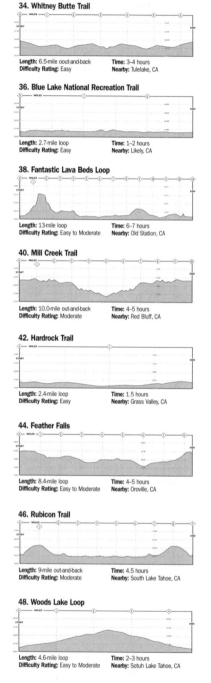

Length: 3.3-mile out-and-back
Difficulty Rating: Easy
Time: 1.5 hour
Nearby: Burney, CA

34. Whitney Butte Trail

Length: 6.5-mile oout-and-back
Difficulty Rating: Easy
Time: 3–4 hours
Nearby: Tulelake, CA

35. Wildlife Viewing Loop

Length: 2.7-mile loop
Difficulty Rating: Easy
Time: 1 hour
Nearby: Alturas, CA

36. Blue Lake National Recreation Trail

Length: 2.7-mile loop
Difficulty Rating: Easy
Time: 1–2 hours
Nearby: Likely, CA

37. Bizz Johnson Trail

Length: 13.4-mile out-and-back
Difficulty Rating: Easy
Time: 6–8 hours
Nearby: Susanville, CA

38. Fantastic Lava Beds Loop

Length: 13-mile loop
Difficulty Rating: Easy to Moderate
Time: 6–7 hours
Nearby: Old Station, CA

39. Chaos Crags Trail

Length: 4.6-mile out-and-back
Difficulty Rating: Moderate
Time: 2.5 hours
Nearby: Mineral, CA

40. Mill Creek Trail

Length: 10.0-mile out-and-back
Difficulty Rating: Moderate
Time: 4–5 hours
Nearby: Red Bluff, CA

41. Monroe Ridge Trail

Length: 3.4-mile loop
Difficulty Rating: Easy to Moderate
Time: 1–2 hours
Nearby: Coloma, CA

42. Hardrock Trail

Length: 2.4-mile loop
Difficulty Rating: Easy
Time: 1.5 hours
Nearby: Grass Valley, CA

43. Independence Trail

Length: 4.2-mile out-and-back
Difficulty Rating: Easy
Time: 2 hours
Nearby: Nevada City, CA

44. Feather Falls

Length: 8.4-mile loop
Difficulty Rating: Easy to Moderate
Time: 4–5 hours
Nearby: Oroville, CA

45. Mount Judah Loop Trail

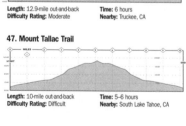

Length: 12.9-mile out-and-back
Difficulty Rating: Moderate
Time: 6 hours
Nearby: Truckee, CA

46. Rubicon Trail

Length: 9-mile out-and-back
Difficulty Rating: Moderate
Time: 4.5 hours
Nearby: South Lake Tahoe, CA

47. Mount Tallac Trail

Length: 10-mile out-and-back
Difficulty Rating: Difficult
Time: 5–6 hours
Nearby: South Lake Tahoe, CA

48. Woods Lake Loop

Length: 4.6-mile loop
Difficulty Rating: Easy to Moderate
Time: 2–3 hours
Nearby: Sotuh Lake Tahoe, CA

49. Bull Run Lake Trail

Length: 7.6-mile out-and-back
Difficulty Rating: Moderate
Time: 4–5 hours
Nearby: Bear Valley, CA

50. South Grove Trail

Length: 4.8-mile loop
Difficulty Rating: Easy
Time: 2–3 hours
Nearby: Arnold, CA

HOW TO USE THIS BOOK

Take a close enough look and you'll find that this little guide contains just about everything you'll ever need to choose, plan for, enjoy, and survive a hike in Northern California. We've done everything but load your pack and tie up your bootlaces. Stuffed with 384 pages of useful Northern California-specific information, *Hike America: Northern California*™ features 50 mapped and cued hikes and 13 honorable mentions, as well as everything from advice on getting into shape to tips on getting the most out of hiking with your children or your dog. And as you'd expect with any Outside America™ guide, you get the best maps man and technology can render. With so much information, the only question you may have is: How do I sift through it all? Well, we answer that, too.

We've designed our Hike America™ series to be highly visual, for quick reference and ease-of-use. What this means is that the most pertinent information rises quickly to the top, so you don't have to waste time poring through bulky hike descriptions to get mileage cues or elevation stats. They're set aside for you. And yet, an Outside America™ guide doesn't read like a laundry list. Take the time to dive into a hike description and you'll realize that this guide is not just a good source of information; it's a good read. And so, in the end, you get the best of both worlds: a quick-reference guide and an engaging look at a region. Here's an outline of the guide's major components.

WHAT YOU'LL FIND IN A *HIKE AMERICA*™ GUIDE. Let's start with the individual chapter. To aid in quick decision-making, we start each chapter with a **Hike Summary**. This short overview gives you a taste of the hiking adventure at hand. You'll learn about the trail terrain and what surprises the route has to offer. If your interest is peaked, you can read more. If not, skip to the next Hike Summary. The **Hike Specs** are fairly self-explanatory. Here you'll find the quick, nitty-gritty details of the hike: where the trailhead is located, the nearest town, hike length, approximate hiking time, difficulty rating, type of trail terrain, and what other trail users you may encounter. Our **Getting There** section gives you dependable directions from a nearby city right down to where you'll want to park. The **Hike Description** is the meat of the chapter. Detailed and honest, it's the author's carefully researched impression of the trail. While it's impossible to cover everything, you can rest assured that we won't miss what's important. In our **Miles/Directions** section we provide mileage cues to identify all turns and trail name changes, as well as points of interest. Between this and our Route Map, you simply can't get lost. The **Hike Information** box is a hodgepodge of information. In it you'll find trail hotlines (for updates on trail conditions), park schedules and fees, local outdoor retailers (for emergency trail supplies), and a list of maps available to the area. We'll also tell you where to stay, what to eat, and what else to see while you're hiking in the area. Lastly, the **Honorable Mentions** section details all of the hikes that didn't make the cut, for whatever reason—in many cases it's not because they aren't great hikes, instead it's because they're over-crowded or environmentally sensitive to heavy traffic. Be sure to read through these. A jewel might be lurking among them.

We don't want anyone, by any means, to feel restricted to just the routes and trails that are mapped here. We hope you will have an adventurous spirit and use this guide as a platform to dive into Northern California's backcountry and discover new routes for yourself. One of the simplest ways to begin this is to just turn the map upside down and hike the course in reverse. The change in perspective is fantastic and the hike should feel quite different. With this in mind, it will be like getting two distinctly different hikes on each map.

For your own purposes, you may wish to copy the directions for the course onto a small sheet to help you while hiking, or photocopy the map and cue sheet to take with you. Otherwise, just slip the whole book in your backpack and take it all with you. Enjoy your time in the outdoors and remember to pack out what you pack in.

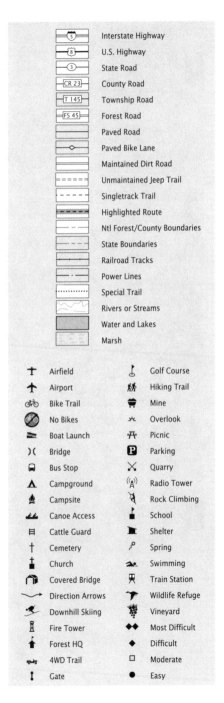

	Interstate Highway
	U.S. Highway
	State Road
CR 23	County Road
T 145	Township Road
FS 45	Forest Road
	Paved Road
	Paved Bike Lane
	Maintained Dirt Road
	Unmaintained Jeep Trail
	Singletrack Trail
	Highlighted Route
	Ntl Forest/County Boundaries
	State Boundaries
	Railroad Tracks
	Power Lines
	Special Trail
	Rivers or Streams
	Water and Lakes
	Marsh

†	Airfield	⚑	Golf Course
✈	Airport	🚶	Hiking Trail
🚲	Bike Trail	⛏	Mine
🚫	No Bikes	↙	Overlook
⛵	Boat Launch	🎋	Picnic
)(	Bridge	**P**	Parking
🚌	Bus Stop	✕	Quarry
▲	Campground	((A))	Radio Tower
⚘	Campsite	⚐	Rock Climbing
⚓	Canoe Access	⚑	School
⊟	Cattle Guard	▬	Shelter
†	Cemetery	⌀	Spring
⚑	Church	⚲	Swimming
⛪	Covered Bridge	⚑	Train Station
⤳	Direction Arrows	⤙	Wildlife Refuge
⛷	Downhill Skiing	❦	Vineyard
⚑	Fire Tower	◆◆	Most Difficult
⚑	Forest HQ	◆	Difficult
🛺	4WD Trail	□	Moderate
⚑	Gate	●	Easy

HOW TO USE THESE MAPS Map Descriptions

1 Area Locator Map

This thumbnail relief map at the beginning of each hike shows you where the hike is within the state. The hike area is indicated by the white star.

2 Regional Location Map

This map helps you find your way to the start of each hike from the nearest sizeable town or city. Coupled with the detailed directions at the beginning of the cue, this map should visually lead you to where you need to be for each hike.

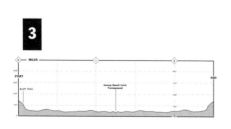

3 Profile Map

This helpful profile gives you a cross-sectional look at the hike's ups and downs. Elevation is labeled on the left, mileage is indicated on the top. Road and trail names are shown along the route with towns and points of interest labeled in bold.

4 Route Map

This is your primary guide to each hike. It shows all of the accessible roads and trails, points of interest, water, towns, landmarks, and geographical features. It also distinguishes trails from roads, and paved roads from unpaved roads. The selected route is highlighted, and directional arrows point the way. Shaded topographic relief in the background gives you an accurate representation of the terrain and landscape in the hike area.

Hike Information (Included in each hike section)

🕐 Trail Contacts:

This is the direct number for the local land managers in charge of all the trails within the selected hike. Use this hotline to call ahead for trail access information, or after your visit if you see problems with trail erosion, damage, or misuse.

🕐 Schedule:

This tells you at what times trails open and close, if on private or park land.

💲 Fees/Permits:

What money, if any, you may need to carry with you for park entrance fees or tolls.

Ⓝ Maps:

This is a list of other maps to supplement the maps in this book. They are listed in order from most detailed to most general.

Any other important or useful information will also be listed here such as local attractions, outdoor shops, nearby accommodations, etc.

A note from the folks behind this endeavor...

We at Outside America look at guidebook publishing a little differently. There's just no reason that a guidebook has to look like it was published out of your Uncle Ernie's woodshed. We feel that guidebooks need to be both easy to use and nice to look at, and that takes an innovative approach to design. You see, we want you to spend less time fumbling through your guidebook and more time enjoying the adventure at hand. We hope you like what you see here and enjoy the places we lead you. And most of all, we'd like to thank you for taking an adventure with us.

Happy Trails!

Introduc

Introduction

Welcome to the wild variety of Northern California hiking! Whether you like it wet, dry, high, low, perfectly level, or very nearly vertical, there's something here for you. Hiking is a wonderful way to explore this diversity because it takes you to places where no roads go, where California's natural beauty remains "untrammeled by man." These trails will take you to roaring waterfalls, silent glades, and wind-whipped peaks. They'll show you alpine meadows swarming with dragonflies and deep verdant forests where ferns grow head-high and colossal trees stand like pillars holding up the sky. And they'll consistently bring you to places where the traces of history seem close enough to touch.

The purpose of this guidebook is to offer readers an opportunity to explore Northern California's many facets. Rather than just throwing together a collection of pleasant hikes, the intent has always been to present excellent hikes that do justice to the history, natural diversity, and character of this region. What you have in your hands is a guidebook to Northern California…by foot. There are hikes here for every level of experience, and at least three of them are wheelchair accessible. Most are day hikes, with some overnighters here and there, and even a couple three-day tours tossed in for good measure.

Northern California Weather

The weather in Northern California is every bit as varied as the landscapes. Along the coast, the Pacific Ocean produces the mild, wet weather that sustains the temperate rainforest of coast redwoods. While the loss of much of this forest has noticeably altered weather patterns in the past 50 years, it is still known for wet winters and foggy summers. Along the Lost Coast, precipitation averages over 100 inches per year, with up to 200 inches in wet years. Thick summertime fog and mild winters help to buffer large temperature swings and account for the milder climate in the coastal regions. (By way of example, the average temperature in San Francisco ranges between 50°F and 60°F.)

A string of mountains stretches nearly unbroken the length of Northern California, creating a rain shadow that leaves the rest of the region considerably drier. The Siskiyou, Klamath, Trinity Alps, Yolla Bolly, and smaller mountain ranges to the south all experience dry, hot summers and wet winters, with heavy snowfall in elevations over 3,000 to 4,000 feet. Temperatures east of the coast ranges can range from well over 100°F in summer to well below zero in winter. The Sacramento Valley goes from hot and sunny in summer to warm and sunny in winter, with cold winter weather increasing as you move north toward the Mount Shasta area.

Along the eastern edge of Northern California, another, larger mountain chain rises up—consisting in equal parts of the volcanic Cascade Range, in the north, and the uplifted Sierra Nevada in the south. Weather in these mountains tends to be slightly wetter on the west side than on the east, as what little moisture escaped the coast range gets trapped by these taller peaks. Modoc and Lassen counties, on the edge of the Great Basin, are dry and hot in summer, with huge snow loads in winter (up to 40 feet in Lassen Volcanic National Park!). The Sierra Nevada and Klamath area mountains also receive a lot of snow, and trails in these areas may be inaccessible from October until well into June. Weather at higher elevations is unpredictable at any time of the year, and rapid temperature changes occur frequently—midsummer snow-storms in the Sierra are not unheard of! To be safe, it is wise to carry a layer of warm clothing and raingear when travelling in any mountainous areas.

Flora and Fauna

With as many microclimates and diverse weather patterns as Northern California has, it's no wonder the vegetation and wildlife vary as much as they do. Of the over 5,000 native plants in California, more than a third of them are endemic to the state.

Sagebrush and pine forests are characteristic of the northeastern corner of the state, where plants must be able to tolerate the meager precipitation and intense summer heat. Jeffrey and ponderosa pines dominate higher elevations, while groves of quaking aspen cluster around streams and springs, and long-leaf mountain mahogany shares dry plains with the sweet-smelling sage. The north coast is famous for its redwood trees—the tallest living things on earth. Under the thick, emerald canopies of these giants, sword ferns carpet the forest floor, occasionally making room for clover-like redwood sorrel, and shade-tolerant tanoak, big-leaf maple, and pungent California laurel.

The Central Valley, once a vast wet plain filled with marsh, lakes, and dense groves of valley oak, is now given over mostly to agriculture, and drained by a network of man-made canals. Little of the original habitat remains, making the isolated groves of valley oak one of the most endangered habitats in the state.

The coast between San Francisco and the Lost Coast alternates between brushy chaparral, coastal scrub, and forested headlands, depending very much on the local microclimates. In the coast ranges, forests become more mixed, with red and Douglas fir, Sitka spruce, incense cedar, sugar pine, and several oak species sharing the space with manzanita and wildflower-filled, grassy meadows. The Klamath region contains a variety of soil types, geology, elevation, and weather patterns that are particularly favorable for conifers. In one small area, 17 species are found growing side by side, creating an astounding pool of diversity that includes several endemic plant species.

The slopes of the Sierra Nevada are divided into five life zones, each with its own distinct flora. The lowest zone, known as foothill oak woodland, is a very prevalent habitat in the state, found on the golden rolling hills around the edge of the Central Valley, the Bay Area, wine country, and the foothills of most mountain ranges. Airy, scattered forests of oak and digger pine are typical of these areas. About half of the 20 or so oak species native to California are endemic to the state, and—unlike oaks in general—all but four of them keep their leaves all year. The small leaves of these ever-green oaks make them drought tolerant, a trait that—together with their general abundance—made acorns a primary source of food for California Indians prior to the influx of European-American settlers.

The next life zone in the Sierras is the lower montane zone, home to Jeffrey pine, Douglas fir, and black oak, as well as some 75 isolated groves of giant sequoia. These are the largest trees on earth, in terms of sheer mass, and are not be confused with their taller but thinner cousins, the coast redwoods. The upper montane zone sees more moisture than lower levels—mostly in the form of snow—and predominantly grows lodgepole pine and red fir, with some bush chinquapin and Sierra juniper mixed in. The subalpine zone hosts whitebark pine and mountain hemlock, often twisted into bizarre shapes by the brutal wind and heavy snow. Above the timberline is the alpine zone, with its low-growing, extremely hardy plants and colorful wildflowers.

Wildlife in the region is easily as impressive as the flora. Half of the insects and invertebrates in the state are endemic, as are 65 of the more than 1,000 native vertebrates. Many of these species have adapted to specific environments. The marbled murrelet and spotted owl, for example, are limited to old-growth forests on the north coast. Wolverine—recently confirmed after years of uncertainty—live in secluded mountain areas, extremely sensitive to habitat loss and human encroachment. Wetlands, scattered along the coast, around the San Francisco Bay Area, and up and down the Sacramento Valley, provide important feeding and breeding grounds for migratory birds, including sandhill cranes, snow geese, and American coot. Osprey nest in the broken tops of tall trees near the rivers they fish.

Tule elk, once numbering in the tens of thousands, were hunted to near extinction before being protected. On the road to recovery, they now survive in protected areas in the Sacramento Valley. A close cousin, the Roosevelt elk, lives in the forests and mountains of the north coast, particularly around Prairie Creek Redwoods State Park. Their numbers are also growing, and herds are spreading into areas to the east and south. Grizzly bears—symbol of the state and once widespread—have been extinct here since the 1920s, but its smaller cousin the black bear is well represented. Mountain lions, seldom seen, roam throughout the state, wherever deer are abundant. Bobcats, coyotes, ravens, raccoons, and skunks are also common. In addition to wolverines, several members of the weasel family are found in forests, including weasels, marten, fisher, and badger. River otter and the larger sea otter play and hunt in secluded waterways and along the coast, respectively.

Seals and sea lions are a common sight along the coast and in coastal estuaries. Harbor seals are the most visable, but California sea lion and northern sea lion are also abundant. Largest of the lot, northern elephant seals can be seen on the coast just south of San Francisco, where they breed. Whale watchers can observe the yearly migrations of the gray whale from any high spot along the coast. Point Reyes, Bodega Head, Klamath, and Crescent City are especially good locations for this.

While threatened by logging, agricultural runoff, dams, and over-development, California's rivers still host impressive seasonal salmon runs. Sockeye, coho, and chinook are some of the monsters that make their way from the ocean up rivers and streams to spawn in the headwaters where they were born.

Wilderness Restrictions/Regulations

Northern California has 11 national forests and two national parks, with 21 wilderness areas between them. Additional wilderness land is managed by the National Park Service, the Bureau of Land Management, and the California state park system. These lands are maintained as reserves of undeveloped land with important biological, cultural, economic, and recreational value. The trick for these agencies is to balance human use without compromising the health and wild character of the wilderness. Permits, access quotas, and fees are part of this effort.

Rules and regulations vary dramatically from region to region, generally becoming stricter with increased use—and consequent potential damage—of the wilderness. Out of the way areas such as the South Warner or Yolla Bolly/Middle Eel Wilderness often require no permits for hikers, while others may require free self-serve permits for overnight use. Heavily visited places like the Sierra Nevada wilderness areas must monitor and regulate use to avoid—or at least reduce—permanent damage. For example, Desolation Wilderness near Lake Tahoe requires fees and permits for all use, including day hikes, as well as for trailhead parking. Due to the ever-present fire danger, campfire permits are required on most public land throughout the state.

Before heading into the backcountry, call the land management agency responsible for your destination, and inquire about permits and regulations that may apply. Staff will often make recommendations about human waste disposal, bear behavior, and campsites that will minimize any negative impact you may have on the wilderness. Please heed this advice, follow regulations, and get required permits. It may seem like a pain, but with six billion people on the planet, wilderness is becoming an increasingly precious commodity. Help keep the wilderness wild.

Thanks for purchasing *Hike America*™: *Northern California*!

Dan Brett
April 2001

Getting around Northern California

● AREA CODES

The coastal areas roughly from Santa Rosa north are covered by the **707** area code, while areas west of the coast range fall under area code **530**, from the Oregon border south to Lake Tahoe. The Sierra Nevada and Gold Country counties south of Tahoe and Interstate 80 fall under area code **209**. The immediate Sacramento area is served by area code **916**, while the Bay Area is split into six area codes: **415** (San Francisco and North Bay), **510** (Oakland), **925** (East Bay), **408** (San Jose and Silicon Valley), **831** (Santa Cruz), and **650** (San Mateo County).

● ROADS

In California, call CalTrans at 1–800–427–ROAD or visit them at *www.dot.ca.gov/hg/roadinfo* for road conditions, closures, and construction status. Also look up *www.ceres.ca.gov/flood/fmap/ncal.html* for updated flood and weather-related road information.

● BY AIR

San Francisco International Airport (SFO) is the region's main airport; a number of smaller airports throughout the state have connections through San Francisco International. When traveling to the Lake Tahoe area, visitors may find it more convenient to fly directly to Reno, Nevada. A travel agent can best advise you on the cheapest and/or most direct way to connect from wherever you're departing. They can also arrange transportation from the airport to your final destination.

To book reservations online, check out your favorite airlines' website or search one of the following travel sites for the best price: *www.cheaptickets.com*, *www.expedia.com*, *www.previewtravel.com*, *www.priceline.com*, *www.travel.yahoo.com*, *www.travelocity.com*, *www.trip.com*—just to name a few. Many of these sites can connect you with a shuttle or rental service to get you from the airport to your destination.

● BY BUS

Greyhound services most major towns and cities in Northern California. Schedules and fares are available online at *www.greyhound.com* or by phone at 1–800–231–2222. A few areas that are off the Greyhound routes, such as the Mendocino Coast, are connected to the network by local buses. Many hiking trails in the San Francisco Bay Area are accessible by public transportation; an excellent online resource for this information is the Bay Area Transit Guide, *www.transitinfo.org*.

● BY TRAIN

Since the early 1990s, California has aggressively worked to expand Amtrak rail service by providing new trains and connecting them to off-line cities with coordinated bus connections. Amtrak's **Capitol Corridor** trains provide frequent service between San Jose, Oakland, and Sacramento; Amtrak Thruway Buses connect these trains to many other destinations including San Francisco, Napa Valley, Santa Cruz, and Lake Tahoe. Amtrak information and reservations are available online at *www.amtrak.com* or by phone at 1–800–872–7245.

The **Coast Starlight** train starts in Los Angeles and serves Oakland, Sacramento, Redding, and Dunsmuir on its way to Seattle. The **California Zephyr** is a long distance train that starts in Chicago and ends in Oakland, stopping in Sacramento and Truckee. **San Joaquin Trains** run from Oakland to the Central Valley with bus connections to Yosemite National Park and Los Angeles. More regional services include **Caltrain**, a commuter rail that runs down the San Mateo Peninsula from San Francisco to San Jose and Gilroy; check out *www.caltrain.org*. **Altamont Commuter Express** (*www.acerail.com*) operates rush hour service from Stockton to San Jose.

❷ VISITOR INFORMATION

For visitor information or a travel brochure, call the California Division of Tourism at 1–800–GOCALIF or visit their website at *www.gocalif.ca.gov*. The state's official site is *www.ca.gov*.

The Hikes

Bay Area & Wine Country

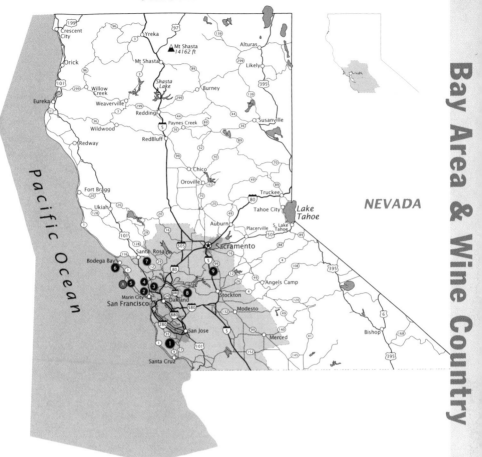

OREGON

Mt Shasta
14162 ft

NEVADA

Pacific Ocean

Lake Tahoe

The Hikes	**Honorable Mentions**
Berry Falls Loop **1.**	**A.** Drake's Estero Trail
Old Railroad Grade Trail **2.**	
Shoreline/Ridge Fire Loop **3.**	
Olompali Trail **4.**	
Sky Trail/Laguna Loop **5.**	
Bodega Head Loop **6.**	
Wolf House Trail **7.**	
Juniper/Summit Loop **8.**	
Willow Slough Trail **9.**	

Bay Area & Wine Country

Dominated by the San Francisco Bay and the cities that surround it, this area is also well endowed with hundreds of miles of hiking trails. The geography of the region—with its extensive waterfront and high, rolling hills—has kept development mostly concentrated along the shores and lowlands, at least until relatively recently. As a result, there's a lot of public park land located surprisingly close to urban areas, giving the recreation-minded Northern Californians plenty of variety and room to play.

The peninsula south of San Francisco sports several state parks, including Big Basin Redwoods State Park—home to fine groves of coast redwoods, and representing the southern end of that tree's historic range. On the east side of the bay, Mount Diablo rises up above the fog, offering impressive views of the surrounding terrain—even as far as Yosemite National Park on clear days. Trails crisscross the park's grassy hillsides and sparse forests, giving hikers a taste of wilderness within sight of the east bay's urban sprawl.

The broad, low valleys north of the bay mark the beginning of Wine Country, where lowlands are dominated by row upon row of grape vines, and young urban professionals cruise from one wine-tasting to the next in polished SUVs. Tucked in among the carefully maintained quaintness, however, are several trails rugged enough to tempt the lug-soled crowd this way. Among other destinations, historic Jack London State Park offers a network of hiking trails (some of which pass through vineyards).

The mountains north of the Golden Gate Bridge are chock full of hiking opportunities. Much of this land falls under the jurisdiction of the Golden Gate National Recreation Area, supplemented by Muir Woods National Monument and Mount Tamalpais State Park. The summit of Mount Tam (as the locals refer to it) offers some of the best views of the bay and surrounding countryside, and is flanked by miles of great trails.

On the coast, the Golden Gate National Recreation Area leads north all the way up to Point Reyes National Seashore—a huge triangle of land neatly separated from the rest of California by the San Andreas Rift. Point Reyes is host to a myriad of microclimates, habitats, and landscapes, including fog-bound shaggy forests, open grassy meadows, rocky hillsides, and miles of gorgeous beaches. One of dozens of possible routes, the Sky-Laguna Loop manages to visit several of these landscapes in a single 10-mile loop.

Overview

Berry Falls Loop

This much-loved trail makes a loop through the heart of Big Basin Redwoods State Park—the oldest of California's state parks. The path follows the courses of fern-carpeted Berry and West Waddell creeks, where plenty of banana slugs, salamanders, and other slimy critters will keep you company. The highlight of the trail is a series of unusual waterfalls on Berry Creek. *(See page 14.)*

Old Railroad Grade Trail

Mount Tamalpais, or Mount Tam as locals call it, has been attracting wanderers for more than a century. There is a little of everything here, including open grasslands, dense laurels, redwood- and fern-filled canyons, and oak knolls. The trail follows the path of an old railroad, and hikers can still see some vestiges of the line along the path. One such remnant is the historical West Point Inn, which was built by the railroad, and is still open for business. Hikers are encouraged to stop by this novel spot for refreshments. *(See page 20.)*

Shoreline/Ridge Fire Loop

The Shoreline/Ridge Fire Loop begins at the remnants of a turn-of-the-century Chinese shrimp-fishing village and explores the dry, oak-woodland hills of the San Francisco Bay Area. The pleasant series of loops provides hikers with plenty of options for longer or shorter hikes. Gorgeous views of San Pablo and San Francisco bays put the visual icing on the trail's cake. *(See page 26.)*

Bay Area & Wine Country

Olompali Trail

This hike strolls through 4,000 years of very colorful history. Beginning as a Coast Miwok village, Olompali Park has a history that continues through Spanish missions, cattle ranches—and even a hippie commune that was once home to the Grateful Dead! An interpretive booklet from the visitor center explains the park's history in greater detail. *(See page 32.)*

Sky Trail/Laguna Loop

This is a strenuous hike, but it offers plenty of variety in return for its toughness. Beginning in dense forest, the trail passes through several native habitats and a recovering burn zone along the way to the beach on Drake's Bay. The trail makes a stop at the summit of Mount Wittenberg, and a short detour takes hikers to Sculptured Beach. Two hike-in campgrounds and a youth hostel are on or near the route, so this trail is perfect for easy overnight trips. *(See page 38.)*

Bodega Head Loop

Spectacular views of the ocean, pocket beaches, and rugged cliffs await hikers on this quick loop around Bodega Head. The wildlife-minded can observe rare birds, gray whales, and sea lions with binoculars from the rocky promontory, which juts out into the Pacific. *(See page 44.)*

Wolf House Trail

This hike is a pleasant walk through meadows and oak forests to the ruins of Jack London's dream house, Wolf House, which burned down before it could be occupied by the famous author. A spur trail leads to London's grave. And the House of Happy Walls contains a museum and visitor center that houses many of the London's personal belongings and photographs. *(See page 50.)*

Juniper/Summit Loop

The loop explores the summit and upper slopes of Mount Diablo, passing through several different habitats and interesting geological features along the way. The north side of the mountain burned in a 1977 forest fire but is recovering nicely. And although the summit is only 3,849 feet high, fans claim you can see more of the Earth's surface from here than from any other peak in North America. On a clear day, you can even make out Half Dome in Yosemite National Park, over 130 miles to the east. *(See page 56.)*

Willow Slough Trail

This ancient valley oak forest is one of the last in California, making it the one of the rarest landscapes in the state. Aside from the trees, many bird species—including the rare sandhill crane—use the preserve as a way station along migratory routes. Others live here full time. Beaver, river otters, and mountain lions also make their homes here. *(See page 62.)*

Berry Falls Loop

Hike Specs

Start: From the Redwood Trail tailhead
Length: 10.4-mile loop
Approximate Hiking Time: 5.5–6 hours
Difficulty Rating: Moderate due to good trails, but there are some steep sections
Terrain: Dirt path along richly forested hills, dry ridges, and waterfalls
Elevation Gain: 2,598 feet
Land Status: State park
Nearest Town: Saratoga, CA
Other Trail Users: Hikers only
Canine Compatibility: Dogs not permitted

Getting There

From San Jose: Head south seven miles on CA 17 from the junction of I-280, and exit onto CA 9 at the Saratoga exit. Head west four miles on CA 9 to the suburb of Saratoga. Follow CA 9 as it turns left and passes through the shopping district before heading out of town. Continue on CA 9 out of Saratoga and up into the Santa Cruz Mountains, climbing seven miles to the ridge and the junction with CA 35. Cross the ridge and continue down the other side another 5.5 miles on CA 9, then take the right fork onto CA 236 at the sign for Big Basin Redwoods State Park, continuing another 3.3 miles to the park headquarters and visitor center. Turn right into the day-use area, and park in the first parking lot on the left. The trail starts on the west side of the parking lot. • **From Santa Cruz:** Head north 13 miles on CA 9 to the town of Boulder Creek, and turn left onto CA 236. Follow CA 236 another 10 miles to the park headquarters. Turn left into the day-use area, and left again into the first parking lot. The trailhead is on the west side of the lot. • **Public Transportation:** Santa Cruz Metro route No. 35 runs to Big Basin Redwoods State Park from Santa Cruz on weekends only. Call (831) 425-8600 for more information, or check out www.scmtd.com for the current schedule. **DeLorme: Northern California Atlas & Gazetteer:** Page 115 C4

The Berry Falls Loop starts at the Redwood Trail trailhead, just across from the Big Basin Redwoods State Park visitor center on the west side of the parking lot. This area is the hub of activity in the park, and there are apt to be crowds on most days. But don't worry. The well-developed network of over 80 miles of trail helps disperse hikers away from the visitor center. This path follows a short section of the Redwood Trail through a showcase grove of the giant trees before crossing Opal Creek and heading south along the opposite bank.

The trail soon shows its true character. The path begins to climb deeper into the forest via a series of switchbacks, and from here, the terrain becomes steeper and the trails more convoluted. The path spends most of its time climbing, descending, or following the contours of hillsides above various creeks. At the junction with the Middle Ridge Road, a sign warns hikers that the trail to Berry Falls is a strenuous one, not suited for a casual stroll. The trail drops down into the West Waddell Creek drainage, first following Kelly Creek then West Waddell Creek downstream to Berry

Creek and the falls. Incidentally, Waddell Creek takes its name from early lumberman William Waddell, who, in the 1860s, built a sawmill near the mouth of the creek, on what is now Waddell Beach. While in the area, in the mid 1870s, Waddell was mauled to death by a grizzly bear—this being when grizzlies still roamed the park in abundance.

During that same time period, the redwoods enjoyed relative security. As recently as 1875, redwood forests covered 53 percent of the land in Santa Cruz County. Members of a Spanish expedition first spotted the giant trees in 1769,

San Jose, at the heart of high-tech Silicon Valley, is the 11th largest city in the United States.

but it was many years before technology had advanced to the point where loggers could profitably harvest the redwoods on a large scale. Even the early 1800s saw lumberjacks milling the logs using a two-person hand saw—a practice that was slow and labor-intensive. But the logging industry was revolutionized in 1840 when the first water-powered sawmill was built north of Santa Cruz on the San Lorenzo River. This industrial advance signaled the end of the redwoods' reign. And by the turn of the century, the groves of Big Basin were some of the last old-growth redwood stands in the county.

Of all the redwood parks in the California State Park system, Big Basin is the oldest. In fact, the park—which contains the largest contiguous stand of coast redwoods south of San Francisco—was the first state park in California. Following a fire in the Santa Cruz Mountains in 1899, local conservationists became interested in saving the last large grove of redwoods from the logger's axe—a threat even greater to the redwoods than fire. The campaign was led by poet and writer Josephine Clifford

Big Basin Redwoods State Park from the ridge east of the park.

15

MilesDirections

0.0 START at the Redwood Trail trailhead. Follow Redwood Trail straight past the restrooms and across Opal Creek via the footbridge.

0.1 Turn left onto Skyline to the Sea Trail.

0.2 The trail veers away from Opal Creek and begins to climb the hill to the right.

0.8 Skyline to the Sea Trail crosses Middle Ridge Fire Road, which runs along the ridge to the left and right. Go straight, continuing down on Skyline to the Sea Trail toward Berry Creek Falls.

1.3 The Sunset/Skyline to Sea Connector Trail heads off to the right. Continue straight on Skyline to the Sea Trail.

2.0 Cross Kelly Creek via a wooden footbridge and continue downstream.

2.2 A short alternate trail goes off to the right. Continue straight.

2.4 The alternate trail rejoins the main path. Continue straight, heading downstream.

2.8 Timms Creek Trail heads right. Continue straight on Skyline to the Sea Trail.

3.7 *[FYI. On the other side of the boulder, to your right, is a 40-foot sheer drop. It's worth a look, but be careful.]*

4.0 The trail descends on wooden steps to West Waddell Creek and crosses the creek on two footbridges. Veer left on the other side, and continue downstream.

4.1 Turn right onto the Berry Creek Falls Trail. (Skyline to the Sea Trail continues left to Rancho del Oso.) Continue uphill toward the falls.

4.2 The trail climbs a little to the Berry Creek Falls overlook. *[FYI. Berry Creek Falls is just over 60 feet tall.]* From here, follow Berry Creek Falls Trail as it continues upstream.

4.6 The trail reaches Silver Falls, which is not quite as tall as Berry Creek Falls, but still impressive. *[FYI. The creek is an unusual color due to oxidized minerals in the ground.]* Follow the trail as it climbs wooden stairs to the top of the falls.

4.7 The trail passes Golden Cascade. *[FYI. This waterfall gets its name from the reddish-yellow color of the rock, and the waterslide shape that plunges down in a series of consecutive small drops.]* Above the Golden Cascade, the trail climbs to the drier forest on the ridge.

5.1 A short trail to Sunset Camp heads left. This junction marks the end of Berry Creek Falls Trail, and the beginning of Sunset Trail. Continue straight along Sunset Trail.

5.3 The trail crosses a small outcropping of white sandstone, surrounded by chaparral.

7.0 Timms Creek Trail heads right at a fork in the trail. Continue to the left, on the Sunset Trail.

9.1 Sunset/ Skyline to the Sea Connector Trail heads right at a fork in the trail. Take the left fork, continuing on Sunset Trail.

9.5 The trail crosses Middle Ridge Fire Road. Continue straight on Sunset Trail toward park headquarters.

9.9 Sunset Trail dead-ends into Dool Trail. Turn right and follow Dool Trail to Opal Creek.

10.0 Dool Trail dead-ends into Skyline to the Sea Trail at Opal Creek. Turn right onto Skyline to the Sea Trail and follow it downstream.

10.3 The trail reaches the junction with Redwood Trail. Turn left onto Redwood Trail and cross over the bridge. Retrace the first 0.1 miles of the hike to the trailhead.

10.4 Arrive back at the trailhead and parking lot.

McCrackin, who worked with artist and photographer Andrew P. Hill and other residents to form the Sempervirens Club. The group, aided by the California Pioneer Society and the Native Sons & Daughters, eventually convinced the state legislature to set aside land for a park. And in 1902, 3,800 acres of old-growth redwood forest were designated California Redwood Park. Other parks were subsequently created, so

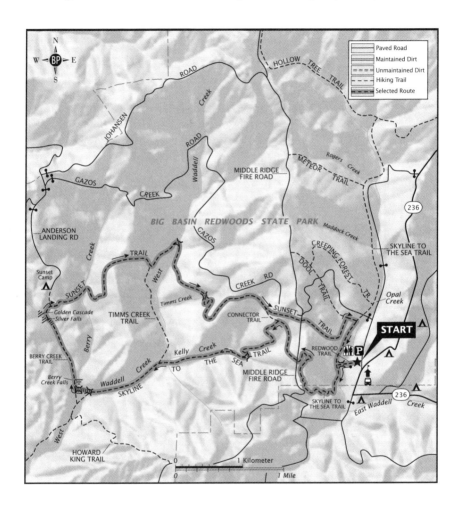

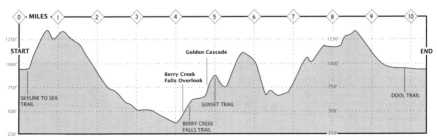

17

the original California Redwood Park had to be renamed Big Basin. The park has continued to grow over the years and now contains more than 18,000 acres.

Berry Falls, the first waterfall the trail encounters, is arguably the most impressive cascade in the park—although there are many falls along the various waterways that can compete. As the trail makes its way up West Berry Creek, it passes the watery grotto of Silver Falls, climbs stairs up the cliff to the top of the falls, and continues onward to Golden Cascade Falls. This third waterfall is a series of plunges over slick rock shaped like a theme-park water slide. The rock base is stained red and orange from minerals in the surrounding earth.

Leaving the waterfalls and West Berry Creek behind, the trail climbs to the ridge, where the vegetation changes drastically. Knobcone pine, buckeye, and chinquapin, better suited to the dry climate on the ridge, replace the humid shadow of redwoods and Douglas fir. For a brief stretch, even this airy forest gives way to chaparral as the trail passes over an outcropping of pale, near-white sandstone. But the trail quickly descends again into deep forest, where the path contours around the upper slopes of the park on the Sunset Trail. The trail eventually drops down into the basin of the park's *hub*—emerging on Opal Creek just upstream of the visitor center and following the waterway down to the first bridge you crossed on this hike. From here, it's just a short jaunt back to the trailhead.

Golden Cascade.

18

Hike Information

Trail Contacts:
Big Basin Redwoods State Park, Boulder Creek, CA (831) 338–8860

Schedule:
Open year round, 6 A.M.–10 P.M.

Fees/Permits:
$3 day-use fee required

Local Information:
San Jose Downtown Association, San Jose, CA (408) 279–1775 or www.sj-downtown.com • San Jose Convention and Visitors Bureau website: www.san-jose.org • Santa Cruz County websites: www.cruzio.com (offers lots of links); www.santacruzguide.com

Local Events/Attractions:
The Tech Museum of Innovation, San Jose, CA (408) 294–8324 or www.thetech.org • Nearby state parks: Castle Rock State Park, Butano State Park, and Ano Nuevo State Reserve (elephant seals can be seen here in season) – www.cal-parks.ca.gov

Accommodations:
Big Basin Redwoods State Park – For camping reservations, call 1–800–444–PARK. (There are nearly 150 campsites within the park.) For concessionaire tent cabins, call 1–800–874–TENT.

Hike Tours:
Ranger-led walks are offered in season. Contact Park Headquarters for up-to-date information.

Organizations:
Mountain Parks Foundation, Felton, CA (831) 335–3174 • Sempervirens Fund,

Los Altos, CA (650) 968–4509 or www.sempervirens.org • Save-the-Redwoods League, San Francisco, CA (415) 362–2352

Public Transportation:
Santa Cruz Metro: (831) 425–8600 or www.scmtd.com – bus service

Local Outdoor Retailers:
Extreme Adventures, Campbell, CA (408) 871–3111 • Extreme Adventures, Campbell, CA (408) 871–3111 • Pit-2-Go, Campbell, CA (408) 559–4278 • Scab, Aptos, CA (831) 685–2835 • Spirited Sports, Campbell, CA (408) 377–9590 • Sports Fever, Campbell, CA (408) 559–3387 • Big 5 Sporting Goods, Capitola, CA (831) 464–3822 • Outdoor World Inc., Capitola, CA (831) 479–1501 • Alexx's Sports Stop, Los Gatos, CA (408) 395–6950 • Any Mountain Ltd., San Jose, CA (408) 871–1001 • REI-Recreational Equipment Inc., San Jose, CA (408) 871–8765 • Valley Athletic Inc., San Jose, CA (408) 291–0520 • Adventure Sports Unlimited, Santa Cruz, CA (831) 458–3648 • Bugaboo Mountain Sports, Santa Cruz, CA (831) 429–6300 • Down Works, Santa Cruz, CA (831) 423–9078 • Jerry's Sports, Santa Cruz, CA (831) 425–7445 • Johnny's Sport Shop, Santa Cruz, CA (831) 423–5443 • Outdoor World Inc., Santa Cruz, CA (831) 423–9555 • Santa Cruz Sports Exchange, Santa Cruz, CA (831) 476–1123 • Play It Again Sports, Soquel, CA (831) 475–1988 • Big 5 Sporting Goods, Watsonville, CA (831) 763–1819 • Sportsmania, Watsonville, CA (831) 722–5824

Maps:
USGS maps: Franklin Point, CA; Big Basin, CA

Old Railroad Grade Trail

Hike Specs

Start: From the Mountain Home Inn
Length: 7.6-mile loop
Approximate Hiking Time: 3.5–4 hours
Difficulty Rating: Moderate due to elevation gain and steep descent
Terrain: Gravel fire road and dirt path through second-growth redwood forest, chaparral, and oak woodland on mountain slopes
Elevation Gain: 2,529 feet
Land Status: Municipal water district and state park
Nearest Town: Mill Valley, CA
Other Trail Users: Cyclists and equestrians
Canine Compatibility: Leashed dogs permitted within Marin Municipal Water District but not on state park trails

Getting There

From San Francisco: Head north on U.S. 101. Five miles north of the Golden Gate, leave U.S. 101 at the Marin City exit, following signs for CA 1 North. Follow CA 1 through Marin City and up the hill 3.1 miles, before turning right onto the Panoramic Highway. Continue another 2.6 miles to Mountain Home Inn. Park in the large lot on the left side of the road. The trail starts across the road and a few yards to the left.
• **Public Transportation:** Weekends only, take Golden Gate Transit bus No. 63 from the Marin City Transfer Center to the Mountain Home Inn. Call (415) 455-2000 for schedule. *DeLorme: Northern California Atlas & Gazetteer:* Page 104 A1

A fascinating history combines with a wide variety of natural habitats to make this hike a treasure. The best feature of this route, though, is undoubtedly the spectacular views. The trail follows the course of the old railroad bed as it snakes its way up the south side of Mount Tamalpais (a.k.a. *Mount Tam*), offering expansive views to the east, west, and south at every turn. With each switchback and the successive gain in elevation, the views get more panoramic and peer farther into the distance. But the trail saves the best for last. At the East Peak, the path shows hikers a sweeping view of the entire northern San Francisco Bay Area.

This region gained popularity in the late 19th Century when crowds of tourists from Mill Valley flocked to the summit and its Tavern of Tamalpais. At this point, cars were not commonplace, and roads had not yet been built here. So the preferred means for sightseers to reach the summit was via rail. The Mount Tamalpais Scenic Railway was constructed in 1896 to help shuttle the masses of visitors up the mountain. The railroad climbed at a steady seven-percent grade for 8.5 snaking miles to reach the summit, which offered spectacular views of the surrounding lowlands and water bodies—even at just 2,571 feet.

The return trip was a special attraction for visitors, who descended the mountain in individual "gravity cars." These cars—each staffed only with a brakeman—coasted down the steady grade to Mill Valley or Muir Woods in a ride that lasted all of 15 minutes. To get the gravity cars started, the passengers were asked to rock back and

forth until the cars started to roll downhill. That's when gravity took over, and the ride began. To get back up the hill, the gravity cars were towed behind the next locomotive leaving for the summit.

The whole trip was very popular in its day, eliciting praise from celebrities like Sir Arthur Conan Doyle, who called the railroad, "more exciting than anything like it in the world." Alas, once the use of automobiles became widespread—and the Pantoll and Ridgecrest roads were built—the railroad became obsolete, and service was finally discontinued in 1930. The tracks and ties have since been removed, but the grade remains and is used now as a trail and fire road.

Since we cannot travel by rail, we'll set off on foot from the Mountain Home Inn, located just off the Panoramic Highway on the lower slopes of the mountain. The first part of the hike traces the route of the Muir Woods Branch Line, which eventually became known as the Mount Tamalpais & Muir Woods Railway. The Muir Woods line met up with the main line at a spot known as the Double Bowknot, so named because the track switches back on itself four times in order to gain 600 feet of elevation in a short space. This section—which brings the total number of turns on the line to 281—helped earn the railroad the nickname "Crookedest Railroad in the World."

View to the north with Lake Lagunitas.

Just above the junction, hikers will find remnants of the old Mesa Station, where trains could pass one another using a *siding*—described as a short section of parallel track that allowed one locomotive to pull off the main line. Part of the concrete sidewalk that separated the siding from the main track is still visible and provides a reference point for visualizing the old station.

Another relic from the *Iron Horse* era is the historic West Point Inn, which stands at the westernmost turn of the line. Originally built as a stopover for passengers waiting for a stagecoach to the coast, the still-rustic inn is now maintained by the West Point Inn Association for the hikers and cyclists who use the trail. The Inn is open to the public for refreshments and overnight accommodations.

Farther up the mountain, time has been less kind to historic railroad structures. The Tavern of Tamalpais—which originally stood near the present-day visitor center and served as the focal point for tourist mobs during the railroad's heyday—is no longer standing. Plans are underway, however, for a small railroad museum to be built alongside a reconstructed section of track. Along with railroad memorabilia, the museum will house a re-creation of one of the original gravity cars.

MilesDirections

0.0 START at the Mountain Home Inn parking lot. Cross the Panoramic Highway and turn left, following the shoulder a few yards, then take the road that forks off to the right. This road forks again immediately; a paved road leads up to left to the fire station, and two gravel roads split off to the right. Take the middle road (Gravity Car Road).

0.1 Another gravel road heads down to the right. Continue straight on Gravity Car Road.

0.2 Pass the locked gate, and continue straight.

0.3 A gravel road heads up to the left. Continue straight.

0.4 *[**FYI.** An opening in the forest allows a good view to the southeast. San Rafael and Bay, San Francisco, and the Oakland Bridge can be seen from here.]*

0.9 At a fork in the road, take the left fork. *[**FYI.** A few yards later, the trail passes what is left of the old Mesa Station.]*

1.1 *[**FYI.** There is a great view to the southwest and east from here.]*

1.2 Gravity Car Road ends at Old Railroad Grade, which switches back to the right, heading down, and continues straight. Go straight on Old Railroad Grade, climbing steadily.

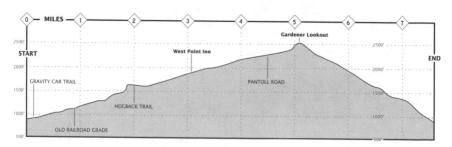

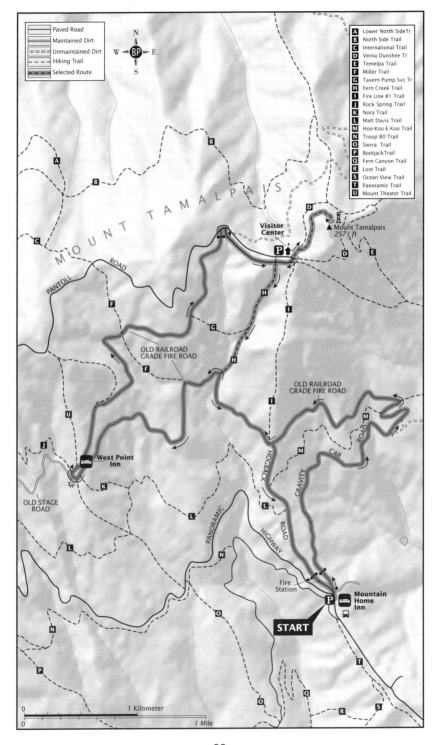

Paved Road
Maintained Dirt
Unmaintained Dirt
Hiking Trail
Selected Route

A Lower North SideTr
B North Side Trail
C International Trail
D Verna Dunshee Tr
E Temelpa Trail
F Miller Trail
G Tavern Pump Svc Tr
H Fern Creek Trail
I Fire Line #1 Trail
J Rock Spring Trail
K Nora Trail
L Matt Davis Trail
M Hoo-Koo-E-Koo Trail
N Troop 80 Trail
O Sierra Trail
P Bootjack Trail
Q Fern Canyon Trail
R Lost Trail
S Ocean View Trail
T Panoramic Trail
U Mount Theater Trail

MOUNT TAMALPAIS

PANTOLL ROAD

Visitor Center

▲ Mount Tamalpais
2571 ft

OLD RAILROAD GRADE FIRE ROAD

OLD RAILROAD GRADE FIRE ROAD

West Point Inn

OLD STAGE ROAD

HOGBACK ROAD

GRAVITY CAR ROAD

PANORAMIC HIGHWAY

Fire Station

START

Mountain Home Inn

0   1 Kilometer
0   1 Mile

1.3 Hoo Koo E Koo Trail joins Old Railroad Grade from the left. Continue straight.

1.4 Hoo Koo E Koo Trail splits off again, heading down to the right. Follow Old Railroad Grade up to the left.

2.0 Hogback Road goes down to the left. (You will take this down on the return trip.) For now, continue straight on Old Railroad Grade.

2.3 Fern Creek Trail goes up to the right. Continue straight.

2.5 Miller Trail heads up to the right. Continue straight on the main grade.

2.7 *[FYI. A view south along Panoramic Highway opens up, as well as another view of San Francisco.]*

3.0 *[FYI. From here, you can see a panorama stretching from Richmond to the Pacific.]*

3.1 The trail reaches the historic West Point Inn. *[FYI. There is a picnic area to the left, and refreshments can be had at the inn.]* Nora Trail heads down to Matt Davis Trail just below the picnic area. Follow the grade up around behind the Inn, where Mount Theater Trail takes off to the left. Continue straight, following the grade.

3.9 Miller Trail crosses the trail. Continue straight.

4.1 Tavern Pump Service Trail heads steeply downhill to the right. Continue straight.

4.5 The trail reaches a locked gate at the junction with Pantoll Road. Turn right onto Pantoll Road, and follow it uphill, keeping to the right as it forks a few yards later.

4.7 Fern Creek Trail goes down to the right. Continue straight.

4.8 The road dead-ends at the Tamalpais summit parking lot and visitor center. The trail continues uphill, just to the left of the restrooms

5.0 *[FYI. There is a good view to the north, as the trail rounds the mountain.]*

5.1 The trail ends at Gardener Lookout on the summit of Mount Tamalpais. This is the turn-around point for this leg of the hike. Retrace the trail to the summit parking lot.

5.4 Back at the summit parking lot, head right, crossing the lot. At the west end of the lot, Fern Creek Trail leads down toward Old Railroad Grade. Take this trail downhill through the brushy vegetation.

5.5 Fern Creek Trail crosses the lower branch of Pantoll Road. Continue straight on Fern Creek Trail.

6.0 Tavern Pump Trail goes up to the right. Continue straight on Fern Creek Trail.

6.4 Fern Creek Trail ends at Old Railroad Grade. Turn left onto Old Railroad Grade and head downhill.

6.8 Turn right onto Hogback Road and head steeply downhill. *[Option. As a milder alternative, retrace Old Railroad Grade and Gravity Car Road to the trailhead.]*

7.0 Hoo Koo E Koo Trail crosses Hogback Road. Continue straight, heading downhill on Hogback Road.

7.2 Hogback Road becomes Throckmorton Trail. Continue straight toward the Throckmorton Fire Station, keeping to the left as you pass a large water tank.

7.4 The trail passes a locked gate, just before reaching Throckmorton Fire Station. Continue past the station, following the paved road down to the left.

7.5 The road ends at Panoramic Highway. Cross the highway and follow the shoulder up to the Mountain Home Inn parking lot.

7.6 Arrive back at the trailhead.

Hike Information

Trail Contacts:
Mount Tamalpais State Park, Mill Valley, CA (415) 388–2070

Schedule:
Open 7 A.M. to sunset, year round. Visitor center at East Peak open daily in summer, weekends the rest of the year.

Fees/Permits:
$5 day-use fee for cars at the summit. Parking at Mountain Home Inn is free.

Local Information:
Marin County websites: www.marin.org (local businesses and travel information); www.visitmarin.org; www.marinhistory.org

Local Events/Attractions:
Mountain Play, May to June, on Mount Tamalpais (415) 383–1100 – outdoor theater

Accommodations:
The West Point Inn: (415) 388 9955 – They have rustic cabins practically on the trail, and they're open Tuesday–Friday, 11 A.M.–6 P.M.; Saturday, 10 A.M.–6 P.M.; Sunday, 11 A.M.–6 P.M.; closed Monday. For reservations call (415) 646–0702, 24 hours a day. Rooms are $30 for adults, $15 for ages 6–18, free for ages 5 and younger. Closed Sunday and Monday nights. • **For local camping information call:** (415) 388 2070 or (415) 456–1286

Restaurants:
The West Point Inn: (415) 388 9955 – have refreshments for hikers

Hike Tours:
The Mount Tamalpais Interpretive Association, San Rafael, CA (415) 258–2410 or www.mtia.net – Leads guided hikes regularly. See their website or call for more information.

Organizations:
Mount Tamalpais Interpretive Association, San Rafael, CA (415) 258–2410 or www.mtia.net

Other Resources:
Website: www.coestudios.com/forge.html – A nice page describing the reproduction of a Mount Tamalpais gravity car.

Public Transportation:
Golden Gate Transit: (415) 455–2000 or www.transitinfo.org – bus service

Local Outdoor Retailers:
Any Mountain: The Great Outdoor Store, Corte Madera (415) 927–0170 • **Marmot Mountain Works,** Kentfield (415) 454–8543 • **Battens & Boards,** San Rafael (415) 499–9316 • **Big 5 Sporting Goods,** Corte Madera (415) 924–3321 and San Rafael (415) 479–6211 • **Champs Sports,** San Rafael (415) 479–8716 • **DemoSport,** San Rafael, (415) 454–3500 • **EEC Fitness Superstore,** San Rafael (415) 453–8498 • **Marin Outdoors** (707) 544–4400 and San Rafael (415) 453–3400 • **Play It Again Sports,** San Rafael, (415) 453–7223 • **T&B Sports,** San Rafael (415) 453–2433 and Santa Rosa, (707) 544–2433 • **Old Town Sports,** Novato (415) 892–0577 • **Oshman's Super Sport USA,** Novato (415) 892–2060 • **Smash,** Novato (415) 898–7997

Maps:
USGS maps: San Rafael, CA

Shoreline/Ridge Fire Loop

Hike Specs

Start: From the China Camp Village trailhead
Length: 5.7-mile loop
Approximate Hiking Time: 2.5 hours
Difficulty Rating: Easy due to mild elevation gain and good trails
Terrain: Dirt path, dirt, and gravel roads travel along the bay shore and rolling, oak-covered hillsides
Elevation Gain: 678 feet
Land Status: State park
Nearest Town: San Rafael, CA
Other Trail Users: Cyclists, joggers, and equestrians
Canine Compatibility: Dogs not permitted

Getting There

From San Francisco: Drive north 18 miles on U.S. 101, and exit at North San Pedro Road. Head east 5.2 miles on North San Pedro Road, and turn left into the parking lot for the China Camp Village Historic Area. The trailhead is to the left of the restrooms near the entrance of the parking lot.
DeLorme: Northern California Atlas & Gazetteer: Page 94 D2

T his hike begins with a quick visit to the China Camp Village site, which consists of a few weather-beaten buildings and a long wooden pier. But don't let the old village's ramshackle appearance dissuade you from exploring the historical site—especially the small museum that tells the story of the Chinese-Americans who settled here in the late 19th Century. These settlers made their living by fishing and processing grass shrimp, mostly for export to the Far East. At its peak, the village was home to nearly 500 residents, but a series of racist and repressive laws passed by increasingly hostile European-Americans all but destroyed the town and its industry. The village currently has only one permanent resident—a descendant of the early Chinese settlers.

With so few physical reminders left, it's difficult to picture the thriving community that once existed here. Ironically, it was the same anti-Chinese sentiment that brought the settlers here in first place that eventually drove them out again. That initial wave of Chinese emigration came in 1848, following the discovery of gold in the California hills. There had been a few Chinese merchants living in the state before this time, but the Asian population exploded toward the middle of the century. The gold rush was a powerful lure, especially for those Chinese immigrants coming from poorer regions in Canton (Guangdong)—most notably an area known as the Four Districts. Conditions there had grown intolerable, largely because of instability brought on by foreign colonial powers and the homegrown opium trade. By the mid

Rat Island and San Pablo Bay.

1800s, the ruling Qing dynasty was in a shambles. And in 1850, the Taiping Rebellion destabilized the region even further.

This disarray stood in sharp contrast to the glowing handbills proclaiming that riches were waiting in America for enterprising men. By 1852, some 20,000 Chinese were pouring into the state every year. The majority of those arriving in San Francisco—known to the Cantonese as *Gam Saan*, or "golden mountains"—were landless peasants seeking jobs as mine laborers.

Although quick to take advantage of the cheap labor, many European-Americans soon developed strong anti-Chinese sentiments. This growing racism led to the passage of a Foreign Miner's Tax, as well as the expulsion of Chinese laborers from min-

MilesDirections

0.0 START at the China Camp Village trailhead, near the parking lot entrance, and to the left of the restrooms. Follow the trail as it heads north parallel to North San Pedro Road.

0.2 An unmarked trail continues north along the road. Turn left, crossing North San Pedro Road, and continuing up the hill on Shoreline Trail.

0.4 Continue straight along the Shoreline Trail.

0.7 The trail arrives at the Park Headquarters and Ranger's Office. Cross the gravel road and continue straight on the other side.

0.9 Peacock Gap Trail heads uphill to the left. Continue straight, along Shoreline Trail.

2.2 *[FYI. The hill ahead and to the right is called Chicken Coop Hill, one of many colorful names applied to geographic features in the park.]*

2.6 The Shoreline Trail continues straight. Turn left instead, and head uphill onto Miwok Fire Trail.

3.1 The Miwok Fire Trail continues straight. Turn left onto Oak Ridge Trail, continuing through the dense oak forest on the narrow dirt path.

3.4 Continue straight on Oak Ridge Trail as it crosses Miwok Fire Trail.

3.7 *[FYI. At an opening in the trees, there is a good view to the right of San Rafael and the Oakland Bridge.]*

4.0 Continue straight on Oak Ridge Trail as it crosses Miwok Fire Trail again.

4.6 As Oak Ridge Trail joins with Peacock Gap Trail, continue straight on Peacock Gap Trail, heading downhill.

4.8 Peacock Gap Trail intersects with Shoreline Trail. Turn right onto Shoreline Trail and retrace the first part of the hike to the trailhead.

5.7 Arrive back at the trailhead.

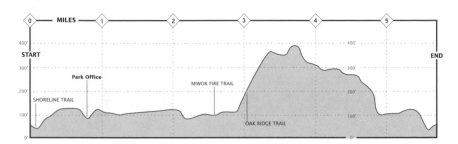

ing camps. And in 1854, California applied the same discriminatory legislation to Chinese-Americans that it already had put into place against blacks and Native Americans: That year, the state Supreme Court ruled that no Chinese person could testify against a white person in court.

The Chinese mining industry had virtually dried up by 1870, when most of the easy surface gold deposits were gone. The displaced miners were frustrated, discouraged, and forced to turn to other occupations. Some found jobs on the railroads, as manual laborers charged with the grueling work associated with building train tracks through the mountains. Others turned to the fisherman's trade they had known in their homeland. Small fishing villages began sprouting up around the San Francisco Bay Area, where the Chinese used traditional techniques and sold mainly to other Chinese or overseas markets. But the prejudice that haunted Chinese mine workers followed them into the fishing trade. And by 1911, increasing pressure and resentment from non-Chinese fishermen prompted the passage of laws outlawing the main Chinese fishing methods.

In spite of all these difficulties, most villages continued to function, and the Chinese-Americans tenaciously refused to abandon their new home. Knowledge of the Chinese-Americans' tough history in the state should provide food-for-thought as you begin the Shoreline/Ridge Fire Loop.

After visiting the China Camp historical site, pick up the trail near the restrooms at the entrance to the upper parking lot. The path heads west and soon crosses North San Pedro Road to ascend into the oak-shaded hills of San Pedro. The trail then lev-

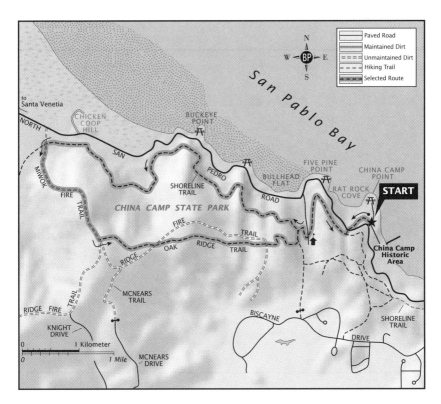

els out and contours gently around the grassy slopes to offer ample views of San Pablo Bay. After passing the large mound on the shore known as Chicken Coop Hill, turn left onto the Miwok Fire Trail, and climb a steep hill for the return trip along the ridge. As you make your way along the Oak Ridge Trail, be sure to take in the breath-taking views over San Rafael and the Richmond-San Rafael Bridge.

These vistas are likely to be enhanced by clear weather and good visibility, a rarity in the Bay Area. Unlike other parts in the region, China Camp State Park averages a stunning 200 fog-free days per year. The mild weather also creates an environment hospitable to beautiful year-round foliage. In late winter, the manzanita produces dazzling white blossoms. And wildflowers put on a display in springtime that includes honeysuckle, milkmaids, and shooting stars. Thanks to the mild weather, any time of year can offer a good hike in the park.

Looking down from the Miwok Trail.

Hike Information

ⓒ Trail Contacts:
China Camp State Park, San Rafael, CA
(415) 456–0766

⊙ Schedule:
Open year round. Museum exhibit open daily, 10 A.M.–5 P.M. Concession stand and fishing pier open weekends only.

ⓢ Fees/Permits:
$5 day-use fee at the China Camp Village area. There are day-use fees at some park areas.

❓ Local Information:
Marin County website: www.marin.org (local businesses and travel information) • General website: www.bahiker.com (everything for the Bay Area hiker)

ⓠ Local Events/Attractions:
Heritage Day, in September – tours of China Camp Village, children's activities, and historic fishing boats

⊖ Accommodations:
China Camp State Park – The park has 30 campsites, plus room for recreational vehicles. Reservations can be made with DESTINET at 1–800–444–7275.

ⓞ Organizations:
Friends of China Camp, San Rafael, CA (415) 456–0766

⊡ Public Transportation:
Golden Gate Transit: (415) 455–2000 or www.transitinfo.org – Bus route No. 23 runs weekdays from the San Raphael Transit Center to North San Pedro Road and Vendola Drive in Santa Venetia near the west end of the park.

⊛ Local Outdoor Retailers:
Any Mountain: The Great Outdoor Store, Corte Madera, CA (415) 927–0170 • Marmot Mountain Works, Kentfield, CA (415) 454–8543 • Battens & Boards, San Rafael, CA (415) 499–9316 • Big 5 Sporting Goods, Corte Madera, CA (415) 924–3321 and San Rafael (415) 479–6211 • Champs Sports, San Rafael, CA (415) 479–8716 • DemoSport, San Rafael, CA (415) 454–3500 • EEC Fitness Superstore, San Rafael, CA (415) 453–8498 • Marin Outdoors, San Rafael, CA (415) 453–3400 • Play It Again Sports, San Rafael, CA (415) 453–7223 • T&B Sports, San Rafael, CA (415) 453–2433; and Santa Rosa, CA (707) 544–2433 • Old Town Sports, Novato, CA (415) 892–0577 • Oshman's Super Sport USA, Novato, CA (415) 892–2060 • Smash, Novato, CA (415) 898–7997

ⓝ Maps:
USGS maps: San Quentin, CA; Petaluma Point, CA

Olompali Trail

Hike Specs

Start: From the west end of the main parking lot

Length: 2.6-mile loop

Approximate Hiking Time: 1–1.5 hours

Difficulty Rating: Easy-to-moderate due to good trail that gets steep in some spots

Terrain: Dirt path and gravel road through oak woodland

Elevation Gain: 789 feet

Land Status: State park

Nearest Town: Novato, CA

Other Trail Users: Equestrians

Canine Compatibility: Dogs not permitted

Getting There

From San Francisco: Head north on U.S. 101 for 29 miles. The Olompali State Park entrance is on the west side of the highway and is only accessible from the southbound lane, so you'll have to continue north until you can turn around, then come back down. From the southbound lane, turn right into Olompali State Park, and follow the entrance road 0.5 miles up to the main parking lot. Visitors must self-register at the bulletin board. The trail begins at the west end of the parking lot. *DeLorme: Northern California Atlas & Gazetteer:* Page 94 C1

The trail follows a short route up through the sparse, oak woodlands and grassy meadows at the heart of Olompali State Park. This airy timberland, which is characteristic of the area, surrounds several old ranch buildings that serve as park headquarters. These oak trees have sustained human societies for hundreds of generations, beginning some 8,000 years ago. By about AD 1100, the people who would later be known as the Coast Miwok had established a major trading village at this spot. In those days, the shores of the bay extended all the way up to where U.S. Route 101 now passes the park. That shoreline dramatically changed during the 1850s, when large-scale hydraulic mining in the Sierra Nevada caused increased sediment in the rivers to partially fill the San Francisco Bay.

The site of the present-day park was a natural choice for prehistoric people looking for a place to settle. Olompali was an optimal location for trade, since it was located near the bay and several rivers. At that time, and indeed until Europeans introduced horses and wagons, water was the preferred mode of long-distance transport. The bay also provided people with a source of food—in the form of fish, waterfowl, and shellfish—and building materials like tule reeds, which were used to construct shelters and small raft-like boats. (Hikers soon will be able to envision more clearly what early life was like here. Descendants of the original inhabitants and other volunteers are recreating a Miwok village, complete with bark and grass huts constructed in the old style.)

The Miwok were alone on this land until the mid 16th Century, when Spanish missionaries began arriving in California. As missionization exercised its influence on the Miwok culture, the residents of Olompali started building structures in the adobe

style. One of these buildings—the home of the last village chief, Camilo Ynitia—is still partially standing and can be seen in the park (It is protected by an enclosing wooden structure.). Archeologists have found other relics from the Miwok era, including several mortars used by the Miwok to pound acorns into flour and an Elizabethan silver sixpence dated 1567. Scientists think this coin probably was left behind when Sir Francis Drake landed on the nearby coast in 1579. They suspect that the coin later made its way to this location via trading.

Olompali Trail as it travels beneath oaks.

The Spanish missions influenced much more than just the building styles of Native Americans. Spanish activities, which began in 1769, resulted in nothing short of the total disruption of native lives and cultures. The colonization effort originally was as a joint military and religious project under Captain Gaspar de Portola and Franciscan Padre Junipero Serra. But the religious aspects of the operation seemed to leave a stronger imprint on the regional peoples than did the military.

Defenders of the missions often argue that the missionaries were well-intended people, seeking only to save souls and bring the gift of civilization to the *wild* and *uncivilized* aboriginal inhabitants of the state. But in most cases, the Native Americans neither wanted nor needed these *gifts*, which often did more harm than good. The Miwoks were slow to convert to Catholicism—and its accompanying feudal Spanish culture. This resistance eventually led the Spanish to try some strange, and dubious, methods of conversion. To boost native participation, missionaries recruited unbelieving neophytes at gunpoint, kept Native Americans incarcerated in the missions, flogged them, and even branded crosses into converts' arms so they could be recaptured should they escape to their former villages. But even as harmful as the missions were to native societies, imported European diseases caused the most

MilesDirections

0.0 START at the west (upper) end of the parking lot. The trail heads uphill through a grassy meadow.

0.1 The trail passes some old barns on the right, then arrives at a junction, marking the start of the loop portion of Olompali Trail. Turn right and continue a few yards before crossing a small creek via a footbridge.

0.2 The trail joins a gravel access road. Turn left and head uphill on the road.

0.3 *[FYI. A Miwok village reconstruction (in progress) can be seen on the left.]*

0.6 *[FYI. The trail passes an old reservoir, once used by the ranch.]*

0.7 The access road continues straight. Turn left and follow the Olompali Trail as it climbs

some wooden steps and continues through the oak forest as a dirt path.

0.9 A defunct section of the trail crosses the path from left to right. Continue straight.

1.0 The Mount Burdell Trail heads to the right, leading to its namesake peak. Continue straight on Olompali Trail.

1.3 The trail crosses a seasonal creek, then hangs a sharp left and begins descending via a series of switchbacks.

1.6 *[FYI. Openings in the trees reveal nice views of the bay and lowlands.]*

2.4 You're now at the end of the loop section of the trail. Turn right and return to parking lot along the first section of the trail.

2.6 Arrive back at the trailhead.

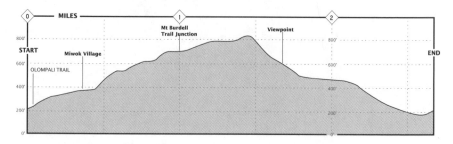

Recreated Miwok Hut.

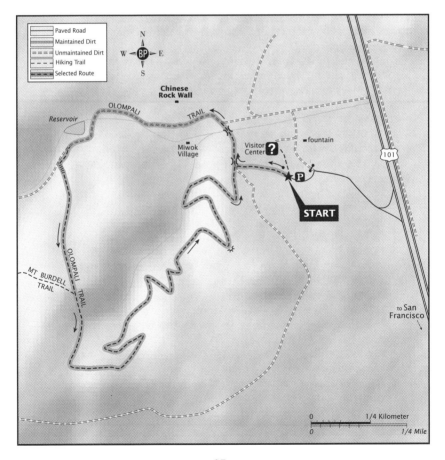

damage. Smallpox, syphilis, and other exotic ailments thoroughly decimated native populations. In fact, the area's Native Americas suffered an estimated decline of over 50 percent from the time the first California mission was established in San Diego in 1769, to the creation of the state's final mission, in Sonoma in 1823.

A few Native Americans did prosper under the Spanish, however. Even Camilo Ynitia, the aforementioned last *hiopu*—or head—of Olompali village, was Christianized and taught European ways by the Franciscan missionaries. This background no doubt helped him acquire Olompali as a land grant from the Mexican governor in 1843. Such grants to Native Americans were rare, and rarer still was the confirmation of that grant by the U.S. government after California joined the Union in 1852. With the decidedly anti-Indian sentiment of the European-Americans of the time, the United States only upheld two such grants to Native Americans. Soon after

Earthquake!

California is a state in motion...literally. The famous San Andreas Fault—which stretches across western North America from Baja California, Mexico, all the way up to southern Mendocino—marks the boundary between the North American Plate and a section of the ocean's crust that is slowly dragging California's western edge northward at a rate of two inches per year.

Most California Indians figured the earthquake to be a supernatural man, or brothers, who shook the earth by running. The earthquake that shook a Spanish Californian expedition in 1769 became the first to enter the history books, but there have been several more since then:

12/8/1812 *An earthquake demolishes Mission San Juan Capistrano, killing 40.*

11/22/1852 *San Francisco's Lake Merced drops 30 feet after a quake.*

10/8/1865 *An earthquake shakes San Francisco. Mark Twain is on hand to witness the spectacle.*

4/18/1906 *The Great Earthquake and Fire in San Francisco. The city is ruined. Jail inmates are moved to Alcatraz Island for safekeeping.*

3/27/1964 *Crescent City is struck by a tsunami (tidal wave) generated by an Alaskan earthquake. Eleven are killed and downtown is destroyed.*

4/14/1969 *Psychics predict an earthquake will cause California west of the San Andreas Fault to fall into the ocean. Ronald Reagan and other politicians arrange to be out of the state, but nothing happens.*

2/9/1971 *San Fernando Earthquake. Sixty-five die. Half a billion dollars in damage.*

10/17/1989 *Loma Prieta, or World Series Earthquake. Santa Cruz and other Bay Area cities hard hit. San Francisco–Oakland Bay Bridge is severely damaged, as are other bridges and overpasses.*

4/25/1992 *Cape Mendocino Earthquake. Fortuna and nearby towns experience damage, especially in old Victorian buildings.*

10/16/1999 *Hector Earthquake (near L.A.) Twenty cars of an Amtrak train are derailed. Blackouts in L.A.*

confirmation of his land grant, Ynitia sold most of his land to James Black and moved to a spot not far away, near the present-day Birkenstock factory. He eventually died—murdered, some say, at the hands of fellow Miwoks angered by his European ways.

In later years, Olompali served various purposes: It was first a ranch and then a Jesuit retreat for the University of San Francisco. The former Miwok village even earned itself a footnote in rock 'n' roll history—as a short-term home for the Grateful Dead. The rockers-in-residence attracted other counter-culture music icons, who frequently visited the ranch. To see a picture of the band lounging on an Olompali hillside, fans can check out the back of the album cover for *American Beauty*. The ranch subsequently housed the so-called *Chosen Family* commune before falling into disuse. It was finally recognized as a historic landmark and preserved as a state park in 1977.

Hike Information

Trail Contacts:
Olompali State Historic Park, Novato, CA (415) 892–3383 or *www.cal-parks.ca.gov*

Schedule:
Open year round, 10 A.M.–7 P.M., daily

Fees/Permits:
$2 day-use fee

Local Information:
Marin websites: *www.marin.org*, *www.visitmarin.org*, and *www.marin history.org*

Local Events/Attractions:
Heritage Day, in May – *Native American dancers, blacksmith demonstrations, Miwok culture and crafts, spring flower walks, lace makers and quilters, and living history presentations*

Organizations:
The Olompali People, Novato, CA (415) 892–3383 • Miwok Archeological Preserve of Marin, 2255 Las Gallinas, San Rafael, CA 94903 or email *mapom@aol.com*

Other Resources:
Website: *www.bahiker.com* (resources for bay area hikers)

Local Outdoor Retailers:
Any Mountain: The Great Outdoor Store, Corte Madera, CA (415) 927–0170 • Marmot Mountain Works, Kentfield, CA (415) 454–8543 • Battens & Boards, San Rafael, CA (415) 499–9316 • Big 5 Sporting Goods, Corte Madera, CA (415) 924–3321; and San Rafael, (415) 479–6211 • Champs Sports, San Rafael, CA (415) 479–8716 • DemoSport, San Rafael, CA (415) 454–3500 • EEC Fitness Superstore, San Rafael, CA (415) 453–8498 • Marin Outdoors, San Rafael, CA (415) 453–3400 • Play It Again Sports, San Rafael, CA (415) 453–7223 • T&B Sports, San Rafael, CA (415) 453–2433; and Santa Rosa, CA (707) 544–2433 • Old Town Sports, Novato, CA (415) 892–0577 • Oshman's Super Sport USA, Novato, CA (415) 892–2060 • Smash, Novato, CA (415) 898–7997

Maps:
USGS maps: Novato, CA

Sky Trail/ Laguna Loop

Hike Specs

Start: From the Sky Trail trailhead
Length: 10.0-mile loop
Approximate Hiking Time: 5–6 hours (overnight possible)
Difficulty Rating: Difficult due to steep trails and elevation gain
Terrain: Gravel road, partially paved road, and dirt path through Bishop pine forests and northern coastal prairie and scrub
Elevation Gain: 2,097 feet
Land Status: National seashore
Nearest Town: Olema, CA
Other Trail Users: Cyclists and equestrians
Canine Compatibility: Dogs not permitted

Getting There

From San Francisco: Drive north on CA 1/ U.S. 101 for seven miles, until the two highways separate north of Sausalito. Follow CA 1 west, then north along the coast, about 26 miles to the town of Olema. At Olema, turn left onto Bear Valley Road and drive north 1.9 miles. Turn left onto Limantour Road and follow it up 3.5 miles before turning left into the Sky Trail trailhead parking lot. The trail begins at the gate on the east side of the lot. **DeLorme: Northern California Atlas & Gazetteer:** Page 93 D5

Considering how close it is to a large urban area, Point Reyes National Seashore has an astoundingly untamed, and varied, character. The high, densely forested eastern side contrasts sharply with the bare, wind-swept prairies and pastures of the western slopes. And in between lie the fire-dependant Bishop pine stands and vast expanses of coyote brush-dominated vegetation, known as northern coastal scrub. The spectacular seashore for which the park is named lies at the outer perimeters of the Point Reyes area. And an impressive list of animals calls this home, including Tule elk, bobcat, black-tailed deer, and the larger axis and fallow deer (two exotic species that were introduced in the 1940s). In addition to the wild animals, 45 percent of native North America bird species have been spotted here.

Shaped roughly like an elongated triangle, Point Reyes sits on the part of the earth's crust known as the Pacific Plate, which is steadily moving north along the North American Plate of the mainland at the rate of about two inches a year. Along its eastern edge, the triangle is partially separated from the rest of the continent by Tomales Bay, a long, thin arm of the Pacific Ocean that marks the rift zone of the famous San Andreas Fault. South of the point, the fault plunges inland, where it periodically wreaks havoc—most notably in nearby San Francisco.

The well-developed trail system at Point Reyes offers ample opportunity for hikers to mix-and-match routes, thereby creating their own perfect trek. This particular loop was chosen because it sees much less use than the Bear Valley trails and passes through most of the habitat types present in the national seashore. As an added bonus, it stops off at the summit of Mount Wittenberg for a bird's-eye view of Drake's

Bay. You also have the option of taking a short detour from Coast Camp down to the beach.

This stretch of coast has been the source of much debate among historians over the years. The dissention stems from questions about the exact point of anchorage chosen by English explorer Sir Francis Drake in the year 1579. Drake was in the midst of his "Voyage of Circumnavigation," a multi-purpose mission that included searching for a secret northwest passage to the Pacific and raiding Spain's many New World holdings, when his ship, the *Golden Hind*, sprang a leak. Drake turned and headed south, seeking a sheltered place along the uncharted California coast to anchor and repair the ship. Most evidence to date indicates that the spot he chose was the nearby Drake's Estero.

The debate was almost settled in 1936 when a brass plate, reputedly left by Drake at the infamous estuary, was recovered. But the discovery proved to be a hoax. Nevertheless, several fragments of Chinese pottery like those held in the *Hind's* hull

Sky Trail and Woodward Valley junction.

MilesDirections

0.0 START at the gate on the east side of the Sky Trail trailhead parking lot. Follow Sky Trail as it heads uphill on a paved access road.

0.1 The trail changes from paved road to gravel road.

0.7 Fire Lane Trail goes off to the right. Continue straight on Sky Trail.

0.8 Sky Trail continues straight leading you to Sky Campground. Turn left onto Horse trail to left, and follow it east toward Bear Valley.

1.0 *[FYI. There is a great view of the valley down to the left from here (weather permitting).]*

1.3 Horse Trail continues straight. Turn right onto Z Ranch Trail, heading to Wittenberg Summit.

1.5 *[FYI. Half way up the incline, there is a good view on the right of Tomales Bay.]*

1.8 Just after entering a grassy alpine meadow, Summit Trail heads up sharply to the left. Mount Wittenberg Trail heads down to Bear Valley on the left, perpendicular to Z Ranch Trail. To the right, Mount Wittenberg Trail heads down to access Meadow Trail, Sky Camp, and Woodward Valley. Turn a sharp left and follow the Summit Trail a short distance to the top of Mount Wittenberg.

2.0 The trail reaches the summit. *[FYI. Enjoy aerial views of the surrounding countryside, mostly to the south.]* Turn around and retrace Summit Trail to the last junction.

2.2 Back at Junction, turn right following the sign directing you to Woodward Valley. Head down Mount Wittenberg Trail toward Woodward Valley.

2.6 Mount Wittenberg Trail joins Sky Trail. To the left, Meadow Trail heads down to Bear Valley. To the right, Sky Trail heads back to Sky Camp. Continue straight, following Sky Trail to Woodward Valley.

3.3 Sky Trail continues straight. Turn right onto Woodward Valley Trail and continue downhill.

4.1 *[FYI. The trail passes through the 1995 burn zone. Plenty of dead and charred trees attest to the ferocity of that blaze.]*

4.3 *[FYI. There is a nice view of Drake's Bay on the left.]*

4.5 *[FYI. As the trail rounds a corner, Limantour Spit can be seen straight ahead.]*

4.7 *[FYI. The trail now passes through the fire recovery zone, characterized by very brushy vegetation.]*

5.1 Woodward Valley Trail ends at the Coast Trail. Turn right onto Coast Trail and follow it toward Coast Camp.

5.7 The trail passes through Coast Camp. *[FYI. Reservations have to be made in advance to camp here, but it's also a nice place to break for lunch, as there are several picnic tables. Don't be surprised to see mountain bikes, which can get here from the west via Limantour Spit and the Coast Trail.]*

5.9 A spur trail branches right and up to access campsites 1–7. Continue straight on Coast Trail.

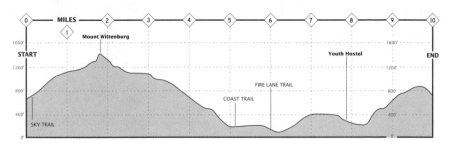

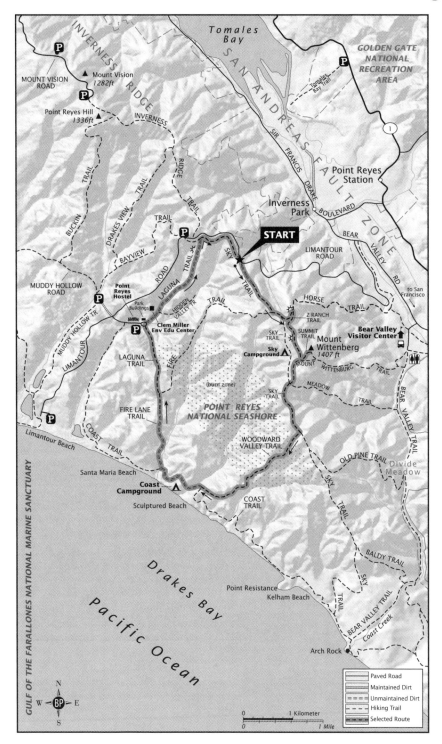

41

6.0 Coast Trail continues straight. Turn right onto Fire Lane, and follow it uphill.

6.4 The dirt road surface of Fire Lane becomes dirt single track.

6.7 Junction. Fire Trail heads right. Laguna trail goes left. Go left.

7.5 Junction. A few park buildings and the Laguna parking lot. Take trail through the trees to the right.

7.7 Junction. Clem Miller Environmental Education Center to left. Hidden Valley Trail is to the right, and straight ahead is our trail.

7.8 Leave the meadow and switchback up. Near the top, trail becomes gravel as it joins old road.

8.1 Top out after steep climb.

8.2 After brief decline, climb again.

8.3 On top again, nice view of Limantour.

9.3 Junction. Bayview to the left, Sky Trail to right. Go right.

10.0 Arrive back at the trailhead.

have been found at area archeological sites, and anthropologists have confirmed that the sailor's descriptions of native people he encountered depict the area's Coast Miwoks. Scientists recently have suggested that Campbell Cove, near the mouth of Bodega Harbor, is the true location of Drake's stopover. Only time—and more research—will settle the debate.

You may occasionally glimpse the ocean once sailed by the *Golden Hind* as you make your way down from Mount Wittenberg to the coast, but you are more likely to notice the charred trees visible on the edge of the forest. Much of the landscape below looks like it is recovering from some type of major devastation. That *something* was the Vision Fire, which burned 14 percent of the national seashore in 1995. The youth hostel and the nearby Clem Miller Environmental Education Center were saved from the surrounding destruction by firefighters. Hostel caretakers will be glad to tell the story of how the building was completely covered with fire-retardant foam during the incident. In the end, only one of the hostel's small outbuildings was lost. The fire initially was very destructive to the local wildlife, but the affected plant communities have been regenerating rapidly. And the Bishop pine—whose cones require the intense heat of fire to release seeds—has taken advantage of the opportunity to repopulate several areas previously lost to cattle ranching.

Cattle ranching has a long and prestigious history at Point Reyes. The Gold Rush of 1849 sparked the intensive cattle ranching, which provided the growing San Francisco population with dairy products. The abundance of grass and fresh water combined with the long growing season created optimal conditions for ranching. By 1867, Marin County was producing 932,429 pounds of butter per year—most of it coming from Point Reyes. Several of the old ranches have shut down, and many park facilities can be found on the sites of these former homesteads. A large portion of Point Reyes, however, is still dedicated to cattle ranching, especially on the western side, where much of the land is still leased to ranchers. Here, the native coastal prairie has largely been replaced with non-native grasses, sparking a serious erosion problem. Although strides have been made to reduce the impact of grazing on the

One of the greeters at the visitor center.

ecosystem, soil conservation authorities say environmental pressures are still above healthy levels.

From the Coastal Trail, the climb back up to the Sky Trail trailhead via the Fire Lane and Laguna trails is long and steep. But the views on a clear day are well worth the effort. A short stint along the Bayview Trail, which runs parallel to Limantour Road, brings you back to the trailhead.

Hike Information

⦿ Trail Contacts:
Point Reyes National Seashore, Point Reyes Station, CA (415) 663–1092 or *www.nps.gov/pore*

⦿ Schedule:
Open daily from sunup to sundown. Visitor Center is open Monday to Friday, 9 A.M.–5 P.M.; weekends and holidays, 10 A.M.–4:30 P.M.

⦿ Fees/Permits:
No entrance fees, but campers must get a permit. Camping costs $10 per site/night for 1–6 people. More for larger groups. Make reservations, Monday–Friday, 9 A.M.–2 P.M., at (415) 663–8054 or fax (415) 663–1597.

⦿ Local Information:
West Marin Chamber of Commerce, Point Reyes Station, CA (415) 663–9232 or *www.pointreyes.org*

⦿ Local Events/Attractions:
Strawberry Festival, in April, at Kule Loklo – *celebration of the First Fruits Ceremony of the Coast Miwok people* • **Habitat Restoration,** regular intervals throughout the year – *Call park for more information at (415) 663–1092* • **Adopt A Trail Program:** (415) 663–1092 – *Volunteer for trail and restoration work.*

⦿ Accommodations:
Point Reyes Hostel, off Limantour Road within the National Seashore (415) 663–8811 – *office hours 7:30–9:30 A.M. and 4:30–9:30 P.M.*

⦿ Organizations:
Point Reyes National Seashore Association, Point Reyes Station, CA 94956 • **Miwok Archeological Preserve of Marin,** 2255 Las Gallinas, San Rafael, CA 94903 or email *mapom@aol.com*

⦿ Public Transportation:
Golden Gate Transit: (415) 923–2000 or *www.transitinfo.org – Bus route No. 65 serves the Bear Valley Visitor Center from the San Raphael Transit Center on weekends and holidays.*

⦿ Local Outdoor Retailers:
Any Mountain: The Great Outdoor Store, Corte Madera, CA (415) 927–0170 • **Big 5 Sporting Goods,** Corte Madera, CA (415) 924–3321 and San Rafael (415) 479–6211 • **Marmot Mountain Works,** Kentfield, CA (415) 454–8543 • **Champs Sports,** San Rafael, CA (415) 479–8716 • **DemoSport,** San Rafael, CA (415) 454–3500 • **Marin Outdoors,** San Rafael, CA (415) 453–3400 • **Play It Again Sports,** San Rafael, CA (415) 453–7223 • **T&B Sports,** San Rafael, CA (415) 453–2433 • **Old Town Sports,** Novato, CA (415) 892–0577 • **Oshman's Super Sport USA,** Novato, CA (415) 892–2060 • **Smash,** Novato, CA (415) 898–7997

⦿ Maps:
USGS maps: Drake's Bay, CA; Inverness, CA

Bodega Head Loop

Hike Specs

Start: From the East parking lot
Length: 1.7-mile loop
Approximate Hiking Time: 1 hour
Difficulty Rating: Easy due to level terrain and short length
Terrain: Dirt path through coastal headlands and windswept grassland and along rocky cliffs
Elevation Gain: 203 feet
Land Status: State park
Nearest Town: Bodega Bay, CA
Other Trail Users: Bird, whale, and sea lion watchers
Canine Compatibility: Dogs not permitted

Getting There

From Bodega Bay: From CA 1, turn west onto East Shore Road and drive 0.3 miles before turning right onto Bay Flat Road, which then becomes West Shore Road. Continue 3.5 miles, then take the left fork in the road and drive another 0.4 miles to the east parking lot. The trail leaves from the east end of the parking lot. *DeLorme: Northern California Atlas & Gazetteer:* Page 92–3 B4

A s you begin the loop, the first thing you see will be Bodega Harbor, with its fishing fleet, and the long sand spit of Doran Beach, which partially encloses the harbor. Located at the south end of a 17-mile string of beaches, Bodega Head is a grassy headland surrounded by steep cliffs and pocket beaches. Attentive hikers can see an astounding variety of wildlife along the trail. Be especially attentive in the cliffs and waters surrounding the head, as that is where the bulk of the wildlife is found.

The name of the bay and town is thought to stem from a visit—circa 1775—by Spain's Juan Francisco de la Bodega y Quadra Mollineda. The sailor parked his schooner, *Sonora,* at the south end of the bay, and in those days, simply landing was enough to warrant having a place named after you.

Even earlier, in 1579, Sir Francis Drake passed this way on a voyage of exploration and plunder, before being forced to stop for repairs in a sheltered bay. Most scholars believe Drake's landing point was an estuary on nearby Point Reyes, but some assert the possibility that the English ship anchored here, near the mouth of the present harbor at Campbell Cove. The latter theory gained support in 1962, when utility workers discovered a stone wall fitting the description of a small fort that Drake had built during his six-week stay. But the debate surrounding the real Drake's Bay continues.

More recently, Bodega Bay and the town of Bodega, located a few miles inland, achieved a kind of infamy as the filming location for Alfred Hitchcock's classic film *The Birds.* The film—which stars Tippi Hedren, Rod Taylor, Jessica Tandy, and Suzanne Pleshette—depicts a quiet fishing village suddenly tormented by swarms of

Cormorant gather on the offshore rocks.

hostile birds. Shot in 1961, the special effects for the picture were so complex that it took two years for the film to be completed. Don't expect to encounter much of the film's ambiance when you arrive in Bodega. The town looks very different now, but movie buffs will find that a few of the buildings seen in the film remain.

There are still a lot of birds here—though you don't have to worry about any mass attack of gulls. All of the birds around Bodega are people-friendly. The natural geology of the headlands and Bodega Harbor provides a variety of habitats ranging from tall rocky cliffs to sheltered salt marshes, providing the birds with both safe nesting sites and direct access to feeding grounds at sea. Aside from the expected seagulls, birdwatchers can find marbled godwits, brown and white pelicans, Hedwicks wrens, northern harriers, and the black-crowned night herons.

The black-footed albatross, looking like a large dark gray seagull with a wingspan of over six feet, occasionally puts in appearances—which is very unusual for a bird that rarely spends time on any land, let alone mainland. Living at sea without fresh

MilesDirections

0.0 START at the end of the east parking lot, near the restroom. Follow the Bodega Head Loop around the edge of the bluffs.

0.1 *[FYI. The trail offers a good view of Bodega Bay from this spot.]*

0.3 *[FYI. An offshore rock on the south side of the head is often occupied by loud and boisterous sea lions. Mats of the succulent ice plant grow on the cliff edges here.]*

0.5 A shortcut leads back to the parking lot on the right. Continue straight around the edge of the bluffs.

0.6 *[FYI. The rocky promontory to the left has a good example of small sea cave at its base.]*

0.8 *[FYI. Cormorants can often be seen down on the rocks to the right.]*

1.1 The trail passes above a sheltered cove and a beach that's impossible to get to safely. *[Note. Do the smart thing and enjoy it from afar.]*

1.2 *[FYI. A memorial to seamen and –women—shaped like the prow of a ship— can be seen to the right.]*

1.3 The trail reaches the west parking lot. *[FYI. This is an excellent spot to look for passing gray whales. A nearby interpretive sign tells more about the watery behemoths.]* The trail back to the east parking lot heads across the meadow, starting next to the restroom and heading past a clump of windblown cypress on the right.

1.5 The trail reaches the east parking lot access road. Turn right, and follow the gravel road back to the parking lot and trailhead.

1.7 Arrive back at the East parking lot and trailhead.

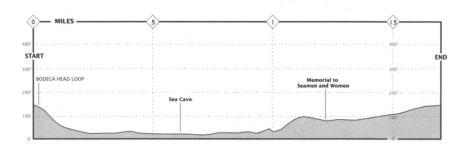

water to drink, the albatross consumes more salt than an average bird. To make up for their high salt consumption, albatrosses have developed a special nasal gland that removes excess salt from their blood. Apparently, all birds have this gland—called the salt gland—but evolution has rendered it inactive in most birds. The salt gland converts the salt to a concentrated fluid that is expelled from the nostrils.

Another star of the native bird population is the rhinoceros auklet— so named for the small white *horn* that grows from the base of its beak during summer. A cousin of the rhinoceros auklet, the tufted puffin, also makes its home here. During the summer months, the tufted puffin has a huge red and yellow bill, a white face, and plume-like eyebrows that sweep back along the side of its head. The bird loses some of its physical pizzazz during the winter months; it sheds the outer layer of its bill, and its plumage turns a somber dark gray.

FYI:
Blue Whales are the largest animals that have ever lived—including dinosaurs.

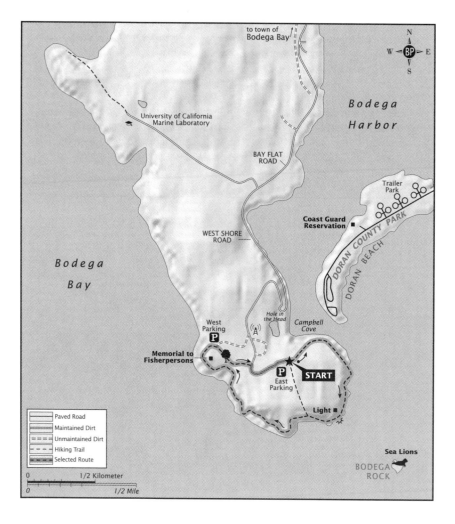

Whale Watching

Although humpbacks, blue whales, and killer whales are all sighted off the California coast, gray whales are most commonly spotted from shore. From November through January, they can be observed as they migrate southward to the warm lagoons of Baja California, where young are born. From February through June, they make their way back to the summer feeding grounds of the Bering and Chukchi seas, swimming a little closer to shore.

From afar, gray whales can be identified by their heart-shaped spout—which is much smaller than the blue whale's—and by the predictable swimming pattern (usually three to four short dives lasting between one and three minutes, followed by a longer dive of five to 15 minutes). Before a deep dive, whales often raise their flukes high in the air, preparing for a vertical descent that, for gray whales, lasts up to 20 minutes. If you are lucky, you may see a whale spyhopping—that is, sticking its head out of the water as if for a better look. Breaching is also seen, although it is much more common in Mexican waters. When a gray breaches, it comes almost straight up, bringing three-quarters of its body out of the water before crashing down on its side with a monstrous splash.

Any high spot along the coast will be good for whale watching, but some of the best locations are Point Reyes, Bodega Head, Mendocino Headlands, beaches along the Lost Coast, and Crescent City.

For those who want to get closer, there are several operators who offer whale-watching boat trips during migration periods. These trips usually depart twice a day and last two to four hours. During peak whale times, knowledgeable members of the volunteer group Stewards of Slavianka visit the park on weekends to talk about whales and to help people spot them.

Cliffs of Bodega Head.

The region's birds aren't the only wildlife worth watching. Due south of Bodega Head is a rock outcrop that's a favorite haul-out spot for sea lions. And an excellent lookout for gray whales is located to the west as you round the head and reach the west parking lot. (See Whale Watching sidebar.)

Hike Information

🕐 Trail Contacts:
Russian River Area State Parks, Duncan Mills, CA (707) 865-2391 or *www.mcn.org/1/rrparks/rrweb.htm*

🕐 Schedule:
Open year round, dawn to dusk

❓ Local Information:
Bodega Bay Area Chamber of Commerce, Bodega Bay, CA 1-877-789-1212 or (707) 875-3422

💡 Local Events/Attractions:
Seafood, Art & Wine Festival, in August, Bodega Bay, CA (707) 824-8404 • **Taste of Bodega's Crab Cioppino,** in November, Bodega Bay, CA • **Bodega Bay Fisherman's Festival,** in April, Bodega Bay, CA (707) 875-3422 – *boat parade, blessing of the fleet, food and crafts*

👥 Organizations:
Stewards of Slavianka, Duncan Mills, CA (707) 869-9177

🛒 Local Outdoor Retailers:
Gualala Sport and Tackle Shop, Gualala, CA (707) 884-4247 • **Old Town Sports,** Novato, CA (415) 892-0577 • **Oshman's Super Sport USA,** Novato, CA (415) 892-2060 • **Smash,** Novato, CA (415) 898-7997 or (707) 884-4247 • **Play It Again Sports,** San Rafael, CA (415) 453-7223 • **T&B Sports,** Santa Rosa, CA (707) 544-2433 • **Sonoma Outfitters,** Santa Rosa, CA (707) 528-1920

🅽 Maps:
USGS maps: Bodega Head, CA

7

Wolf House Trail

Hike Specs

Start: From the kiosk in the left-hand corner of the parking lot
Length: 1.2-mile out-and-back
Approximate Hiking Time: 1 hour
Difficulty Rating: Easy due to shortness of hike and partially paved trail
Terrain: Dirt, gravel, and paved trail through oak woodland and grassland
Elevation Gain: 326 feet
Land Status: State park
Nearest Town: Glen Ellen, CA
Other Trail Users: Dog owners
Canine Compatibility: Dogs permitted

Getting There

From Santa Rosa: Head east on CA 12, 15 miles, then turn right onto Arnold Drive. In Glen Ellen, turn right onto London Ranch Road. Drive a mile or so to the park entrance, then left to the trailhead parking lot. The trailhead is at the kiosk on the far end of the lot.
• **Public Transportation:** From San Francisco, take the Golden Gate Transit route No. 80 to the Santa Rosa Transit Center. Transfer to Sonoma County Transit route No. 30, and ride to the intersection of Arnold Drive and London Ranch Road in Glen Ellen. Walk or bicycle uphill one mile on London Ranch Road to the park entrance, then left to the trailhead parking lot. *DeLorme Northern California Atlas & Gazetteer:* Page 94 B1

J ack London was an adventurer, socialist, dreamer, and one of the most successful authors of his time. He gained fame at a relatively early age with the publication of *Call of the Wild* and *The Sea Wolf*. An author of the people, London bucked the writing establishment and wrote directly to the average Joe rather than for an intellectual elite. By time he died, at the age of 40, the prolific author had written more than 50 books and hundreds of short stories, articles, and essays.

Around 1905, Jack moved to the country with his second wife, Charmian, in search of a peaceful lifestyle and with the dream of founding a London "ancestral home." He took over the already-existing vineyard, began raising pigs and draft horses, built a reservoir-fishpond and tried out various wild ideas—including a failed attempt to market the Australian eucalyptus tree as a fast-growing hardwood. He had modest success with the vineyard and most of his other efforts, but the cost of maintaining his farm while financing his experiments and building projects forced him to keep up a frenetic writing pace in order to pay the bills.

As you enter the park, there are two parking areas, one on either side of the entrance road. The one to the right is for a network of longer hiking trails that lead to the lake and to the farmhouses of the original winery and homestead, known as Beauty Ranch. These trails connect to the much-larger Bay Area Ridge Trail, which as the name suggests, circles the San Francisco Bay Area along the surrounding mountain ridges.

To the left of the entrance road is the parking lot for the visitor center, museum, and the short trail to the ruins of Wolf House. At the west end of the lot are a small information kiosk and a trail heading up into the forest. The path to Wolf House leads through typical California oak woodlands and tops out by a large chestnut tree next to a sun-drenched meadow of blonde grass. Grasslands like this one originally earned California the nickname the Golden State, despite later assumptions that the moniker stemmed from the discovery of gold in the mountains.

The first stop along the trail is at the House of Happy Walls, which was built by Charmian after her husband's death. Today, the house serves as a visitor center and museum, and contains many of Londons' personal belongings and photographs. There's also a shop that sells maps of the park and books by London.

Along the way to Wolf House, a side trail leads to the spot where Jack London's ashes were buried. The location—on a quiet, fenced-in knoll—is marked by a large red rock taken from the ruins of Wolf House and identified with a plaque. London's (and later Charmian's) ashes were placed beneath this rock, per the author's wishes, and lie near the much older graves of two settlers' children.

Continuing down the main trail, you finally reach the ruins of London's home. The author began construction of his dream abode, which he called Wolf House, in 1910. It took three years to finish the house—built of raw volcanic stone and unpeeled redwood logs—but the Londons never lived in it. The night before they were scheduled to move in, the house mysteriously burned to the ground. The cause of the fire was never determined, although some people suspect that the blaze was the result of arson. The fire remains a mystery to this day. Only the house's stonework and first-floor walls remain, but it is easy to imagine what the final construction must have looked like. (If your imagination fails you, photographs of the impressive Wolf House and a scale model are in the visitor center.) A hole in the floor surrounded by the stone arches of the interior walls marks what was once the swimming pool. And stark stone chimneys stretch upward, leaving second-story fireplaces eerily suspended in mid-air. Take some time to look around what was to be London's monument, and consider the irony of a house built to last forever that didn't last a night.

London planned to rebuild the house, but the loss left him under financial pressure to keep writing, and the demands of the farm kept him perpetually busy. In 1916, overworked and in poor health, London died of chronic gastrointestinal uremic poisoning. He had ignored doctor's orders to slow down and change his habits, choosing instead to stubbornly continue his frantic pace to the end. The park and Wolf House ruins remain as a tribute to this driven man.

Return along the same trail to the parking lot.

MilesDirections

0.0 START from the Kiosk at the end of the parking lot.

0.05 The trail leads to the House of Happy Walls, former home of Jack's widow, and current museum and park visitor center.

0.3 The dirt trail intersects with a paved way. To the left, the path continues to Wolf House, to the right, it returns to the parking area. Turn left.

0.4 The trail climbs a mild hill. *[**FYI.** In season you'll find blackberries thriving on the right.]*

0.5 *[**Side-trip.** A dirt spur trail on the left leads 0.7 mile to Jack London's marked grave.]*

0.6 Wolf House ruins. This is the turnaround point. Return the way you came.

1.2 Arrive back at the parking lot.

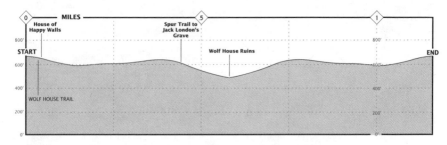

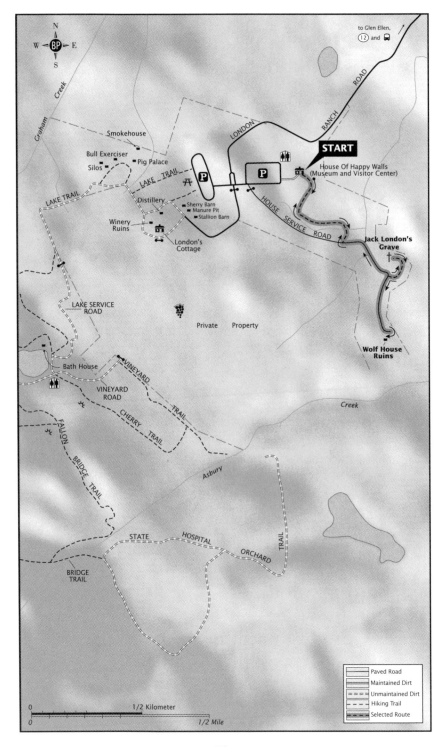

Wolf House ruins.

Hike Information

Trail Contacts:
Jack London State Historical Park, Glen Ellen, CA (707) 938–5216 or www.parks.sonoma.net/JLPark.html or www.cal-parks.ca.gov

Schedule:
The park is open daily, 9:30 A.M.–7 P.M. in the summer; and 9:30 A.M.–5 P.M. the rest of the year. The House of Happy Walls is open daily (except Thanksgiving, Christmas, and New Year's Day), 10 A.M.–5 P.M.

Fees/Permits:
$6 per car ($5 for seniors)

Local Information:
Sonoma County website: www.sonoma.com (tourist and recreation information)

Local Events/Attractions:
Wine Country Film Festival, in July and August, Jack London State Historical Park, Glen Ellen, CA – Held at the park's outdoor Sebastiani Theater. Call (707) 935–3456 for information • Heart of the Valley Barrel Tasting, in February, in Kenwood and Glen Ellen, CA (707) 833–5501– wine-tasting event held over a weekend • Olive Oil Festival, in May, B.R. Cohn Winery: (707) 938–4064 • The Sonoma Cattle Company: (707) 996–8566 – offers guided horseback riding in Jack London and Sugarloaf state parks

Accommodations:
Sugarloaf Ridge State Park: (707) 938–1519 – Call for camping information.

Organizations:
Valley of the Moon Natural History Association, 2400 London Ranch Road, Glen Ellen, CA 95442

Other Resources:
Jack London website: www.sunsite.berkeley.edu/London – This site is dedicated to Jack London. It lists his works as well as biographies and other publications relating to the author.

Public Transportation:
Sonoma County Transit: (707) 576–7433 or www.transitinfo.org – Bus route No. 30 stops at Arnold Drive and London Ranch Road in Glen Ellen from Santa Rosa. (Walk or bicycle one mile to the park entrance.)

Local Outdoor Retailers:
Sonoma Outfitters, Santa Rosa, CA (707) 528–1920

Maps:
USGS maps: Glen Ellen, CA
A trail map is available from the museum.

8   Juniper/Summit Loop

Hike Specs

Start: From the Juniper Campground Turnout
Length: 4.5-mile loop
Approximate Hiking Time: 2.5 hours
Difficulty Rating: Easy-to-moderate due to some steep spots
Terrain: Dirt path and dirt, gravel, and paved roads through oak- and chaparral-covered hillsides
Elevation Gain: 1,291 feet
Land Status: State park
Nearest Town: Walnut Creek, CA
Other Trail Users: Cyclists
Canine Compatibility: Dogs not permitted

Getting There

From San Francisco: Head east on I-80 for eight miles, before turning onto I-980 and continuing east another three miles. From here, turn onto CA 24 and follow it east for 16 miles to the junction with I-680. Take I-680 south seven miles and exit at Diablo Road in Danville. Head east on Diablo Road one mile. Turn right at the stoplight (this is still Diablo Road) and drive another 2.2 miles, before turning left onto Mount Diablo Scenic Boulevard. About 3.9 miles later, come to the entrance station and pay the fee. Continue up this road 3.2 miles and turn right onto the Summit Road. Drive another 2.4 miles to the Juniper Campground and park in the oversized turnout. The trail starts at the picnic area at the north end of the turnout.
DeLorme: Northern California Atlas & Gazetteer: Page 105 A6

L ocal hikers and friends of Mount Diablo like to tell visitors that the view from the mountain's summit encompasses more of the earth's surface than any other point on the planet. While such boasts may be difficult to prove, it is easy to see how they came about. Rising up on the edge of California's broad Central Valley, Mount Diablo has little to obstruct its panoramic views to the north, east, and south. On the western side, low, rolling hills spill into the San Francisco Bay, beyond which the city guards its portal to the Pacific Ocean. The list of landmarks visible from the peak on a clear day is long, and includes Yosemite National Park to the east, the Farallon Islands to the west, and Lassen Peak to the north—which is within sight even 181 miles away!

The hike is most popular during the springtime, when the trail is alive with varied and abundant wildflowers. Mount Diablo fairy lantern, Indian warrior, Johnny-jump-up, and mosquito-bill join the state flower, California poppy, in painting the hillsides vibrant shades of red, orange, blue, and yellow. The second, longer portion of this loop explores the open, grassy hillsides of the southern and western mountain slopes, which are particularly pretty when the wildflowers are in full bloom.

But spring is not the only time to try this hike. The area's mild climate allows for pleasant hiking in any season. Snow is rare, even in the depths of winter, so the trail is open and accessible year round. The path gets less crowded during the fall and winter off-season, so hikers can wander the area in solitude. But in late summer and early

View to the north over the Bay Area "soup."

autumn, visitors will not be alone on the trail: Hikers should be on the lookout for a harmless—if unsettling—surprise as mature male tarantulas scurry across the trails in search of the opposite sex.

Despite their bad image, tarantulas are not aggressive to humans and need not inspire great fear. In fact, their bite is said to be no worse than a bee sting—which isn't too bad considering the tarantula is North America's largest spider and can have a leg spread of up to six inches. The furry spiders usually stay underground in their burrows. But when males reach maturity, they leave home in search of a mate. These mature spiders—now between seven and 10 years old—have a tough mating ritual. They must first locate the larger females by scent and somehow entice their potential partners out of the burrow. The males then have to skillfully avoid being attacked and eaten by the females as they attempt to procreate. After mating, the female retreats into her den, lays a multitude of eggs, and encases them in a broad, flat cocoon of silk. The eggs hatch six to seven weeks later, and the young tarantulas stick around for another week or so before setting out to find their own dens. For the males, post-mating life is short—even if they survive the experience. They don't return to their burrows after mating, choosing instead to wander aimlessly above ground. The male tarantula eventually succumbs to either the season's increasingly cold, rainy weather or predators like snakes, birds, and the highly specialized tarantula hawk wasp. (This insect lays its eggs inside spiders they have paralyzed with a

MilesDirections

0.0 START to the right of the campground entrance, at the Laurel Group Picnic Area. Head uphill, to the right, on Juniper Trail.

0.2 At this point the landscape changes from dense forest to chaparral. Rock Ridge Trail heads left; continue straight on Juniper Trail.

0.8 The trail passes a large broadcasting tower.

1.0 The trail crosses Summit Road. As you reach the road, follow it to the right about 20 yards, then turn left where the path resumes, continuing uphill on Juniper Trail.

1.1 As you reach the Lower Summit Parking Lot, continue straight across the lot, heading due east toward the summit.

1.2 Beyond the parking lot, continue up Summit Road, taking the right fork in the road (this is the beginning of the summit loop). Juniper Trail continues just past the fork, on the left. Follow the trail up through a patch of thick forest to the summit.

1.3 Pass another radio tower on the right side.

1.4 Juniper Trail ends at Mount Diablo Summit (3,849 feet). The visitor center and observatory is straight ahead, across Summit Road and the small parking lot. After seeing the summit, retrace the last 0.3 miles to the Lower Summit Parking Lot.

1.7 Back at the Lower Summit Parking Lot, continue straight past the junction with Fire Loop Trail, and turn left onto Summit Trail at the upper end of parking lot.

2.0 North Peak Trail heads left, toward Prospector's Gap. A sharp curve in Summit Road, known as the Devil's Elbow, passes close by on the right. Follow the shoulder of the road around the corner, and continue on Summit Trail as it continues downhill to the left.

2.1 The path changes to dirt road. Continue to the right on Summit Trail.

2.5 The trail joins Summit Road. Follow the shoulder to the left for 20 feet, then turn left again as Summit Trail resumes, heading downhill on a narrow dirt path.

2.8 The dirt path widens to become a road as you near a large water tank.

2.9 The trail passes by some restrooms and a small picnic area. Frog Pond Road heads left. Continue straight around the water tank, which is to your right.

3.0 A small portion of the old trail heads straight, now closed for plant rehab. Take the new section of Summit Trail to the left.

3.1 The trail surface becomes paved road as you reach a junction. To your left, Green Ranch Road leads to Frog Pond Road. Continue straight on Summit Trail/Green Ranch Road a few yards, to the junction with Summit Road. Cross Summit Road at the pedestrian crossing, and continue down the dirt road (still Summit Trail) on the other side.

3.2 Summit Trail continues straight. Turn right onto Juniper Trail, and follow it uphill.

3.3 The trail crosses a gravel deck, near a bend in Summit Road. Follow Juniper Trail north as it resumes on the other side.

3.5 After passing through the lush gorge of Jill Creek, the trail emerges onto an open, grassy hillside

4.0 Upon reaching the apex of a grassy knoll, continue straight along the bottom edge of Juniper Campground.

4.2 Mitchell Canyon Trail heads left as Juniper trail reaches the junction with a gravel road. Turn right onto Deer Flat Road/Juniper Trail.

4.3 Deer Flat Road/Juniper Trail becomes paved road as it continues uphill through Juniper Campground, past the restrooms.

4.5 Arrive back at the trailhead.

potent sting. When the eggs hatch, the wasp larvae make an extended meal of the still-living spider.)

Though most will never see the local tarantulas, there's plenty to see along this hike. The trail begins at the Laurel Group Picnic Area above the Juniper Campground and continues up the hill into a patch of dense, shady forest. The path soon leaves the forest and the landscape changes, giving way to a scraggly chaparral that covers the broad, rolling hillsides in tangled masses. The trail offers a clear view

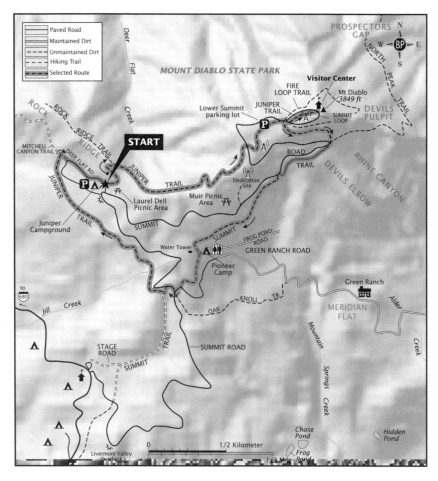

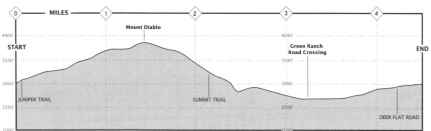

of wide suburban valleys to the west and north that is marred only by a few radio towers near the top. Beyond the Lower Summit parking lot, the trail enters a young oak forest for the last stretch to the summit. The saplings stand is a reminder of the area's last major wildfire, which swept through in 1977. For those with extra time, the interpretive Fire Loop Trail—which starts at the Lower Summit parking lot—provides some insight into the recovery process with a short, self-guided tour around the summit.

The visitor center at the summit is an example of the so-called *Park Service Rustic* style of architecture made popular during the 1930s by the Civilian Conservation Corps (CCC) crews. These Depression-era builders constructed this and other similar structures in parks across the country to help alleviate the national crush of unemployment and poverty. The rough, stone-walled visitor center houses a museum and an observation deck for admiring the spectacular Mount Diablo view.

The mountain has been called by many names over the years. To the Miwok people who lived here in antiquity it was known as *Oj-ompil-e* or *Supemenenu*. The Ohlone/Costanoan tribes called it *Tushtak*, and to the Nisenan, it was *Sukku Jaman*. When the Spanish arrived in the late 18th century, they called the peak *Cerro Alto de los Bolbones*—"high place of the Bolbones"—after a sub-group of Bay Miwok people who lived at its base. The name Mount Diablo stems from a legend—of which there are several versions—about a group of Spanish soldiers looking for Native Americans who had escaped from the missions in San Francisco and San Jose. In one of the oldest versions, the soldiers came upon a village in a willow thicket and surrounded it. As night fell, the Miwok villagers were able to slip away unnoticed, and the angry Spanish cursed the thicket as *monte del diablo*—"thicket of the devil." The

Juniper Trail below the Summit Road—watch for falling cars.

name was later mistranslated by English-speaking settlers as "mountain of the devil" and applied to nearby Mount Diablo. Another version of the legend tells of a group of terrified Spanish soldiers wandering in the wilderness. On the slopes of a high mountain, they were startled by a wildly plumed native medicine man. The superstitious soldiers promptly mistook this vision for the devil himself. American author Bret Harte created his own myth in an 1863 short story entitled "The Legend of Monte del Diablo." The protagonist of this tale is a Spanish priest who meets Beelzebub high on the mountain's summit. The priest turns down the dark one's offer to stem the Yankee tide, in return for renouncing his holy vows. The story ends with the two doing battle, and the priest finally waking up, as if from a dream.

Hike Information

Trail Contacts:
Mount Diablo State Park, Clayton, CA (925) 873–2525 or *www.cal-parks.ca.gov*

Schedule:
Open year round, 8 A.M. to sunset, but may close due to extreme fire danger

Fees/Permits:
Day-use fee $5

Local Information:
Contra Costa County websites: *www.c4.net* or *www.co.contra-costa.ca.us*

Local Events/Attractions:
SummerFest, in June, Danville, CA (925) 837–4400 – *arts, crafts, music and food* • **Art & Wine Festival,** in June, Walnut Creek. (925) 934–2007

Accommodations:
Mount Diablo State Park, Clayton, CA 1–800–444–7275, or (916) 638–5883 – *for camping reservations within the park*

Hike Tours:
Mount Diablo Interpretive Association: *www.mdia.org – hosts guided hikes*

Organizations:
Mount Diablo Interpretive Association: *www.mdia.org*

Public Transportation:
County Connection: (925) 676–7500 – *Bus route No. 110 from the BART station in Concord serves the north end of Mount Diablo State Park* • **The Bay Area Transit Outdoors:** *www.transitinfo.org/ Outdoors/Mount_Diablo.html – This guide provides bus to trail information.*

Local Outdoor Retailers:
Any Mountain Ltd. Concord, CA (925) 674–0174 • **Champs Sports,** Concord, CA (925) 687–0534 • **Frank Culum,** Concord, CA (925) 689–4587 • **Recreational Equipment Inc.** Concord, CA (925) 825–9400 • **Sportmart,** Concord, CA (925) 687–6300 • **Sports 4 All,** Concord, CA (925) 671–9808 • **Hogan's,** Pleasant Hill, CA (925) 686–1985 • **Transition Sports Inc.,** Orinds, CA (925) 253–8399 • **Play It Again Sports,** Pleasant Hill, CA (925) 825–3396 • **Big 5 Sporting Goods,** Walnut Creek, CA (925) 932–4196 • **Copeland Sports,** Walnut Creek, CA (925) 935–8601 • **Sunrise Mountain Sports,** Walnut Creek, CA (925) 932–8779

Maps:
USGS maps: Clayton, CA; Diablo, CA

Willow Slough Trail

Hike Specs

Start: From the Willow Slough Trail trailhead

Length: 3.7-mile loop

Approximate Hiking Time: 2 hours

Difficulty Rating: Easy due to flat terrain and good trail

Terrain: Dirt path, dirt road, and boardwalk through old-growth valley, oak woodland, and meadows

Elevation Gain: 47 feet

Land Status: River preserve

Nearest Town: Galt, CA

Other Trail Users: Hikers only

Canine Compatibility: Dogs not permitted

Getting There

From Sacramento: Take I-5 south 22 miles, get off at the Twin Cities exit, and head east on Twin Cities Road (E13). Turn right on Franklin Boulevard and drive south 1.5 miles. Willow Creek Slough Trail trailhead is on the left side, at the preserve entrance. The visitor center is 0.5 miles farther down the road, also on the left. *DeLorme: Northern California Atlas & Gazetteer:* Page 96 B3

T he Cosumnes River Preserve is very young, as parks go, having been established in the early 1990s as a joint effort of the Nature Conservancy, the Bureau of Land Management, and several other public and private entities. The spot was chosen for its now-unique combination of undammed rivers and remnant old-growth valley oak—one of California's most endangered landscapes. Why are these resources so rare? When European settlers came into the area, they found 800,000 acres of riparian oak woodlands and immediately began converting them to firewood. Now, just one percent of the old-growth valley oak remains, and the preserve is charged with protecting part of it.

Prior to white settlement, California's Central Valley consisted of several large lakes, wetlands, meandering rivers, and the accompanying riparian vegetation and wildlife. Farmers and cattle ranchers began transforming the area by draining the wetlands and clearing the forests. Later, as cities and urban areas grew, more of the rivers were dammed, straightened, and/or diverted to control flooding and provide water for the urban masses. As a result, most of the Central Valley today bears little resemblance to the original landscape. The Cosumnes River is one of the last rivers originating in the Sierra Nevada to remain undammed, and as a result, winter floods often cover its banks and the surrounding land with water. This flooding is key to the rejuvenation of valley oak forests—not only because it deposits a nutrient-rich layer of silt on the riparian land, but it also keeps rodent populations in check, giving more acorns the chance to germinate and reducing the damage done to seedlings.

All along the trail, numbered posts mark specific natural features of interest to hikers. And for a 50-cent donation, you can pick up brochure with more detail at the visitor center. The center also has interpretive displays and hands-on activities for

kids, as well as restrooms and a picnic area. The route is fairly straightforward: Wander down the east side of the slough; turn left to follow the Cosumnes River upstream a short distance; head inland; and double back to the main trail.

The trip begins behind the gate at the preserve entrance. Immediately to the right is the head of the slough. Depending on the time of day, the slough either can be full

Willow Slough.

of water or resemble an empty mud puddle. Interestingly, the slough is dependent on the tides—even though the preserve is nearly 100 miles from the ocean. The preserve's low elevation (on average less than 10 feet above sea level) overrides the distance and allows the tides to be felt. High tide in San Francisco Bay backs up the fresh water coming down the Cosumnes River, raising the water line by as much as four feet. When the tide is out, the mud on the riverbanks offers a good opportunity to see a variety of animal tracks.

To the left of the trail is a tule marsh, where several species of waterfowl spend their time. Among these are Canada geese, tundra swans, various ducks, and the preserve's most prized visitors—the sandhill cranes. If you're hiking in the fall or winter, listen for the loud rattling calls of the cranes in the grass. With luck, you may see them bow and dance, leaping into the air with wings spread like feathered ballerinas in their courtship displays.

As you come to a bend in the river, there is a bench that serves as a good vantage point to observe beaver, great blue herons, and other park inhabitants while you eat lunch. Look around on the tree trunks, and try to spot signs of the previous season's high water mark.

MilesDirections

0.0 START from the Willow Slough Trail trailhead. The ditch to the right is the head of Willow Slough.

0.1 A spur trail heads left. Continue to the right, following the sign for Willow Slough Trail.

0.2 A short spur trail goes right to the slough. Continue straight

0.3 There is a picnic area to the right.

1.0 A dirt road heads off to the left here. This is the returning branch of the loop. Continue on the trail to the right.

1.2 A short spur trail goes off to the right, accessing the river.

1.4 The trail crosses under the railroad bridge.

1.7 *[FYI. The bench here is a good place to watch birds and other wildlife.]*

2.1 Cross the access road, continuing straight.

2.3 Cross under the railroad bridge again and turn right, following the access road.

2.5 Turn left onto the trail, leaving the road.

2.6 End of loop. Turn right and retrace the first portion of the trail.

3.7 Arrive back at the Willow Slough Trail trailhead.

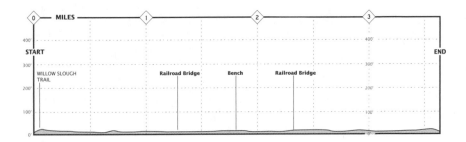

Continuing on, the trail turns back inland on the way back to the main trail. The path travels through a large open meadow with a scattering of oaks before the loop passes twice under the tracks of the Union Pacific Railroad. The railroad company works with the preserve managers to protect the habitat adjacent to the tracks.

After rejoining the main trail, spend a few minutes waiting quietly by the edge of the tule marsh on your way back to the trailhead. In places like this, silence is often rewarded.

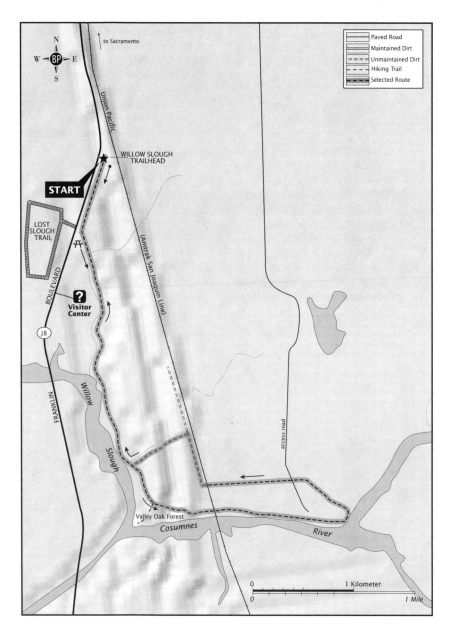

Hike Information

🕐 Trail Contacts:
Consumnes River Preserve, Galt, CA (916) 684–2816 or *www.cosumnes.org*

🕐 Schedule:
The trail is open every day from dawn to dusk. Visitor center is open most weekends, 9 A.M.–5 P.M., and intermittently during the week, contingent on volunteer availability.

💲 Fees/Permits:
No fees or permits required

❓ Local Information:
Sacramento Convention & Visitors Bureau, Sacramento, CA (916) 264–7777 or *www.oldsacramento.org*

💡 Local Events/Attractions:
Fall Workday Extravaganza, in October, Consumnes River Preserve, Galt, CA (916) 684–2816 – *Volunteers help with maintenance and research activities* • Sandhill Crane Festival, in November, Consumnes River Preserve, Galt, CA (916) 684–2816

• Lodi Grape Festival, mid September, Lodi, CA (209) 369 2771 or *www.grape-festival.com* • Harvest Festival, in April, Sacramento, CA (707) 778–6300 or *www.harvestfestival.com* • The Great River Otter Amphibious Race – Sacramento River Kinetic Art Challenge, in August, Sacramento, CA (916) 446–7704 or *www.riverotter.com* • Gold Rush Days, August–September, Sacramento, CA • Heritage Holidays, in December, Sacramento, CA (916) 264–7031 or *www.oldsacramento.org* • California State Indian Museum, Sacramento, CA (916) 324–7405 – *open daily, 10 A.M.–5 P.M.* • California State Railroad Museum, Sacramento, CA (916) 445–6645 (24-hour info) or (916) 445–7387 (office) – *open daily, 10 A.M.–5 P.M.* • Wells Fargo History Museum, Sacramento, CA (916) 440–4263 – *open daily, 10 A.M.–5 P.M.* • Golden State Museum, Sacramento, CA (916) 653–7524 or *www.ss.ca.gov/museum/intro.htm* – *open Tuesday–Saturday, 10 A.M.–5 P.M.; Sunday,*

Tule marsh and valley oak.

12 P.M.–5 P.M. • **Old Sacramento Historic District,** Sacramento, CA (916) 558–3912 (event hotline) or (916) 264–7031 (office) or *www.oldsacramento.com*

Hike Tours:

Consumnes River Preserve, Galt, CA (916) 684–2816 – *Volunteer Naturalists lead nature walks about twice a month, beginning at 9 A.M. Call for more information.*

Organizations:

The Nature Conservancy: *www.tnc.org/ infield/State/California – The Nature Conservancy has 13 preserves in California, many with hiking trails.*

Local Outdoor Retailers:

Big 5 Sporting Goods, Lodi, CA (209) 366–1514 • **Lodi Sporting Goods,** Lodi, CA (209) 368–7993 • **Adventure Sports,** Sacramento, CA (916) 971–1800 • **All American Sports Fan,** Sacramento, CA (916) 442–5066 • **Athletics Unlimited,** Sacramento, CA (916) 483–2352 • **Big 5 Sporting Goods,** Sacramento, CA (916) 488–5060 • **Champs Sports,** Sacramento, CA (916) 393–4482 • **Copeland's Sports,** Sacramento, CA (916) 429–9199 • **Peak Adventures,** Sacramento, CA (916) 278–6321 • **Sierra Outfitters,** Sacramento, CA (916) 922–7500 • **Athletic Supply Of California,** Stockton, CA (209) 952–1887 • **Big 5 Sporting Goods,** Stockton, CA (209) 957–3095 • **Champs Sports,** Stockton, CA (209) 478–8280 • **Copeland Sports,** Stockton, CA (209) 957–6441 • **Javier's Sporting Goods,** Stockton, CA (209) 462–1480 • **Play It Again Sports,** Stockton, CA (209) 474–1944 • **Sports Station,** Stockton, CA (209) 956–6475 • **Sundance Sports,** Stockton, CA (209) 477–3754

Maps:

USGS maps: Bruceville, CA
A trail map is available from the visitor center for a small donation.

Know Your Pinnipeds

Is it a seal or a sea lion?

All pinnipeds—which means *wing-* or *fin-footed*—descended from land-dwelling animals, although it's thought that *phocids* (true seals) share a common ancestor with otters, while *otariids* (eared seals) are more closely related to bears. The most obvious visual difference between true seals and eared seals is the way they move on land. True seal's hind flippers are fused together and directed rearward like a whale's flukes. When on land, true seals have to inch along on their bellies like a caterpillar. Eared seals, on the other hand, can tuck their hind flippers under them and support their weight with the front flippers, allowing for a means of locomotion closer to that of a land dwelling animal. In the water, true seals propel themselves forward primarily with the hind flippers, while eared seals use their fore flippers to swim.

What might you see? And where?

If you see light gray animals with dark spots, these are likely harbor seals. They tend to stick close to shore, and are commonly seen around docks and wharves. Males and females of this species are about the same size averaging between 200 and 300 pounds. At the other end of the scale is the Northern elephant seal. The name stems from the sizable schnozz that males develop when they reach sexual maturity. Like the harbor seal, the elephant seal is a *phocid* (or true seal), although that's where the similarity ends. Elephant seals show a strong sexual dimorphism—meaning, the males of the species grow much larger than females. While the females are impressive enough at up to 2,000 pounds, old bulls can reach a stately 5,000 pounds and 18 feet in length.

Recent research has shown that the elephant seals are master divers, able to hold their breath for up to two hours and dive to depths of nearly a mile. Nearly hunted to extinction for their blubber, elephant seals are making a comeback and can often be seen near Chimney Rock on Point Reyes and at Año Nuevo, south of San Francisco.

California sea lions, the most abundant representatives of the *otariids* (or eared seals), are commonly observed up and down the coast and are very playful. They can often be seen lounging out on rocks or swimming in groups, and tend to express themselves through loud, raucous barks. These guys are often blamed by fishermen for declining fish stocks, in spite of several million years of co-evolution.

Stellar sea lions—a threatened species—have been reduced to a few scattered breeding colonies in California. Though relatively quiet in its colonies, when a Stellar sea lion does vocalize, the cry is less a bark than a bold roar. These guys are the largest of the sea lions, with heads broad and bear-like and bodies stretching up to 10 feet and weighing 2,000 pounds.

Another resident of these waters is the Northern fur seal (a.k.a. the Alaska fur seal). Rarely seen on shore, the fur seal can sometimes be seen sleeping on its back on the open ocean with its flippers in the air. The fur seal has a shorter, blunter snout than other seals and sea lions, in addition to a thicker coat and the most obvious ears of all the resident pinnipeds.

Honorable Mentions

Bay Area & Wine Country

Compiled here is an index of great hikes in the Bay Area and Wine Country region that didn't make the A-list this time around but deserve recognition. Check them out and let us know what you think. You may decide that one or more of these hikes deserves higher status in future editions or, perhaps, you may have a hike of your own that merits some attention.

(A) Drake's Estero Trail

This is an invigorating 9.0-mile out-and-back across the grass-covered headlands of Point Reyes National Seashore. North of San Francisco, head west on Sir Francis Drake Road and continue up through the town of Inverness. At mile 8.5, turn left onto the signed road leading to the Estero Trail, and continue another mile to the trailhead. Follow the gravel trail past arms of the estuary and through dairy pastures to the Drake's Head Trail. Go left on this, and follow it to the top of a cliff overlooking Drake's Bay.

For more information contact Point Reyes National Seashore, Point Reyes Station, CA (415) 663–1092 or visit *www.nps.gov/pore*. *DeLorme: Northern California Atlas & Gazetteer:* Page 93 D5

Redwood Coast

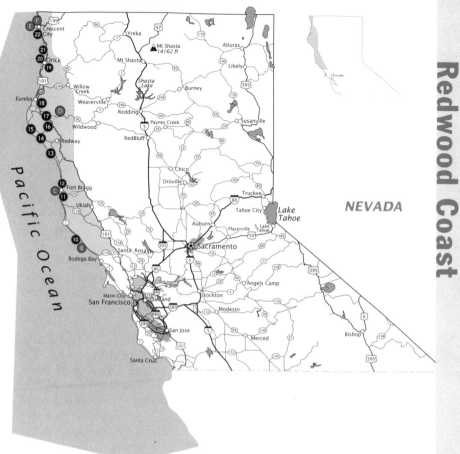

OREGON

NEVADA

Pacific Ocean

The Hikes

Honorable Mentions

Redwood Coast

This area covers a 240-mile swath of the Northern California coast from Sonoma County up to Del Norte County and the Oregon border. At the northern end of this strip lie the largest examples of primal old-growth forests in the state, chief among them the stately redwood groves that have been a source of tourist amazement—and logging controversy—for the past 100 years. The best groves are preserved in several state parks and one national park, spread out sparsely up the coast and clustering into a patchwork of parks in Humboldt and Del Norte counties. The newest of these tree *museums* is the Headwaters Forest Reserve, created in 1999 when the state and federal governments purchased the land from Pacific Lumber Company, after years of protests and negotiations. The reserve still has limited public access, but one trail is open for day use.

Farther south, the coast range makes a frontal assault on the Pacific, marching up to the water with row upon row of steep-sloped ridges. The unwelcoming coastline has effectively discouraged human development and resulted in roughly 40 miles of largely untouched shoreline, collectively known as the Lost Coast. Several fine trails explore this lush and rugged landscape. Kings Peak, at just over 4,000 feet, is not the tallest of peaks, but with its foothills practically dangling into the Pacific, the view from the summit is nonetheless remarkable. Nearby Sinkiyone Wilderness State Park offers a narrow strip of meadows and elk-haunted forests, long-since abandoned homesteads, and great hiking trails.

The Mendocino and Sonoma coastline—accessed by the long, snaking ribbon of California 1—is a rugged and rocky shelf, riddled with natural bridges, sea caves, blowholes, and rock-studded coves. The sea is equally rough, with undertows, rip tides, and large, crashing waves that still tempt a few brave surfers out into the fray. Beaches, where they exist, tend to be narrow strips in sheltered coves, but waters are rarely safe for casual swimming. Grassy meadows run along the level tops of coastal bluffs, where trails explore the erosive power of the sea. Seals and sea lions ply the waters close to shore, and spouts of ocean spray betray the presence of migrating gray whales in deeper water. Other hikes follow narrow ravines from sheltered coves to lush, verdant forests and mossy waterfalls upstream.

Overview

Coastal Trail: Fisk Mill to Stump Beach on the Bluff Trail

Whale watchers, be on the lookout! This hike visits a prime spot to see the huge mammals in their natural habitat. The trail is a short hike along steep bluffs overlooking offshore rocks, which are home to harbor seals. Deep gullies and surge channels are also interesting features found along this rugged stretch of coast. (*See page 78.*)

Russian Gulch Trail

The trail leads up through a lush coastal canyon filled with ferns, maples, berries, and second-growth redwood trees to a 36-foot waterfall. On the coast, hikers can view the Punchbowl, a collapsed wave tunnel with a diameter of 100 feet. The Punchbowl resembles a large crater churning at its base with waves injected through a tunnel from the nearby shoreline. (*See page 84.*)

Ten Mile Beach Trail

This trail is an old logging road, now closed to the motorized vehicles due to several washed-out sections. The path leads past MacKerricher Dunes, one of the coast's longest dune systems and Inglenook Fen, a coastal wetland. The fen shelters rare plants, like marsh pennywort and rein orchid, and is home to several endemic insect species. (*See page 90.*)

Lost Coast Trail

This relatively easy piece of the Lost Coast Trail follows a narrow strip of grassy meadows nestled between driftwood-strewn beaches and densely forested slopes. Observant hikers can spot pelicans, gray whales, and harbor seals in the water, as well as Roosevelt elk in the woodlands. For those who want to spend more time here, there are two excellent walk-in campgrounds along the trail. The complete Lost Coast Trail covers over 25 miles of shoreline that are inaccessible by other means. *(See page 96.)*

King Peak Trail

This short, steep hike to Kings Peak—the highest point in the King Range at 4,087 feet—offers 360-degree views of the rugged Lost Coast. The trail passes through oak, alder, madrone, and old-growth fir forests and emerges onto bare, knife-edge ridges before reaching the peak.
(See page 102.)

Mattole Beach Trail

This hike is a beach bum's paradise. The trail begins at the Mattole River Estuary and offers three miles of beautiful black sand beaches, dunes, and tide pools that lead to an abandoned lighthouse. Along the way, there is plenty of secluded beach to comb. Hiking beneath the cliffs at Punta Gorda can be dangerous at high tide,

so be sure to plan your hike during low tide. Because low tide comes at different times every day, hikers will need to consult a tide calendar. This information usually is posted at the trailhead. *(See page 106.)*

Bull Creek Flats Loop

This trail takes hikers on a classic stroll through the Rockefeller Forest, one of the largest tracts of contiguous uncut coastal redwoods in the world. The path wanders among the majestic trees, many of which are individually named for peculiar traits—like the Flatiron Tree, known for its distinctive cross-section. Beneath the canopy, plant-lovers will find a variety of floral gems, including giant horsetail, iris, blue blossom, and sweet-scented bedstraw. *(See page 112.)*

Drury-Chaney Loop

This trail is named for two leaders of the Save-the-Redwoods League, Newton B. Drury and Ralph Works Chaney. The path showcases their namesake redwood groves, protected along with several other acres as part of Humboldt Redwoods State Park. Hikers will also encounter wild cucumber, false lily-of-the-valley, and California laurel. *(See page 118.)*

Headwaters Trail

The hike leads through one of Northern California's most controversial pieces of real estate, the infamous Headwaters Forest. This infamous parcel of land includes old-growth redwood forest that was saved from the chainsaw through the much-publicized *Headwaters Deal* of 1999. The trail is the only path in the preserve that presently is open to the public. It passes by the site of a former mill town called Falk, gone now except for some plants that once decorated residents' gardens. The hike culminates on the edge of the old-growth Headwaters Grove at a vista point overlooking Hole in the Headwaters—a controversial piece of land within the preserve that was exempted from the agreement. *(See page 124.)*

Tall Trees Grove Loop

A short, but impressive walk through the world's tallest trees. Besides redwoods, there are also rhododendrons, giant ferns, and moss-hung maple trees, as well as access to wild Redwood Creek. The drive to preserve this grove led to the establishment of Redwood National Park. A permit is required to visit the Tall Trees Grove and is available free of charge from the visitor center just south of Orick. There they will give you the code for the combination lock on the gate (changed on a regular basis) and answer any questions you might have. (*See page 130.*)

Skunk Cabbage Section of the Coastal Trail

This trail is a veritable cornucopia of habitats that leads through massive spruce and melancholy alder stands, into deep green canyons, and along pristine coastal bluffs. Along the way, hikers have a chance to see abundant wildflowers and the very plant that gives the trail its name, the skunk cabbage. Very quiet, observant naturewatchers might even be lucky enough to catch a glimpse of elk through the trees. (*See page 136.*)

Fern Canyon/James Irvine Double Loop

This hike is an invigorating stroll through ancient forests along meandering streams to the ocean and the magical Fern Canyon. Roosevelt elk are plentiful in the park—especially along Gold Bluffs Beach, where the trail turns and returns through the forest to the trailhead. Fern Canyon and the adjacent bluffs still show signs of human activity dating to the late 1800s, when the area was the site of gold mining operations. (*See page 140.*)

Damnation Creek Trail

This hike follows a steep but very scenic trail, which offers the best of old-growth redwoods and rugged coastline. In spring, the trail is sprinkled with a variety of wildflowers—most notably the distinctive three-leafed trillium, a showy native flower with white and pink blossoms. The trail ends at a beach next to a small, natural rock arch, carved by waves. Excellent tide pools can be explored at low tide. *(See page 146.)*

Coastal Trail
Fisk Mill to Stump Beach

Hike Specs

Start: From the Fisk Mill north parking lot
Length: 2.6-mile out-and-back
Approximate Hiking Time: 1.5–2 hours
Difficulty Rating: Easy to Moderate due to a couple of steep sections and a poorly maintained trail
Terrain: Dirt path through Bishop pine forests and open meadows and along a rocky coastline
Elevation Gain: 290 feet
Land Status: State park
Nearest Town: Walsh Landing, CA
Other Trail Users: Hikers only
Canine Compatibility: Leashed dogs are permitted only in picnic and parking areas, and are not allowed on the trail itself.

Getting There

From Santa Rosa: Drive six miles west on CA 12, then turn right onto CA 116 and follow it about 28 miles to the junction with CA 1. Go north 20 miles on CA 1, continuing past the main entrance to Salt Point State Park and the Stump Beach parking areas to the Fisk Mill parking area at the northernmost end of the park. Turn left into the Fisk Mill parking area and immediately turn right, following this road 0.2 miles to the north parking lot. The trail begins on the west side of the lot at the sign for the Bluff Trail. *DeLorme: Northern California Atlas & Gazetteer:* Page 82 D2

The Mendocino Coast has some of California's most dramatic coastline scenery. Steep-walled cliffs drop off into crashing surf. Enormous waves slam against offshore rocks and explode in a wall of spray. Deep coves shelter hidden beaches. And the constant attention of the ocean carves caves and natural bridges into the rock. In short, it's a fine place to take a stroll.

Salt Point State Park harbors a variety of terrain within its 6,000 acres. Gerstle Cove Marine Reserve, also within park boundaries, is one of the first underwater parks in California, protecting the diversity of marine life found here. Aside from the rocky coast, the park offers a variety of habitats that includes grasslands and forests of Bishop pine. There are also stands of second-growth redwoods, and even a small pygmy forest.

In the past, this area was home to several groups of southwestern Pomo Indians, also known as Kashia (or Kashaya) Pomo. Archeologists found evidence of their villages by studying the garbage dumps of yesteryear, called middens. Since the Pomo did not have plastic and metals in those days, most of what went into a midden was biodegradable and has long since turned to dirt. What remain are bones, less perishable artifacts, and—above all—shells. Shellfish was a popular item on the Native American menu, and it's still possible to identify old settlements up and down the coast by the profusion of broken shells in and on the ground. (**Note:** *These sites are valuable for archeologists, so don't disturb them.*)

This hike, one of several short walks within Salt Point State Park, starts at the Fisk Mill parking area at the north end of the park. The path plunges into a shady forest

Geology on display.

dominated by Bishop pine and winds around in the enchanting woods a bit before revealing the first ocean vista. The views here are so striking that most people are likely to spend the majority of their time on this hike gawking at the magical landscape around them. As the trail continues, it ducks in and out of the forest—and later into open grassland—offering new surprises with each visit to the edge.

The earth here also is undergoing constant changes, due in part to a series of streams that course through the region and slowly erode the natural landscape. Where water has bared the bones of the earth, you can see layers of sedimentary rock, which sometimes tend to tilt up at odd angles. The streams that descend from the forests form shallow pools as they encounter bedrock, shortly before taking the final plunge to the sea. Near the halfway point of the hike, a tiny creek careens over the brink of the coastal cliffs, forming a waterfall framed against a background of emerald green plant life. For aspiring postcard photographers, it doesn't get any better than this.

The trail climbs gently as it continues across broad meadows and eventually reaches the entrance to Stump Beach Cove, where it turns inland and skirts the cliffs.

MilesDirections

0.0 START from the west side of the parking lot at the sign for the Bluff Trail. The short spur trail enters the trees and almost immediately joins the Bluff Trail. A short spur leads straight a few yards to a view of the ocean. Turn left, heading south on the Bluff Trail.

0.2 *[FYI. The forest opens to reveal an oceanic panorama on your right. Waves crashing on the rocks can make for spectacular displays.]*

0.3 *[FYI. A picnic area is on the left side of the trail.]* A spur trail heads off to the left, accessing the south parking lot. Continue along Bluff Trail to the right.

0.4 An unofficial path leads off to the right. Continue to the left on Bluff Trail.

0.7 Another unofficial path leads across the meadow to the highway. Continue to the right on the main trail.

1.0 The trail forks here, with one branch going up and over a rock outcropping and the other continuing along the cliffs. Take either one, because they rejoin in a couple hundred feet.

1.1 The trail follows the coastline as it takes a turn eastward. *[FYI. Below you is a nice view of Stump Beach Cove.]*

1.2. The trail descends a steep slope into a ravine and crosses a small footbridge over the creek.

1.3 The trail spills you onto the beach at Stump Beach Cove. This beach is the turn-around point. Return the way you came.

2.6 Arrive back at the trailhead.

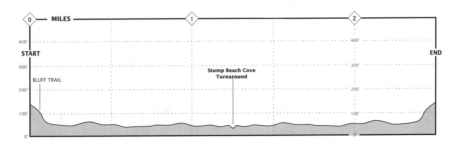

A sweet spot for a nap.

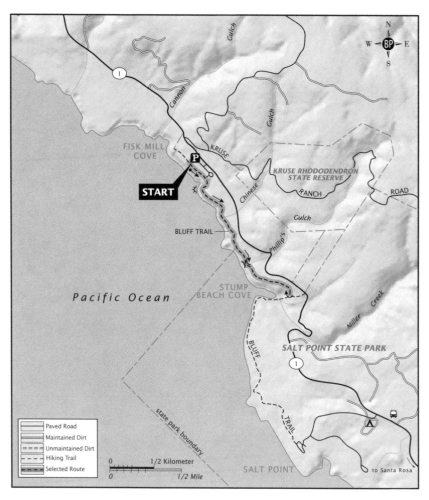

There are extensive kelp beds in and around the cove, and it's easy to imagine Aleutian hunters in the early 19th Century plying the waters in their kayaks and searching for the sea otter that once fed here in large numbers. The Aleuts were working for enterprising Russian fur-traders, probing down the coast from their Alaskan settlements and seeking pelts from the increasingly rare animal. They eventually hunted the otters to the brink of extinction, but the web-footed mammals now are protected by the Endangered Species Act and are making a slow recovery.

Heading east above Stump Beach Cove, the trail passes close to the edge of the tall, dark cliffs that rim the cove. From this vantage point, a natural bridge can be seen in the jagged rock below. The path then leads past the site of a recent forest fire as it re-enters the woodland. As a parting shot, the trail offers a steep scrabble down a gully before crossing the small creek and dropping down the last few feet to Stump Beach. Here you can kick off your shoes and go beachcombing. Be sure to check out the mounds of bullwhip kelp that wash up on the beach regularly.

Sonoma Coast and kelp beds.

Hike Information

Trail Contacts:
Salt Point State Park, Jenner, CA (707) 847-3221 or *www.cal-parks.ca.gov*

Schedule:
Open year round. The visitor center is open daily, 8 A.M.–4 P.M.

Fees/Permits:
$5 per car, day-use fee

Local Information:
Sonoma County websites: *www.sonoma.com* (an excellent place for planning a trip here) or *www.comnetsolutions.com/comnet/sonoma* • **Driving and Ocean Condition Recording:** (707) 847-3222

Accommodations:
Salt Point State Park, Jenner, CA 1-800-444-7275 or 1-800-274-7275 *– There are several camping areas within the park. Call for reservations. Several spots are available for cyclists and hikers on a fist come/first served basis.*

Hiking Tours:
Salt Point State Park, Jenner, CA (707) 847-3221 *– Walking tours are occasionally given by park interpreters. Call for specific information.*

Public Transportation:
Mendocino Transit Authority (MTA): 1-800-696-4682 or *www.transitinfo.org* *– Bus route No. 95 runs once daily along CA 1 between Point Arena and Santa Rosa. The bus will drop you off at any safe location, and you must flag the bus to be picked up. The bus runs inbound to Santa Rosa in the morning and outbound from Santa Rosa in the afternoon. In Santa Rosa, Golden Gate Transit offers connections from San Francisco.*

Local Outdoor Retailers:
Gualala Sport and Tackle Shop, Gualala, CA (707) 884-4247 • **Sonoma Outfitters,** Santa Rosa, CA (707) 528-1920 • **Catch A Canoe & Bicycles Too,** Mendocino, CA (707) 937-0273 • **Big 5 Sporting Goods,** Ukiah, CA (707) 462-2870 • **Diamond Jim's Sporting Goods and Liquor,** Ukiah, CA (707) 462-9741 • **Freedom,** Ukiah, CA (707) 462-3310 • **GI Joe's Outdoor Store,** Ukiah, CA (707) 468-8834

Maps:
USGS maps: Plantation, CA A trail map is available from the visitor center, or at Fort Ross State Park.

Russian Gulch Trail

Hike Specs

Start: From the first gate, just before the campground
Length: 7.0-mile loop
Approximate Hiking Time: 3 hours
Difficulty Rating: Moderate due to some steep sections
Terrain: Pavement, gravel, and dirt path through second-growth redwood forest and riparian streamside habitat
Elevation Gain: 979 feet
Land Status: State park
Nearest Town: Mendocino, CA
Other Trail Users: Cyclists (for a short section)
Canine Compatibility: Dogs not permitted

Getting There

From Fort Bragg: Drive south six miles on CA 1 to Russian Gulch State Park. Turn right at the entrance sign, then immediately left again, which brings you to the park entrance booth. Follow the entrance road 0.2 miles, as it curves around and passes under the highway. Park in the lot just before the first gate, which is locked in winter. The trail starts at the gate. *DeLorme: Northern California Atlas & Gazetteer:* Page 73 B5

Officially called the Falls Loop Trail, this double loop passes through a narrow valley filled to the brim with diverse plant life. The thick, moss-covered maples, alders, and willows that live along the stream give way to mature second-growth redwood forest as the path climbs the steep North Trail to the ridge. From there, the trail drops back to the valley floor and begins the second loop, which brings you to the base of a 36-foot waterfall.

The ancient redwoods in this valley were among the first to be chopped down by European settlers. Beginning in 1852, San Francisco engineer and promoter Harry Meiggs erected a sawmill on the nearby Big River to harvest the trees. In those days, the process of felling the giants was long and labor-intensive. But the difficulties involved in transporting the lumber provided the logging industry with a true challenge. Much of the demand for redwood lumber came from the central part of the state, where the gold rush had turned San Francisco into a boomtown. The era's great Victorian *painted ladies*—large, ornate wooden mansions—were built from redwood, as was everything from railroad ties to shingles to grape vine pickets for California's vineyards. The redwood tree served as a near-perfect building material. It was easy to work, easy to split, and more resistant to rot and insect damage than almost any other wood.

In the years following the gold rush, California's population exploded. Lumber barons quickly made plans to exploit the great forests of the north in order to keep up with heavy demands, but many of those dreams went bust under the weight of the difficult logistics and harsh realities of transporting the wood. Steep, muddy hillsides

and numerous flood-prone waterways in Redwood Country effectively blocked any road-building efforts, while stormy seas and treacherous coasts made shipping equally dangerous.

The challenges involved in harvesting the redwoods often sparked inventive solutions. The trees were so large that new tools and techniques had to be developed in order to fell them. Special two-man crosscut saws—sometimes over 20 feet long—were developed to cut through the mammoth trees. And because the trees tend to swell at the butt, chopping them down at their base was incredibly tough. So inventive foresters devised a system whereby notches were cut in the trunk to support scaffolding, allowing lumberjacks to make the cut 4–10 feet above the ground—where the trunk was noticeably smaller in diameter—and thus easier to cut. Foresters also had to figure out a way to prevent the redwoods from shattering as they hit the ground from their great height. To solve this problem, beds of branches and forest litter were prepared to cushion the impact. The giant trees then had to be cut into pieces (a process known as *bucking*) and taken to the mill. Even after the bucking, the redwood logs were enormous, making transportation out of nearly impenetrable forests and steep ravines difficult at best. The treacherous terrain meant overland

MilesDirections

0.0 START at the parking lot just before the first gate. Head past the gate, following the paved road through the campground.

0.2 Turn left onto the narrow dirt North Trail, and follow it up as it climbs several switchbacks..

0.6 The trail reaches the top of the ridge and levels out.

0.8 *[FYI. The circle of trees on the right sprouted from an old-growth stump, long since rotted away.]*

0.9 The trail crosses the Horse Trail. Continue straight.

1.4 Boundary Trail heads to the left. Continue straight.

1.9 North Boundary Trail heads left. Continue straight.

2.0 The trail crosses two small wooden bridges.

2.5 Descending with several switchbacks, the trail drops back down to the valley bottom.

2.6 North Trail connects to Falls Loop Trail. Turn left onto Falls Loop Trail, then take the left fork, as the trail splits. This is the beginning of the loop section of the trail.

3.0 The trail crosses a long footbridge.

3.1 *[FYI. The regenerative power of redwoods is shown again by the trees growing out of an old stump on the left.]*

3.3 Cross a bridge and follow the trail as it climbs a series of wooden steps.

3.4 An unmarked trail continues straight. Take the right fork, continuing on the main trail to the waterfall.

3.5 Cross the creek on a wooden bridge below the small but scenic waterfall, and follow the trail as it heads up the other side, passing by the top of the falls before climbing steps that have been hewn into the rock.

3.6 An unmarked trail heads left. Take the right fork, following the main trail uphill.

4.0 The trail levels out on top of a low ridge.

4.7 The trail descends to a creek, then joins an old skid road. Turn right on the dirt road and continue downstream.

5.1 Cross a wooden bridge and return to the main junction, where the loop section of the trail ends. Continue straight, retracing the short section of trail to the junction with North Trail. Keep going straight, on the paved main trail back to the campground. (This section of trail is open to bicycles.)

5.6 Road turns to gravel. *[FYI. Several species of ferns are growing everywhere in this moist canyon-bottom, even high in the trees. Maples, willows, and alders grow along the creek, contrasting their light foliage with the dark green of the coniferous forest beyond.]*

6.6 South Trail heads off to the left. Continue straight.

6.8 North Trail heads uphill to the right. Continue straight, retracing the first part of the trail to the parking lot and trailhead.

7.0 Arrive back at the trailhead.

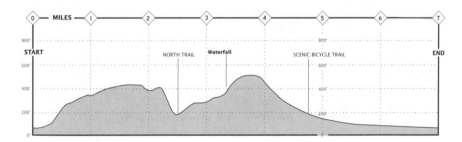

travel was virtually impossible for many years. Though dangerous, the only avenue open during this time was moving the lumber by sea.

The north coast of California is rocky and hazardous, with few good harbors and lots of punishing surf. There is a long history of shipwrecks on the coast, and for a while, salvaging wrecks was something of a local pastime. Conditions along the Mendocino Coast are about as rough as the California shoreline gets. In fact, the only ports available are small, rock-strewn coves known as *dog holes*.

Even getting the lumber on board the schooners was a complicated process. Builders constructed elaborate chutes that were suspended by cables anchored in the rocks. From these chutes, the wood was pushed onto the ships as they bobbed in the surf. Many ships were lost on the jagged rocks using this method, but it proved profitable enough for the practice to continue until better modes of transport were devised. If you look closely, you can still see some of the worn, rusty iron rings once used to anchor the cables along the jagged rocks of the headlands.

Another reminder of the area's logging past is the park's mature second-growth. Although it cannot replace the unique habitat of an ancient forest, the second-growth harbors an impressive amount of vegetation. Full-blown trees often stand atop

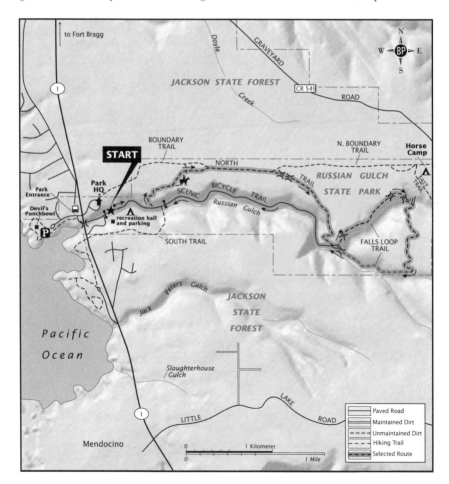

Mouth of Russian Gulch.

old redwood stumps, either as new offshoots of the original tree or as another species that found purchase on the rotten hulk and sent out roots to find the ground. Redwoods are famous for their regenerative abilities. And by producing new shoots, felled or toppled trees can continue to grow, forming new trunks and branches in a potentially limitless cycle. Another phenomenon peculiar to redwoods is the *fairy ring*—or cathedral trees—that form when a redwood stump sends up shoots around the circumference of its base. When the shoots mature, they form a circle of living pillars that have become very popular settings for weddings and other events.

This hike serves as a relaxing journey through a verdant wonderland. Beyond the photogenic waterfall, the trail climbs the opposite ridge and returns along another branch of the creek to the spot where the loops join. From here, you return to the trailhead along an old road that hugs the valley floor as it parallels the creek. Before you leave the park, take a few minutes to check out the Devil's Punchbowl, a collapsed wave tunnel in the middle of a meadow. The Punchbowl is an excellent demonstration of the erosive power of waves.

Hike Information

Trail Contacts:
Russian Gulch State Park, Mendocino, CA (707) 937-5804 or *www.mcn.org/1/ mendoparks/mendo.htm*

Schedule:
Open year round, dawn to dusk. Campground is closed from November 1 to March 31.

Fees/Permits:
$5 day-use fee. Camping is $16.

Local Information:
Fort Bragg-Mendocino Coast Chamber of Commerce, Fort Bragg, CA 1-800-726 2780 or (707) 961-6300 or *www.mendocinocoast.com*

Local Events/Attractions:
Annual Fort Bragg Whale Festival, in March, 1-800-726-2780 – *whale watching, boat show, wine tasting, lighthouse tours, and live music* • **Freedom Run,** in July, (707) 468-8024 – *half marathon, 10K* • **Harvest Festival,** in October, (707) 964-1228 – *craft fair, fiddle contest, and food booths*

Public Transportation:
Mendocino Transit Authority (MTA): 1-800-696-4682 or *www.transitinfo.org* – *Bus route No. 60 stops at CA 1 and Point Cabrillo road just north of the park entrance from Fort Bragg and Mendocino Monday through Friday. In addition, the MTA's CC Rider bus provides one daily roundtrip from Santa Rosa with Golden Gate Transit connections from San Francisco.*

Local Outdoor Retailers:
The Outdoor Store, Fort Bragg, CA (707) 964-1407 • **Pete's Sporting Goods,** Lakeport, CA (707) 263-4413 • **Catch A Canoe and Bicycles Too,** Mendocino, CA (707) 937-0273 • **Big 5 Sporting Goods,** Ukiah, CA (707) 462-2870 • **Diamond Jim's Sporting Goods and Liquor,** Ukiah, CA (707) 462-9741 • **Freedom,** Ukiah, CA (707) 462-3310 • **GI Joe's Outdoor Store,** Ukiah, CA (707) 468-8834 • **Ronnie's Basics,** Ukiah, CA (707) 462-0535 • **Luna's Market and Sportshop,** Willits, CA (707) 459-5775

Maps:
USGS maps: Mendocino, CA

Ten Mile Beach Trail

Hike Specs

Start: From the Laguna Point parking lot
Length: 10.4-mile out-and-back
Approximate Hiking Time: 4–5 hours
Difficulty Rating: Easy due to flat terrain and partially paved trail
Terrain: Using pavement, gravel, and sandy beach paths, tour beaches, dunes, and a salt marsh
Elevation Gain: 305 feet
Land Status: State park
Nearest Town: Fort Bragg, CA
Other Trail Users: Equestrians and cyclists
Canine Compatibility: Leashed dogs permitted

Getting There

From Fort Bragg: Drive north three miles on CA 1, and turn left into Mac Kerricher State Park. After passing the entrance station, continue 0.4 miles to the first junction, turn left and continue 0.4 miles down to Lake Cleone. Turn right just past the lake and pass under the bridge, continuing another 0.2 miles to the Laguna Point parking lot. The trail starts near the entrance to the parking lot, on the east side of the road. *DeLorme: Northern California Atlas & Gazetteer:* Page 63 D5

It is easy to imagine that you're walking some post-apocalyptic stretch of highway as you follow the torn and battered tarmac north along Ten Mile Beach. The bridge passing over the park entrance road is one of the better-preserved sections of the old Haul Road, which once connected area loggers to the mill in Fort Bragg. The story of this road is also the story of the park, as the histories of both of them are intertwined and can be traced back to the man the park was named after, Duncan MacKerricher. Canadian-born MacKerricher and his new bride Jessica sailed for California from New York in 1864. In those days, the voyage was a long one that involved departing in pre-canal Panama and traveling by rail across the isthmus. The voyage continued on the Pacific side by ship to San Francisco, where the MacKerrichers boarded another vessel and headed north along the dangerous north coast. MacKerricher found work in the mill for a while, then signed on as an assistant with the local Indian Agent. At that time, the Mendocino Indian Reservation occupied the land north of Fort Bragg—including the current site of the state park—and the fort existed to oversee it. The reservation eventually was relocated to the Round Valley, but MacKerricher stayed on and set up shop as a dairy farmer.

In 1915, the Union Lumber Company obtained MacKerricher's permission to build an extension of the California Pacific Railroad from Fort Bragg to the Ten Mile River. Loggers used the new route to transport wood from the river to the mill. The railroad hugged the coast, following a trail used for centuries by the Coast Yuki and neighboring Pomo Indians as they traveled up and down the coast. In 1949, the well-worn tracks were taken up and replaced with a paved logging road, allowing the logs to be moved by truck instead of train car.

But being so close to the ocean has been hard on the road, which had to be repaired many times over the years. By 1968, the cost to maintain the road had become prohibitive and it was abandoned. At this point, the land adjacent to the road had already been sold to the state in the 1950s for use as a park. The state acquired the stretch of road in 1995, and MacKerricher State Park was complete.

As the trail continues north into the park's less-visited areas, hikers will notice a break in the dunes through which a small pond is visible. This is Sandhill Lake, and it forms the centerpiece of one of California's rarest landscapes. Inglenook Fen, home to dozens of rare, indigenous species, belongs to the category of wetland known as

MilesDirections

0.0 START at the entrance to the parking lot. Follow the short gravel trail that heads east (away from the ocean) through the bushes. Follow this about 150 feet, then turn left onto the paved road (now closed to cars).

0.3 At the first washed-out section of the road, there is a steel tunnel going under the raised roadbed, partially rusted and collapsed at the ends. *[**FYI.** Mats of ice plant cover the ground next to the trail.]*

0.4 Horse Trail goes off to the right. Continue straight along the old road.

0.8 The trail passes several houses on the right. At this point, the state park is just a thin strip of beach and dunes.

1.1 A spur trail goes down to the right, then curves left and passes through a culvert under the road to access the beach. Continue straight along the old road.

1.4 The old road is washed out here. Take the short gravel trail down to the beach and continue along the upper edge of the beach.

1.6 A creek comes out of the dunes, often vanishing into the sand before it reaches the ocean.

1.8 Keep to the left of the posts in the sand on the edge of the dunes.

2.0 The road resumes after a long absence. Climb back up onto it and continue on the old road.

2.1 The beach is very narrow at this point, and waves frequently reach the old road, causing it to wash out in places. Continue straight along the remaining pavement.

2.3 The road has been completely washed out. Continue straight, north along the beach.

2.4 The road resumes. Climb back onto it and continue north. *[**FYI.** The ground to the right is covered with thousands of crushed seashells. These are midden heaps left from pre-contact Native American settlements, and are protected archeological sites.]*

2.7 *[**FYI.** The marsh to the right is Inglenook Fen. A few buildings from an old cattle ranch remain on the edge of the dunes. In January, you can hear hundreds of frogs chirping in the fen.]*

3.5 The vegetation is now changing to include more brush and even some small trees.

5.0 The old road is half buried in spots by the surrounding dunes, which are larger here than they have been. The trail curves inland along the banks of Ten Mile River, on the left.

5.2 The trail reaches the park boundary where CA 1 bridges Ten Mile River. This is the turn-around point for the hike. Return the way you came.

10.4 Arrive back at the trailhead.

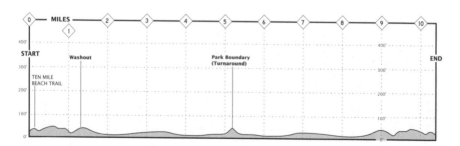

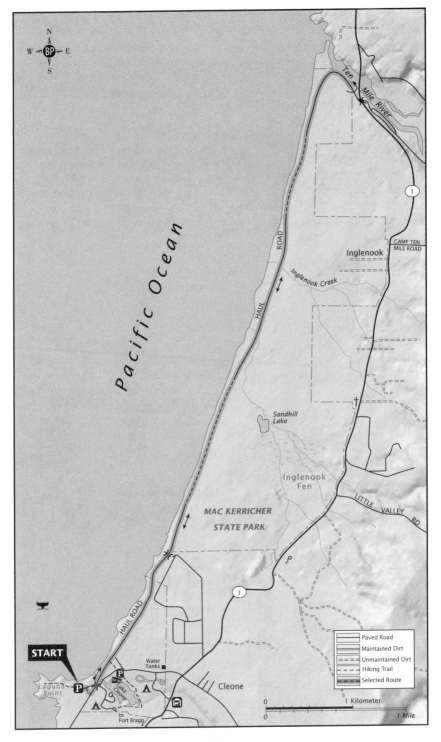

N
W - BP - E
S

Pacific Ocean

Ten Mile River

1

HAUL ROAD

Inglenook Creek

Inglenook

CAMP TEN MILE ROAD

Sandhill Lake

Inglenook Fen

LITTLE VALLEY RD

MAC KERRICHER STATE PARK

1

HAUL ROAD

START

Laguna Point

P

P

Water Tanks

Lake Cleone

Cleone

to Fort Bragg

Paved Road
Maintained Dirt
Unmaintained Dirt
Hiking Trail
Selected Route

0   1 Kilometer
0   1 Mile

coastal fen. Floristically speaking, a fen is somewhere between a bog and a marsh. The difference lies in the soil and the plants that grow in those soils. In a marsh, grasslands are flooded or partially flooded, and the soil is mostly mineral. In a bog, the soil is mostly organic—made up of decaying plant matter that allows the formation of thick peat moss layers. A fen has aspects of both, with a mixture of mineral and organic soils that allows some formation of peat. Inglenook Fen was created about 5,000 years ago when the formation of dunes along the beach blocked the outflow of water from the fen's drainage.

If fate had been less kind, Inglenook Fen could easily have wound up as a parking lot for a shopping mall before its uniqueness was discovered. The fen's special gifts were not really uncovered until the 1960s when scientists began studying the wetlands and realized that this was more than just your run-of-the-mill damp spot. Within this small area are dozens of endemic insect species—species found nowhere else in the world—and a variety of rare plants. Some of these plants are typically found only in arctic zones, a fact that has sparked suspicions that the Inglenook plants

Ten Mile River.

are remnants of the last ice age. But there's more: A 1970s study discovered over 500 arthropods living here; of those, many were previously unknown to science.

Though incredibly rare now, fens were originally commonplace. At the time of European contact, they were found interspersed all along the Northern California coast. But today, Inglenook Fen is the last one existing in the state. While the trail does not go through the fen (the protected land is far too fragile an environ to withstand much human contact), it does travel through the dunes on the fen's western edge. Hikers will have plenty of opportunity to admire the fragile ecosystem from this vantage point. The state park system is working to preserve the rare habitat, so please respect the restrictions and stay on the path.

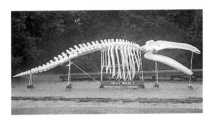

The trail continues through the northern dunes until it reaches the turnaround point at the broad mouth of the Ten Mile River. Return the way you came.

Hike Information

● Trail Contacts:
Russian River-Mendocino Sector, MacKerricher State Park: (707) 937-5804

● Schedule:
Open year round, with reduced facilities from October through February

● Fees/Permits:
No day-use fee, but camping costs $16

● Local Information:
Fort Bragg-Mendocino Coast Chamber of Commerce, Fort Bragg, CA 1-800-726-2780 or (707) 961-6300 or www.mencdocinocoast.com

● Local Events/Attractions:
Annual Fort Bragg Whale Festival, in March, 1-800-726-2780 – *whale watching, boat show, wine tasting, lighthouse tours, and live music* • **Freedom Run,** in July, (707) 468-8024 – *half marathon, 10K* • **Harvest Festival,** in October, (707) 964-1228 – *craft fair, fiddle contest, and food booths*

● Hike Tours:
MacKerricher State Park: (707) 937-5804 – *There are seasonal ranger-led hikes. Call for more information.*

● Organizations:
Ten Mile Coastal Trail Foundation, Fort Bragg, CA (707) 964-9340 or www.mcn.org/1/10milecoastaltrail.

● Local Outdoor Retailers:
The Outdoor Store, Fort Bragg, CA (707) 964-1407 • **Catch A Canoe and Bicycles Too,** Mendocino, CA (707) 937-0273 • **Big 5 Sporting Goods,** Ukiah, CA (707) 462-2870 • **Diamond Jim's Sporting Goods and Liquor,** Ukiah, CA (707) 462-9741 • **Freedom,** Ukiah, CA (707) 462-3310 • **GI Joe's Outdoor Store,** Ukiah, CA (707) 468-8834 • **Ronnie's Basic,** Ukiah, CA (707) 462-0535 • **Luna's Market & Sportshop,** Willits, CA (707) 459-5775

● Maps:
USGS maps: Inglenook, CA; Fort Bragg, CA

13

Lost Coast Trail

Hike Specs

Start: From the Needle Rock visitor center
Length: 4.4-mile out-and-back
Approximate Hiking Time: 2 hours
Difficulty Rating: Easy due to good trails and little elevation gain
Terrain: Dirt path through coastal bench lands, meadows, and sparse forest
Elevation Gain: 915 feet
Land Status: State park
Nearest Town: Shelter Cove, CA
Other Trail Users: Equestrians
Canine Compatibility: Dogs not permitted

Getting There

From Redway: Head west 10.7 miles on Briceland Road and take the left fork (still Briceland Road), following the sign for Whitethorn and Shelter Cove. Continue another two miles, then take the left fork again (still Briceland Road) to Whitethorn. Drive 8.8 miles and turn left at the signed junction leading to Sinkyone Wilderness State Park. From here, it's another 3.2 miles along a narrow dirt road (still Briceland Road) to the Needle Rock visitor center. The trail starts a few feet back up the road from the parking lot, on the west side of the road. **DeLorme: Northern California Atlas & Gazetteer:** Page 62 A4

A s a crow flies, Sinkyone Wilderness State Park is scarcely 10 miles from the busy U.S. Route 101 corridor. But down on the ground, the traveler quickly learns why the area is known as the Lost Coast. Travel in this region is difficult when conditions are optimum; during the winter rainy season, it can be near impossible. The result is a feeling of total isolation. And when the weather is right, the effect can be downright paradisiacal. For some, the park can be difficult to reach—the main road in is virtually a jeep trail, after all—but hikers are rewarded with gorgeous scenery and relative privacy. This hike includes the option of a short spur trail to the beach and a chance to see the park's resident herd of Roosevelt elk, which were reintroduced here in 1982.

Though relatively undeveloped now, the region bustled with inhabitants in the past. Before Europeans began emigrating and settling the West, the Northern California coastline had one of the highest population densities in North America—and the Lost Coast, home to the Sinkyone Indians, was no exception. The Athabaskan-speaking tribe represents a line of human occupation that may reach back more than 14,000 years. The Sinkyone spent the summer months on the coast, harvesting the abundant sea life, before moving inland to spend the winter in permanent villages on the banks of the South Fork Eel River. To survive, they hunted seals and sea lions; collected ocean fish, seaweed, and shellfish; and gathered a variety of roots, nuts, seeds, and berries in the area. They also foraged for acorns, a major staple of the Sinkyone diet, in the tanoak groves that thrived on the coast. The native Californians set fires in the groves to clear out the undergrowth and make it easier to collect the acorns. These burnouts had an environmentally helpful side

Two young bulls, or "spikes."

MilesDirections

0.0 START at the Needle Rock visitor center parking lot. Hike back up the road 100 yards to the Horse Camp building. Follow the narrow footpath as it veers off from the road to the left, passing just below the Horse Camp building and heading north.

0.1 The trail crosses a small creek on a tiny footbridge.

0.2 *[FYI. Needle Rock is visible in the surf to the left. Due to natural erosion, the moniker is no longer quite accurate.]*

0.3 Cross a wooden bridge. (A short spur trail leads straight ahead to Streamside Camp.) Follow the main trail as it switches back to the left and continues north.

0.6 Low Gap Trail heads to the right. Continue straight.

0.8 *[FYI. After crossing a creek via a wooden bridge, an old dam is visible to the left after crossing, left over from the homesteaders who used to live here.]*

1.0 The eucalyptus stand to the right of the trail marks Jones Beach Camp, site of a former homestead. A spur trail from the entrance road leads to the right. Continue straight, and cross the creek via a footbridge. The rusted remains of a vintage automobile can be seen on the left.

1.1 *[Side-trip. Jones Beach Trail, on the left, leads down 0.2 miles to the ocean.]* Continue straight.

1.5 The trail skirts the edge of a long narrow pond. *[FYI. Herds of Roosevelt elk are often seen here.]*

1.8 The trail heads inland, following Whale Gulch.

1.9 *[FYI. Mats of periwinkle can be seen on both sides of the trail.]*

2.2 The trail reaches the Whale Gulch stream crossing. The Lost Coast Trail continues on the other side, but this is the turnaround point for this hike. Return the way you came.

4.4 Arrive back at the trailhead.

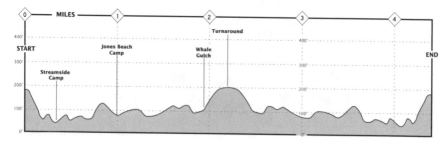

effect: They improved the health of the groves by removing the insect-infested, rotten acorns from the forest bed.

The Sinkyone population declined rapidly during and after the Gold Rush, when settlers poured into the area to look for land. Inevitable tensions arose between the newcomers and the native Sinkyone. And as was often the case, the Native Americans were forced to cede in these situations. One of the most famous instances of the Sinkyone-settler conflict is the story of Sally Bell. In the 1930s, the elderly Sinkyone woman told white friends about her childhood on the Lost Coast in the 1860s. The episode that figured most prominently in the tale was the night Bell saw her family massacred by U.S. soldiers and how she survived by hiding in the bushes.

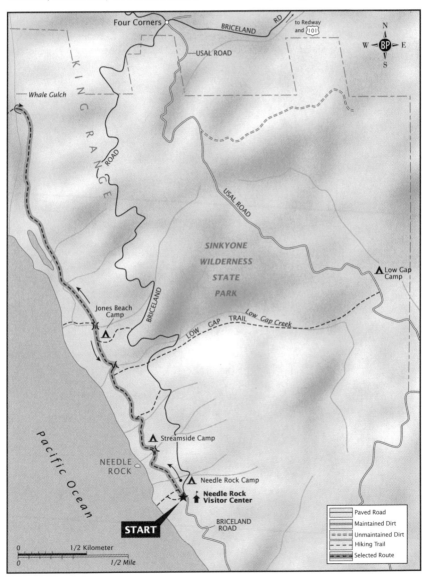

Bell's life story inspired an activist arrested in 1983 to give Police the name Sally Bell in place of her own to call attention to logging on one of the Lost Coast's last remaining old-growth redwood groves. Eventually, over 7,000 acres of the groves were purchased from the Georgia-Pacific lumber company. Nearly half of that land was added to the state park, doubling the park's total acreage. The remaining 3,800 acres were bought by the InterTribal Sinkyone Wilderness Council, a non-profit consortium of Native American tribes. The council plans to manage the area as a unique park, with land-use guidelines inspired by the ancient stewardship ethics of native Californian tribes.

The hike begins at the Needle Rock visitor center, where you can see the first of many relics of the park's past habitation. The visitor center itself is housed in what once was a ranch house belonging to dairyman Calvin Cooper Stewart and his family. Both of the walk-in campsites are located on former homesteads; and if you look carefully, you can find other vestiges of the pioneer era. These artifacts range from a

small dam and an abandoned railroad bed, to a rancher-planted eucalyptus grove, to the rusted skeleton of a vintage automobile.

The homesteaders left another important mark on the region: the disappearance of the tanoak groves. Settlers originally grazed livestock in the meadows and harvested tanoak bark, which was used in commercial leather tanneries. But the practice of stripping the trees of bark and leaving them to rot eventually resulted in the disappearance of the indigenous tanoak groves. In time, settlers turned their focus to logging and established a town and sawmill at Bear Harbor, where 300 workers were employed by the turn of the century. The remoteness and inaccessibility eventually took its toll, and the highways were built around—rather than through—the convoluted King Range.

The turnaround point for this hike is Whale Gulch. But hikers with more time can continue along the path as far as the Mattole River Estuary, some 35 trail miles north of here. (See *Hike 15* for the northernmost three miles.)

Hike Information

🕐 Trail Contacts:
Sinkyone Wilderness State Park, Whitethorn, CA (707) 986–7711

🕐 Schedule:
Open year round, from dawn to dusk

💲 Fees/Permits:
$3 day-use fee from May to September; $2 fee from October to April. Camping is $11 from May to September; $7 from October to April.

❓ Local Information:
Eureka-Humboldt County Convention & Visitor's Bureau, Eureka, CA 1–800–346–3482 or (707) 443–5097 • Humboldt County websites: *www.visithumboldt.com, www.co.humboldt.ca.us, www.redwoodvisitor.org,* and *www.humguide.com* • Links to individual state parks: *www.cal-parks.ca.gov*

🎎 Organizations:
California Coastal Trails Foundation, Trails Coordinator, P.O. Box 20073, Santa Barbara, CA 93120

🎒 Local Outdoor Retailers:
Adventure's Edge, Arcata, CA (707) 822–4673 • The Outdoor Store, Arcata, CA (707) 822–0321 • Big 5 Sporting Goods, Eureka, CA (707) 444–3682 • Bucksport Sporting Goods, Eureka, CA (707) 442–1832 • Northern Mountain Supply, Eureka, CA (707) 445–1711 • Picky Picky Picky Inc., Eureka, CA (707) 444–9201 • Pro Sport Center, Eureka, CA (707) 443–6328 • Sports Exchange, Eureka, CA (707) 444–3644

Ⓝ Maps:
USGS maps: Bear Harbor, CA

King Peak Trail

Hike Specs

Start: From the Lightning Trailhead
Length: 5.0-mile out-and-back
Approximate Hiking Time: 3 hours
Difficulty Rating: Moderate to Strenuous due to steep switchbacks and elevation gain
Terrain: Dirt path through densely forested slopes and along exposed ridges
Elevation Gain: 2,017 feet
Land Status: Bureau of Land Management land
Nearest Town: Shelter Cove, CA
Other Trail Users: Equestrians
Canine Compatibility: Dogs permitted

Getting There

From Redway: Head west 10.7 miles on Briceland Road and take the left fork (still Briceland Road), following the sign for Whitethorn and Shelter Cove. Continue another two miles, then take the right fork (Shelter Cove Road), and drive another 4.5 miles. Turn right onto King Peak Road and drive 8.5 miles, then take the left fork (Lightning Road) and continue another six miles to the Lightning Trailhead, located on the left side of the road. The trail starts at the bulletin board.
DeLorme: Northern California Atlas & Gazetteer: Page 52 C3

The King Range is a convoluted, crumpled mass of ridges and steep-walled valleys that was formed by the violent meeting of three plates of the earth's crust. Just offshore lies the point of convergence, where the North American plate—upon which the King Range sits—and two oceanic plates collide. The range has risen 66 feet in the last 6,000 years, a feverish pace of activity by geologic standards. This phenomenal growth has made life interesting for archeologists, who have found ancient sites high up in the hills that were once located near the shore. Most of these sites

consist of middens—the refuse and compost heaps of tribal groups who gathered on the coast in summer to harvest the bountiful shellfish and other oceanic edibles. The bulk of what is found in the middens is the unde-cayed shells and bones of animals eaten long ago. But scientists occasionally are lucky enough to turn up artifacts that shed some light on how the original inhabitants lived. The upward growth of the mountains—aside from making the middens easier to date by measuring the rate of elevation—has preserved the sites from the ravages of storm-caused erosion on the dunes. (**Note:** *It should go without saying that any archeological sites found by hikers should be left undisturbed.*)

The King Range is unlike other California mountains, in that the coastal mountains here edge right up to the sea, providing little or no room for the development that is so common along the rest of the California coastline. The steepness of the terrain makes it difficult to build and maintain roads, and seismic activity keeps the ground unstable. Furthering the problems for developers, the King Range gets heavy rainfall in the winter—even by regional standards. Precipitation averages 100-plus inches per year. And in wet years, 200 or more inches are possible—making this one of the wettest spots in the United States. Bad weather easily renders the steep, windy dirt and gravel roads impassable, even to 4WD vehicles. All of these factors conspire to keep the area largely undeveloped, allowing the King Range to maintain a feeling of remoteness and deserve the nickname the *Lost Coast*.

But humans have not always been so dependant on roads. Prior to European arrival, this stretch of coastline was one of the most densely populated areas in North America. The Sinkyone Indians and their ancestors have lived here for more than 6,000 years, enjoying the abundance of plant and animal life found in the forestal and

Hike Information

Trail Contacts:
Arcata Resource Area, U.S. Bureau of Land Management, Arcata, CA (707) 825–2300

Schedule:
Open year round

Fees/Permits:
Permits required only for organized groups

Local Information:
Eureka-Humboldt County Convention & Visitor's Bureau, Eureka, CA 1–800–346–3482 or (707) 443–5097 • **Humboldt County websites:** *www.visithumboldt.com, www.co.humboldt.ca.us, www.redwoodvisitor.org,* and *www. humguide.com* • **Links to individual state parks:** *www.cal-parks.ca.gov*

Accommodations:
There are several primitive campgrounds within the King Range Conservation Area. Most of them cost $5–$8 per night.

Local Outdoor Retailers:
Adventure's Edge, Arcata, CA (707) 822–4673 • **The Outdoor Store,** Arcata, CA (707) 822–0321 • **Big 5 Sporting Goods,** Eureka, CA (707) 444–3682 • **Bucksport Sporting Goods,** Eureka, CA (707) 442–1832 • **Northern Mountain Supply,** Eureka, CA (707) 445–1711 • **Picky Picky Picky Inc.,** Eureka, CA (707) 444–9201 • **Pro Sport Center,** Eureka, CA (707) 443–6328 • **Sports Exchange,** Eureka, CA (707) 444–3644

Maps:
USGS maps: Honeydew, CA

coastal habitats. Though their numbers have greatly diminished, the Sinkyone still live in the area and use certain sites for ceremonial purposes. Such places generally are not open to the public.

As you head up the path from the Lightning Trailhead, you pass through a woodland supporting thick undergrowth and characterized by oak, alder, and madrone. This terrain gradually gives way to a mature stand of fir, and the trail starts its steep climb up switchbacks to the ridge. Don't expect to find the redwood, which is so common in surrounding lands, here. The King Range is subjected to hot, dry winds in the summer months that cancel out the effects of winter's prodigious rainfall, making the climate unsuitable for the giant trees. In place of redwoods, hikers should look for patches of the more drought-tolerant old-growth fir forests.

Farther up the ridge, the vegetation changes once again. The climate and land now favor smaller hardwoods and scrubby chaparral. The view begins to open up, and it's possible to see the Mattole River Valley to the north, the Eel River to the east, and the snow-capped peaks of the Yolla Bolly-Middle Eel Wilderness to the southeast.

MilesDirections

0.0 START at the Lightning Trailhead bulletin board. Follow the King Peak Trail as it heads into the forest behind the sign.

0.4 An unmarked trail heads left. Continue straight, keeping to the main trail.

0.7 (A spur trail heads right at the sign, apparently leading to Big Rock Camp—not found on maps.) Follow the main trail as it curves right, climbing uphill.

1.4 The trail tops out on a long ridge. *[FYI. A glimpse of the ocean can be seen through the trees on the left.]*

1.7 An alternate route to King Peak heads left. Take the right fork, keeping to the main stem of King Peak Trail.

2.0 To the right, King Crest Trail heads northwest. Turn left, following King Crest Trail south to King Peak.

2.2 The trail crosses an exposed knife-edge ridge, offering a great view to the north.

2.4 The trail dips into a saddle and heads left, skirting a steep drop-off to the right.

2.4 King Crest Trail continues to the left toward Saddle Mountain Road. Take the right fork, following King Peak Trail to the summit.

2.5 An unmarked trail continues to the left, back down to King Crest Trail. Take the right fork, which climbs another 20 feet to the summit of King Peak. This is the turnaround point. Enjoy the awesome views, then return the way you came.

5.0 Arrive back at the trailhead.

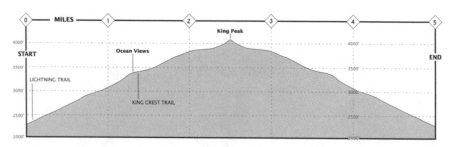

The ridge is not far from King Peak, which is marked by an old three-sided stone shelter nestled into the hillside. The hut provides refuge for unfortunate wanderers caught off-guard by sudden storms. This vantage point showcases the peak's 360-degree view, adding the western panorama of the coast to what was visible from the ridge. It might be tempting to stick around to watch a sunset from here, but remember, it's 2.5 miles down an already-shadowy eastern slope back to the trailhead.

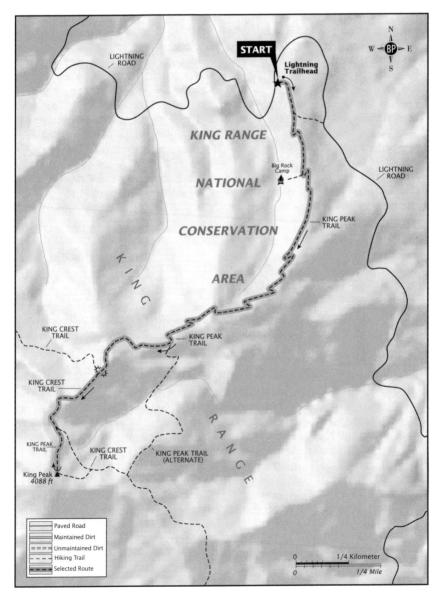

Mattole Beach Trail

Hike Specs

Start: From the Mattole Estuary Campground and day-use area

Length: 6.2-mile out-and-back

Approximate Hiking Time: 4–5 hours

Difficulty Rating: Easy to Moderate due to soft sand and stream crossings

Terrain: Dirt and sand path through grassy dunes and black sand beaches

Elevation Gain: 445 feet

Land Status: Bureau of Land Management land

Nearest Town: Petrolia, CA

Other Trail Users: Equestrians and beachcombers

Canine Compatibility: Dogs permitted (however, the black sand beaches can be hard on paws)

Getting There

From Eureka: Head south 11 miles on U.S. 101, leaving the highway at the Fernbridge/Ferndale exit. Turn right onto CA 211 and continue four miles through downtown Ferndale. Turn right onto Centerville Road, drive west one block, then turn left onto Mattole Road. Follow this windy road 28 miles south through forest and cattle range to the tiny town of Petrolia. Continue through town and over the Mattole River before turning right onto Lighthouse Road. Head west five miles to the campground and day-use area at the Mattole Estuary. The trail starts at the information board. *DeLorme: Northern California Atlas & Gazetteer:* Page 52 B1

Down at the end of Lighthouse Road near the tiny hamlet of Petrolia is a sandy little car-campground nestled in the dunes near the mouth of the Mattole River. A walk along the broad beach here reveals copious amounts of driftwood—some of it old stumps the size of an automobile. Many bird species frequent the estuary, and harbor seals often lounge about on nearby sandbars. From here, there are great views of the cliffs north toward Cape Mendocino.

At the southern end of the campground/parking lot is a bulletin board where fees are deposited and information gathered. From here, the Mattole Beach Trail leads south past an archeological site and along the dunes before dropping hikers firmly onto the black sand beach that will serve as trail for the remainder of the hike.

Unlike many black sand beaches that have volcanic origins, this one—along with the hills above it—is made of crumbly sandstone called graywacke. Though actually dark gray, the sand appears black when wet, providing a stark contrast to the white foam of the surf that washes up onto the beach. The result is beautiful, but be warned: The graywacke is coarser than the quartz sand of other beaches, so people hiking barefoot should expect abrasions and sore feet. Even dogs are not immune and are likely to suffer tender paws if they are not used to the scratchy surface. Some hikers advise bringing canine booties if the dog is not accustomed to the rough turf or if you plan a longer walk along the coast.

Most of the hike is accessible at all times, but the area surrounding Punta Gorda can be hazardous at high tide, when the waves crash up against the cliffs. The ocean here is known for having treacherous riptides and undertows, and sneaker waves can suddenly sweep the unwary out to sea. So it's strongly advised that you pay attention to tide charts and plan your hike around them. The Arcata Bureau of Land Management office should be able to help you determine when it's safe to traverse the point, as well.

Mouth of the Mattole.

Aside from personal safety, there is another advantage to hiking at low tide—the chance to explore world-class tide pools in the exposed rocks below the beach. Convoluted crags and crevices create an ideal habitat for numerous mussels, urchins, and anemones, all easily observed in astounding numbers when the tide is out. Low tide also unveils a multitude of marine life, so plentiful that tidepoolers must be very careful not to step on anything that might object. High or low tide, hikers should watch their step when moving around on the slippery rocks and always keep an eye on incoming waves.

MilesDirections

0.0 START at the information board. Head south through the locked gate and along the dunes.

0.2 The trail comes to a fenced archeological area. Turn right following along the fence to the interpretive exhibit. After seeing the exhibit, continue south along the fence and the dunes.

0.5 The trail crosses a small creek, which sometimes disappears into the sand before reaching the sea.

0.7 *[FYI. Deep gullies have been carved into the dunes by the creek.]*

0.9 Head down a steep bank and across the creek, continuing south between the bluffs and the ocean.

1.5 The bluffs are closer to the water here, forcing the trail onto the beach. *[Note. The trail can be dangerous at high tide, since so-called "sneaker waves" can catch hikers by surprise. Be careful.]*

2.1 The trail rounds Punta Gorda. *[Note. This is the most dangerous point on the trail during high tide, since the beach is particularly narrow here. Around the corner, the beach becomes much wider (and safer) again. Avoid this section during high tide.]*

2.8 A couple of private cabins huddle beneath the bluffs on the left. Wade across Four Mile Creek, and continue south along the beach on the other side. There is no bridge over Four Mile Creek, but it is generally fordable even in winter.

3.0 Cross a small creek. The lighthouse is now visible ahead to the left.

3.1 Reach Punta Gorda Lighthouse. This is the turnaround point for the hike. Return the way you came, making sure to time your return to avoid high tide around Punta Gorda.

6.2 Arrive back at the trailhead.

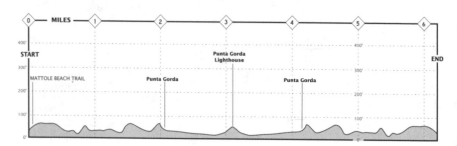

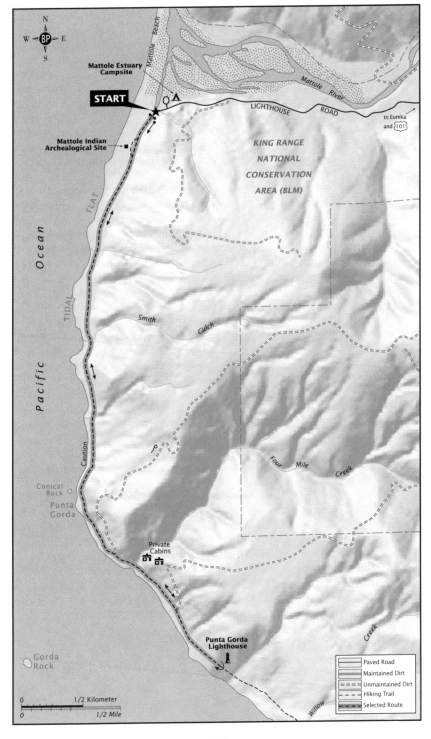

N
W—BP—E
S

Mattole Estuary
Campsite

START

Mattole Beach

Mattole River

LIGHTHOUSE ROAD

to Eureka
and (101)

Mattole Indian
Archealogical Site

KING RANGE
NATIONAL
CONSERVATION
AREA (BLM)

Ocean

FLAT

Smith

Gulch

TIDAL

Four   Mile   Creek

Pacific

Caution

Conical
Rock

Punta
Gorda

Private
Cabins

Punta Gorda
Lighthouse

Gorda
Rock

Creek

	Paved Road
	Maintained Dirt
	Unmaintained Dirt
	Hiking Trail
	Selected Route

Willow

0   1/2 Kilometer
0   1/2 Mile

These rock habitats can be divided into five different zones based on the amount of time they're under water or exposed to air. The highest level is the *splash zone*, which is rarely underwater but is kept wet by the splashing of the waves. This is mostly the domain of shore birds like the marbled godwit, black-bellied plover, and western sandpiper. A small crustacean called the rock louse also manages to live here as long as its gills are kept moist by the waves. Below the splash zone is the *high intertidal zone*, which is covered at high tide but exposed for long periods. Limpets, barnacles, and periwinkles can be found in this area.

The *middle intertidal zone* gets limited exposure to the air and has the strongest wave action of the five zones. Limpets, goose barnacles, mussels, and ocher sea stars thrive here because they have developed a means of hanging on to the rocks. Plants and animals that need to be wet most of the time inhabit the *low intertidal zone*. While these creatures require a lot of water, they can't be fully submerged in still waters. The intertidal creatures need waves to bring them food in the form of plankton, or they need to be close to sunlight. Some types of seaweed grow here, and anemones and urchins are present in large numbers. The urchins hollow out cup-shaped depressions in the rocks to protect themselves from the waves and have become so numerous that some of the rocks appear to have been honeycombed by the prickly, purple plankton-eaters.

The *subtidal zone* is the area that is never exposed to air, even at the lowest of low tides. The constant water source makes the subtidal zone a safe haven for creatures in danger of drying out, which migrate down to this area during low tide. Nudibranchs, marine relatives of slugs and snails that can have wild shapes and colors, are some of the most interesting subtidal zone inhabitants.

> **FYI**
>
> The first oil well in California was drilled in Petrolia in 1865, giving the town it's first export—and its namesake—petroleum.

Between Punta Gorda and the lighthouse lies Four Mile Creek. The trail traverses a wide but shallow crossing that may require hikers to take off their shoes and wade through the water—at least in winter. Don't stray from the path here, as the cabins on the north bank of the creek are private, and trespassing is not appreciated.

Up ahead is the Punta Gorda Lighthouse, a structure originally built in 1910 following the tragic wreck—just offshore—of the passenger ship *Columbia*, in which 87 people died. When the lighthouse was constructed, a small village of lighthouse keepers and their families sprung up nearby. But the town of Punta Gorda disappeared in 1951 once modern navigation equipment forced the then-obsolete lighthouse to close. Though it has been out of service for some 50 years, the building and squat tower are well kept, and hikers can climb the tower and admire the view—provided they can squeeze through the narrow opening at the top of the staircase.

Be sure to give yourself plenty of time to return to the trailhead before high tide.

Sea star.

Hike Information

🕒 Trail Contacts:
Arcata Resource Area, Bureau of Land Management, Arcata, CA (707) 825–2300

🕐 Schedule:
Open year round

💲 Fees/Permits:
$1 day-use fee. $5 camping fee.

❓ Local Information:
Eureka-Humboldt County Convention & Visitor's Bureau, Eureka, CA 1–800–346–3482 or (707) 443–5097 • **Humboldt County websites:** *www.visithumboldt.com, www.co.humboldt.ca.us, www.redwoodvisitor.org,* and *www.humguide.com* • **Links to individual state parks:** *www.cal-parks.ca.gov*

🍴 Accommodations:
Mattole Estuary Campground, at the trailhead, costs $5 per vehicle.

👫 Organizations:
California Coastal Trails Foundation, Trails Coordinator, P.O. Box 20073, Santa Barbara, CA 93120

🎒 Local Outdoor Retailers:
Adventure's Edge, Arcata, CA (707) 822–4673 • **The Outdoor Store,** Arcata, CA (707) 822–0321 • **Big 5 Sporting Goods,** Eureka, CA (707) 444–3682 • **Bucksport Sporting Goods,** Eureka, CA (707) 442–1832 • **Northern Mountain Supply,** Eureka, CA (707) 445–1711 • Picky Picky Picky Inc., Eureka, CA (707) 444–9201 • **Pro Sport Center,** Eureka, CA (707) 443–6328 • **Sports Exchange,** Eureka, CA (707) 444–3644

🅝 Maps:
USGS maps: Petrolia, CA

Bull Creek Flats Loop

Hike Specs

Start: From the Big Tree parking area
Length: 9.2-mile loop
Approximate Hiking Time: 4.5 hours
Difficulty Rating: Easy to Moderate due to long, flat trail
Terrain: Dirt path, packed gravel, and a tiny section of paved road through old-growth and second-growth redwood forests, and meadows
Elevation Gain: 900 feet
Land Status: State park
Nearest Town: Fortuna, CA
Other Trail Users: Equestrians
Canine Compatibility: Dogs not permitted

Getting There

From Eureka: Head south 47 miles on U.S. 101 to Humboldt Redwoods State Park. Exit at Mattole Road and turn right. Follow Mattole Road west 4.6 miles, and turn left at the sign for Rockefeller Forest: Tall Tree, Flatiron Tree, and Giant Tree. Follow this road 200 feet to the parking area. The trail begins at the bulletin board. *DeLorme: Northern California Atlas & Gazetteer:* Page 52 B4

This hike is a botanist's dream. From the mammoth redwood trees to the smallest mosses, the Rockefeller Forest is literally full of plants. And this trail showcases some of the park's most spectacular plant life. The path begins at the Big Tree parking area and immediately crosses the creek to visit some of the forest's so-called celebrity trees. These "famous" redwoods are well known for characteristics that make them special—even among the already unique trees. Among these stars are the Flatiron Tree, so named for its unusual cross-section, and the Giant Tree, noted for its size. The Giant Tree is not the tallest redwood on record, but it is considered by some to be the world's champion redwood by virtue of its combined height, circumference, and crown size.

Leaving these celebrity redwoods behind, the trail heads east through the heart of the Rockefeller Forest. Officially termed a temperate rainforest, this park has been shown to possess over seven times the biomass of tropical rainforests. Biomass is the recorded sum of all living and dead organic material in a given place. And there is an estimated 1,800 tons of it per acre in the old-growth stands of the park. From the dense mats of moss and ferns underfoot to the thick canopy suspended by the redwoods up to 350 feet overhead, almost everything you see here is—or was once—alive.

But the boundary between life and death in redwoods is difficult to pin down. Walking through the musty forest, you'll frequently see adult trees growing out of old trunks that are half-decayed and have long since fallen. Most of these are sprouts from the original tree and are genetically identical to it. Even when a log is rotten and completely dead, it is a host for a complex multitude of life—including an estimated 700 species of plants, lichen, mosses, and fungi; 3,228 different invertebrates; and a slew of various birds and mammals. Dead trees that remain upright, known as *snags*,

provide vital habitat for over 100 species of birds and mammals, including the famous spotted owl and the marbled murrelet.

Intermingled with the mammoth trees are a host of more abundant—if less impressive—plants, including redbud, Oregon grape, and maidenhair ferns. In moist, low-lying spots, you can find the unique giant horsetail. This plant looks like a relic of the dinosaur age. And as a matter of fact, it is. Horsetails have such high silica content that early European settlers used them to scrub pots. Those same settlers found copious quantities of miner's lettuce, a plant named, obviously, because it's edible.

About 150 years ago—not long in the life of a redwood, which can grow to be 2,000 years old—the first European-Americans made their way to this remote area and found the Sinkyone-Lolangkok people. The tribe's name was taken from their location: *Sin-ke-kok* was the word for the South Fork of the Eel River, and *Lolangkok*, for Bull Creek—the later term distinguished this group from its southern cousins, the Shelter Cove Sinkiyone. The Lolangkok and other local tribes developed cultures that took full advantage of their region's abundant plant- and wildlife, without damaging those resources. The  tribes subsisted largely on acorns from the nearby oak groves and salmon that spawn in area rivers and streams. Before using the acorns, the Lolangkok repeatedly ground and soaked the nuts to remove the bitter tannin. The end product was boiled as soup or baked into bread. These foods were supplemented with other plants, fish, and the occasional deer.

The Lolangkok also made good use of the region's native trees, finding ways to utilize almost every part of the redwood tree. They hollowed out the logs to form dugout canoes and split the trees into planks for building houses. The bark and roots served as cordage and basket-making material, as did many other native plants.

Sadly, the Lolangkoks suffered the same fate as most other California tribes. Confronted by land-hungry—and often violent—settlers, and the new diseases and alcohol they brought, the native population dwindled. Probably numbering close to 2,000 people in 1850, the population fell to just a handful by 1920.

Initially, the trees didn't fare much better. In the early part of the 20th Century, logging threatened to destroy the remaining ancient redwood groves. Some forward-thinking conservationists formed the Save-the-Redwoods League to combat the destruction. The group's goal was to purchase lands and turn them into parks. After taking a tour through the area, business tycoon J. D. Rockefeller was moved to donate

$2 million to the league. The funds were used to purchase the 10,000 acres along Bull Creek, now named the Rockefeller Forest. It is through this forest that the Bull Creek Flats Loop wanders.

Even the most jaded local finds some surprises in these deeply shaded groves—whether it is peculiar bulging burls, cavernous burned-out trunks, or mossy hulks lying prone on the forest floor like beached sea monsters. The urge to photograph is strong here. But if you want to see anything but dark blurs on the developed film, bring along a flash and a tripod. The canopy doesn't let much light in, even on sunny days.

After crossing Bull Creek again, a side trail leads around the Rockefeller Loop before returning up the other side of the creek to the trailhead. This side of the stream has more second-growth and several small glades laced with giant horsetail, sweet-scented bedstraw, and the ubiquitous redwood sorrel. Return the way you came, along the south bank of Bull Creek.

MilesDirections

0.0 START at the bulletin board in the Big Tree parking area. Cross Bull Creek, either via the temporary summer bridge or by wading in the off-season (be careful), and then follow Bull Creek Flats Loop as it heads left along the creek.

0.05 A spur trail to the right leads a few yards to the Flatiron Tree. Continue straight on Bull Creek Flats Loop.

0.2 Cross over a small creek on a wooden bridge.

0.3 Johnson's Camp Trail heads uphill to the right. Continue straight, keeping parallel to Bull Creek.

1.0 *[FYI. The trail passes some good examples of hollow redwood logs, some of them big enough to walk through.]*

1.4 Cross a small meadow, continuing straight.

1.7 The trail crosses a small bridge.

1.9 *[FYI. Keep an eye out for the Giant Braid, standing alongside the trail. This living curiosity consists of three redwood trunks that have grown twisted together.]*

3.3 The trail skirts the base of an enormous log, making what seems like a U-turn. Follow it anyway, because it eventually doubles back again.

3.4 The trail begins to climb the only incline of the trail.

4.4 As the trail levels out, you can see the little flood plain (flat) of Bull Creek below to your left.

4.5 Burlington-Bull Creek Trail continues straight. Turn left and follow the Bull Creek Flats Loop down to the flat.

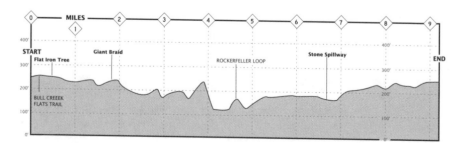

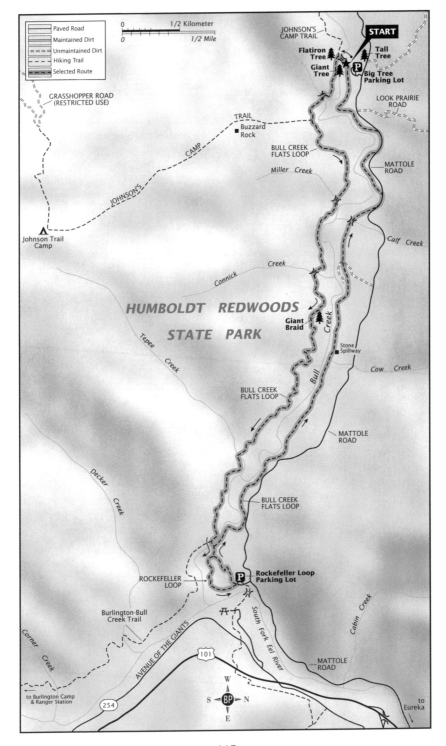

4.6 Cross Bull Creek. There is a large log conveniently down alongside the trail, spanning the creek in a natural bridge. Cross on the log or wade the creek. Once on the other side, Bull Creek Flats Loop heads left back up the other side of Bull Creek. Continue straight to explore the short Rockefeller Loop, which will return you to this junction shortly.

4.7 Rockefeller Loop begins here. Turn right and follow the trail through a prime redwood grove.

5.0 A log hanging over the trail has had an arch cut out of it, to allow easier passage for hikers.

5.1 To the right is the parking lot for the Rockefeller Loop. Continue straight on the trail.

5.4 Reach the end of Rockefeller Loop. Turn right and return to the junction with Bull Creek Flats Loop. At the junction, turn right and head upstream on Bull Creek Flats Loop.

The flats across from the Rockefeller Loop.

6.6 [*FYI. Passing close to the creek, the trail crosses a nice example of a stone French drain.*]

7.2 The trail crosses a small bridge over a side stream.

8.2 The trail joins Mattole Road briefly. Continue straight on the road shoulder a few yards until the trail resumes, heading down to the left.

8.4 An unmarked trail veers off to the left. Continue along the right fork.

8.5 The trail joins Mattole Road again briefly. Continue straight along the road shoulder.

8.7 A picnic area has been set up in a turnout to the left of the road. Cross this open area and continue on Bull Creek Flats Loop as it enters the forest on the other side of the clearing. The trail enters the woods near the creek.

9.0 Cross a small wooden bridge

9.2 Arrive back at the Big Tree parking area and trailhead.

Hike Information

● Trail Contacts:
Humboldt Redwoods State Park, Weott, CA (707) 946–2409 or *www.humboldtredwoods.org*

● Schedule:
Open year round. Footbridges over Bull Creek are removed for the winter season.

● Local Information:
Eureka-Humboldt County Convention & Visitor's Bureau, Eureka, CA 1–800–346–3482 or (707) 443–5097 • **Humboldt County websites:** *www.visithumboldt.com, www.co.humboldt.ca.us, www.redwoodvisitor.org,* and *www.humguide.com* • **Links to individual state parks:** *www.cal-parks.ca.gov*

● Local Events/Attractions:
Avenue of the Giants Marathon, in May, (707) 766–3655 – sponsored by the Six Rivers Running Club

● Accommodations:
Humboldt Redwoods State Park, Weott, CA 1–800–444–7275 – *There are three campgrounds within the park with a combined total of 249 campsites, available on a first-come, first-served basis. Reservations are recommended during the peak season.*

● Hike Tours:
Humboldt Redwoods State Park, Weott, CA – *Ranger-guided walks are scheduled from time to time. Check with the visitor center for more information.*

● Organizations:
Humboldt Redwoods Interpretive Association, Weott, CA (707) 946–2263 • **Save-the-Redwoods League,** 114 Sansome Street, Room 605, San Francisco, CA 94104

● Other Resources:
Humboldt Redwoods State Park, The Complete Guide by Jerry and Gisela Rohde. Illustrations by Larry Eifert.

● Local Outdoor Retailers:
Big 5 Sporting Goods, Eureka, CA (707) 444–3682 • **Bucksport Sporting Goods,** Eureka, CA (707) 442–1832 • **Northern Mountain Supply,** Eureka, CA (707) 445–1711 • **Picky Picky Picky Inc.,** Eureka, CA (707) 444–9201 • **Pro Sport Center,** Eureka, CA (707) 443–6328 • **Sports Exchange,** Eureka, CA (707) 444–3644

● Maps:
USGS maps: Weott, CA; Bull Creek, CA

17 · Drury-Chaney Loop

Hike Specs

Start: From the Drury-Chaney Grove turnout
Length: 2.5-mile loop
Approximate Hiking Time: 1–1.5 hours
Difficulty Rating: Easy due to shortness and lack of elevation gain
Terrain: Dirt path through old-growth redwood forest
Elevation Gain: 104 feet
Land Status: State park
Nearest Town: Scotia, CA
Other Trail Users: Hikers only
Canine Compatibility: Dogs not permitted

Getting There

From Eureka: Head south for 31 miles on U.S. 101, and exit at the sign for the Avenue of the Giants at Pepperwood. Turn left onto the Avenue of the Giants and drive 2.8 miles to the trailhead. Drury-Chaney Trailhead is a small turnout on the right side, marked by a low wooden sign for Newton B. Drury-Ralph W. Chaney Groves. *DeLorme: Northern California Atlas & Gazetteer:* Page 52 A4

Surrounded by impenetrable forests, daunting mountain ridges, and unpredictable waterways, Humboldt Redwoods State Park is home to a remnant of millennia-old ancient forest that remained unaltered into the 20th Century. The region, which contains the Drury-Chaney Loop, was once home to the Sinkyone-Lolangkok people, who used the streams and forests as a source of food, shelter, and materials. In spite of thousands of years of occupation by Native Americans, the land remained virtually unaltered. It was not until the first European-Americans began appearing in the 1850s that native populations saw a quick decline—due to imported diseases, depletion of the traditional food sources, and violence at the hands of settlers.

The area underwent another change in 1914 when the Northwestern Pacific Railroad first connected the region to the outside world. The Redwood Highway soon followed in 1922, sparking increased tourism and large-scale commercial logging. As regional tourism grew, the pressures of new development and road building caused some residents to become increasingly alarmed about the rapid pace of change. Their chief concern was the imminent threat to the groves of ancient redwoods on the alluvial flats of Bull Creek and South Fork Eel River, which were being damaged by the hordes of tourists and threatened by plans for a new road. To combat the feared destruction of the trees, three of the country's most prestigious naturalists—Henry Fairfield Osborn, Madison Grant, and John C. Merriam—came to the area in 1917 to study the mammoth forests. They left with a fervent desire to protect these unique treasures from the logger's axe and formed, along with other prestigious preservationists, the Save-the-Redwoods League in 1919. Franklin K. Lan, then secretary of the interior, was chosen as the group's first president.

Over the next few years, the league managed to secure several groves with state funding and private contributions. The bulk of these donations were obtained

Notches in this old stump held the loggers' platform.

through a successful memorial grove program, whereby large donors could name different groves. These lands were eventually transferred to the state of California and made into a state park. In 1931, the heart of the park—the Bull Creek Flats and Dyerville redwoods—finally was acquired from a reluctant Pacific Lumber Company. Business leaders like J. D. Rockefeller were among those who supported the effort. In fact, Rockefeller donated $2 million, which was then matched by funds from a state bond act.

Thus was born the Humboldt Redwoods State Park, which now protects over 53,000 acres of forest—including 17,000 acres of old-growth. One of every five remaining old-growth redwood trees is found in this park—tribute to the effort that went into creating the park but a sad reminder of the ancient forests' destruction. Of the original two million acres standing when Europeans first arrived, less than 93,000 remain. Some 80,000 acres are now protected in parks. The remaining 10,000-plus acres rest in private hands and are thus always in danger of being logged.

MilesDirections

0.0 START at the Drury-Chaney Trail trailhead. Follow Drury-Chaney Trail into the forest, heading west.

0.3 *[FYI. A bay laurel arches over the trail. This tree can be identified by the pungent smell.]*

0.7 The trail reaches a junction with a gravel access road. Cross the road and continue straight on Drury-Chaney Trail on the other side. *[FYI. To the left, just past this junction, is an old-growth stump with a 10-inch diameter tree growing out of it.]*

0.8 This junction marks the beginning of the loop portion of the hike. Turn right and continue that way.

1.0 *[FYI. To the left is an old growth stump with several notches cut into it. These are from the old logging method of building small platforms around the tree to allow cutting above its swollen base.]*

1.1 The trail passes through Irving Grove. Ignore the many false trails going off perpendicular to the main path, and continue straight along Drury-Chaney Trail.

1.7 Cross a little wooden footbridge and continue straight

1.9 The trail crosses another bridge and shortly thereafter reaches the end of the loop portion of the hike. Turn right onto the first leg of the trail, and return the way you came.

2.5 Arrive back at the trailhead.

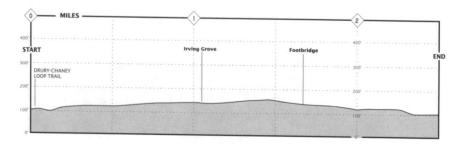

The Drury-Chaney Loop Trail passes through some of the Save-the-Redwoods League's memorial groves, two of which are dedicated to early league leaders Newton B. Drury and Ralph Works Chaney. Drury was secretary of the Save-the-Redwoods League back in the 1920s, during the club's most acquisitive years. And Chaney was the league's president from 1961 to 1971. He is credited with bringing the dawn redwood to this country from its native China.

In 1948, a Chinese forester named T. Wang found an unusual tree growing from the roof of a small temple in a remote part of China. When compared to ancient fossils, the specimen was determined to be a type of sequoia. The new tree was dubbed the dawn redwood and given the scientific name *Metasequoia glyptostroboides*. It was an important discovery, because the only other closely related trees are the coast redwood (*Sequoia sempervirens*) and the giant sequoia (*Sequoiadendron giganteum*), both of which now occur naturally only in California. Millions of years ago, when the earth's climate was warmer, sequoias covered a much larger portion of the globe, including parts of Europe and Asia. As the climate changed, the sequoias' habitat

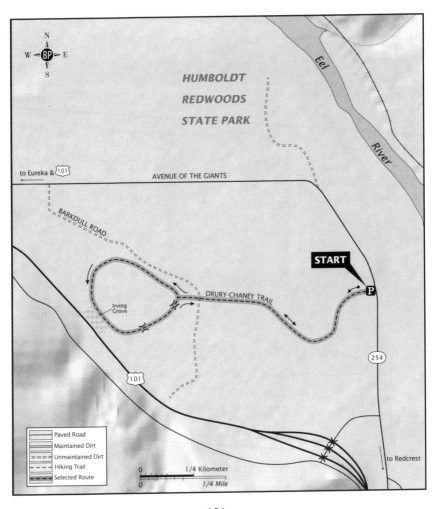

121

shrank until only the California redwoods remained—until the dawn redwood was discovered halfway around the world.

Chaney, then a paleontologist from the University of California at Berkley, traveled to China to see the new discovery first-hand. After some squabbling with customs officials in Hawaii, Chaney was allowed to bring samples into the United States. Back at the university, he cultivated seedlings from these samples, from which most of the dawn redwoods grown in this country originate.

The hike begins at a small grassy spot along the famed Avenue of the Giants and quickly enters the deep shadow of the redwood forest. Just like in other groves of this type, there are abundant redwood sorrel, huckleberry, tanoak, and several species of fern growing under the redwood canopy. And California bay laurels—also known as pepperwood for the aromatic smell of their crushed leaves—are scattered along the first part of the trail.

Strolling among giants.

Hike Information

ⓒ Trail Contacts:
Humboldt Redwoods State Park, Weott, CA (707) 946–2409 or *www.humboldt redwoods.org*

⊙ Schedule:
Open year-round. Seasonal bridges are removed in the winter, and high water in late winter and spring can restrict access.

❓ Local Information:
Eureka-Humboldt County Convention & Visitor's Bureau, Eureka, CA 1–800–346–3482 or (707) 443–5097 • Humboldt County websites: *www.visithumboldt.com, www.co.humboldt.ca.us, www.redwoodvisitor.org,* and *www.humguide.com* • Links to individual state parks: *www.cal-parks.ca.gov*

ⓠ Local Events/Attractions:
Avenue of the Giants Marathon, in May, (707) 766–3655 – sponsored by the Six Rivers Running Club

⊜ Accommodations:
Humboldt Redwoods State Park, Weott, CA 1–800–444–7275 – *There are three campgrounds within the park with a combined total of 249 campsites, available on a first-come, first-served basis. Reservations are recommended during the peak season.*

ⓗ Hike Tours:
Humboldt Redwoods State Park, Weott, CA – *Ranger-guided walks are scheduled from time to time. Check with the visitor center for more information.*

ⓘ Organizations:
Humboldt Redwoods Interpretive Association, Weott, CA (707) 946–2263 • Save-the-Redwoods League, 114 Sansome Street, Room 605, San Francisco, CA 94104

ⓑ Other Resources:
Humboldt Redwoods State Park, The Complete Guide by Jerry and Gisela Rohde. Illustrations by Larry Eifert.

ⓧ Local Outdoor Retailers:
Big 5 Sporting Goods, Eureka, CA (707) 444–3682 • Bucksport Sporting Goods, Eureka, CA (707) 442–1832 • Northern Mountain Supply, Eureka, CA (707) 445–1711 • Picky Picky Picky Inc., Eureka, CA (707) 444–9201 • Pro Sport Center, Eureka, CA (707) 443–6328 • Sports Exchange, Eureka, CA (707) 444–3644

ⓝ Maps:
USGS maps: Scotia, CA: Redcrest, CA

18

Headwaters Trail

Hike Specs

Start: From the Headwaters Trail trailhead
Length: 11.2-mile out-and-back
Approximate Hiking Time: 4–5 hours
Difficulty Rating: Moderate due to steep hills on the second half of the hike
Terrain: Pavement, gravel road, and dirt road over riparian lowland and steep, forested hills
Elevation Gain: 1,770 feet
Land Status: Bureau of Land Management land
Nearest Town: Eureka, CA
Other Trail Users: Hikers only
Canine Compatibility: Leashed dogs permitted

Getting There

From Eureka: Take U.S. 101 to the south end of Eureka, and exit left (east) onto Herrick Road, then turn right onto Elk River Road. Follow Elk River Road south 1.7 miles to a fork in the road. Take the right fork (still Elk River Road) and continue another 3.4 miles to a bend in the road with a bridge on the right. Turn right, crossing over the bridge, and continue another 0.9 miles (still on Elk River Road) until the road dead-ends at the Headwaters Forest Reserve parking area. The trail starts at the bulletin board on the left. ***DeLorme: Northern California Atlas & Gazetteer:*** Page 42 C3

T here are at least two major reasons why people come to the Headwaters Forest Reserve—to see the land at the heart of the Headlands controversy and to visit the former town of Falk. The town is referred to as the former town of Falk, because it is, for all practical purposes, no longer there. From roughly 1884 to 1937, Falk was a bustling little mill town where loggers scrambled to convert acres of old-growth forest into lumber to be sold in distant ports. But all that remain now are the wild-looking, overgrown remnants of once-orderly orchards and a pair of ornamental yew trees that once guarded the walkway to someone's front door.

The town gets its name from Noah Falk, a latecomer to the Gold Rush who moved west in 1854. Upon his arrival, Falk was promptly recruited as a carpenter for a new sawmill in Mendocino. He later married and in 1867 moved to Eureka with his new bride. Falk was hoping to make a career as a baker here. But once again, he got sidetracked with an offer of employment from Eureka's leading citizen, William Carson, the timber baron whose mansion still stands as the town's milestone of Victorian architecture. Falk worked for the Carson Lumber Company for two years before venturing into the lumber business for himself, creating Falk, Chandler & Co. He ran several successful milling operations before finally beginning work in a valley just southeast of Eureka, along the Little South Fork of the Elk River. The sawmill built in that valley came to be known by the Falk name, as did the bustling town that sprung up around the mill. A spur railroad was built to carry the freshly milled lumber to Bucksport—now part of Eureka—where it was loaded onto ships for transportation south. With a forest full of trees at hand and a ready transportation system to ferry lumber to the coast, the Falk Mill was soon a hive of activity.

At its peak, the town was home to around 400 people, including mill workers and their families. But the mill was closed in 1937. With no other reason for people to stay, the population quickly dwindled. By 1979, Falk was a ghost town, and landowners burned and bulldozed the last remaining structures to avoid paying liability insurance.

The Headwaters Trail starts at the newly constructed trailhead and follows the old road—now closed to all but pedestrian traffic—for about a mile, past blackberries and alders, to the old town site. A leaflet that points out some of the more obvious signs of former life here can be picked up at the trailhead. A sign marks the meadow that was once the center of Falk. From here, the trail continues southeast into the heart of the preserve. Watch your step, as the path's surface soon switches from asphalt to gravel, and eventually, to dirt.

People who continue past the Falk town site generally do so to get a glimpse of what sparked the so-called *Headwaters Deal* hubbub. Details of the land venture—far less quaint than the particulars of the Falk tale—involve years of heated debate and protest demonstrations that are still fresh in local resident's minds. The controversy centers on the Headwaters Grove, a nearly 3,000-acre grove of old-growth redwoods located in the hills just east of Fortuna. The grove, which lies between isolated forests

in Humboldt Redwoods State Park and Redwood National Park, is an important link for the gene pools of plants and animals in those two areas. The grove provides critical habitat for the endangered marbled murrelet and shelters the headwaters that are home to the equally threatened coho salmon.

MilesDirections

0.0 START at the Bulletin Board. Follow the paved Headwaters Trail east through an alder forest.

0.1 [*FYI. Cherry trees can be seen on the left side of the trail. These trees once grew in the gardens of Falk residents. The houses are gone, but the trees remain.*]

0.3 [*FYI. The pair of yews on the right once flanked the entrance to someone's front yard. A cement paving stone can be seen between the yews.*]

0.6 The trail surface changes from pavement to gravel.

1.0 [*FYI. The town of Falk once occupied the clearing to the left and the surrounding lands. The forest is encroaching rapidly on the town site, and almost nothing remains of the buildings.*]

2.8 [*FYI. An old truck has found a resting place in the underbrush on the right. During the protests that led to Headwaters Grove being saved from logging, protestors pushed this vehicle into the road to block logging equipment.*]

3.0 South Fork Trail goes left along the narrow strip that hems in the Hole in the Headwaters. Continue to the right on the main trail, which changes from gravel to dirt.

3.1 Cross the steel logging bridge over the South Fork Elk River. The trail heads steeply uphill from here, and the going can be slippery and muddy after heavy rains.

3.8 Cross another logging bridge, continuing uphill.

5.0 The old bridge that used to span this creek has been removed. Follow the narrow footpath down to the right. Cross the creek and follow the footpath back up the other bank until it rejoins the road. Continue uphill on the road.

5.4 An old log deck is visible on the right. [*FYI. In the logging days, this was used as a place to stack logs, prior to loading them onto trucks for transport to the sawmills.*]

5.5 This is the official end of the trail. You can catch a glimpse of the old-growth Headwaters Grove straight ahead. Follow the road as it curves left to the vista point.

5.6 Reach the vista point. This is another old logging deck, next to a recovering clearcut. Due to the lack of trees, there is a good view to the left of the ocean and the south end of Eureka. Straight ahead, on the other side of the ridge, is the "Hole in the Headwaters." This spot is the turnaround point for the hike. Return the way you came.

11.2 Arrive back at the trailhead.

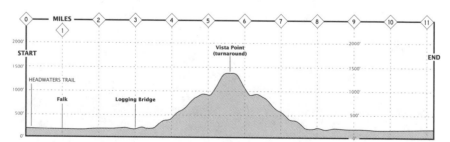

126

In the early 1980s, Headwaters Grove was the largest unprotected stand of old-growth redwoods in the world and belonged to the Pacific Lumber Company (PALCO). Over the years, Pacific Lumber had developed a reputation as an environmentally responsible company, with practices that were a model of sustainable forestry. That was before 1985, however—the year Charles Hurwitz's MAXXAM Corporation acquired the Pacific Lumber Company in a hostile takeover. In addition to looting the company's pension fund and selling off major assets, Hurwitz stepped up logging in an effort to pay off the huge debt incurred by the takeover. Pacific Lumber's forestry practices changed. The company began using clearcuts as the preferred cutting method and applying diesel-based herbicides to the cleared slopes. Environmentalists were horrified and began seeking ways to protect the remaining old-growth groves. With the help of sympathetic lawmakers, several attempts were made beginning in 1989 to pass legislation authorizing the purchase of the groves for public parkland. But the Headwaters forest contained prized old-growth groves, worth millions as lumber, and Pacific Lumber was in no mood to part with the trees so easily. In 1995, Pacific Lumber announced it would begin logging in the Headwaters, at which point things immediately began heating up. Activists took to the woods—while the Environmental Protection Information Center and the Sierra Club took to the courtroom—in an attempt to stop the logging. A series of court battles ensued, which delayed the logging but failed to win lasting protection for the Headwaters.

Finally, in late 1996, MAXXAM and government officials reached a complex agreement. It involved money—lots of it—and included a Habitat Conservation Plan and Sustained Yield Plan that would cover Pacific Lumber's remaining forestland. It took three years to hammer out the agreement, and the *deal* was finally sealed in the spring of 1999. State and federal governments purchased the Headwaters Grove, along with 5,000 acres of second-growth and a smaller old-growth grove, for $380 million. Ironically, the final plan was bitterly opposed by many environmental-

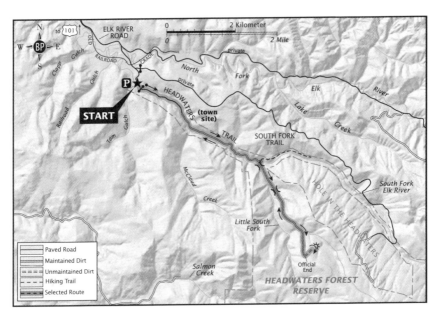

The Kinetic Sculpture Race

Way back in 1969, Ferndale artist Hobart Brown converted his son's tricycle into a mobile sculpture. Intrigued, a metal-sculpting friend built his own contraption and challenged Brown to a race. One thing led to another, and by the time race day rolled around, 12 contestants found themselves locomoting down Main Street in a variety of human-powered monstrosities, to the cheers and laughter of the assembled townsfolk. The Kinetic Sculpture Race was born!

The race was a resounding success, and became a yearly event in Ferndale, until the crowds drawn by the spectacle began to outgrow the tiny dairy hamlet. The start of the event moved from Ferndale to Eureka, finally settling on college town Arcata, while the length of the course grew from its original three-block street run to the present three-day, 38-mile Tour-de-Farce. Entries must now be land, sea, and sand-worthy, in addition to being totally people-powered—as they are required to traverse streets and dunes, and make three water crossings, including a stretch of Humboldt Bay with over a mile of open water! Over the past 30 years, the Kinetic Sculpture Race has spawned similar events in other cities, and even in countries as far away as Australia.

The race takes place over the three days of Memorial Day weekend, beginning on the Plaza in Arcata, making two mandatory evening stops, and ending the third day where it all began, in downtown Ferndale. Entries have become very sophisticated, with decorated multi-person human-powered sculpture/vehicles of breathtaking design racing alongside last-minute garage contraptions made of leftover bicycle parts. The only limits to creativity are the laws of street- and nautical legality, as presided over by the local police and coast guard. Volunteer Kinetic Kops ensure the race's often bizarre and zany rules are obeyed, although bribery is not only permitted, but encouraged—as attested by the awarding of the Best Bribe prize at race's end. Other awards include Best Performance, Best Costume, the Outrageous Award, and Worst Honorable Mention.

For more information on the Kinetic Sculpture Race, call (707) 786-4477 or visit www.humguide.com/kinetic.

ists, because it left out several small groves of old-growth forest and gave Pacific Lumber permission to "take" (or carry out operations that may result in the death of) endangered species on its remaining land. Perhaps the biggest environmental sticking point with the deal, however, was the so-called Hole in the Headwaters area—a 1,000-acre parcel of land within the Headwaters Forest Reserve that may still be logged by Pacific Lumber. Inclusion of the hole has prompted many environmentalists to continue fighting the Headwaters deal.

The trail leads past Falk into second-growth forest, climbing a series of steep slopes into the heart of the preserve and ending on the northern fringe of the Headwaters Grove. The turnaround point is a vista point—an old logging deck— which offers a view over Eureka to the northwest and Hole in the Headwaters to the north. Return the way you came.

Hike Information

Trail Contacts:
Bureau of Land Management, Arcata, CA (707) 825–2300 or *www.ca.blm.gov/ arcata/headwaters.html*

Schedule:
Open year round

Fees/Permits:
No fees or permits required

Local Information:
Eureka-Humboldt County Convention & Visitor's Bureau, Eureka, CA 1–800–346–3482 or (707) 443–5097 • Humboldt County websites: *www.visithumboldt.com, www.co.humboldt.ca.us, www.redwoodvisitor.org, and www. humguide.com* • Links to individual state parks: *www.cal-parks.ca.gov*

Restaurants:
Roy's Club, Eureka, CA (707) 442–4574

Hike Tours:
Bureau of Land Management, Arcata, CA (707) 825–2300 – *Rangers guide hikes to Falk and to the edge of Headwaters Grove from the south. Call for more information.*

Other Resources:
Earth First website: *www.enviroweb.org/ headwaters-ef/* – *the environmentalists'*

side of the Headwaters saga • **Pacific Lumber Company website:** *www.palco.com/hforest.htm – Pacific Lumber's point of view* • **Headwaters website:** *www.ceres.ca.gov/headwaters – maps and detailed forest data* • **Charles Hurwitz website:** *www.jail hurwitz.com – more about the man behind the mischief, with a bit of a bias*

Local Outdoor Retailers:
Adventure's Edge, Arcata, CA (707) 822–4673 • Big 5 Sporting Goods, Eureka, CA (707) 444–3682 • Bucksport Sporting Goods, Eureka, CA (707) 442–1832 • Northern Mountain Supply, Eureka, CA (707) 445–1711 • The Outdoor Store, Arcata, CA (707) 822–0321 • Picky Picky Picky Inc., Eureka, CA (707) 444–9201 • Pro Sport Center, Eureka, CA (707) 443–6328 and McKinleyville, CA (707) 839–9445 • Sports Exchange, Eureka, CA (707) 444–3644

Maps:
USGS maps: McWhinney Creek, CA; Fields Landing, CA

Tall Trees Grove Loop

Hike Specs

Start: From the Tall Trees Grove Trail trailhead
Length: 5.2 miles, partial loop
Approximate Hiking Time: 2 hours
Difficulty Rating: Moderate, due to steep return trip
Terrain: Dirt path through second- and old-growth forests and alluvial flats
Elevation Gain: 628 feet
Land Status: National park
Nearest Town: Orick, CA
Other Trail Users: Hikers only
Canine Compatibility: No dogs allowed on trail

Getting There

From Eureka: Drive north 42 miles on U.S. 101 to the town of Orick. Stop at the visitor center (open 9 A.M.–5 P.M.) at the south end of town, and pick up a free permit. Just north of Orick, turn right onto Bald Hills Road and drive east 6.4 miles, then turn right onto the gravel Tall Trees Grove Access Road. Unlock the gate using the combination you were given with your permit, and after closing the gate behind you, continue another 5.6 miles to the trailhead. The trail begins next to the small pavilion. *DeLorme: North California Atlas & Gazetteer:* Page 33 C4

A living relic from the days of the dinosaur, the giant redwood is truly an awe-inspiring sight. Walking deep in a primeval forest, with rays of sunlight filtering down through the fog between the trees, it's not hard to imagine yourself wandering the planet millions of years ago, when such forests covered much of the globe. One of three surviving species of redwood, the coast redwood (*Sequoia sempervirens*) is the tallest tree on earth, often growing well over 300 feet tall. The closely related giant sequoia (*Sequoiadendron giganteum*) grows only in the south-central Sierra Nevada range in and around Sequoia-Kings Canyon National Park. The giant sequoia is the largest living thing on earth, in terms of sheer mass, but with an average height of 225 feet, it falls far short of the coast redwood in height. The third relative is a distant cousin of the other two: The dawn redwood is a much smaller, unremarkable tree found in China, and sometimes grown in the U.S. as an ornament.

The coast redwood grows only on the Pacific Coast of Northern California, where the mild climate and heavy fog provide ideal growth conditions for these silent giants. Of the estimated two million acres of old-growth redwoods existing here at the time of European arrival, only about three percent survive today. The rest have fallen to the axe, and more recently, the chainsaw. Of the remaining groves, more than half are protected on public land.

The logging of old-growth forests, a source of very heated debate in the area, is seen as a vital source of jobs and revenue by some, and as wasteful destruction of irreplaceable habitat by others. As forests were depleted and public outcry became louder, stronger environmental laws were enacted to protect species endangered by the loss of habitat. This further reduced timber jobs—the result being that the timber industry supporters increasingly blamed environmentalists for their loss of prosperity.

Feeling small.

Both fronts have become increasingly embittered, and as outside pressures grow to end the logging of old-growth, loggers become ever more militantly anti-environment. The low point of the conflict saw local schools banning a Dr. Seuss children's book (*The Lorax*), which depicted the tragic depletion of an imaginary forest for short-term gain.

Created in 1968, Redwood National Park is tiny as national parks go, and is split up into four isolated subsections, surrounded by state parks and private land. Nonetheless, it is still possible to find something approximating backcountry in the large southern end of the park, which encompasses the lower drainage of Redwood Creek.

Although the Tall Trees Grove was within the original boundaries of the park, most of the surrounding land was not included until 1978, by which time most of it had already been clearcut by the timber company. Twenty years of recovery have stabilized the topsoil and allowed a primary red alder forest to grow up, mixed with

MilesDirections

0.0 START next to the pavilion. Trail guides are located in a box at the trailhead, with descriptions corresponding to numbered posts along the path. Follow the trail as it heads downhill into the forest.

0.1 Emerald Ridge Trail to Dolason Prairie heads left. Continue Straight on Tall Trees Grove Trail.

0.3 A section of old-growth log has been removed to make way for the trail. *[FYI. This is a good opportunity to count the rings of an old-growth tree (if you have some time).]*

0.4 A spring wells up from under the stump on the right side of the trail.

1.1 *[FYI. At this spot, the historic Trinidad Trail used to head east and west. It has all but disappeared now.]*

1.5 The trail passes a restroom on the right, and enters Tall Trees Grove.

1.6 The trail forks, marking the start of the loop portion of the trail. Take the left fork. Shortly past the junction, Redwood Creek Trail heads left. Keep going straight.

1.7 *[FYI. The official world's tallest tree is on the right, a magnificent double-trunked redwood.]*

1.8 The trail enters a grove of big-leaf maple, thriving in the riparian zone along Redwood Creek.

1.9 *[FYI. As you pass under several large bay laurels (a.k.a. pepperwood trees), the pungent smell of the leaves is discernable from the trail.]*

2.6 The loop ends, back at the fork in the trail. Turn left and return the way you came.

5.2 Arrive back at the trailhead.

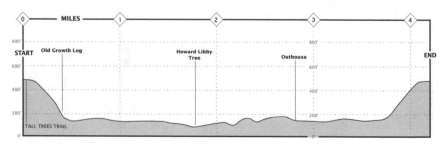

young second-growth redwoods and other species, but it will be another thousand years until a true old-growth forest stands here again, if ever.

Fortunately, you can still experience the real thing in the surviving ancient redwoods of Tall Trees Grove. The sheltered, fog-drenched location and nutrient-rich soil of the small floodplain provide ideal conditions for truly mammoth timber. Here, on the edge of Redwood Creek, stand the tallest trees on Earth. The world-record holder—a double-trunked beauty first surveyed by a *National Geographic* crew in 1963—stands a full 367.8 feet tall (over 60 feet taller than the statue of liberty and its base combined). The second, third, and sixth tallest trees in the world are also in this grove.

You access the grove via a locked gate off of Bald Hills Road, and a long, windy ex-logging road leading down through the young second-growth of the upper slopes.

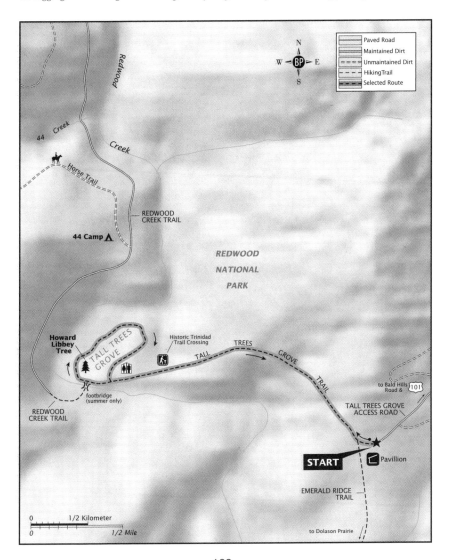

At the end of the road is the trailhead for Tall Trees Grove, and a small pavilion with a guest book for hikers. The first leg of the hike is a steep downhill, cool and shady beneath the dense canopy far above, with giant ferns and rhododendron thickets to both sides.

Big leaf maple.

Eventually the trail reaches the flood plain and flattens out. This is where the giants are, well marked along the loop with signs. At several spots along the loop, it's possible to access the rocky bar alongside Redwood Creek, which is an excellent place to break out the food and have lunch. If you keep quiet, you have a good chance of spotting some of the abundant wildlife here.

An alternative to the gate and windy access road is to park at the Redwood Creek trailhead—at the foot of the Bald Hills road—and hike up the much longer Redwood Creek Trail to the grove. This route involves crossing the creek a few times. There are temporary bridges installed in the summer, but if you're planning to go in winter or spring, it's best to avoid this route. The creek is generally high during the rainy season and can become a raging torrent with spring snowmelt or heavy rainstorms.

Hike Information

Trail Contacts:
Redwood National and State Parks, Crescent City, CA (707) 464–6101 or www.nps.gov/redw

Schedule:
Open year round

Fees/Permits:
A free permit is required to access the trail, obtainable at the Redwood National Park Visitor Center, just south of Orick on U.S. 101. With the permit, you'll receive the combination for the gate.

Local Information:
Eureka-Humboldt County Convention & Visitor's Bureau, Eureka, CA 1-800-346-3482 or (707) 443-5097 • Humboldt County websites: www.visit humboldt.com, www.co.humboldt.ca.us, www.redwoodvisitor.org, and www.humguide.com • Links to individual state parks: www.cal-parks.ca.gov

Local Events/Attractions:
Annual Banana Slug Derby, in August, Prairie Creek Redwoods State Park • Discovery Ride, in October, Redwood National and State Parks

Accommodations:
National and State park campsites: 1-800-444-7275 to reserve • Car camping is allowed free of charge on the Freshwater Lagoon spit south of Orick.

Organizations:
Redwood Natural History Association, Crescent City, CA (707) 464–6101 ext. 5095 • North Coast Redwood Interpretive Association, Prairie Creek Redwoods State Park, Orick, CA (707) 464–6101 ext. 5300

Local Outdoor Retailers:
Adventure's Edge, Arcata, CA (707) 822–4673 • Big 5 Sporting Goods, Eureka, CA (707) 444–3682 • Bucksport Sporting Goods, Eureka, CA (707) 442–1832 • Northern Mountain Supply, Eureka, CA (707) 445–1711 • The Outdoor Store, Arcata, CA (707) 822–0321 • Picky Picky Picky Inc., Eureka, CA (707) 444–9201 • Pro Sport Center, Eureka, CA (707) 443–6328 and McKinleyville, CA (707) 839–9445 • Sports Exchange, Eureka, CA (707) 444–3644

Maps:
USGS maps: Bald Hills, CA; Rodgers Peak, CA

Skunk Cabbage
Section of the Coastal Trail

Hike Specs

Start: From the Skunk Cabbage Trail trailhead
Length: 10.5-mile out-and-back
Approximate Hiking Time: 5–6 hours
Difficulty Rating: Moderate due to length and some steep sections
Terrain: Dirt path through a temperate swamp and second-growth forests with some old-growth, as well as along coastal bluffs and beaches
Elevation Gain: 1,703 feet
Land Status: National park
Nearest Town: Orick, CA
Other Trail Users: Hikers only
Canine Compatibility: Dogs not permitted

Getting There

From Eureka: Drive north 42 miles to the town of Orick. Just north of town, turn left at the sign for Skunk Cabbage Trail trailhead and continue another 0.6 miles to the trailhead. The trail begins where the road ends. *DeLorme: Northern California Atlas & Gazetteer:* Page 32 B3

There is no one thing that makes this hike so special. Rather, it's the combination of a unique array of habitats and the trail's mood of isolation that earns it a place on the list of top regional hikes. The first section of the trail follows the path of an old logging road that cuts through a forest ravaged long ago—not surprising, given its proximity to the logging town of Orick. Nevertheless, there are still a number of remnant old-growth giants scattered throughout the area. Some of these redwoods were left as seed trees or were deemed unsuitable for the mill because they were twisted or hollow. Others were only broken stumps at the time the area was logged and remain in nearly the same condition, thanks to redwood's natural rot-resistance.

The second-growth forest that has replaced the ancient redwoods is comprised mainly of spruce and alder, trees that create a somber, isolated mood. The addition of a swamp along the floor of the drainage further darkens the area's atmosphere. This wetland is filled with exotic-looking skunk cabbage, unflatteringly named for the strong odor of the leaf that surrounds its flower spike. A relative of the calla lily, the skunk cabbage blooms in the spring and summer. A single burst of tiny blossoms is partially covered by a bright yellow hood, an arrangement that compliments the plant's large, waxy leaves. The root and young leaf are edible—after sufficient cooking to

remove the unpleasant calcium oxalate present in the plant—and were used as a food source by some Native Americans and early miners. Another relative of skunk cabbage—called *taro*—was a traditional staple in the diets of many Polynesians.

After crossing the swamp, the trail heads up a fern-lined ravine and eventually reaches the crest of the coastal bluffs at the junction with the now defunct South Beach Access Trail. The bluffs are steep and brushy here, so the trail ducks back inland to follow the ridge north through the forest. This part of the forest has that *lived-in* look that's achieved only where large mammals regularly visit. In this case, the large mam-

Hike Information

Trail Contacts:
Redwood National and State Parks, Crescent City, CA (707) 464–6101 or *www.nps.gov/redw*

Schedule:
Open year round

Fees/Permits:
No fees or permits required

Local Information:
Eureka-Humboldt County Convention & Visitor's Bureau, Eureka, CA 1–800–346–3482 or (707) 443–5097 • Humboldt County websites: *www.visithumboldt.com, www.co.humboldt.ca.us, www.redwoodvisitor.org,* and *www.humguide.com* • Links to individual state parks: *www.cal-parks.ca.gov*

Local Events/Attractions:
Annual Banana Slug Derby, in August, Prairie Creek Redwoods State Park • Discovery Ride, in October, Redwood National and State Parks

Accommodations:
National and State park campsites: 1–800–444–7275 to reserve • Car

camping is allowed free of charge on the Freshwater Lagoon spit south of Orick.

Organizations:
Redwood Natural History Association, Crescent City, CA (707) 464–6101 ext. 5095 • North Coast Redwood Interpretive Association, Prairie Creek Redwoods State Park, Orick, CA (707) 464–6101 ext. 5300

Local Outdoor Retailers:
Adventure's Edge, Arcata, CA (707) 822–4673 • Big 5 Sporting Goods, Eureka, CA (707) 444–3682 • Bucksport Sporting Goods, Eureka, CA (707) 442–1832 • Northern Mountain Supply, Eureka, CA (707) 445–1711 • The Outdoor Store, Arcata, CA (707) 822–0321 • Picky Picky Picky Inc., Eureka, CA (707) 444–9201 • Pro Sport Center, Eureka, CA (707) 443–6328 and McKinleyville, CA (707) 839–9445 • Sports Exchange, Eureka, CA (707) 444–3644

Maps:
USGS map: Orick, CA

mals aren't humans—they're Roosevelt elk. Game trails crisscross the ridges and hollows, and there are many open, flat spaces under the canopy where elk like to bed down. While elk are commonly seen in the meadows along U.S. Route 101 north of Orick and in Prairie Creek Redwoods State Park, it's fairly unusual to see them in the forest. But you have a good chance of glimpsing one of the beasts in this area. In any setting, keep a healthy distance from the elk, which are unpredictable.

The trail soon pops onto the bluffs again and quickly drops down to follow the beach northward. There are fields of driftwood on the beaches here, and some of the pieces are quite large. It's not uncommon for floods to wash old stumps and logs out to sea, where waves bring many of them back onto nearby beaches. In fact, some areas here seem to attract the stuff like a magnet.

The hike ends at the creek crossing where Davison Road leaves the woods and heads north along Gold Bluffs Beach. The bluffs are pushed back here and drop off

MilesDirections

0.0 START at the Skunk Cabbage Trailhead. Follow the Skunk Cabbage Trail (a.k.a. Coastal Trail) west into the forest.

0.4 The trail crosses a small wooden bridge.

0.5 *[FYI. The swamp below to the right is full of the trail's namesake skunk cabbage.]*

1.2 The trail does an S-curve and crosses a wooden bridge over the swamp.

1.8 Cross another bridge and follow the trail as it heads up the canyon.

1.9 The trail begins to switchback up.

2.2 *[FYI. The white-barked stand of trees across the canyon are red alder.]*

2.4 A spur trail used to lead down to the beach on the left, but has been closed due to trail deterioration. There is a good view of the ocean from here. Continue to the right, following the main trail.

3.1 The trail begins to descend to the beach.

3.3 The trees open up briefly to offer another view of the ocean.

3.5 *[FYI. This area is heavily trafficked by elk. There are game trails and bedding areas everywhere around the trail.]* Continue straight.

3.9 The trail exits the forest and switchbacks down the bluffs to the beach. At the bottom, turn right and head north along the narrow beach. There is no visible trail from here until the turnaround point.

4.4 The trail crosses a small creek. On the right is a large field of driftwood.

5.3 The trail reaches a wide creek. Davison Road is visible as the trail exits the forest on the left and heads north along the dunes. This is the turnaround point for the hike. Return the way you came.

10.5 Arrive back at the trailhead.

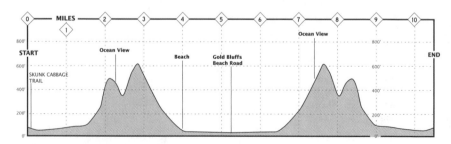

vertically from the ridge, leaving ochre cliffs of exposed dirt and rock perched above low, grassy dunes. If the scene looks a little unnatural, that's because it is. These "Gold Bluffs" were created by hydraulic mining operations, which reached their peak in the late 1800s. Mining had been occurring here since the 1850s, when gold was discovered on the bluffs, but it wasn't until prospectors cleaned out the "free" deposits of gold with placer mining techniques that miners switched to the rougher hydraulic system. Gold-seeks aimed water cannons at the bluffs to wash away their soil and soft rock, a process that left the heavier gold behind. Eventually, this method also proved unprofitable, and mining in the area stopped by the 1920s.

Return the way you came.

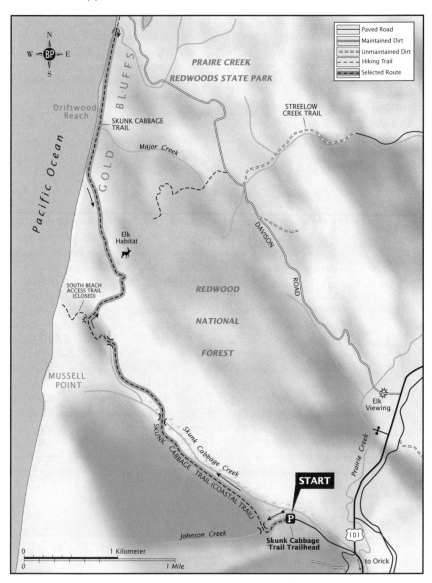

Fern Canyon/James Irvine
Double Loop

Hike Specs

Start: From the visitor center trailhead

Length: 10.0-mile loop

Approximate Hiking Time: 4–5 hours

Difficulty Rating: Easy to Moderate due to stream crossings and a couple of steep sections along good trails

Terrain: Dirt and gravel path through old-growth redwood forests and lush fern-lined canyons

Elevation Gain: 619 feet

Land Status: State park

Nearest Town: Orick, CA

Other Trail Users: Hikers only

Canine Compatibility: Dogs not permitted

Getting There

From Eureka: Take U.S. 101 north 47 miles and exit at Newton B. Drury Scenic Parkway. Turn left at the stop sign, pass under the highway, and head north another mile along the parkway to the Prairie Creek State Park entrance, on the left. The trail starts at the large trail sign opposite the parking lot. *DeLorme: Northern California Atlas & Gazetteer:* Page 32 A3

The trail begins near the Prairie Creek State Park visitor center and immediately delves into some of the most impressive old-growth redwood forest in California—or the world, for that matter. This park and its neighbor state-owned redwood parks are considered by many to be the crown jewels of California's state park system. Their prestige is one of the main reasons the parks have not been incorporated into the surrounding national park as was originally planned.

When Redwood National Park was created in 1968, the founders stipulated that Prairie Creek, Del Norte Coast, and Jedediah Smith state parks would eventually become part of a larger, consolidated national park. There was a good deal of resistance to the plan, though—in particular from the state park employees, who were loath to lose control of their beloved groves. By the early 1990s, public pressure to consolidate had become intense, and all parties sat down at the table to hammer out an agreement. The result of this bargaining was a kind of loose confederation of parks: In what is now known officially as Redwood National and State Parks, the state parks remain autonomous but share a management plan with the national park system.

Whatever you call it, this is a wonderful place to take a hike. The James Irvine Trail departs from the visitor center and parallels a tributary of Prairie Creek as it flows through the lush ancient forest. The trail then tops a low ridge and enters the Fern Canyon drainage, a leafy jumble of green tumbling gently down to the ocean.

As you cross the wooden footbridges over the upper reaches of Fern Canyon, you will no doubt notice the strange shape of the streambed, which has steep, narrow walls and unexpected depth. At times, the creek bed seems more like a Southwestern slot canyon than a Redwood Country creek. This topographic idiosyncrasy was

caused by the intense mining activity that took place here in the late 1800s, when the hunger for gold led people to do some very strange things.

Gold fever took hold of California in the 1850s, prompting prospectors to scour the state for the next mother lode. With so many miners tearing into the earth, it was only a matter of time before somebody noticed the telltale glint in the sand at the base of the Gold Bluffs. Thus beach mining commenced near Fern Canyon. But mining gold from the beach was labor-intensive and provided meager returns at best.

The mouth of the canyon.

Pioneer Edson Adams acquired the land around Fern Canyon soon after gold was discovered there and promptly rented it out to a larger gold mining operation. Before long, a tiny community of half a dozen buildings had been established on the north rim of the canyon at Lincoln Prairie. The trail passes the *prairie*—actually a small meadow—just before it reaches the mouth of the canyon. But don't expect to see much of the old mining town. Nothing but ghosts and memories remain of the short-lived town that briefly thrived here.

The beach here originally was much narrower, and the waves crashed right up against the base of the bluffs. The constant pounding from the waves played a major roll in the difficult process of beach mining. The force of the surf forced parts of the bluffs to break off, prompting opportunistic miners to quickly load any promising dirt onto pack mules and haul it to a spot above the bluffs that was safe from the tides. The beach gold was found in the form of a fine dust that was bonded to the sand and sediment. So miners had to use a two-step process to isolate the precious mineral.

Hike Information

🕑 Trail Contacts:
Redwood National and State Parks, Crescent City, CA (707) 464-6101 or www.nps.gov/redw

🕐 Schedule:
Open year round. The visitor center is generally open 9 A.M. to 5 P.M.

💲 Fees/Permits:
$5 day-use fee

❓ Local Information:
Eureka-Humboldt County Convention & Visitor's Bureau, Eureka, CA 1-800-346-3482 or (707) 443-5097 • **Humboldt County websites:** *www.visit humboldt.com, www.co.humboldt.ca.us, www.redwoodvisitor.org,* and *www.hum guide.com* • **Links to individual state parks:** *www.cal-parks.ca.gov*

🎯 Local Events/Attractions:
Annual Banana Slug Derby, in August, Prairie Creek Redwoods State Park • **Discovery Ride,** in October, Redwood National and State Parks

🍴 Accommodations:
National and State park campsites: 1-800-444-7275 to reserve. There are sev-eral public and private campgrounds in the area. Car camping is allowed free of charge on the Freshwater Lagoon spit south of Orick.

👥 Organizations:
Redwood Natural History Association, Crescent City, CA (707) 464-6101 ext. 5095 • **North Coast Redwood Interpretive Association,** Prairie Creek Redwoods State Park, Orick, CA (707) 464-6101 ext. 5300

🎒 Local Outdoor Retailers:
Adventure's Edge, Arcata, CA (707) 822-4673 • **Big 5 Sporting Goods,** Eureka, CA (707) 444-3682 • **Bucksport Sporting Goods,** Eureka, CA (707) 442-1832 • **The Moonstone Factory Store,** Arcata, CA (707) 826-8970 • **Northern Mountain Supply,** Eureka, CA (707) 445-1711 • **The Outdoor Store,** Arcata, CA (707) 822-0321 • **Picky Picky Picky Inc.,** Eureka, CA (707) 444-9201 • **Pro Sport Center,** Eureka, CA (707) 443-6328 and McKinleyville, CA (707) 839-9445 • **Sports Exchange,** Eureka, CA (707) 444-3644

Ⓝ Maps:
USGS maps: Orick, CA; Fern Canyon, CA

Another factor in the decline of productivity may have been the increase of ocean-deposited sand—primarily the result of the rampant use of hydraulic mining elsewhere in the state. Hydraulic mining is a particularly destructive surface-mining method that involves washing away topsoil with high-pressure water jets to uncover any buried gold. In California, miners turned to hydraulic mining only after most of the *easy* nuggets had been recovered by placer mining techniques like panning for gold. The legacy of hydraulic mining is evident in the enormous rock mounds found along nearby riverbanks and in the forever-altered regional ecology. The sediment from hydraulic mines in the Sierra Nevada caused severe flooding in low-lying towns and eventually left San Francisco Bay partially filled, altering its shape and environment forever. Even the sediment that made it to the ocean often found its way back to the beaches of California. These particles increased the sand bars at the mouths of rivers and made them more difficult to navigate.

The shape of Fern Canyon—with its near-vertical walls and flat base—is itself a product of hydraulic mining. Although stripped of plant life by the mining industry, years of inactivity have allowed the flora to recover nicely. The canyon is a gorgeous example of the lush plant life that thrives in these temperate rain forests. Every square inch of the canyon walls is covered with greenery, much of which belongs to one of several species of fern. Lady fern, wood fern, five-finger fern, deer fern, leather leaf fern, and sword fern all grow in the canyon and the surrounding forests, along with a host of mosses and other small plants.

After seeing the canyon, return to the visitor center along the Clintonia and Miner's Ridge trails, which pass through some excellent old-growth groves. And shutterbugs should take note of the straight section of trail along the ridge: It's an excellent place to photograph people walking below the towering giants.

MilesDirections

0.0 START at visitor center trailhead. (This is the large wooden sign next to a display case with elk antlers.) Go down the wooden steps and across the bridge on James Irvine Trail.

0.05 Prairie Creek Trail heads right toward Zig-Zag Trail. Continue straight.

0.1 Nature Trail goes left toward Miner's Ridge Trail. Keep going straight on James Irvine Trail.

0.2 West Ridge Trail heads right. Continue straight.

1.0 The trail crosses a wet spot via a wooden walkway. *[FYI. Skunk cabbage, a relative of the lily, grows all around.]*

2.0 The trail descends some wooden steps and crosses a small creek on a footbridge.

2.5 After descending via some steps, the trail crosses a lush, narrow gully and heads up the

opposite side. *[FYI. You're now in the drainage of Home Creek, which flows through Fern Canyon downstream.]*

2.8 Clintonia Trail heads up to the left, toward the junction with Miner's Ridge Trail. Continue straight on James Irvine Trail.

3.0 The trail descends some steps and crosses two small bridges in quick succession.

3.4 Cross another footbridge.

3.5 The trail crosses a deep, narrow ravine via a footbridge. *[FYI. The ravine was formed by hydraulic gold mining in the late 19th Century.]*

3.7 Climb the steps to the right, still following James Irvine Trail.

3.8 The trail tops out high on the slope above

Home Creek, then begins to descend again.

3.9 At this point, the trail crosses a bridge at the upper end of Fern Canyon.

4.0 Friendship Ridge Trail heads up to the right. Continue straight on James Irvine Trail.

4.3 Fern Canyon Loop Trail heads left. You will eventually return to this point via that trail, but continue straight for now, on James Irvine Trail.

4.4 *[FYI. The meadow on the left is called Lincoln Prairie, and was once a gold-mining camp.]*

4.5 Descend on the steps to the mouth of Fern Canyon. *[FYI. This is an excellent opportunity to picnic or explore nearby Gold Bluffs Beach. To do this, head right 100 feet, then left a few more yards to the Fern Canyon trail-*

head.)] To continue the hike, turn left onto Fern Canyon Loop Trail and head up the narrow, vertical-walled canyon. The trail crosses the creek several times, so expect to get wet feet when it has been raining. (It's worth it.)

5.0 Follow the trail up the steps on the left up to the rim of the canyon.

5.2 Fern Canyon Loop Trail ends at James Irvine Trail. Turn right and follow James Irvine Trail back to the junction with Clintonia Trail.

5.5 Friendship Ridge Trail heads up to the left. Continue straight.

6.7 Turn right onto Clintonia Trail, which heads steeply uphill toward the ridge.

7.0 The trail tops out on the ridge, and passes three memorial redwood groves, dedicated to the philanthropists (and their loved ones) who helped preserve these groves for inclusion in the park.

7.7 Clintonia Trail dead-ends at Miner's Ridge Trail, which heads right (toward Gold Bluffs Beach), and left (toward the visitor center). Turn left onto Miner's Ridge Trail and follow it southeast along the ridge.

9.1 The trail begins to drop down off the ridge.

9.6 Cross the footbridge and continue straight.

9.8 Miner's Ridge trail ends at the junction with Nature Trail. Turn left onto Nature Trail, and head toward the visitor center.

9.9 Turn right onto James Irvine Trail and retrace the first 0.1 miles to the trailhead.

10.0 Arrive back at the trailhead.

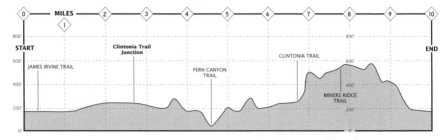

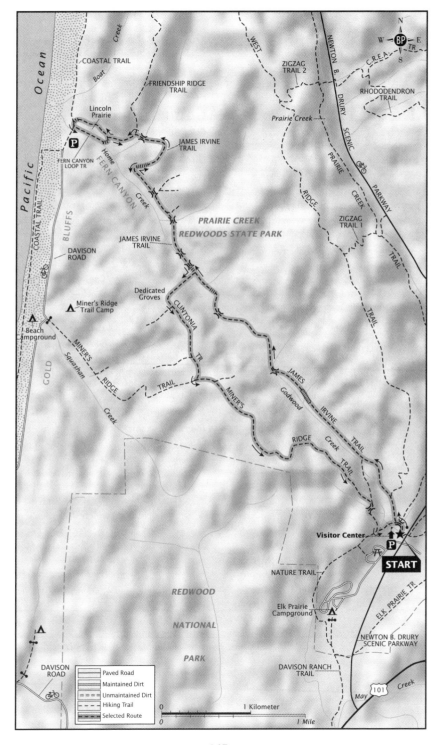

Damnation Creek Trail

Hike Specs

Start: From the Coastal Trail turnout
Length: 3.4-mile out-and-back
Approximate Hiking Time: 2 hours
Difficulty Rating: Moderate-to-strenuous due to steep, but well maintained, trail
Terrain: Dirt path and asphalt road (closed to cars) through old-growth redwoods and coastal scrub, as well as along rocky beach
Elevation Gain: 1,630 feet
Land Status: State park
Nearest Town: Crescent City, CA
Other Trail Users: Cyclists
Canine Compatibility: Dogs not permitted

Getting There

From Eureka: Take U.S. 101 north for 67 miles. North of the Klamath River, the highway briefly skirts the ocean at Wilson Creek and False Klamath Cove before climbing steeply. As the highway veers inland away from the coast, it enters old-growth redwood forest. Park at the first turnout on the right, where the Coastal Trail crosses U.S. 101. Start hiking where the Coastal Trail heads into the forest on the opposite (north) side of the road. ***DeLorme: Northern California Atlas & Gazetteer:*** Page 22 C3

The dark and secluded Damnation Creek lies entirely within the boundaries of Del Norte Redwoods State Park, one of the three state redwood parks nestled in among the patchwork of lands that make up Redwood National Park. With only 6,400 acres, it is the smallest of the three parks. But what it lacks in size, it makes up for in show: It has some 3,200 acres of old-growth and oversees eight miles of pristine coastline. The rugged sea cliffs here are tall and inhospitable to humans, a feature that allows easy beach access only via the Redwood-lined Damnation Creek Trail and the Footsteps Rock Trail at the southern tip of the park

It's likely that the creek—and trail—got their intimidating name because of the area's difficult nature. The perilous terrain also kept the Native Americans away prior to European contact: There were no permanent Indian villages along this stretch of coast before Europeans began settling the region. The nearest major settlements originally were on Pebble Beach—at present-day Crescent City to the north and near the mouth of Wilson Creek to the south.

The land south of Wilson Creek traditionally was considered Yurok territory, while the territory north of Wilson Creek—including Damnation Creek—was generally regarded as Tolowa country. The tribes shared a number of cultural traits, like the use of tooth-like dentalia shells for currency and the custom of women wearing basket hats. But the Tolowa differed from the Yurok in having clearly defined, politically powerful chiefs. And there was occasional violent conflict between the two groups, usually in the form of raids.

Both the Tolowa and the Yurok nations have survived, but the Tolowa have been reduced to a tiny fraction of their former numbers and are no longer federally recognized as a tribe. The Yurok have fared better in that sense. With a tribal roll of over

4,000 members, they are considered the largest Native American tribe in California (at the time of writing).

The first part of the hike follows a piece of the Coastal Trail along a defunct section of the original U.S. Route 101. If you scrape a few inches of duff off the trail, you'll find the pavement still mostly intact—right down to the yellow dividing line. The highway was diverted several years ago to avoid the coastline's slow but persistent slide into the ocean. Even today, this phenomenon keeps the highway between Wilson Creek and the trailhead in constant need of repair.

The upper portion of the trail roughly follows the footsteps of Northwest California's patron pioneer, Jedediah Smith—one of the most famous 19th-century mountain men. In 1827, the 30-year-old Smith set out from Utah's Great Salt Lake to explore the area in hopes of opening new trade routes and new sources for beaver

Salmon Berry.

Wild Iris.

Redwood Sorrel.

Trillium.

and otter skins. Smith's journey was not without peril. He survived dangerous river crossings, a battle with Mojave Indians that cost him most of his men and all his horses, and a trek across the brutal Mojave Desert. He finally arrived in Southern California, only to be taken into custody by Mexican authorities suspicious of American intentions. After placating the Mexican governor, Smith was released and allowed to continue his exploration. He re-supplied and made his way up the Sacramento Valley, cutting west along a tributary of the Trinity River and trapping furs as he went. Smith followed the river down to its confluence with the Klamath, and from there, he continued downstream to the ocean. Smith and his party headed north from the mouth of the Klamath along the coast, reaching the Damnation Creek area in early June of 1828. The difficulties of traveling with large pack animals

MilesDirections

0.0 START at the junction of the Coastal Trail and U.S. 101. The trail curves and heads west toward the coast.

0.1 The trail drops down onto an abandoned section of U.S. 101, which is now nearly buried beneath redwood needles and duff. Turn right onto the old highway (now part of the Coastal Trail) and head north.

0.5 *[FYI. To the left of the trail is a small boulder inset with a bronze plaque as a monument to Henry Solon Graves, who was a local forester, educator, and administrator in the early 20th century. Henry's monument was placed here by Save-The-Redwoods League in 1925.]*

0.7 Damnation Creek Trail heads right (0.6 miles) to U.S. 101. Continue straight on the Coastal Trail.

0.8 An alternate fork of Damnation Creek Trail heads right to U.S. 101. The Coastal Trail continues north to Crescent City. Turn left onto Damnation Creek Trail and head downhill.

1.0 Halfway down to the beach, the trail begins a series of sharp switchbacks and descends rapidly.

1.3 As the trail nears the ocean, the forest changes from predominantly redwoods to predominantly spruce and fir, which are more tolerant of the salty sea air. *[FYI. Big balls of leather ferns are visible high in the trees to the right.]*

1.5 The trail crosses a wooden foot bridge over a shallow ravine.

1.6 After crossing another wooden bridge, the trail enters the coastal scrub habitat zone, with low bushes and a grassy meadow that is full of wildflowers in the spring.

1.7 Follow the faint path down to the right and down a series of wooden steps to the beach. The last few steps are rock. *[Note. Be careful, because they can be slippery.]* This is the turnaround point for this hike. Return the way you came.

3.4 Arrive back at the trailhead.

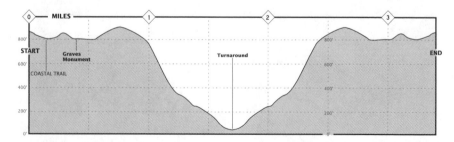

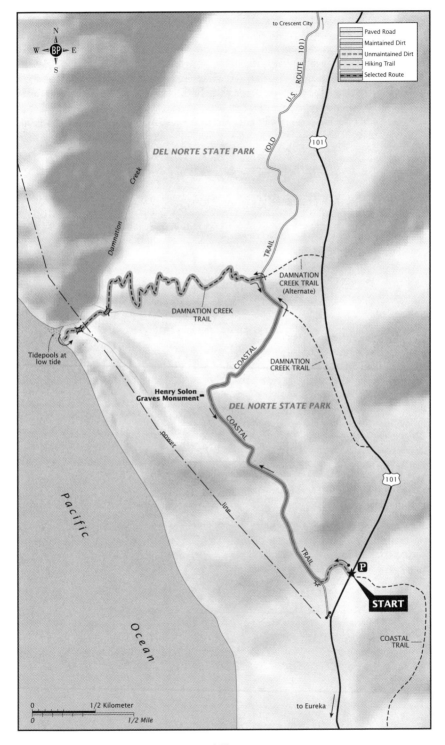

to Crescent City

	Paved Road
	Maintained Dirt
	Unmaintained Dirt
	Hiking Trail
	Selected Route

U.S. ROUTE 101 (OLD)

101

DEL NORTE STATE PARK

Damnation Creek

TRAIL

DAMNATION CREEK TRAIL (Alternate)

DAMNATION CREEK TRAIL

COASTAL

DAMNATION CREEK TRAIL

Tidepools at low tide

Henry Solon Graves Monument

DEL NORTE STATE PARK

COASTAL

power

line

101

TRAIL

P

START

Pacific

Ocean

COASTAL TRAIL

to Eureka

N
W — E
S
BP

0   1/2 Kilometer
0   1/2 Mile

149

in Redwood Country were daunting, to say the least. Once you see the jumbles of giant logs and dense vegetation that cover the forest floor here, you'll understand why. The journey was so difficult that the expedition sometimes managed to travel less than two miles a day!

Smith eventually made it to Fort Vancouver on the Columbia River, sold his share of the trapping business, and returned to his Rocky Mountain haunts a wealthy man. He continued to explore, however, and figures prominently in the history of several other western states. As his last adventure, Smith got involved in the Santa Fe fur trade. He was killed in 1831 by Comanche Indians on the Cimarron River.

Smith and his men were often on the brink of starvation during their travels. They survived by trading with the Native Americans they encountered. Oral history accounts of these meetings survive among several local tribes and confirm the route Smith described in his journals. They also provide an interesting counterpoint to the often one-sided history of the West.

From the old highway, the Damnation Creek Trail descends steeply through the dense forest that lines the deep Damnation Creek gully. The abundant fog creates an eerie, dramatic backdrop for the hike. As you make your way down through the tangled forest to the seemingly forgotten coastline, leather ferns perch high above the trail in the crooks of wind-twisted spruce and pine trees. The trail ends at a pristine, rocky cove, complete with stone arches and dramatic offshore rocks. At low tide, these rocks reveal tide pools full of marine life. Mussels, sea urchins, anemones, and starfish can all be found here, clinging to the surf-pounded rocks. In spring, look for a splash of color in the tiny meadow above the beach, as wildflowers come into bloom.

Return the way you came.

Hike Information

● Trail Contacts:
Del Norte Redwoods State Park, Crescent City, CA (707) 464–6101 ext. 5064 or 5120

● Schedule:
Open year round

● Fees/Permits:
No fees or permits required

● Local Information:
Del Norte Chamber of Commerce, Crescent City, CA 1–800–343–8300 or *www.northerncalifornia.net*

● Accommodations:
Hostelling International Redwood National Park, Klamath, Ca (707) 482–8265 or *www.norcalhostels.org – There is a youth hostel at the mouth of Wilson Creek* • **Del Norte Redwoods State Park,** Crescent City, CA 1–800–444–7275 – *Campgrounds in the state park are open from April 1st to October 1st. Call to reserve a campground site.*

● Organizations:
Redwood Natural History Association, Crescent City, CA (707) 464–6101 ext. 5095 • **North Coast Redwood Interpretive Association,** Prairie Creek Redwoods State Park, Orick, CA (707) 464–6101 ext. 5300

● Local Outdoor Retailers:
Adventure's Edge, Arcata, CA (707) 822–4673 • **Big 5 Sporting Goods,** Eureka, CA (707) 444–3682 • **Bucksport Sporting Goods,** Eureka, CA (707) 442–1832 • **Northern Mountain Supply,** Eureka, CA (707) 445–1711 • **The Outdoor Store,** Arcata, CA (707) 822–0321 • **Picky Picky Picky Inc.,** Eureka, CA (707) 444–9201 • **Pro Sport Center,** Eureka, CA (707) 443–6328 and McKinleyville, CA (707) 839–9445 • **Sports Exchange,** Eureka, CA (707) 444–3644

● Maps:
USGS maps: Childs Hill, CA; Sister Rocks, CA

Redwood Coast

Compiled here is an index of great hikes in the Redwood Coast region that didn't make the A-list this time around but deserve recognition. Check them out and let us know what you think. You may decide that one or more of these hikes deserves higher status in future editions or, perhaps, you may have a hike of your own that merits some attention.

Ⓑ Russian Cemetery Trail

A short 1.2-mile out-and-back hike from the reconstructed Russian fort to the accompanying orthodox cemetery. Fort Ross State Historic Park is located on CA 1, roughly 55 miles north of San Francisco. The trail heads seaward from the fort, curving around to the left toward a small sheltered cove. From here, the trail climbs through thick vegetation along a tiny creek to the cemetery, located on a low hill behind the fort. For more information, contact Fort Ross State Historic Park, Jenner, CA (707) 847–3286. *DeLorme: Northern California Atlas & Gazetteer:* Page 82 D2&D3

Ⓒ Ecological Staircase Nature Trail

A nice, easy 5.0-mile out-and-back stroll through a variety of landscapes, from grassy headlands to riparian streamside forest, mature second-growth to pygmy forest. From Fort Bragg, head south three miles on CA 1 to Jug Handle State Reserve. From the information board on west side of the parking lot, the trail makes a quick trip to the coastal bluffs before curving around to the right and heading inland. The trail ends at a short loop through a pygmy forest, caused by hardpan, mineral-leached soils. For more information contact: Mendocino Sector Headquarters, c/o Russian Gulch State Park, Mendocino, CA (707) 937–5804. *DeLorme: Northern California Atlas & Gazetteer:* Page 73 A5

Ⓓ Memorial/Baird Double Loop

An easy 1.5-mile double-loop hike through old-growth and second-growth redwoods. The trail is accessed via a seasonal (summer) footbridge over the Van Duzen River. From Eureka, head south 20 miles on U.S. 101, then east 17.5 miles on CA 36 to Grizzly Creek Redwoods State Park. For more information contact: Grizzly Creek Redwoods State Park, Carlotta, CA (707) 777–3683. *DeLorme: Northern California Atlas & Gazetteer:* Page 53 A4&A5

(E) Coastal Trail – Crescent Beach Trail

An easy 4.4-mile out-and-back from the Crescent Beach Information Center to the Crescent Beach Overlook. The trail passes through meadows and patches of forest between bluffs and ocean. Excellent bird and whale watching. From Crescent City take U.S. 101 south out of town and turn right onto Enderts Beach Road. Follow this road to the Crescent Beach Information Center. For more information contact: Redwood National Park, Crescent City, CA (707) 464–6101. *DeLorme: Northern California Atlas & Gazetteer:* Page 22 C2

(F) Boy Scout Trail

A 7.4-mile out-and-back trail through old-growth redwoods and boggy skunk cabbage patches to the trail's namesake Boy Scout Tree, a double-trunked giant, and a little farther to a picturesque waterfall. From Crescent City, head east one mile on Elk River Road, turning right on Howland Hill Road and continuing 2.7 miles to the Boy Scout Tree trailhead. At 2.8 miles up the trail, a spur heads right a few yards to the Boy Scout Tree. The main trail continues another 0.4 miles to the waterfall and turnaround point. For more information contact: Jedediah Smith Redwoods State Park, Crescent City, CA (707) 464–6101 ext. 5064 or 5112. *DeLorme: Northern California Atlas & Gazetteer:* Page 22 B2&B3

Coastal Mountains

OREGON

Crescent City
199
29
96
Yreka
97
139
Alturas
Mt Shasta 14162 ft
299
Likely
Orick
27 28
1
Mt Shasta
H
89
27
G
5
30
395
26
Willow Creek
Shasta Lake
Burney
101
299
Weaverville
25
299
349
119
Eureka
Redding
Susanville
211
Weaverville
1
44
44
36
Wildwood
Paynes Creek
89
16
36
Redway
24
RedBluff
89
99
32
70
70
Chico
49
89
Oroville
162
70
Truckee
80
Fort Bragg
20
20
Tahoe City
Lake Tahoe
NEVADA
Ukiah
128
20
49
Placerville
S. Lake Tahoe
Auburn
50
89
101
128
23
16
88
Santa Rosa
25
4
505
80
16
108
395
116
5
99
Bodega Bay
20
49
80
26
49
Angels Camp
Marin City
580
Oakland
Stockton
4
120
San Francisco
880
132
Modesto
140
6
280
99
San Jose
Merced
41
Bishop
168
1
35
152
145
395
101
Santa Cruz

The Hikes

Honorable Mentions

Coastal Mountains

While not as high or dramatic in scenery as the Sierra Nevada, the mountains that stretch up and down the Northern California coast are nevertheless full of surprises for hikers willing to get off the beaten track. Bounded largely by U.S. Route 101 in the west and Interstate 5 in the east, only a few major roads cross the range to access the national forests and wilderness areas that lie tucked within. Steep, curvy roads are the rule here, and the resulting time delays further reduce the crowds that would otherwise spoil the solitude.

Civilization tends to keep a low profile here, and the major towns keep, for the most part, to the valleys east and west of the ranges. Along U.S. Route 101, the major towns are Ukiah, Willits, and Eureka—none of which are particularly large by Bay Area standards. Redding and the smaller Red Bluff are the *hubs* of civilization in the Sacramento Valley.

Aside from extensive holdings by major timber companies, most of the land in the Coastal Mountains is managed by the U.S. Forest Service (e.g. Klamath, Six Rivers, Shasta-Trinity, and Mendocino), with a few patches of BLM land in between. The area's unique geology includes frequent outcroppings of gray-green serpentine rocks, the makeup of which creates special challenges to plant life growing in serpentine-derived soils. As a result, many native plants have made special adaptations to survive in these soils. Serpentine, along with its position on the boundaries of several habitat zones, has made the Klamath *knot* of mountains home to an astounding biological diversity. At the heart of this is the Marble Mountain Wilderness, a jumble of peaks and valleys studded with lakes and green meadows. The nearby Trinity Alps Wilderness has miles and miles of excellent trails—and scenery that rivals that of its Swiss namesake. The region also boasts world-class whitewater recreation and—at higher elevations—exquisite alpine lakes that serve as destination points for hikers.

Farther south—and even more remote—are the Yolla Bolly and Snow mountains. Granted, there are fewer lakes and less spectacular scenery in the Yolla Bolly/Middle Eel Wilderness than in the two areas up north, but the Yolla Bollys are so secluded that the place is a haven for wildlife. The area is home to plenty of black bear, coyotes, deer, fox, bobcat, and mountain lion...even a few of the rare and elusive wolverines. It's a wonderful area for secluded hiking and camping.

At the southern end of the Coastal Mountains region is Clear Lake, a natural body of water that was once home to extensive tule marshes. Pomo Indians, who lived along the lakes shores since prehistoric times, made extensive use of the tule plant, and archeological evidence of large villages has been found at Anderson Marsh State Park, on the southeastern end of the lake. Of course there are trails there, too.

Coastal Mountains

Anderson Marsh Loop

This hike is an easy stroll through prime bird and wildflower habitat and is especially impressive in the springtime when the meadows are in full bloom. Birders will find a wealth of species, but take note: They are best viewed in the morning. Archeology buffs will also be rewarded on this hike. The park was once the site of a Pomo Indian village and has yielded useful archeological information. A 19th Century ranch house, typical of early European settlers, serves as a museum and visitor center for the park. *(See page 160.)*

North Yolla Bolly Loop

This hike is a great loop through one of Northern California's least-traveled wilderness areas. The trail makes stops at a picturesque lake and a mountain summit before traversing a long ridge, offering fabulous views of the coast range and beyond. The Yolla Bolly/Middle Eel Wilderness is home to abundant wildlife, including martens, mountain lions, and even the elusive wolverine. *(See page 166.)*

Stuart Fork Trail to Emerald and Sapphire Lakes

These tantalizingly named lakes lie at the end of a trail that crosses one of the largest alpine meadows in the Trinity Alps. There are numerous reminders of the gold mining activity that took place here in the past, including ditches, cabin ruins, and the remains of a dam on Sapphire Lake. This is a long trail and hard to follow in spots (especially above Morris Meadows), so be aware of your limitations before attempting this hike. *(See page 172.)*

Water Dog Lakes Loop

This trail visits a little-used corner of the Trinity Alps Wilderness that was scorched by a huge forest fire in 1999. A short side trip leads to an old cabin that was spared by the fire. Part of the trail was used as a mule-train route in the 19th Century. During its use, settlers traveled this passage to ferry supplies from Arcata to the Scott River Valley. *(See page 178.)*

Haypress-McCash Loop

The Haypress Trail leads deep into the Marble Mountains Wilderness and passes through the scene of a recent forest fire, where hikers can witness nature healing itself. Higher up, the trail travels through a series of alpine meadows before climbing a steep slope and returning along the McCash Loop. This return route highlights the loop's exposed ridge and panoramic views. But there are only a few sources of water along the ridge portion of the trail, so be sure to come prepared. Fill up your water bottle before you get there, or bring enough to last the entire trip. Also, be aware that hunting season begins in September. *(See page 184.)*

Kelsey Trail

The historic Kelsey Trail is an old supply route that was built in the 1850s. The passage was used to bring supplies from Crescent City to the homesteaders and miners in the Scott Valley, as well as to the military post at Fort Jones. On the return trip, traders brought gold and local commodities to the coast. The trail passes through beautiful alpine country, visits three lakes, and overlaps a section of the Pacific Crest Trail. *(See page 190.)*

Devil's Punchbowl Trail

The dramatic Devil's Punchbowl is revealed at the last moment, after climbing a steep trail and topping a low ridge. It hides below the trail and is surrounded on three sides by steep rock walls. This part of the Klamath Mountains is famous for its botanical diversity. As many as 15 or 16 different species of conifer grow near each other in this area. The Siskiyou Wilderness also boasts an unusually high number of unique plant species that flourish here but cannot grow anywhere else in the world. *(See page 196.)*

Crags Trail

The views of the Crags up close and of Mount Shasta in the distance more than make up for the energy expenditure involved in climbing the trail. The strangely shaped crags and crevices invite exploration, and with steep slopes that plunge into thick forest on all sides, the Crags truly feel like an island in the sky. Be sure to take your sunglasses, because the sun reflecting from the white granite at the summit can be blinding. *(See page 202.)*

23   Anderson Marsh Loop

Hike Specs

Start: From the trailhead behind the ranch house
Length: 2.8-mile loop
Approximate hiking time: 1.5–2 hours
Difficulty Rating: Easy due to flat terrain and smooth trails
Terrain: Mowed meadow, boardwalk, and dirt path through grassland, oak woodland, riparian woodland, and freshwater marsh
Elevation Gain: 152 feet
Land Status: State park
Nearest Town: Lower Lake, CA
Other Trail Users: Hikers only
Canine Compatibility: Dogs not permitted

Getting There

From Ukiah: Head north six miles on U.S. 101, then east on CA 20, continuing about 46 miles to the other end of Clear Lake. Turn south onto CA 53 and drive eight miles to the park entrance. The park is just off the highway on the right-hand side, between the towns of Clear Lake and Lower Lake. *DeLorme: Northern California Atlas & Gazetteer:* Page 84 A1

A bundant natural beauty, ancient Pomo Indian heritage, and a carefully preserved example of an early settler's house all await visitors at Anderson Marsh State Historic Park. The site was chosen as a state park because the Anderson house so typifies how average European settlers lived while the area was being settled around 1855. The 1,000-acre park contains several archeological sites documenting the presence of native people as many as 10,000 years ago. The area was home to the Southeastern Pomo, one of California's largest native populations before the arrival of Europeans sparked a sharp decline in the population. Descendants of the Pomo still live nearby.

Ecologically speaking, the park protects within its boundaries a large portion of the remaining tule marsh on Clear Lake. This marsh, dominated by its namesake tule reed, is only a tiny remnant of the huge marsh that once surrounded the lake. But it still provides habitat for several species of birds, mammals, fish, amphibians and reptiles.

Tules (*Scirpus acutus*) are long, whip-like aquatic plants that grow in a habitat similar to that of cattails and are very important to Clear Lake's health. The tule marsh acts as a filter for the lake, removing noxious (and smelly) varieties of blue-green algae and other pollutants. The tules also provide cover for area wildlife. Many species of fish spend at least part of their lives sheltered among the reedy plants. For the Pomo Indians, tules were an important building material. Tule mats were used to cover bent-pole lodges and to cover shade structures that provided relief from the summer sun. Because tules are naturally buoyant, they were used in bundles to build

canoe-shaped rafts for fishing and transport. Sometimes, enormous floating mats were constructed, from which a whole family would embark on an extended fishing tour.

The featured loop starts at the back corner of the ranch house, near the old out-house. The trail passes first through a short section of grassland, once used as winter cattle pasture by the Andersons—a typical pioneer family who settled here and built the surrounding house and barns. Beyond the grassland, you cross through a section of seasonal marsh via a long boardwalk. Vines of wild grape can be seen hanging from the trees, and in the late summer months, they dangle bunches of grapes just out of the eager hiker's reach.

Anderson Marsh.

The first of two channels the trail passes over is the original course of the creek, which was straightened in 1938 to increase the outflow of Clear Lake, thereby draining much of the original marsh. When the water recedes in summer, the shallower bends of the original creek bed run dry. The muddy oxbows left behind are a good place to examine the tracks of some of the park's inhabitants. The typical cloven hooves of black-tailed deer seem omnipresent. And if you spend some time, you'll probably see the tracks of raccoons, which look very much like tiny human hands.

The trail skirts a section of the main Cache Creek channel, which is home to several species of waterfowl in spite of the buildings and human activity on the other side of the creek. Mallards are common, as are black phoebes. Keep an eye open for the Western grebe, a duck-shaped bird with a pointed yellow-green bill and a black patch covering the top of its head and eyes. (The bird is easily distinguished from its drab brown cousin the pied billed grebe.)

Beyond the boardwalk, the trail can become wet and overgrown in the spring, as high water levels sometimes prevent park staff from cutting back the prodigious growth. Occasionally, hikers may stumble upon local crayfish on the trail, surprising the crustaceans into a defensive position. But if you leave them alone, the crayfish are harmless. Passing through the heavy grasses and head-high weeds, tiny tunnels and paths can be seen running off perpendicular to the trail. These mini-paths are frequented by small mammals and ground-dwelling birds.

Just past the first junction, the trail reaches the slightly raised section in the landscape known as the *ridge*. From here, you have a good view of the whole trail-accessible portion of the park. The landscape has become a sparse oak woodland. This is the part of the park where the Pomo had a village in prehistoric times. There's not

MilesDirections

0.0 START from the trailhead behind the ranch house.

0.2 Follow the boardwalk over the oxbows of Cache Creek.

0.6 A short spur trail leads off to the right, offering a view of the creek.

1.1 Turn right at the junction. *[FYI. Immediately on the right is the rock outcropping called Ridge Point; a good vantage point for observing the local fauna.]*

1.4 *[FYI. There is a snag on the right with tons of holes in it, many of which have been stuffed with acorns by industrious woodpeckers.]*

1.5 McVicar Trail heads off to the right. We continue to the left.

2.0 Turn right at the junction onto the Ridge Trail, heading toward the ranch.

2.8 Arrive back at the parking lot.

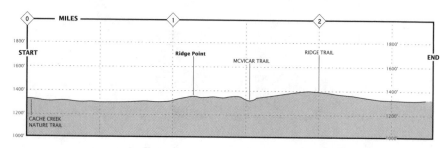

much to see in the way of historical reminders, but if you do happen across any artifacts, do the right thing and leave them where they are.

At the next junction, the McVicar Trail leads off to the right, leading to the McVicar Wildlife Sanctuary, and offering good views of the expansive tule marsh that occupies this end of Clear Lake. The trail is about 1.8 miles out-and-back to this point, and there is a picnic area at the turnaround point. (**Note:** *Poison oak is prevalent here. See sidebar.*)

Back on the main loop, the trail continues through oak woodland and passes an old dead tree—called a *snag*. The snag has hundreds of holes bored into it, some of which are stuffed with acorns. This is the work of the acorn woodpecker, which uses the tree to store reserves for the winter. As it turns colder, the seasonal rains help leach out a bitter tannins from the acorns. The woodpecker uses the acorns, along with insects attracted by the acorns to sustain itself through the winter.

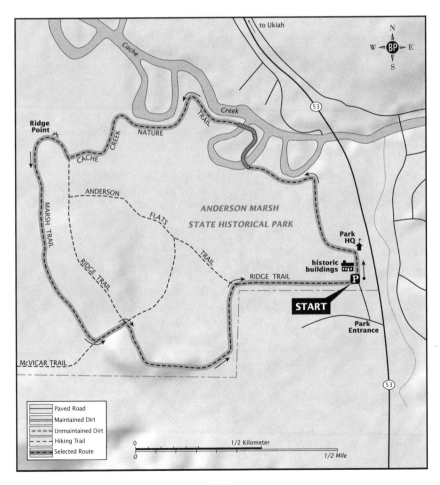

Let the Hiker Beware: Poison Oak (*Rhus diversiloba*)

This unpleasant plant is found in abundance throughout the region and can turn an otherwise enjoyable trip into an itchy-scratchy misery. Poison oak uses the same toxin as poison ivy and poison sumac to produce the dreaded rash of tiny red bumps, which itch like crazy and keep you scratching all night long—much to the discomfort of the afflicted and the annoyance of tent-mates.

There are some products on the market that either protect the skin from the oils or lessen the itching after the fact, but they are expensive and are not perfect. The best advice is, simply, DON'T TOUCH IT! Learn to recognize the familiar three-leaf pattern and the oak-leaf shape of the leaves, and you'll soon see poison oak lying in wait on the edges of trails and beneath trees. If you do touch the plant, wash immediately with lots of COLD water, and you should be able to rinse away most of the toxic oil. It's not a good idea to wash with warm water, as this opens the pores of the skin and lets the poison in that much faster.

The good news? Poison oak does not grow above 5,000 feet, so you should be safe in the high country. Good luck!

Acorn storage for woodpeckers.

Hike Information

◐ Trail Contacts:

Anderson Marsh State Historic Park, Lower Lake, CA (707) 944–0688 or (707) 279–2267 or *www.calparks.ca.gov*

◑ Schedule:

The gate is open from Wednesday to Sunday, 10 A.M.–5 P.M., and the house is open for guided tours Thursday through Sunday, 10 A.M.–4 P.M. (closed from October to March or April). Trails are accessible year round even if the gate is closed.

⑤ Fees/Permits:

$3 voluntary day-use fee

◑ Local Events/Attractions:

Anderson Marsh State Historic Park: Heron Festival, second weekend in April – *includes water tours via canoe to areas not usually accessible to visitors* • **Anderson Marsh State Historic Park:** Blackberry Festival, second weekend in August – *Celebrates the blackberry harvest. There are archeological and historical tours given, and several special events, including live music and, of course, blackberry pie* • **Anderson Marsh State Historic Park: Native American Cultural Heritage Celebration,** third Saturday in May

◑ Hike Tours:

The Redbud Audubon Society, Clearlake, CA (707) 994–2024 – hosts a nature walk the first Saturday of every month at 9 A.M.

◒ Accommodations:

There are numerous hotels and rental cabins in Clear Lake, most of them reasonably priced.

🛉 Organizations:

Redbud Audubon Society, Clearlake, CA (707) 994–2024 • **Anderson Marsh Interpretive Association,** Lower Lake, CA (707) 994–0688

◐ Other Resources:

An Interpretive Trail Guide to the Natural Features of Anderson Marsh State Historic Park by Susanne Scholz – *This little book covers the flora, fauna, and natural history of the park, and is available in the ranch house.*

🏬 Local Outdoor Retailers:

Big 5 Sporting Goods, Ukiah, CA (707) 462–2870 • **Diamond Jim's Sporting Goods and Liquor,** Ukiah, CA (707) 462–9741 • **Freedom,** Ukiah, CA (707) 462–3310 • **GI Joe's Outdoor Store,** Ukiah, CA (707) 468–8834

Ⓝ Maps:

USGS: Lower Lake, CA; Clearlake Highlands, CA. A trail map is available in the ranch house, when open.

North Yolla Bolly Loop

Hike Specs

Start: From the Rat Trap Gap trailhead
Length: 12.6-mile loop
Approximate Hiking Time: 7–8 hours (either as a long day hike or an overnight stay)
Difficulty Rating: Moderate to Strenuous due to steep switchbacks and occasionally sketchy trail
Terrain: Dirt path through dense forests, along exposed ridges, and across alpine meadows
Elevation Gain: 3,639 feet
Land Status: National forest
Nearest Town: Wildwood, CA
Other Trail Users: Equestrians, anglers, and hunters (in season)
Canine Compatibility: Dogs permitted

Getting There

From Eureka: Take U.S. 101 south 20 miles to CA 36 and turn left. Drive east 80 miles and turn right onto paved FS 30, two miles before the town of Wildwood. Take FS 30 south 20 miles through Shasta-Trinity National Forest to Pine Root Saddle. Turn left onto FS 35 (also paved) and follow it 11 miles to Stuart Gap. Turn left here, following the sign for FS 35, and continue to the junction with FS 45. The Rat Trap Gap trailhead is located on the southwest corner of this junction. *DeLorme: Northern California Atlas & Gazetteer:* Page 55 C5

Perhaps the most striking feature of the Yolla Bolly/Middle Eel Wilderness is its remoteness. Standing at the colorfully named Rat Trap Gap trailhead, it's hard to imagine that California is the country's most populous state. In fact, it can be difficult to imagine that the area is populated at all, because the remoteness and low profile of the Yolla Bollys attract few visitors. The wilderness' twisting gravel roads and lack of lakes—which are usually a focal point in backcountry areas—make for a true hermit's hideaway.

Those seeking casual recreation may often overlook the Yolla Bolly/Middle Eel Wilderness, but the area is popular among hunters, who are attracted by the abundant game. Aside from big game such as black tail deer and black bear, plenty of other animals thrive in the absence of human development, including wild turkeys, mountain lions, grouse, quail, bobcats, and a few rare Northern spotted owls. Marten, otters, and weasels—all members of the Mustelidae (or weasel) family—also live here.

The presence of another musteline animal, the secretive wolverine, has recently been confirmed within the wilderness. Once thought to be extinct in California, these powerful predators are now known to survive in more remote parts of the Sierra Nevada and northern coastal ranges. Also known as the skunk bear, carcajou, and woods devil, the wolverine is one of the least known and least understood of North America's large predators. Wolverines rarely exceed 45 pounds in weight, but they are known as tenacious hunters that occasionally prey on animals as large as moose (especially in deep snow, when large animals have difficulty running away). Like bears, however, they are omnivores and consume mostly roots, berries, fish, and small

Looking down from North Peak.

game. Native Americans and early fur trappers, who knew the wolverine as a skilled raider of food caches, grew to hate the critter. The settlers' distaste helps account for the beast's unflattering name—which means "glutton"—as does its scientific name, *Gulo gulo*. Once thought to inhabit a enormous range across North America, the pop-

MilesDirections

0.0 START at Rat Trap Gap trailhead.

0.1 The trail forks. Take the right (straight) fork, following North Yolla Bolly Trail to North Yolla Bolly Lake.

2.3 The trail enters the Yolla Bolly Middle Eel Wilderness.

2.5 The forest opens to reveal a nice view to the north. The trail skirts a deep ravine with exposed bedrock on other side.

2.7 Small stream crossing. There is no bridge, but you'll find good stepping stones.

2.9 *[FYI. Excellent view to the north of distant Mount Shasta.]*

3.2. The trail circles right, around a low, jagged ridge and heads up the other side.

3.4 Reach North Yolla Bolly Lake. The trail circumnavigates the north and west sides of lake, then begins switchbacking up.

4.0 *[FYI. Mount Lassen and the central valley are visible from here, when the weather allows it.]*

4.7 Turn left on Pettijohn Trail and head south toward Chicago Camp.

6.1 Trail reaches the saddle on the ridge, with great views to the north and south. *[FYI. North Yolla Bolly Peak is now visible on the left.]* Turn left on the ridge, then follow the trail as it dips down through the trees on the north side of the ridge.

6.8 The trail enters a small meadow with a nice spring and a well-developed campsite. The trail becomes faint and climbs straight up on the east side of the meadow, switching back and forth up the slope. When in doubt, look for rock cairns and keep climbing.

7.2 Near the saddle of the short ridge between two peaks, the trail appears to fork. Take the left fork across a small meadow.

7.3 The trail tops out at the saddle. Turn left to climb the north peak. There is no trail, but it is an easy scramble up the bare slope to the highest point.

7.7 Arrive at North Yolla Bolly Mountain's north peak (7,863 feet). Return to the saddle you just left.

8.1 Back at the saddle, continue straight along the short ridge and climb up to the south peak.

8.3 The trail tops out on North Yolla Bolly Mountain's south peak. Follow the ridge east, slightly to the left.

8.6 The trail follows the ridge in and out of meadows and trees. The path is faint, but hard to lose if you follow the cairns and stay on the ridge.

9.3 *[FYI. To your left is the head of Beegum Basin.]*

9.5 As a bald hill looms before you, the trail ducks into the forest on the south side of the ridge.

10.4 The trail again enters dense woods, after several open patches, and heads downhill.

10.9 Reach a junction. Turn left on Cold Fork Trail.

11.5 The trail exits the wilderness.

12.5 Back at that first fork in the trail. Turn right.

12.6 Arrive back at the trailhead.

ulation and future of the animal are now uncertain. But the U.S. Fish & Wildlife Service has denied a petition to list the wolverine as an endangered species, citing lack of scientific population data for the animal as its reason.

While stomping through the Yolla Bolly/Middle Eel Wilderness on an overnight hike, your chances of seeing a wolverine rank somewhere between winning the lottery twice and getting struck by lightning while standing on your head in the bathtub, but it doesn't really matter. Just knowing they're out there adds a dimension of adventure to the hike.

From Rat Trap Gap, the trail first contours in and out of several deep gullies before coming to North Yolla Bolly Lake. This small lake on the northern face of the mountain often freezes over in the winter, and it sometimes stays frozen until mid June. But once it has thawed, the lake is a nice spot to spend some time—especially in the morning, when the sun lights the water with a soft glow. After this idyll, the trail climbs a series of switchbacks over a flank of the mountain before dropping down

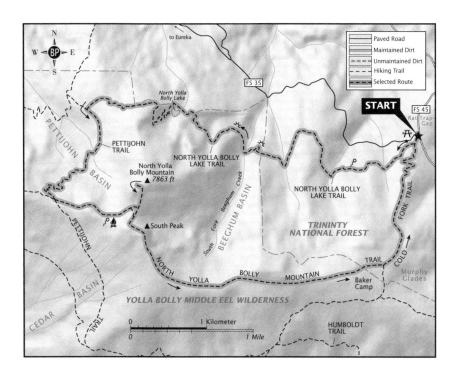

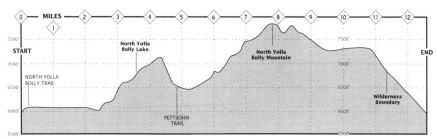

again and joining the Pettijohn Trail. The trail climbs south from these green meadows to a ridge, where the whole of the wilderness opens up before you.

The Yolla Bolly/Middle Eel Wilderness lies smack in the middle of the Coast Range, amid a sea of low ridges and nameless forested hills. Towns are few and far between out here, and when they do exist, they tend to be loose confederations of outlying homesteads rather than clustered villages. People live out here because they like to be alone.

Attracted by the sparse population, mild-to-hot weather, dense tree cover, and inaccessibility, the area has become known as a haven for marijuana growers. Legal or not, the *Devil's weed* is a major cash crop for the area—especially in nearby Humboldt County—and adds a noticeable boost to the local economy. At the height of the drug war, it was common to see Drug Enforcement Agency helicopters scanning the hills for large-scale growers. Things have calmed down in recent years, although occasionally large busts are still made.

View of South Peak from North Peak.

The name Yolla Bolly comes from a Wintun Indian phrase meaning "snow-covered mountain." The Wintun (or Wintu) was a group of Penutian-speaking people who lived in the western Sacramento Valley and its adjacent foothills. Nearly wiped out by land-hungry white settlers, the Wintun still survive today, albeit in much smaller numbers. The wilderness is also named for the Middle Fork Eel section of the Eel River, which flows northwest from here and enters the Pacific Ocean a few miles south of Humboldt Bay.

From the ridge, the trail turns east again, stopping off at North Yolla Bolly Mountain before following a long, sandy ridge to the Cold Fork Trail and back to the trailhead.

Hike Information

🌐 Trail Contacts:
Shasta-Trinity National Forest, Yolla Bolly Office, Platina, CA (530) 352–4211 or (530) 352–4212 or www.r5.fs.fed.us/shastatrinity

🕐 Schedule:
Open year round, although access is hindered from May to October by snow

💲 Fees/Permits:
No fees or permits required—except for campfire permits which are available at ranger stations.

❓ Local Information:
Trinity County Visitor Information: (530) 623–6101 or 1–800–487–4648 or www.trinitycounty.com • **Tehama County websites:** www.tehamacounty.com or www.discoverredbluff.com

💡 Local Events/Attractions:
Watch grass grow.

🎒 Local Outdoor Retailers:
Outdoor Outfitters, Anderson, CA (530) 365–5210 • **Pro Image,** Anderson, CA (530) 365–3677 • **J & B Sports,** Cottonwood, CA (530) 347–5170 • **Paradise Sporting Goods,** Paradise, CA (530) 877–5114 • **Sport Wild Sporting Goods,** Red Bluff, CA (530) 527–3225 • **Tops Mini Mart,** Red Bluff, CA (530) 527–1859 • **Big 5 Sporting Goods,** Redding, CA (530) 223–2006 • **Camps Sporting Emporium,** Redding, CA (530) 241–4530 • **Redding Sports Ltd.,** Redding, CA (530) 221–7333 • **Rhino-Gear,** Redding, CA (530) 222–1599 • **Sports Fever,** Redding, CA (530) 222–3387 • **American Outdoors,** Shasta Lake, CA (530) 275–6490 • **Brady's Sport Shop,** Weaverville, CA (530) 623–3121 • **Westside Outdoorsman,** Willows, CA (530) 934–2638

🅝 Maps:
USGS maps: North Yolla Bolly, CA

Stuart Fork Trail to Emerald and Sapphire Lakes

Hike Specs

Start: From the Stuart Fork Trail trailhead
Length: 30.0-mile out-and-back
Approximate Hiking Time: 3 days
Difficulty Rating: Moderate to Strenuous due to long length and sketchy trail between Emerald and Sapphire lakes
Terrain: A mile of gravel road and dirt path through dense mountain forests, alpine meadows, and rocky glacial valleys
Elevation Gain: 4,576 feet
Land Status: National forest and wilderness area
Nearest Town: Weaverville, CA
Other Trail Users: Equestrians and anglers
Canine Compatibility: Dogs permitted

Getting There

From Redding: Head west 52 miles on CA 299 to the town of Weaverville. Turn right onto CA 3 and head north 13 miles to the bridge over the Stuart Fork arm of Claire Engle Reservoir. Just past the bridge, turn left onto an unsigned paved road. Drive up this road three miles, past the Trinity Alps Resort to Bridge Camp campground and the Stuart Fork Trail trailhead. The trail starts at the locked gate. *DeLorme: Northern California Atlas & Gazetteer:* Page 45 A5

When pitted against the postcard perfection of Lake Tahoe, Yosemite, or the Redwoods, out-of-the-way places like the Trinity Alps simply get lost in the shuffle. "All the more for the rest of us!" winks the small crowd of knowing enthusiasts who regularly visit the broad alpine meadows and sparkling lakes of California's second-largest wilderness area. While not exactly devoid of human activity, the area sees only a fraction of the use that comparably scenic places in the Sierras report.

Part of the reason for the hike's relative quiet lies in the fact that the Trinity's most impressive peaks are hidden from view by lower ridges until you are actually in the wilderness. From all the surrounding highways and towns, the mountains appear to be a jumble of rugged, scraggly, and generally unimpressive hills. And for most casual hikers, the adage holds true: Out of sight, out of mind.

But hidden within this knot of convoluted geography are sharp glacier-scrubbed peaks, soft grassy meadows, and numerous granite-bound lakes of the highest caliber. They don't call them the Trinity Alps for nothing. The resemblance to the mountains' European namesake is startling—especially when standing in the middle of Morris Meadows on a summer day with the sun lighting up patches of snow on the surrounding peaks.

This hike runs through what is known as the White Trinities, named for the bleached gray of the granite bedrock that lies exposed through much of this portion of the wilderness. By way of contrast, the western edge of the wilderness (including the Water Dog Lakes and the Devil's Backbone) is known as the Green Trinities, due

to its heavy forest cover. Another area is called the Red Trinities after the reddish soils and rocks found there.

The White Trinities account for the highest part of the wilderness, though the peaks are still short by Sierra Nevada standards. The highest point—just above Mirror Lake—is Thompson Peak, at 9,002 feet. Surprisingly, Morris Meadows is only 4,400 feet above sea level, even though it's truly alpine in character. Treeless granite crags close in on both sides as you head up the valley toward Emerald Lake, leaving no doubt that you are in *real* mountains.

The trail starts at Bridge Camp on Stuart Fork, just past the historic Trinity Alps Resort. The access road to the trailhead passes right through the resort, with its vintage cabins crowded along the rushing creek. The resort was originally a cattle ranch, dating from the 1850s. The ranch changed hands many times until Anna and Anton Weber & Sons purchased it in 1924. The Webers developed the resort and built cabins along the creek—naming each cabin after a California county. They also built a dining room that spanned the creek, but this was destroyed in a flood in 1955.

Emerald Lake.

MilesDirections

0.0 START at Stuart Fork Trail trailhead. Follow the gravel road behind the locked gate.

0.3 At the fork in the road, take the right fork.

0.9 Reach Cherry Flat and the Trinity Alps Wilderness boundary. The trail narrows and becomes a dirt path. Continue straight.

1.0 Cross a small stream via well-spaced rocks.

1.1 A false trail heads to the left. Follow the more obvious right path.

1.2 The trail crosses a small stream with a minor waterfall. The stream is dry in late summer.

2.9 A spur trail goes left, down to the Stuart Fork of the Trinity River. Go straight, keeping to the main path.

3.2 The trail drops down onto a flat next to the river. *[FYI. Nice camping spots here.]*

3.8 The trail climbs a bit, offering a first view, to the left, of the snow-capped White Trinities.

4.0 *[FYI. After dropping down onto the flats again, a few more good camping spots become obvious on the left.]*

4.2 Cross a 35-foot-long bridge over Deep Creek. Directly below, you'll notice a 15- to 20-foot-tall waterfall. Spur trails head down on both sides of the bridge to access the creek

5.3 At the junction, the Alpine Lake Trail heads up to the left. Go straight.

5.6 The trail now parallels an old mining diversion ditch, long unused. Another view of the White Trinities opens to the left.

7.2 The trail crosses Salt Creek on stepping stones.

7.4 An equestrian trail bypassing the Deer Creek bridge goes straight. Hikers should follow the path on the left down to the bridge.

7.8 *[FYI. A spur trail goes left to several campsites near the river.]* Continue on the main path across the Deer Creek bridge. *[FYI. Nice swimming holes await in the creek below.]*

7.9 A spur trail goes down to the right to access Deer Creek. Continue straight.

8.0 The equestrian bypass trail rejoins the main path from the right.

8.3 Deer Creek Trail heads off to the right at the junction. Continue straight.

8.5 A view to the left of several snowy peaks heralds the southern end of Morris Meadows. Continue straight.

8.6 Reach Morris Meadows proper. *[FYI. Camping spots can be found on all sides of the meadow.]* The trail becomes faint here. Continue due north, keeping to the left side of the meadow until the trail reappears near the trees.

9.4 North end of Morris Meadows. There's a great view to the left of Bear Gulch.

9.7 The trail re-enters the forest, continuing up-valley to Emerald Lake.

10.3 The forest opens again in a small meadow. *[FYI. There is a nice swimming (or fishing) hole to left.]*

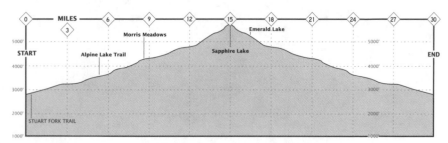

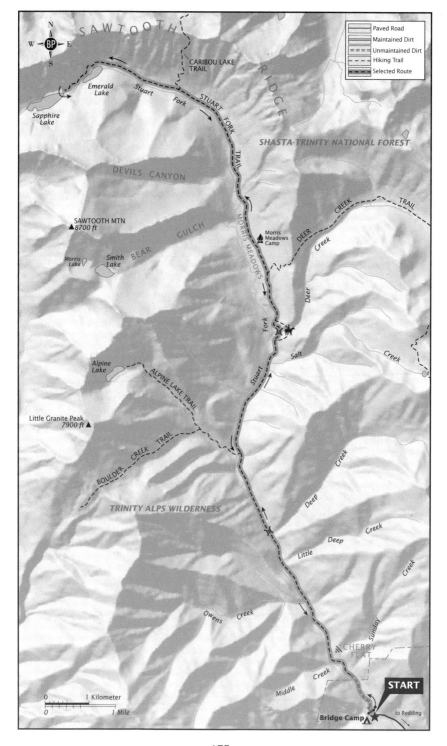

12.4 Come to a junction. The Caribou Lake Trail goes right, climbing steeply to the crest of the ridge. [**Side-trip.** If time permits, a short trip up the Caribou Lake Trail leads to a summit vista that takes in aerial views of Emerald and Sapphire lakes upstream and Morris Meadows downstream.] Continue straight to Emerald Lake.

13.5 The first view of the waterfalls below Emerald Lake opens before you.

13.9 Reach Emerald Lake. [**FYI.** Be sure to check out the old stone dam at the lake's outlet, a reminder of past mining activity.] The trail continues up the right side of the lake to Sapphire Lake.

14.1 [**FYI.** There is a good campsite below to the left.]

14.3 The trail becomes rocky and brushy, in places hard to find. When in doubt, follow cairns and keep going up-valley.

15.0 Reach Sapphire Lake and the turnaround point. [**FYI.** Excellent swimming in season. There are also plenty more relics from the old mining days, including part of a dam, cables, pulleys, and miscellaneous chunks of iron.] Return the way you came.

30.0 Arrive back at the trailhead.

From the campground at Bridge Camp, the trail follows a gravel road to the wilderness boundary at Cherry Flat. At this point, the trail surface changes to dirt and plunges into the forest. There are quite a few good camping spots along the way, but most people choose to hold out for the open space at Morris Meadows, about eight miles from the trailhead. Luckily, the Meadows are huge; so several groups can camp there without overcrowding spoiling the fun.

From here, the trip up the canyon to Emerald and Sapphire lakes can be done as a day trip, or you can transfer base camp as you travel. Be forewarned that campsites are scarce around the lakes, and the best spots are likely to be taken unless you're traveling outside the peak season. As always in wilderness camping, the early bird gets the proverbial worm. For all practical purposes, the trail ends at the eastern edge of Sapphire Lake (the turnaround point for this hike), but especially experienced and/or thick-headed hikers can follow a faint path that quickly degenerates into a brushy

Remains of a dam at Sapphire Lake.

bushwhack as it heads up the north side. Hidden from view on a rocky shelf at the head of the valley is Mirror Lake, which is arguably the heart of the Trinity Alps. Few people venture up there—and when you see what's involved in reaching it, you'll understand why. Thick brush growing on fields of uneven rocks and near-vertical cliffs block the path of would-be adventurers, making Mirror Lake a destination option only for the most experienced hikers. Besides, it doesn't get much better than Sapphire Lake. Deep crystal blue in color, the lake is surrounded by jumbled white granite boulders, rock ledges made for diving, and dramatic towering cliffs. It also has a fair share of brook and rainbow trout, for those inclined to dangle a line. Just be sure you have obtained a fishing license first.

Obvious features of both Emerald and Sapphire lakes are the remnants of human activity near the respective outlets. Both lakes were tamed by rock dams hand-built back in 1898. The dams were used to regulate water flows through a series of ditches, pipes, siphons, and tunnels that culminated nearly 30 miles away at the LaGrange hydraulic mine fields on Oregon Mountain, west of Weaverville. Cables, pulleys, pipes, and other rusting hunks of iron and steel can be seen along the trail, especially on the rocky slope between the two lakes.

Return the way you came.

Hike Information

◷ Trail Contacts:
Shasta-Trinity National Forest, Weaverville Ranger District, Weaverville, CA (530) 623-2121 or www.r5.fs.fed.us/shastatrinity

◷ Schedule:
Open year round, although access is hindered from November to June by snow

$ Fees/Permits:
A free backcountry permit is required, available at the ranger station. Self-service permits can be obtained when ranger station is closed.

❓ Local Information:
Trinity County Visitor Information: (530) 623-6101 or 1-800-487-4648 or www.trinitycounty.com

💡 Local Events/Attractions:
Joss House State Park, Weaverville, CA (530) 623-5284 or (530) 225-2065 or www.park.ca.gov – *oldest Chinese temple in continuous use in California* •

J.J. Jackson Museum & Historic Park, Weaverville, CA (530) 623-5211 – *local and gold mining history, plus black-smithing demonstrations*

● Accommodations:
Trinity Alps Resort & Restaurant, Trinity Center, CA (530) 286-2205

🛒 Local Outdoor Retailers:
Big 5 Sporting Goods, Redding, CA (530) 223-2006 • **Camps Sporting Emporium,** Redding, CA (530) 241-4530 • **Redding Sports Ltd,** Redding, CA (530) 221-7333 • **Rhino-Gear,** Redding, CA (530) 222-1599 • **Sports Fever,** Redding, CA (530) 222-3387 • **American Outdoors,** Shasta Lake, CA (530) 275-6490 • **Brady's Sport Shop,** Weaverville, CA (530) 623-3121

Ⓝ Maps:
USGS maps: Thompson Peak, CA; Mt. Hilton, CA; Siligo Peak, CA; Rush Creek Lakes, CA; Caribou Lake, CA

Water Dog Lakes Loop

Hike Specs

Start: From the Bear Hole Trail trailhead

Length: 14.7-mile loop

Approximate Hiking Time: 10 hours (recommend 2 days)

Difficulty Rating: Moderate-to-strenuous due to steep sections and some sketchy trail

Terrain: Dirt path and dirt road through dense forest, along exposed ridges, and across alpine meadows

Elevation Gain: 3,771 feet

Land Status: National forest and wilderness area

Nearest Town: Willow Creek, CA

Other Trail Users: Equestrians and cattle ranchers

Canine Compatibility: Dogs permitted

Getting There

From Eureka: Head north 10 miles on U.S. 101, and exit onto CA 299 east. Drive 42 miles to the town of Willow Creek. Turn left onto CA 96, and head north another 14 miles, past the town of Hoopa, to Big Hill Road. Turn right onto Big Hill Road and reset your mileage counter. At mile 1.5, the road turns to gravel and continues up into the hills. At mile 6.5, take the left fork, heading uphill. At mile 8.1, take the right fork, and at mile 8.7, take the left fork. At mile 9.9, take the right fork. Mile 11.6 marks the boundary of the Hoopa Reservation, and the beginning of national forest land. The road is paved from this point. Turn right onto a dirt road at mile 13.9, following the sign for Bear Hole and Mill Creek trailheads. Drive up this road to a fork in the road, mile 15.1. Take the middle fork, and continue to another fork, mile 16.6. This time take the left fork, and continue the last 0.4 miles to the trailhead parking. The trailhead is reached by crossing the log footbridge or wading the creek. *DeLorme: Northern California Atlas & Gazetteer:* Page 34 D1

The Water Dog Lakes Loop begins in a hollow known as Bear Hole, which might have been named back when the Great Griz still roamed these hills—and indeed there's a place called Grizzly Camp just a few miles south along the ridge. The name still fits, though, as the area supports a large population of the grizzly's smaller cousin, Ursus americanus (known to most of us as the black bear). Hikers who tread lightly and keep still stand a good chance of seeing bears anywhere along the trail, especially in the early evening. While these bears are not quite as sophisticated (or fearless) as their Sierra Nevada relations, it's still a very good idea to carefully hang food when camping in the Trinity Alps.

From the trailhead, the path quickly climbs up the western slope of Horse Trail Ridge. The flat, round meadow at Crogan Hole marks the beginning and end of the loop section of this hike, and is also a good spot to have lunch. Once on the ridge, a short jaunt south brings you to an old cabin known as Trinity Summit Cabin. The

old station is somewhat the worse-for-the-wear after serving half a century as shelter for rangers, ranchers, hunters, hikers, and even a few skiers. Inside the cabin, numerous visitors have left messages scrawled on the walls. Some of the graffiti dates as far back as the 1950s, long before the area received wilderness designation—which means that some of these scribblers could very well have driven their jeeps up here. Although the Trinity Alps were set aside as a primitive area in 1932, it wasn't until 1984 that the area was added to the National Wilderness Preservation System, thus banning such activity. The area's relatively recent designation explains why there are some old roads running through boundary areas such as Crogan Hole. As of this writing, the Forest Service had begun work on removing culverts and rehabilitating some of these roads.

After returning to the junction with Crogan Hole Trail, the hike continues north along Horse Trail Ridge, while the historic mule train route turns right to cross the hellishly narrow Devil's Backbone (see the Honorable Mentions). The Devil's Backbone Trail dates back to pre-wilderness designation and even pre-Forest Service days. It was originally used as part of a mule train circuit that ran from the Scott River area, 60 miles inland from Klamath, to Arcata, which is on the coast. In the 19th Century, pack trains were the only way to get anything in or out to the miners, prospectors, and farmers of the interior. Ingenious packers found ways to bring food,

View east from the summit over burned Trinity Alps Wilderness.

MilesDirections

0.0 START at Bear Hole Trail trailhead. Turn left at the corral and head uphill on Bear Hole Trail.

0.7 The trail crosses a small bog, where the trail surface often turns to deep mud.

1.9 Cross Tish Tang-a-Tang Creek.

2.3 The trail crosses a meadow and heads uphill.

2.6 The trail enters a large, flat meadow known as Crogan Hole. Turn right onto the old road now called Bret Hole Trail and cross the meadow.

2.7 Turn left shortly after the trail re-enters the trees and continue uphill on Bear Hole Trail.

3.0 Come to a small stream crossing.

3.5 The forest opens into a meadow. [Note. In summer, the small stream that flows through here is the last water source before the ridge. The next source of water on this hike is found at Water Dog Lakes.] An alternate trail to the ridge goes up to the right (very faint). Continue on the main trail, heading slightly to the left.

3.7 Reach Horse Trail Ridge. Turn right on Horse Trail and follow the ridge to Trinity Summit Cabin.

4.0 The alternate trail from mile 3.5 joins Horse Trail from the right. Continue straight.

4.4 Nice western view from the rocks on the right.

4.7 Reach Trinity Summit Cabin. *[FYI. Graffitti on the walls of the cabin dates back to the 1950s. In the back room on the upper right*

corner of the doorjamb is a message from the author, left when I was working on trails here for the Forest Service.] Turn around and return to the Bear Hole Trail/Horse Trail junction.

5.7 From the Bear Hole Trail/Horse Trail junction, continue straight (north) along the ridge.

6.3 The trail passes through a long meadow, frequented by cattle in late summer.

7.2 Follow the trail as it descends downhill to the left.

7.7 The trail appears to fork here. A false trail goes straight. Continue on the right fork.

7.9 Reach East Water Dog Lake. The trail passes the lake on the northern edge, following the line of trees.

8.1 Reach West Water Dog Lake. The trail is faint, but marked by occasional rock cairns. Turn left onto Water Dog Lakes Trail, near the edge of the lake, and follow the cairns uphill.

8.4 The trail crests the flank of North Trinity Mountain and heads down the other side.

8.9 Cross a small stream.

9.3 The Mill Creek Trail trailhead is just a few yards to the right from this junction. Turn left onto Bret Hole Trail, an old road. Follow it as it contours around back to Crogan Hole.

12.2 Reach Crogan Hole. Turn a sharp right at the cedar standing alone in the meadow, and retrace the first part of Bear Hole Trail to the trailhead.

14.7 Arrive back at the Bear Hole Trail trailhead.

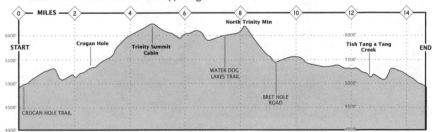

pipes, pottery, bridge cables, and even the occasional piano in on the backs of sure-footed mules.

Every mule train had a bellboy, who rode up front and rang a bell to warn oncoming traffic on the narrow trails. The bellboy was an important member of the team, because it's virtually impossible to back up a long line of fully loaded mules safely, and there are few spots along most mountain trails wide enough for passing. On the treacherous Devil's Backbone, a bellboy would have been very useful. The trip across the narrow, knife-edged ridge was a dangerous one, especially where the trail is steep and seems to consist mostly of loose pebbles. You may wonder why those old-time

> **FYI**
>
> *The rivers for which Six Rivers National Forest is named are: Smith River, Klamath River, Trinity River, Eel River, Mad River, and Van Duzen River.*

trailblazers chose to roller-coaster up and down the ridge instead of just contouring around and maintaining the same elevation. The reason is simply that trees have an annoying tendency to fall down. And in a place where trees are often four to six feet in diameter, it makes sense to put the trail up on an exposed ridge, where a fallen tree

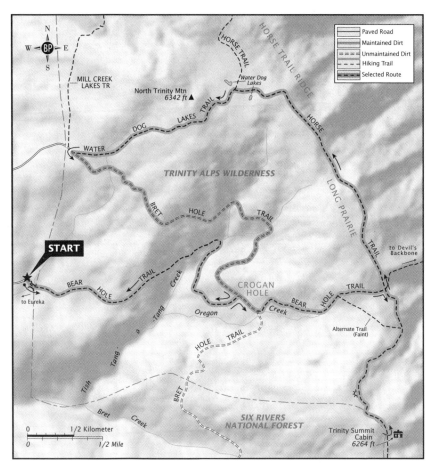

isn't such a problem. Anyone who has ever gone on a pack trip can tell you, there's work enough to be done without having to cut out logs around every corner!

In later years, Horse Trail Ridge was also used extensively by pack trains—just what the name suggests—and packers had a camp in the meadow that opened on the

Welcome to Bigfoot Country

The legend of giant, hairy creatures walking around on two legs in the dense forests of North America is a familiar one to most people. Bigfoot and Sasquatch are the most common names for this animal, said to be shaped something like a human or large ape, standing anywhere from six to 10 feet tall, covered with long, thick hair, and possessing a body odor that could halt an army. Reports of sightings date back to pre-Columbian times, and many Indian tribes have stories that tell of these "forest people," who inspired fear and were given wide berth by humans.

While Bigfoot sightings have been reported in almost every state and province in North America, most come from the Pacific Northwest region of the United States, and British Columbia in Canada. Miners and loggers have been reporting encounters for years, and some of them have received considerable attention. Aside from eyewitness accounts, most of the evidence for the existence of these encounters comes in the form of plaster casts of Sasquatch footprints. Some of these are obvious hoaxes, but others have led to serious examination by biologists and anatomists, which has produced ambiguous results. Anatomists have concluded that the shape of the feet points to a very different type of locomotion than that used by humans, one that would be appropriate for a very heavy creature walking bipedally in mountainous forest habitat. Other casts preserve so much detail that dermal ridges (like in fingerprints) are visible, something experts say would be almost impossible to fake.

Visit www.bfro.net to read about the latest Bigfoot research, conducted by the Bigfoot Field Researchers Organization—"the only scientific organization probing the Bigfoot/Sasquatch mystery." Judge for yourself.

The highest concentration of Bigfoot sightings has come from the area around Bluff Creek, a minor stream that joins the Klamath River a few miles above the confluence with the Trinity River in Northern California. It was here, in 1967, that the famous Patterson film was shot, showing an obviously female Bigfoot running along a dry streambed for several seconds before disappearing in the trees. Many people were convinced of the film's authenticity, but many more were not. Skeptics of Bigfoot ask why, if these creatures do exist, have we never found a body or skeleton? And how could they exist in such secrecy when surrounded by human habitation? At the same time, much of the evidence is impossible to discount completely, even by scientific experts. For Bigfoot, the jury is still out.

Bigfoot enthusiasts will want to visit the Willow Creek-China Flat Museum, at the intersection of CA 299 and CA 96, in Willow Creek. This local history museum features a Bigfoot wing with a plaster cast footprint collection. Open mid April through October, 10 A.M.–4 P.M., and by appointment the rest of the year. Visit www.bfro.net/news/wc museum.htm for more information.

ridge north of the junction. Hikers are better served by continuing up the ridge and camping near one of the two Water Dog lakes, where camping is much nicer. Springtime is the best time to visit, as the lakes and streams are full, and the meadows are in full bloom. Salamanders are abundant in the clear waters and provide a nice diversion as you pump water or soak your feet. Unfortunately, later in summer the cows arrive. By September, the lakes have partially dried up, and the cows have churned the banks into a deep muddy mess.

From the lakes, the trail heads west again over a flank of North Trinity Mountain before dropping down toward the Mill Creek Lakes trailhead and returning to Crogan Hole via an old road. This area was severely affected by the 1999 Megram Fire, which started as a lightning strike in August and raged through 125,000 acres of national forest, adjacent private land, and Hoopa Indian Reservation land before being controlled in November. Take a look around as you pass through. You are witnessing the early stages of forest regeneration.

From Crogan Hole, retrace the first part of the hike to the trailhead.

Hike Information

🛈 Trail Contacts:
Six Rivers National Forest, Lower Trinity Ranger District, Willow Creek, CA (530) 629–2118 or *www.r5.pswfs.gov/sixrivers*

🕐 Schedule:
Open year round, though snow limits access in winter and spring

💲 Fees/Permits:
No permits required—except free campfire permit, which is available at the ranger station.

❓ Local Information:
Willow Creek Chamber of Commerce, Willow Creek, CA (530) 629–2693 or 1–800–628–5156 or *www.willow creekchamber.com*

☺ Local Events/Attractions:
Swimming holes: There are several good ones along the Trinity River around Willow Creek and Hoopa. Ask the locals for their favorites.

🛏 Accommodations:
Limited space for primitive camping is available at the trailhead and along the forest access road.

📖 Other Resources:
The Bellboy: A Mule Train Journey by Margret S. McClain – A children's book based on the experiences of a local bellboy during the late gold rush days. The Devil's Backbone is the highlight of the story.

🎒 Local Outdoor Retailers:
Adventure's Edge, Arcata CA (707) 822–4673 • **The Moonstone Factory Store,** Arcata CA (707) 826–8970 • **The Outdoor Store,** Arcata CA (707) 822–0321 • **Big 5 Sporting Goods,** Eureka CA (707) 444–3682 • **Bucksport Sporting Goods,** Eureka CA (707) 442–1832 • **Northern Mountain Supply,** Eureka CA (707) 445–1711 • **Picky Picky Picky Inc,** Eureka CA (707) 444–9201 • **Pro Sport Center,** Eureka CA (707) 443–6328 and McKinleyville (707) 839–9445 • **Sports Exchange,** Eureka CA (707) 444–3644

🗺 Maps:
USGS maps: Trinity Mountain, CA; Tish Tang Point, CA.

Haypress-McCash Loop

Hike Specs

Start: From the Haypress Trail trailhead
Length: 12.2-mile loop
Approximate Hiking Time: 2 days
Difficulty Rating: Moderate to Difficult due to occasionally steep and poorly maintained trails
Terrain: Dirt path through dense conifer forest, across alpine meadows, and along exposed ridges
Elevation Gain: 2,712 feet
Land Status: National forest and wilderness area
Nearest Town: Orleans, CA
Other Trail Users: Equestrians, anglers, and hunters (in season)
Canine Compatibility: Dogs permitted

Getting There

From Eureka: Take U.S. 101 north 10 miles, then exit onto CA 299, heading east. Drive 42 miles to Willow Creek, turn left onto CA 96 and continue 48 miles to the Salmon River. Turn right onto Salmon River Road and left again onto FS 15N17. Drive 14 miles, following the signs for Wilderness Trailheads. Turn right onto FS 15N17E and drive 1.5 miles to the Haypress Trail trailhead. *DeLorme: Northern California Atlas & Gazetteer:* Page 34 A1

The hike begins at the Haypress Trail trailhead—which is, without a doubt, the most-used wilderness trailhead in the Ukonom/Orleans Ranger District. Despite that claim, the path is positively lonely compared with more famous destinations. Crowds will not be a problem here. The trail enters the woods at the bulletin board, twists immediately into two small switchbacks, and then contours for the first two miles around the hillside far above roaring Haypress Creek. Along the way, the path passes through an area that burned-over in 1997. The undergrowth is beginning to regenerate, but the older fir trees were traumatized in the fire and continue to die off. As these older trees die, the forest's canopy opens, allowing more sunlight to reach the ground and encouraging primary vegetation like alder to grow.

Leaving the burn area, the trail passes through the first of several meadows in a larger meadow complex. This grassland was a major attraction for European settlers who lived here following the Gold Rush. The meadow provided hay—in fact, the trail got its name from a hay press set up here by some industrious settlers—and pastures for cattle grazing. It was said that 500 head of cattle could feed here during the season, and even now, the grass provides for cows grazed each summer by a private permit-holder. If you have a strong aversion to cow patties, visit the forest before the cows arrive in mid July.

The trail's main junction is at Haypress Meadows, the largest of the meadows in this complex and a good place to stop for a scenic lunch. You'll notice the remains of two posts on the flat part of the junction. These are left over from the days when a

telephone wire stretched through the wilderness to the fire lookout on Medicine Mountain. Now, fires are spotted from airplanes, and phone lines—besides being hard to maintain—are considered unfitting for a wilderness area. But if you're observant and look up into the trees, you can spy the occasional porcelain insulator, from which the telephone wire originally was strung.

After following the meadows, the trail heads up through dense forest. It eventually pops out on Sandy Ridge—a point that offers sweeping views of the surrounding mountains and valleys. A short 0.1-mile spur trail leads down to Round Meadow, a grassland whose flat ground and easily accessible water supply make it a good campsite candidate.

A pack train climbs Sandy Ridge.

MilesDirections

0.0 START from Haypress Trail trailhead.

0.3 The trail enters the Marble Mountains Wilderness.

0.4 *[FYI. In summer, thimbleberries cover the forest floor here.]*

1.0 Cross the long wooden bridge over a bog.

1.3 *[FYI. This is the edge of a 1997 forest fire.]*

1.5 At the far edge of the burn, there is a small bridge and the beginning of Haypress Meadows. *[FYI. Corn lilies bloom in August, giving the meadows the appearance of a wild field of corn.]*

2.0 Reach Haypress Creek. This is a larger stream crossing, but not dangerous except during unusually high snow melt periods, although wet feet are possible. The trail climbs to left as you reach the other side.

2.2 The trail drops down into a tiny meadow. *[FYI. Possible campsite.]*

2.3 At the junction, take the right trail (still Haypress) following the sign for Monument Lake, Let'er Buck Trail, and Halfmoon Trail. *[Note. There are often cows in this area after the middle of July, so watch your step.]*

2.4 Let'er Buck Trail heads off to the right. Continue straight on Haypress Trail, following signs for Torgerson Trail and Monument Lake.

3.5 After crossing a stream at a small meadow, follow the trail as it hooks to the right.

3.6 Torgerson Trail heads left uphill. Continue straight on Haypress, following the sign for Halfmoon Meadow. *[Option. Torgerson Trail intersects McCash Loop at its upper third, so this could work as a smaller loop, although Torgerson is very steep.]*

3.7 After crossing the small stream, the trail veers right, and forks shortly thereafter. The Halfmoon Trail continues on the right fork, passing through Halfmoon Meadow. Take the left fork instead, and continue on the Haypress Trail up Sandy Ridge. *[FYI. There is a 12-inch-diameter tree sticking upside-down in the earth at this junction. This is a tree top that broke off in a storm and impaled the edge of the trail. Although it blocks the trail signs slightly, it was left where it fell, just to impress people.]*

4.5 Round Meadow Trail heads right, leading down to Round Meadow. *[FYI. This is a possible place to camp.]*

4.9 There is a small stream crossing the trail here. *[Note. This is the last source of water along this hike until you reach the upper end of Long Meadow, so tank up. You can pitch a tent on a little flat spot here, but it isn't the best camping spot.]*

5.1 *[Side-trip. A short spur trail leads to an overlook on the right, known as Pickle Camp.]* From here, you have a good view of Medicine Mountain, due south.

5.5 Turn left onto McCash Loop Trail, following the sign for Torgerson Trail and Long Meadow. The faint path leads up at a steep incline diagonally westwards, climbing up to the crest of the ridge.

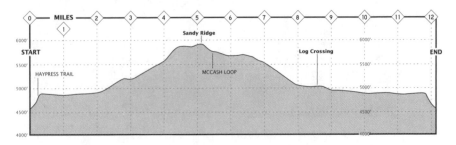

Once the trail joins the McCash Loop, water becomes scarce until shortly before Long Meadow, so be sure to have enough to make it through comfortably. The last water source in the summer is a trickle that comes out of the hill at Pickle Camp. In spring and early summer, remaining snow cover should be enough to serve your needs.

The McCash Loop part of the district is infrequently traveled or maintained, a situation that has both good and bad points. Because it doesn't receive much attention, the trail is likely to be scattered with fallen trees and other debris. But that means that the *wild* experience you came for will be stronger here. If you're quiet, you'll

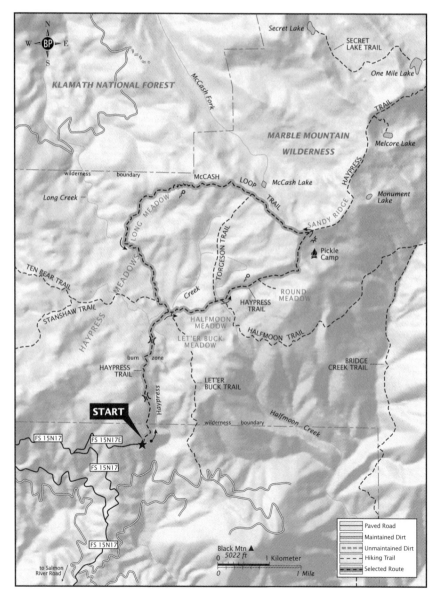

5.7 The trail descends down the north side of the ridge, opening a vista to the right of the McCash Creek drainage.

5.9 A pond is visible below and to the right, but it would be a hard, steep scrabble down to it from here.

6.0 Back on the ridge crest, Torgerson Trail heads left. Continue straight, following the sign for Long Meadow.

6.5 The trail crosses back to the north side of the ridge, and there's a steep drop off to the right, at the bottom of which is McCash Lake. *[**Note.** The lake is very difficult to reach from here, and is not recommended.]*

7.7 The trail levels out below an enormous incense cedar. *[**Note.** There is running water below the trail to the left.]*

8.7 Descending into Long Meadow proper, the trail skirts the trees on the right side of the clearing. *[**FYI.** Another cow haven, in late summer.]*

8.8 Slow water stream crossing. There are no rocks to cross on, but a huge log is down parallel to the trail. You can cross on this if you're not afraid of heights. The trail doubles back on the other side of the creek, continuing to the left, along the edge of the meadow.

8.9 The trail turns right and climbs straight up a steep 40-foot slope, leveling out on a low bench.

9.0 The trail drops down into Haypress Meadows and curves left, crossing to the other side of the meadow.

*[**Note.** This section can be very muddy, especially if cows are around.]* The path follows along the northeast edge of the meadow. *[**Note.** When in doubt look for blazes on trees: a vertical rectangle below a square.]*

9.2 The trail once again crosses the meadow, aiming slightly right and following the general drainage of the meadow. It enters the forest on the opposite side.

9.5 The trail crosses another small meadow and skirts its left edge.

9.6 Stanshaw Trail goes off to the right. Continue straight on McCash Loop, following the sign for Haypress.

9.7 The trail enters another meadow and crosses two branches of Haypress creek, both fairly easy to cross.

9.8 You're now back at the first Haypress/McCash Loop junction. Turn right on Haypress Trail and follow the first portion of the trail back to the trailhead.

12.2 Arrive back at the Haypress Trail trailhead.

Night snake sunning itself.

probably spot area wildlife faster than you would on a busy trail. The Roosevelt elk moved back into the area a few years ago and are once again at home in the Marbles. It is fairly common to see a herd browsing at dusk or to hear their peculiar grunts, whistles, and wheezy calls as they communicate with each other. You can expect the solace and quiet of the trail to be broken in September, when hunters converge on the area to hunt deer and elk. If you plan on being out in the woods at this time of year, consider investing in a bright orange hat or vest.

At Long Meadow, the trail relents from the ups and downs of the upper McCash Loop to become much easier and nearly level. And as an added bonus, there are several good campsites with nearby water supplies on the edge of the meadows. You're now back in cow country, so watch out for cow patties in the meadows. Although the cows don't show until July, the patties have a remarkably long *shelf life* and are present throughout the year. Consider building a cooking fire with them: It was good enough for the pioneers, and you can beautify the neighborhood as you cook.

The trail continues down through Long Meadow, over a low plateau, and through upper Haypress Meadows before reconnecting with the Haypress Trail at the main junction. Turn right down Haypress and retrace the first two miles of the route to the trailhead.

Hike Information

● Trail Contacts:

Orleans Ranger District, Orleans, CA (916) 627–3291 or *www.r5.fs.fed.us* – *This is the Region 5 home page, with general Forest Service information and links to the individual national forests in California. Some permits are available online.*

◐ Schedule:

May be closed from November through June due to snow. Contact Ranger Station for current conditions.

ⓢ Fees/Permits:

No fee and no permit are required for hiking and camping. A permit is required for campfires.

◉ Local Events/Attractions:

Whitewater recreation: *You'll find world-class whitewater on the Salmon River in spring. Several companies offer rafting tours on the Salmon and Klamath rivers.*

● Accommodations:

Oak Bottom Campground (Forest Service) is two miles up the Salmon River from CA 96.

⊕ Local Outdoor Retailers:

Adventure's Edge, Arcata CA (707) 822–4673 • **The Outdoor Store,** Arcata CA (707) 822–0321 • **Big 5 Sporting Goods,** Eureka CA (707) 444–3682 • **Bucksport Sporting Goods,** Eureka CA (707) 442–1832 • **Northern Mountain Supply,** Eureka CA (707) 445–1711 • **Picky Picky Picky Inc,** Eureka CA (707) 444–9201 • **Pro Sport Center,** Eureka CA (707) 443–6328 and McKinleyville (707) 839–9445 • **Sports Exchange,** Eureka CA (707) 444–3644

Ⓝ Maps:

USGS maps: Somes Bar, CA; Ukonom Mountain, CA; Ukonom Lake, CA • **USFS maps:** available from Orleans Ranger Station

Kelsey Trail

Hike Specs

Start: From the Kelsey Trail trailhead
Length: 14.4-mile out-and-back
Approximate Hiking Time: 2 days (recommend 3 days)
Difficulty Rating: Moderate to Difficult due to length, elevation, and occasionally sketchy trail
Terrain: Dirt path through conifer forests, across alpine meadows, and along exposed rocky ridges
Elevation Gain: 5,523 feet
Land Status: National forest
Nearest Town: Fort Jones, CA
Other Trail Users: Anglers, equestrians, and hunters (in season)
Canine Compatibility: Dogs permitted

Getting There

From Yreka: Drive south four miles to CA 3, and head west to Fort Jones. Turn Right on Scott River Road and drive 9.9 miles to the fork in the road at Quartz Valley. Continue on the right fork another nine miles to the bridge at Bridge Flat Campground. Immediately after crossing the bridge, turn left onto the gravel road and head up 0.5 miles, turning right onto another gravel road just before the bridge. Follow this road up another 0.2 miles to the Kelsey Trail trailhead. *DeLorme: Northern California Atlas & Gazetteer:* Page 24 C3

L eaving the trailhead behind, the first few miles of the path follow the course of Kelsey Creek up into the heart of the Marble Mountains. Heavy forests cling to the steep sides of the canyon, and small streams frequently cross the trail as it steadily ascends. As in any mountain range, the water levels vary greatly with the time of year and rainfall. So beware that the mild-mannered Kelsey Creek can turn into a raging torrent at times, a fact that's evidenced by logjams that can be seen in the creek bed throughout the year. In fall, the area puts on a display of brilliant fall foliage. Maples, cottonwoods, and several shrubs—including poison oak— turn bright reds and yellows, contrasting with the dark green of the surrounding conifers and the deep shadows of the canyon.

The Kelsey Trail was built in 1855 by an enterprising young man named Ben Kelsey and his crew. Observing the flourishing gold-mining camps in the Klamath Mountains, Kelsey decided a supply trail was needed, and managed to convince the towns of Crescent City and Yreka to fund its construction. The Gold Rush in this part of California was just getting underway, and thousands of miners were pouring into the area in the hope of striking it rich. Until Kelsey came along, mules packed in most supplies from San Francisco—a long and tedious journey. Kelsey realized that a serviceable trail between Crescent City and the Scott River Valley would enable supplies to be brought up by ship to Crescent City Harbor and packed a much shorter distance to the mountain camps.

Kelsey and his crew started blazing the trail in late spring, striking out from Crescent City and reaching the Klamath River near Happy Camp by mid summer. The crew then disbanded, and Kelsey went to Yreka with a few men. From there, a new crew was hired, and the trail's 120-mile stretch was finished from the opposite end. Mule trains soon were bringing in supplies and equipment and taking out gold and other area commodities for delivery to the coast. The trail's heyday lasted a short 25 years, until the expanding railroad enabled even easier access to the rugged mountain camps. By this time the Gold Rush had fizzled anyway—ending in disappointment for most—and the population in the mountains dwindled as the miners left.

A lonesome pine on the ridge.

MilesDirections

0.0 START from the Kelsey Trail trailhead.

0.2 An extension of Kelsey Trail heads right Bridge Flat Campground. Continue to the left, heading west on Kelsey Trail.

1.6 In the creek below the trail is an enormous log jam, left over from a past flood.

1.9 There is a fork in the stream below. Kelsey Creek comes down on the left, and a seasonal creek (dry in summer) joins it from the right. *[FYI. There are some nice pools in Kelsey Creek that might be suitable for swimming when the water is the right level.]*

2.0 The trail begins climbing a series of switchbacks.

2.1 The trail crosses a small creek, which offers a nice little cascade above the trail.

2.3 Reach the wilderness boundary.

2.4 The trail crosses a small creek.

3.3 Another small creek crosses the trail.

3.4 Maple Falls is visible through the trees to your left.

3.5 *[Side-trip. A spur trail to the left leads down 30 yards to an old packer's camp, adjacent to the top of the waterfall.]*

4.4 The trail crosses a creek and comes to a split-rail fence. This fence keeps the cattle within the allotment boundaries in the wilderness (I know what you're thinking). There is a sliding-rail gate, which you can open to get through, or just climb over. The trail continues straight ahead.

4.8 Reaching the first big meadow, there is a signed junction. Turk Valley Trail heads up to the right. This is the return loop of the hike. Continue straight to Paradise Lake on Kelsey Trail.

5.0 The trail crosses a small meadow, passing to the right of a large Cottonwood tree with a gnarly base.

5.4 A cow path heads off to the left. Continue straight on Kelsey Trail.

5.6 A great view of the cliffs above Paradise Lake looms ahead.

6.0 After a steep climb, the trail tops out on the end-moraine that formed Paradise Lake.

6.2 Kelsey Trail reaches the junction with the Pacific Crest Trail (PCT) on the shore of Paradise Lake. [FYI. Great camping here.] To the left, the PCT heads south past Black Marble Mountain. Turn right onto the PCT/Kelsey Trail when you're ready and head north.

6.6 The trail crosses a little creek and continues up through a meadow. Above you to the left are some impressive and colorful cliffs.

7.0 The trail crests a side ridge and curves to the left on the other side.

7.2 After topping out on the main ridge, the trail continues along the crest, offering views to the east and west.

7.3 Far below to your left is Bear Lake.

7.4 Kelsey Trail goes down to the left at this junction, while the PCT/Kelsey Trail continues

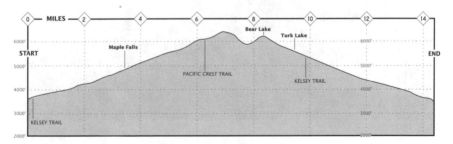

There's little left to remind hikers of the trail's history. The climate here produces vigorous plant growth, which tends to cover old signs and tracks in a hurry. But the trail still winds through an area just as wild as it was 150 years ago. And it's easy to imagine an old-time mule string loaded down with supplies, wearily making its way down the trail.

After crossing the split-rail cattle fence, the trail opens onto its first big meadow. Far above, a vertical wall of rock stretches across the horizon like a giant amphitheater. At the base of these cliffs is Paradise Lake, but you still have a bit of a climb to get there. The glacial end-moraine that holds the water in the lake appears as a steep wall at the upper end of the valley, and the trail switchbacks up this steep slope before finally topping out at the aptly named Paradise Lake. As with many special places, the lake is popular and can get crowded in the summer. But as fall rolls around and the days start to get a little cooler, you could have the place all to yourself. Sunrise on the cliffs is well worth spending the night for, as the morning sun turns the cold rock into a massive wall of glowing red. You might even catch a glimpse of the resident river otter that sometimes basks on the tiny island in the lake.

If you have the time and inclination, detour a couple of miles south down the Pacific Crest Trail to Black Marble Mountain. Water has heavily eroded the white limestone and marble around the base of the cliffs, a process that has formed the eerie shapes and caves typical of such landscapes (known as *karst*). This area is a geologist's dream. With so many different kinds, shapes, and colors of rock stacked on top of each other and exposed to view, it's a great place to explore.

After a short hike north from Paradise Lake, along a narrow, rocky ridge, you'll arrive at Bear Lake. Like Paradise, two-acre Bear Lake is nestled down under a cliff

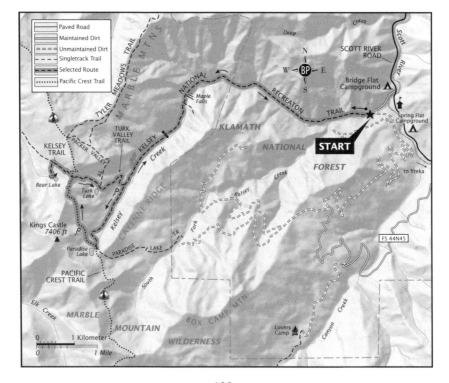

straight, and Turk Valley Trail heads right. Turn left onto Kelsey Trail and head steeply downhill.

8.0 Kelsey Trail leads to the right. Continue straight on the spur to Bear Lake.

8.1 Reach Bear Lake. Backtrack to the PCT junction when you're ready.

8.7 Once you're back at the ridge junction with PCT, Kelsey Trail, and Turk Valley Trail, continue straight down the other side of the ridge on Turk Valley Trail.

8.8 The trail becomes indistinct as it descends the rocky slope. Keep to the left side of the draw, and the trail will become more obvious farther down.

9.1 The trail empties into a meadow. Continue straight, aiming just to the left of the fir trees ahead.

9.2 Passing a large incense cedar, the trail curves to the right and down through the trees to Turk Lake. If you lose the trail, you'll find it again shortly on the shore of the lake.

9.4 Reach Turk Lake. Follow the lake shore around to the left.

9.4 On the far edge of the small clearing, a faint path leads away from the lake, heading east. This is the way back to the Kelsey Trail. After crossing a small seasonal creek, keep to the right, following the ridge down.

9.7 An unsigned trail leads off to the left. Continue straight down.

9.8 Turk Valley Trail reaches the junction with Kelsey Trail. Turn left and return to the trailhead, retracing the first part of the hike.

14.4 Arrive back at the trailhead.

How the Marble Mountains got their name—fields of marble lie below Black Marble Mountain (near to this hike).

and surrounded by forest. There are several good camping spots split into secluded pockets by the trees along the lakeshore. In addition, the fishing in Bear Lake—which has self-sustaining populations of Eastern brook and rainbow trout—is supposed to be the best of the three lakes on this hike.

Turk Lake rests on the other side of the ridge and is without a doubt the least visited of the three lakes, as you can tell by the faintness of the trail. This lake is less impressive than the either Paradise or Bear, but it's still a nice place to enjoy the area's solitude and wilderness.

When you're ready, the faint trail by Turk Lake brings you back to the meadow that lies far below Paradise Lake. From there, head back down Kelsey Creek to the trailhead.

Hike Information

🕐 Trail Contacts:
Fort Jones Ranger District, Fort Jones, CA (530) 468–5351

🕐 Schedule:
Open year round, but snow limits access from early winter through late spring. Call the ranger station for current status.

💲 Fees/Permits:
Permits are not required to use the wilderness, but a campfire permit is required to build fires.

❓ Local Information:
Scott Valley Chamber of Commerce, Fort Jones, CA (530) 468–5442 • **Siskiyou County Visitor's Bureau:** 1–800–446–7475 • **Siskiyou County website:** *www.visitsiskiyou.org* • **National forest website:** *www.r5.fs.fed.us (links to individual forests in Region 5)* • **California Office of Tourism:** *www.gocalif.ca.gov/index2*

🍴 Accommodations:
Bridge Flat Campground: *At Bridge Flat, just north of the bridge on the right side, overlooking the river. There are a limited number of spaces, but camping is free* • **Spring Flat Campground:** *Within a few minutes of the trailhead. Accessed from Scott River Road* • **Indian Scotty Campground:** *Within a few minutes of the trailhead. Accessed from Scott River Road.*

🛒 Local Outdoor Retailers:
Don's Sporting Goods, Yreka, CA (530) 842–5152 • **Etna Hardware and Sporting Goods,** Etna, CA (530) 467–3905

🅝 Maps:
USGS maps: Marble Mountain, CA; Grider Valley, CA • **USFS maps:** *A Guide to the Marble Mountain Wilderness and Russian Wilderness.* A simple Xeroxed map of the area is often made available at the trailhead.

Devil's Punchbowl Trail

Hike Specs

Start: From the Doe Flat Trail trailhead
Length: 10.6-mile out-and-back
Approximate Hiking Time: 5–6 hours
Difficulty Rating: Difficult due to a very steep climb
Terrain: Dirt road and path through dense, mountain forests and along exposed granite ridges
Elevation Gain: 3,076 feet
Land Status: National forest and wilderness area
Nearest Town: Hiouchi, CA
Other Trail Users: Equestrians, anglers, and hunters (in season)
Canine Compatibility: Dogs permitted

Getting There

From Crescent City: Drive north three miles on U.S. 101, and turn right onto U.S. 199. Continue 24 miles and turn right onto paved FS 16 (FS 17N05) at the sign for Little James Creek Road, three miles past the hamlet of Patrick Creek. Follow this up one mile and take the left fork, then continue another six miles before taking the left fork again (always following signs for FS 17N05). Drive another three miles up and turn left at the large, flat gravel log deck. Half a mile up this gravel road, take the right fork. Continue two miles, take the left fork, and drive the last mile and a half to the Doe Flat Trail trailhead parking lot, at the end of the road. At the end of the parking lot is a short trail to tent camping sites. The trail to Devil's Punchbowl begins on the east side of the lot, to your right as you come in. ***DeLorme: Northern California Atlas & Gazetteer:*** Page 23 B6

Though the Siskiyou Wilderness is not known for its stunning vistas, there are exceptions, of course—like the Devil's Punchbowl. But for the most part, any glimmer of panorama remains hidden behind a curtain of dense trees. And, yes, the mountains are relatively modest in height. The highest peak in the range stands at just over 8,000 feet— a mere foothill if it were in the High Sierras. But these lackluster descriptions should not (and do not) deter hikers from visiting this region. Those who come to Siskiyou are not drawn to the flashiness of the landscape. They are drawn to the park's secretive, brooding nature; its deep, dark forests; and its mist-shrouded slopes. This is not a place of open spaces and endless views; it is a place of dark nooks and hidden crannies, deep valleys and shaggy, nameless hills. The wilderness is also an example of a unique, biologically diverse environment that boasts upwards of 14 different species of cone-bearing trees growing in close proximity. Among those conifers are the mountain hemlock, red fir, Jeffrey pine, Alaska yellow cedar, coastal Western hemlock, and Brewer spruce. This famed diversity is due, at least in part, to the area's high-metal, low-nutrient serpentine soils, which promote special plant adaptations and give the Smith River its characteristic gray-green color.

The Devil's Punchbowl is every bit as dramatic as its name suggests. Almost completely surrounded by steep, rocky cliffs and jagged spires, the Punchbowl is straight out of a fantasy novel. That feeling of otherworldliness is heightened as you hike the trail from the valley up to the lake. The difficult route will prompt J.R.R. Tolkien fans to feel empathy for Frodo—and the special agony of an arduous journey whose completion seems simultaneously just around the corner and just out of reach. Uncounted switchbacks climb at an excruciating pitch up the slope, and the trail tortures hikers by always appearing to end just ahead. Right when you start to celebrate reaching the top, you find there's still more climbing to do. But never fear. As with Frodo's journey to Mordor, endurance is rewarded. The Punchbowl, once you reach it, satisfies all but the most jaded of hikers.

MilesDirections

0.0 START at the Doe Flat Trail trailhead. The trail heads east and enters the Siskiyou Wilderness almost immediately.

0.7 The Buck Lake Trail heads right. Continue straight, downhill.

1.5 *[FYI. There is a fair camping spot on the right.]* The trail continues downhill.

2.0 *[FYI. Here is another campsite on the right.]*

2.4 The gravel road surface ends at a large berm. Climb over the berm and continue downhill on Doe Flat Trail as it becomes a dirt path. Just past the berm on the left is an old mining site. Nothing but a hole and the ruins of a cabin remain here now.

3.1 Doe Flat Trail dead-ends at a junction. Devil's Punchbowl Trail heads to the right, and Young's Valley Trail heads northeast toward the junction with Clear Creek Trail. Turn right onto Devil's Punchbowl Trail. Just before crossing Doe Creek, a false trail heads left at an apparent fork in the trail. Take the right fork across the creek.

3.3 The trail begins the steep ascent up countless switchbacks.

3.8 The trail rounds a corner just past a rock outcropping, offering a nice view to the east and north.

4.0 Here is the first view south, including the crags above Devil's Punchbowl.

4.4 The trail passes a large cedar tree just before entering an open rocky area.

4.6 The trail becomes hard to follow here. Climb over the rock outcropping that blocks the path, and follow the rock cairns roughly in a straight line due south between the peaks.

4.9 The trail passes a little pond on the right, prior to reaching Devil's Punchbowl.

5.3 Reach Devil's Punchbowl. Stay awhile, then return the way you came.

10.6 Arrive back at the trailhead.

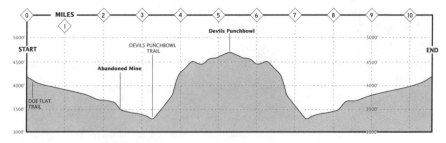

The whole journey begins at the Doe Flat Trail trailhead at Siskiyou Gap—which, at 4,100 feet, is the lowest pass in a 25-mile radius of the surrounding Siskiyou range. The trail wanders down a wide valley through dense forest and streamside vegetation to a point just above the confluence with Clear Creek. The trail crosses Doe Creek here and begins the heart-thumping climb to the Punchbowl, during which all lost elevation is recovered in a fraction of the distance. About half of the trail stretching from the pass to this junction is actually a former road that remains from the area's pre-wilderness days. Indeed, before the Siskiyou range was designated an official wilderness area in 1984, hikers drove in to Doe Flat and began their hikes from there.

FYI

The Smith River is named for Jedediah Smith, an early fur trapper and explorer.

Although humans never settled the immediate area, the mountains were very important to the people who lived nearby. Three Native American cultures shared this high country, regarding it as a place of great spiritual importance and power. To

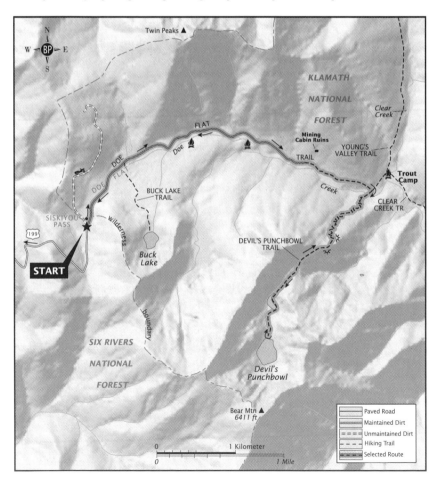

the northwest, the Tolowa lived in the Smith River region. The east, on the upper Klamath River, was Karuk country. And the Yuroks lived to the south and southwest. All three groups revered the high Siskiyou and ventured into the range only to worship in sacred shrines, conduct spiritual training, and negotiate with other tribes. The mountains even had their own kind of hierarchy: Lower slopes were used for personal medicine, while higher places were considered more powerful and reserved for more important rites. The evil sites also were located on high and avoided at all costs.

These lands are not simply ancient ritual grounds. Native Americans still feel strongly about the Siskiyou Mountains—something the U.S. Forest Service learned first-hand in the late 1970s when the agency tried to build a road through the middle of the range. Dubbed the *GO Road* because it would link the towns of Gasquet (on the Smith River) and Orleans (on the Klamath), the road came under heavy fire from Native American groups who said the road would intrude on their sacred lands and infringe upon their religious freedom. Building the GO Road was, they said, akin to putting an autobahn through the Vatican. The case went to court and was tied up

View of the ridge above Devil's Punchbowl.

for several years before Congress passed the California Wilderness Act of 1984, which designated a large portion of the area protected wilderness but exempted the strip needed to complete the GO Road. The case was finally argued before the U.S. Supreme Court, which decided that the road would not infringe upon Native Americans' right to practice their religion. It seemed the road would be built, but with the surrounding land designated official wilderness, there would be no logging and, thus, less need for a road. The matter was laid to rest in 1990, when Congress passed legislation creating the Smith River Recreation Area, providing further protections on the land, and effectively putting a quiet end to the GO Road.

So while you hike through the sullen beauty of the Siskiyous, remember to have some respect. After all, you are in somebody's house of worship.

Hike Information

🌓 Trail Contacts:
Gasquet Ranger Station, Gasquet, CA (707) 457–3131

🕐 Schedule:
Open year round, though snow limits access from November through June

💲 Fees/Permits:
No fees or permits required, except for free campfire permit, available at the ranger station

❓ Local Information:
The Crescent City/Del Norte County Chamber of Commerce, Crescent City, CA (707) 464–3174 or 1–800–343–8300

💡 Local Events/Attractions:
Jedediah Smith State Park, three miles east of Crescent City on U.S. 199 •

Darlingtonia Nature Trail, milepost 17.9 on U.S. 199 – *a short, 0.2-mile nature trail that visits a bog full of Darlingtonia californica, the insectivorous California pitcher plant*

🏕 Accommodations:
Campgrounds: *There is a campground at the trailhead, as well as four developed campgrounds along U.S. 199. Call 1–800–280–2267 for reservations.*

🏬 Local Outdoor Retailers:
Coast-to-Coast Stores, Crescent City, CA (707) 464–3535 • **Escape Hatch Sport And Cycle Shop,** Crescent City, CA (707) 464–2614 • **Hastings Sporting Goods,** Crescent City CA (707) 465–1895 • **Loring's Lighthouse Sporting Goods,** Brookings, OR (541) 469–2148

🅝 Maps:
USGS maps: Devil's Punchbowl, CA

Crags Trail

Hike Specs

Start: From the Vista Point parking area

Length: 5.4-mile out-and-back

Approximate Hiking Time: 3.5 hours

Difficulty Rating: Moderate to Difficult due to steepness and elevation, despite excellent trails

Terrain: Dirt path through dense coniferous forests and alongside exposed granite formations

Elevation Gain: 2,546 feet

Land Status: State park and national forest

Nearest Town: Dunsmuir, CA

Other Trail Users: Hikers only

Canine Compatibility: Dogs not permitted

Getting There

From Yreka: Take I-5 south 52 miles to the Castella exit. Leave the highway and turn right. Drive one mile to the park entrance and turn right into the park. Just past the entrance station, turn right again, and continue up to the Vista Point parking area at the road's end. *DeLorme: Northern California Atlas & Gazetteer:* Page 36 C3

The Castle Crags are on the eastern-most edge of what geologists call the Klamath Mountain Province. This province includes the Siskiyou, Marble, Russian, and Trinity Alps ranges, and the rocks here are mostly sedimentary and volcanic. But during the Jurassic era, huge bodies of molten granite (called *plutons*) intruded these rocks in several places. These islands of hard rock weathered slower than the surrounding landscape and were eventually left standing bare as the softer rocks around them eroded away. The spires and domes of Castle Crags—sculpted from the original monolith by the persistent forces of nature—are the remains of one such pluton.

The Crags had pretty much assumed their present form by the time Native American groups began living around their base. Thousands of years later, European settlers discovered the region. In 1855, after an enormous influx of gold miners into the area, hostilities broke out with the Native American. The fight, known as the Battle of Castle Crags, took place between Castle Lake and Battle Rock at the northwestern end of the Crags. The battle marked the beginning of the Modoc War—one of the last *Indian Wars* —and ended in 1872 with the last desperate battles between the U.S. Calvary and a small group of Modoc Indians, reluctantly led by a man known as Captain Jack. (See *Captain Jack & the Modocs* on page 208.)

The trail to the heart of the Crags begins at the curve in the road below the Vista Point parking lot. It plunges into dense forest and quickly begins to climb the steep grade to the summit. The first portion of the trail follows Kettlebelly Ridge, which was a once part of the California-Oregon Toll Road used by early settlers.

The Pacific Crest Trail (PCT) soon crosses the path under one of the park's less-pleasant features—a battery of power lines that cut a swath across the landscape

through the park. Unlike the PCT hikers, you soon leave the power lines behind as the trail continues up the ridge through the woods.

Farther along, a sign heralds the short trail to Indian Springs. A side-trip to the springs is well worth the trouble, especially on a hot day when the weather conspires with the elevation gain to drain the liquid from hikers' bodies. Beyond the tiny creek

Mount Shasta in the distance.

is a wall of rock, and there's a spot to the right where a stream of water squirts from the stone at just the right height and angle to fill a water bottle (filtration is recommended). For additional cooling off, you can climb down a few feet and stand near the spray from the rocks below the spring.

If you are lucky, you may run into one of the park's more colorful characters on your way up. Johnny Ollie is a volunteer, who comes up about twice a week to work on the trails—which explains why they're in such good shape at a time when most parks and forests are hurting for maintenance funds. A spry 85 years young, Johnny has been to the top of the Crags 307 times, as of this writing. He also has hiked the Appalachian Trail and the Pacific Crest Trail, as well as having climbed Mount Rainier, Mount Hood, Mount Whitney (from all four sides), and Mount Shasta. If you happen to meet him, take a minute to chat, and be sure to thank him for his hard work!

Eventually, all the climbing pays off with an upward view of the Crags looming above you. A few minutes later, you'll find yourself climbing up between them. The trail becomes rougher here, and parts of it are carved out of the rock (for lack of a better alternative). Take it slow, and be sure to stay within the boundaries of the trail.

MilesDirections

0.0 START at the curve in the road just below the Vista Point parking area.

0.2 Crags Trail forks here. To the right, Root Creek Trail leads to Root Springs. Take the left fork.

0.3 The trail reaches the junction with the Pacific Crest Trail, as power lines buzz overhead. Continue straight ahead.

0.6 Reach a junction with Bob's Hat Trail on the left. Continue straight.

0.8 Reach the wilderness boundary.

1.2 *[FYI. Here is the first good view of the crags.]*

1.4 Come to a junction with Indian Springs Trail going off to the left. The trail leads 0.24

miles to Indian Springs. Continue straight ahead on Crags Trail.

1.5 Enter national forest land. Nice view of Castle Dome.

1.8 The trail begins a steep ascent.

2.1 You are now up in the crags, and the trail gets a little rough in spots.

2.6 The trail tops out and curves to the right. Follow the rows of stones that mark the path.

2.7 The trail ends at a cable guardrail, with views down into the Root Creek drainage. Return the same way you came.

5.4 Arrive back at the trailhead and Vista Point parking area.

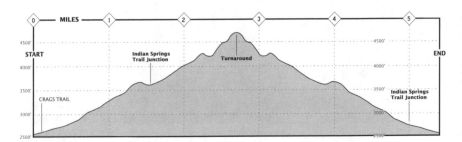

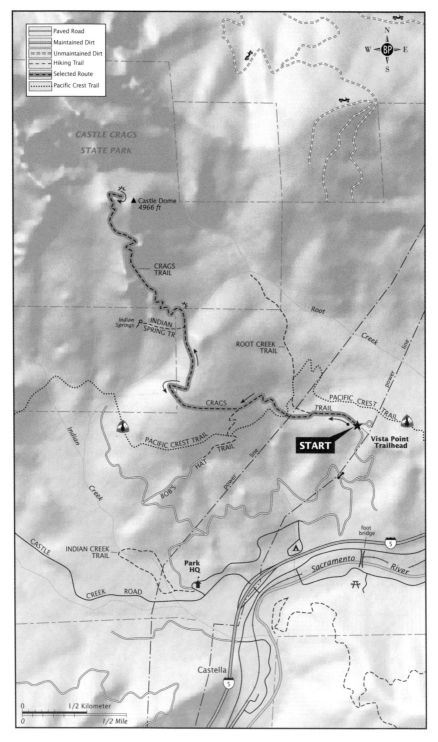

Paved Road
Maintained Dirt
Unmaintained Dirt
Hiking Trail
Selected Route
Pacific Crest Trail

CASTLE CRAGS
STATE PARK

N W BP E S

▲ Castle Dome
4966 ft

CRAGS
TRAIL

Indian
Springs   INDIAN
SPRING TR.

Root

Creek

power line

ROOT CREEK
TRAIL

PACIFIC CREST TRAIL

CRAGS   TRAIL

PACIFIC CREST TRAIL

START

Vista Point
Trailhead

Indian

Creek

BOB'S   HAT   TRAIL

power line

CASTLE

INDIAN CREEK
TRAIL

CREEK   ROAD

Park
HQ

foot
bridge

5

Sacramento   River

Castella

5

0   1/2 Kilometer
0   1/2 Mile

The Castle Crags from the half-way point.

The State of Jefferson

Since Oregon and California achieved statehood, there have been voices calling for a redrawing of lines to allow better representation of the people in extreme Northern California and Southern Oregon. As early as 1852, citizens of this area, frustrated and under-represented by the distant governments in Sacramento (California) and Salem (Oregon), attempted to create a new state named Shasta. When this failed, they tried again the next year with the name Klamath, and the next with Jackson—but always in vain. Things were quiet for a while, until sentiment began to stir again in the 1890s, and grew slowly but steadily until the early 1940s, when citizens, angry about poor road conditions and the resulting impairment of local industry, decided to act. On November 17, 1941, representatives from the counties involved met in Yreka and decided to research the possibility of forming a new state. A newspaper contest was held to choose a name for the state. Jefferson (after Thomas Jefferson) was the winning entry. The state seal depicted a gold pan with two Xs— echoing the local sentiment of having been double-crossed by state governments.

The State of Jefferson Citizen's Committee began stopping traffic at the border, welcoming travelers to the new state, and handing out a Proclamation of Independence. As the movement grew, it began capturing national attention, and San Francisco Chronicle reporter Stanton Delaplane was sent up to document the proceedings, eventually winning the Pulitzer Prize for his colorful reporting of the rebellion. The climax came on December 4, 1941, when Judge John C. Childs of Del Norte County was elected Governor of Jefferson, and Hollywood newsreel film companies were on hand to record the subsequent parades, road barricades, and celebrations. The newsreels were to be shown nationwide on December 8, but history chose to pre-empt the occasion with the Japanese bombing of Pearl Harbor. The nation entered WWII, and the State of Jefferson movement died a quiet death. Or did it?

As you reach the nearly level area just below the summit, the crushed white rock can be blinding under full sun, making a pair of sunglasses very welcome. To the right, the round hump of Castle Dome is outlined against the sky. The dome shows the exfoliation—slabs of rock peeling off like the layers of an onion—that is so typical of granite formations in Yosemite National Park and throughout the Sierras.

The trail ends at a chasm between Castle Dome and the rest of the Crags. Far below and to the left are the headwaters of Root Creek, which curves around the eastern base of the Crags before spilling into the Sacramento River. In the distance ahead is the omnipresent profile of Mount Shasta.

Take some time at the top to look around and enjoy some of the other vistas available between the various formations. Some scrabbling will bring you a little higher to the summit of the smaller dome. From here, the view is almost 360 degrees. Return the way you came.

Hike Information

Trail Contacts:
Castle Crags State Park, Castella, CA (916) 235–2684

Schedule:
Open year round, but winter snow and rain make the trail difficult or impassable at times. Call for current conditions.

Fees/Permits:
$5 per vehicle day-use fee

Local Information:
Dunsmuir Chamber of Commerce website: www.dunsmuir.com • National forest website: www.r5.fs.fed.us (links to individual national forests in Region 5) • State Park website: www.cal-parks.ca.gov • California Office of Tourism website: www.gocalif.ca.gov/index2

Local Events/Attractions:
Annual Fourth of July Celebration, Mount Shasta City, CA – three days of parades and live entertainment • Cool Mountain Nights, Labor Day weekend, Mount Shasta City, CA – street dance, concerts, and other activities

Accommodations:
Castle Crags State Park, Castella, CA – There are 64 developed campsites in the park. Reservations are recommended in the summer and can be made by calling MYSTIX at 1–800–444–7275. There are also two walk-in primitive camping areas. Check with the park office to use these.

Hike Tours:
Ranger-guided walks are occasionally scheduled. Check the park bulletin board or office for times and places.

Local Outdoor Retailers:
Dunsmuir True Value Hardware, Dunsmuir, CA (530) 235–4539 • McCloud General Store, McCloud, CA (530) 964–2934 • Mountain Rising Recreational Equipment Rental & Reservations, Mount Shasta, CA (530) 926–2809 • Sportsmen's Den, Mount Shasta, CA (530) 926–2295 • The Fifth Season, Mount Shasta, CA (530) 926–3606

Maps:
USGS maps: Dunsmuir, CA; Seven Lakes Basin, CA • USFS maps: A guide to the Mount Shasta Wilderness and Castle Crags Wilderness. Trail maps are also available at the park entrance station.

Captain Jack &
The Modocs

On November 29, 1872, a group of Modoc Indians awoke to find their camp surrounded by 38 heavily armed troopers of the First Cavalry. When the Modoc chief came out to talk to them, he was informed that his people were to surrender their weapons and return to the Klamath reservation in the north. As the Indians were dropping their rifles in a pile, one of them, known to the whites as Scarfaced Charlie, refused to give up his pistol. A lieutenant drew his pistol to force him, and shots were fired. The Modocs fled south to the southern shores of Tule Lake, amidst the natural defenses of the lava beds.

The Modoc chief was named Kientpoos, but the white settlers knew him as Captain Jack. He was a peace-loving leader and had tried to cooperate with the whites, even going so far as to abandon his ancestral home on the Lost River and peacefully retreat to the reservation established on Klamath Indian land. The Klamaths did not welcome the newcomers, however, and made life for them very difficult. The government also failed to supply the Modocs with the rations and supplies they had promised, and so Captain Jack led his people back home. The settlers on the Lost River did not want the Modocs there, and pressured the government until, finally, soldiers were sent to remove them.

The same morning of Captain Jack's encounter with the soldiers, white settlers attacked another band of Modocs, led by a sub-chief called Hooker Jim. Several members of the band were killed. This group also fled south, killing white settlers along the way, before meeting up with the main group at a natural fortification called the Stronghold. Hooker Jim's rampage angered Captain Jack—he knew this meant they would now all be hunted down—but he allowed the band to join him.

On January 17, 1873, the army attacked the Stronghold. Although they had over 200 soldiers and another 100 Oregon and California volunteers, the army was unable to gain any ground on Jack's 51 warriors. The terrain was torturous and made a direct assault impossible, not to mention that a thick fog covered the scene. The numerous natural trenches and breastworks allowed the Modocs to repel the attackers, and by day's end, the army had lost 37 soldiers; the Modocs, none. The army withdrew and waited.

As time passed, after several newspapers documented the conflict, public sentiment in the East called for a peaceful resolution to the conflict. A delegation was formed, headed by General E.R.S. Canby. Talks began, but little success. The army was unwilling to grant the Modoc a reservation on the Lost River, and Captain Jack refused to surrender Hooker Jim's band. All the while, the army ranks swelled with reinforcements, making the situation even more hopeless for the Modocs.

Concerned that their chief would soon surrender, several of the Modoc warriors confronted Captain Jack at a council and goaded him into promising to assassinate General Canby. At the next peace talk, after Canby again refused to remove the army and leave the Modocs in peace, Captain Jack drew his pistol in frustration and shot Canby in the head, killing him instantly.

Three days later, the strengthened army attacked the Stronghold with mortars and waves of infantrymen. After two days, the Modocs—cut off from water and desperate—fled south in the middle of the night, leaving the soldiers to find an empty stronghold in the morning.

The army pursued the ragged band (with the help of Tenino Indian scouts) to the Warm Springs reservation in Oregon. There was more fighting—with Jack's band, at one point, nearly wiping out an advance patrol—but the strain of such a detached existence was too much for the Modocs, and the remaining band split up into smaller groups and scattered.

In the end, Hooker Jim's band surrendered, and then led the army to Captain Jack's group. Betrayed by the man who had incited the army's vengeance and who helped bully him into murdering General Canby, Captain Jack received a mock trial and was hanged, along with three of his warriors. Hooker Jim went free. The remaining 153 Modocs were removed to Indian Territory. In 1909, 51 surviving Modocs were at last allowed to return to a reservation in Oregon.

(If you'd like to hike the Captain Jack's Stronghold Historic Trail in the Lava Beds National Monument, see Honorable Mention I in the Lava Lands section on page 272 for details.)

Coastal Mountains

Compiled here is an index of great hikes in the Coastal Mountain region that didn't make the A-list this time around but deserve recognition. Check them out and let us know what you think. You may decide that one or more of these hikes deserves higher status in future editions or, perhaps, you may have a hike of your own that merits some attention.

(G) Red Cap Lake Loop/Devil's Backbone Trail

A moderate to difficult 8.0-mile loop hike. Climb up through heavy forests to fish-filled Red Cap Lake, tucked in below steep rocky slopes. The loop climbs to the northern end of the historic Devil's Backbone Trail, and returns along the ridge. From Red Cap Lake, the adventurous can attempt the difficult 16.0-mile out-and-back hike over the full length of the Devil's Backbone Trail. From Eureka, you can reach the trailhead by heading north 10 miles on U.S. 101, then east 42 miles on CA 299 to the town of Willow Creek. Turn left (north) onto CA 96 and continue 40 miles to Orleans. Just past Orleans, on the other side of the bridge, turn right onto FS 10N01. Follow this road to the trailhead. For information contact: Orleans Ranger District, Orleans, CA (916) 627–3291. *DeLorme: Northern California Atlas & Gazetteer:* Page 34 C1

(H) Wooley Creek Trail

A 10.0-mile out-and-back up the lush Wooley Creek canyon to an historic cabin, with the option for much longer hikes. From Eureka, head east on U.S. 101 to Willow Creek, then north 40 miles on CA 96 to Salmon River Road, and east six miles to the Wooley Creek Trail trailhead. The trail climbs a hill at the mouth of the creek, then rounds the corner and follows the drainage upstream to the cabin (and beyond). For more information contact: Orleans Ranger District, Orleans, CA (916) 627–3291. *DeLorme: Northern California Atlas & Gazetteer:* Page 34 A1 & B1

Lava Land

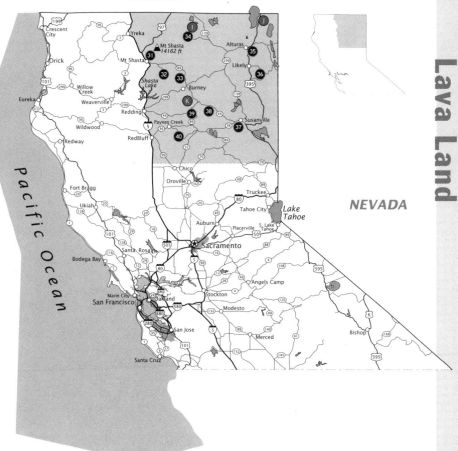

Lava Land

OREGON

NEVADA

Pacific Ocean

The Hikes

Horse Camp **31.**
McCloud River Trail **32.**
Burney Falls Trail **33.**
Whitney Butte Trail **34.**
Wildlife Viewing Loop **35.**
Blue Lake National Recreation Trail **36.**
Bizz Johnson Trail **37.**
Fantastic Lava Beds Loop **38.**
Choas Crags Trail **39.**
Mill Creek Trail **40.**

Honorable Mentions

I. Highgrade National Recreation Trail
J. Captain Jack's Stronghold Trail
K. Tamarack Trail

Lava Land

This little known and sparsely populated area is home to some of the state's most spectacular and fascinating geology. Fueled by the intense subterranean friction of plate tectonics, volcanic activity has continuously reshaped the landscape of this region right up to the present day. The most recent activity took place in Lassen Volcanic National Park, where the last major eruption occurred in the early 20th Century, and where sulfur vents and fumaroles still hint at the forces at work far below the surface. Lassen is one highlight of this area, but by no means the only one. Other attractions include the otherworldly landscape of Lava Beds National Monument, whose natural wonders include a labyrinth of lava-tube caves, sinkholes, spatter cones, and glass flows, as well as the monolithic majesty of Mount Shasta. Capped with a glistening cloak of perennial snow, Shasta's dormant (not dead) cone is visible from many of Northern California's high spots, shining like a beacon for the climbers, skiers, hikers, and new age seekers who visit her year round.

Redding, located on Interstate 5 at the northern end of the Sacramento Valley, is the springboard for most visitors to the area. To the north and east of this small city, the Lassen area stretches out its broad horizons, crisscrossed by narrow ribbons of lonely highway interrupted only rarely by small ranching towns.

In the extreme northeast corner of the state, Alturas serves as the hub of activity for visitors to the wide, sage-covered high plains and low mountains ranges of Modoc National Forest—home to herds of wild horses. Lying on the Pacific Flyway, the large lakes and wetlands in the area support a wide array of migrating birds, mostly during spring and fall. Blue Lake, nestled at the foot of the Warner Mountains, is home to beaver and bald eagle, and is encircled by the relaxing Blue Lake National Recreation Trail.

Roughly 70 miles south from Alturas, as the crow flies, Susanville sits on the edge of Nevada's Great Basin, backed by the southernmost extreme of the Cascade Range. The Bizz Johnson Trail, a prime example of a successful Rails-to-Trails project, follows an old spur line through the rugged Susan River canyon from Susanville to Westwood.

South of Lassen Volcanic National Park, on the edge of the Sacramento Valley, lies a unique low-elevation wilderness named for Ishi—lone survivor of a Yana Indian sub-tribe—who remained hidden from the modern world until 1911. Early settlers regarded the Ishi Wilderness as a hot and brushy wasteland, but the area has a strange enchanting quality worth exploring.

Overview

Horse Camp

This walk through the forested lower slopes of Mount Shasta is the first portion of the climb to the mountain's summit, which stands at 14,162 feet. Shasta is volcanic in origin and rises like a near-perfect cone from the flat plains below. Historic Horse Camp, at 7,400 feet, is the usual staging point for the summit attempt and the turnaround point for this hike. The best time to wander in this area is in the fall, between summer heat and heavy snows. (*See page 218.*)

McCloud River Trail

This trail provides access to the McCloud River, which is hard to reach in most places. Keep your eyes peeled, as the area is home to abundant wildlife. Observant—and lucky—hikers can spot mountain lions, black bears, mule deer, bald eagles, and the occasional (very rare) wolverine. (*See page 224.*)

Burney Falls Trail

Leave the majority of tourists behind at Burney Falls—famous as one the most beautiful falls in California—and continue hiking down through ponderosa pine, Douglas fir, and incense cedar to the shores of Lake Britton. Along the way, the trail passes a chalk bluff formed of diatomaceous earth. The crumbly substance grinds down into a powder that is effective at combating garden pests. (*See page 230.*)

Whitney Butte Trail

The trail starts at the Merrill Ice Cave and skirts Whitney Butte en route to the Callahan Lava Flow. The lava flow is a jagged wasteland of jumbled and twisted black rock, stretching off to the southern horizon. Stark landscapes and harsh high-desert beauty await the well-prepared hiker who carries plenty of water and adequate sun protection. *(See page 236.)*

Wildlife Viewing Loop

Modoc National Wildlife Refuge, along with other area refuges, is home to one of North America's most impressive collections of migratory birds. Some 245 species have been sighted here, along with as many as 500 bald eagles at a time. The wildlife-viewing loop skirts the wetlands that are so attractive to waterfowl and raptors. Be on the lookout for tundra swans, sandhill cranes, red-tailed hawks, and other birds. And don't forget your binoculars. *(See page 240.)*

Blue Lake National Recreation Trail

The animal tracks on this trail often outnumber the footprints left by hikers. Be sure to watch for wildlife even as you enjoy this relaxing commune with nature. And don't worry about the sun: About 80 percent of the trail, which circles Blue Lake, is shaded by large ponderosa pines. *(See page 244.)*

Bizz Johnson Trail

This trail follows the mild grade of a historic rail line along the scenic Susan River. In spite of its proximity to the town of Susanville, the trail has a secluded character to it, and wild camping is allowed (away from the trailheads). Basalt formations along the canyon walls give the scenery a dramatic touch, and several railroad bridges and two tunnels are thrown in for good measure. *(See page 248.)*

Fantastic Lava Beds Loop

This trail makes a brief stop-off at an impressive cinder cone volcano before circling the aptly named Fantastic Lava Beds and Painted Dunes. All of these sites showcase the park's recent volcanic history. The path continues around Snag Lake and visits some gorgeous aspen groves before returning to Butte Lake and the trailhead. *(See page 254.)*

Chaos Crags Trail

This short hike climbs up through airy coniferous forests to the base of dramatic Chaos Crags, a series of volcanic plug domes surrounded by a skirt of talus slopes. A tiny lake awaits hikers at the top, as do excellent views of Table Mountain and the surrounding terrain. *(See page 260.)*

Mill Creek Trail

Follow this meandering path into the heart of the Ishi Wilderness—named after the last "wild Indian" in California, who secretly maintained his traditional lifestyle in these canyons until the early 1900s. Though low in elevation, this hike gives visitors a glimpse of what many of California's foothills must have looked like prior to European settlement. *(See page 266.)*

31

Horse Camp

Hike Specs

Start: From the Bunny Flat trailhead
Length: 4.0-mile out-and-back
Approximate Hiking Time: 2 hours
Difficulty Rating: Easy to Moderate due to easy trail, but high elevation
Terrain: Dirt path through sparse coniferous forest and along open rocky slopes
Elevation Gain: 1,017 feet
Land Status: National forest and private land
Nearest Town: Mount Shasta City, CA
Other Trail Users: Equestrians (only during the day)
Canine Compatibility: Dogs not permitted

Getting There

From Yreka: Take I-5 south to Mount Shasta, and get off at the second exit for Mount Shasta City. Follow Lake Street 1.2 miles through the center of town, continuing as the road curves left and becomes the Everitt Memorial Highway. Follow this highway up the lower slopes of the mountain 10.3 miles to the Bunny Flat parking lot. *DeLorme: Northern California Atlas & Gazetteer:* Page 36 AB4

T he first thing you'll notice upon entering the Mount Shasta region is that the mountain dominates everything around it. It attracts— and, yes, even creates—weather systems. Because the mountain is so big, it takes away all sense of scale. You only really begin to get a feel for its size when you realize that you have been driving past it for some time, and it still hasn't moved in your field of vision. The closer you get, the more impressive it is.

The 14,162-foot-tall Mount Shasta is the second-highest peak (second to Mount Rainier) in the Cascade Mountain Range, which stretches from here to British Columbia. The mountain is, technically speaking, a *stratovolcano*—that is, it was created by both slow-flowing lava and violent eruptions. Though currently dormant, the volcano is far from extinct. In fact, there have been numerous eruptions in the last 3,400 years. On average, a blast occurs every 250 to 300 years. So perhaps we should be on the lookout, seeing as the last eruption occurred about 200 years ago. In the meantime, enjoy the peace and tranquility and the five glaciers on its massive flanks.

Not surprisingly, many people past and present have revered the mountain as a holy place. Members of the Wintu, Modoc, Shasta, Okwanuchu, Pit River, and Karuk tribes all considered the mountain sacred, and sites on the lower slopes were used to conduct vision quests, healing ceremonies, and the training of medicine men and women. Numerous myths and legends have sprung up surrounding Mount Shasta, most focusing on magical beings who reside on or in the mountain. Chief among these beings are the Lemurians. According to legend, the Lemurians were res- idents of a lost continent that is now covered by the Pacific Ocean. As their conti- nent began to sink, they made their way eastward and fashioned great caves within the slopes of Mount Shasta. Legend has it that they still reside in the caves, are total-

Horse Camp, just below the tree line.

The causeway built by "Mac" Olberman, the first caretaker.

ly self-sufficient, and manage to stay perfectly hidden. Other residents include the Yaktavians—master bell-makers who "used their bells to hollow out underground cities and produce light and power for the cities," according to a 1945 article by Frederick Morrison. Through the years, there also have been reports of UFOs, dwarves, Ascended Masters, and the occasional Bigfoot sighting (but we won't go into that). Many people in Mount Shasta City will be happy to tell you more.

The hike begins at the Bunny Flat trailhead, already high on the lower slopes of the mountain at 6,990 feet. The trail heads up through the sparse forest, offering glimpses of the summit between the trees as you pad along the well-worn trail. It's a pleasant, but largely uneventful two miles. The thrill comes simply from being so close to the mountain. Once you get a taste of Mount Shasta, you may find yourself planning a return visit for a summit attempt.

Horse Camp lies just below the timberline on a patch of land that is owned and managed by the Sierra Club. The historic stone cabin was built in 1922—when the Sierra Club was just a small *club* of friends—as an emergency shelter for climbers. J.M. "Mac" Olberman, the first caretaker, lived in the cabin, maintained the area and the camp, and constructed the remarkable Olberman's Causeway. The Causeway is a stone-paved path leading up a quarter-mile from the cabin to the slope below Helen Lake. Remarkably, the Causeway is made entirely of on-site rocks and small boulders from the area.

Though Mac retired in 1934 at the age of 72, there's still a caretaker at the cabin during the climbing season. And the structure is always open for emergency use. There are several campsites around the cabin that are open to the public. (The club requests a $5 donation for campers with tents and a $3 contribution for bivy sack

MilesDirections

0.0 START at the Bunny Flat trailhead.

0.1 The narrow dirt trail reaches a junction with an old jeep trail. Turn left on this.

0.8 A rain gauge is standing on the right side of the trail.

1.2 Sand Flat trail heads left. Continue to the right on the main trail.

1.7 Reach the wilderness boundary.

2.0 Reach Horse Camp Cabin and the turn-around point. Return the way you came.

4.0 Arrive back at the Bunny Flat trailhead.

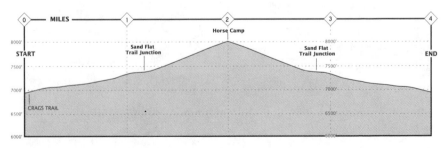

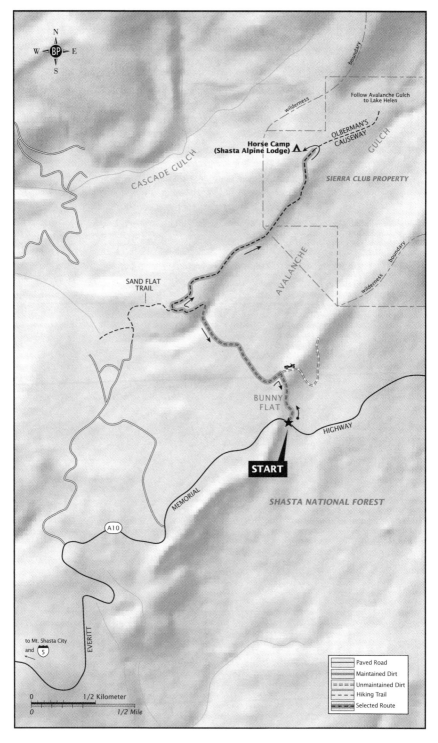

The Mysterious Stone Circles

If you stop at the Interstate 5 rest area north of Mount Shasta City with some daylight left, find a picnic table to stand on and take a moment to examine the sagebrush steppe surrounding you. If you look carefully, you'll notice that the ground is divided into a regular pattern of low, raised mounds, each encircled by a flat ring of stones. These are the infamous stone circles that have puzzled residents and scientists alike for years.

The dirt within these circles is mostly free of larger stones, and the ring around them consists of almost nothing but stone, filling what seems to be a shallow ditch around the mounds. The circles are spread out across 600 acres of the Scott River Valley, apparently at random, but all are more or less 60 feet in diameter and about two feet high.

Originally, they were thought to be the remains of Native American agricultural activity, but this theory was later discounted when no human artifacts were found in the excavated mounds—not to mention it's unlikely that Native American's would attempt growing crops in such an inhospitable landscape. Eventually the geologists took over, suggesting that the formations were the result of frost-heave activity, or some strange type of erosion. Some people have even suspected gophers!

None of the theories has been proven satisfactorily, and to this day, the stone circles remain a mystery.

A nearly snow-bare Mt. Shasta.

sites.) In addition to the cabin and campsites, the club maintains a spring well and two very nice solar composting toilets for the use of climbers and hikers. This "honor" system works even with no supervision because climbers have developed an ethical code that prohibits theft and abuse of public facilities. It's amazing to see an unlocked cabin filled with firewood, furnishings, and a bookshelf—completely free of vandalism and ready to help half-frozen climbers should they need it. Please observe the climber's code, and leave the cabin as you found it.

From here, return the way you came. (If you're looking to do a little more hiking, continue up to Helen Lake, above the timberline at 10,443 feet. Be sure you're prepared for bad weather if you attempt this hike, as storms can appear out of nowhere on the mountain. Warm clothing and raingear are highly recommended.)

Hike Information

◑ Trail Contacts:
Mt. Shasta Ranger Station, Mount Shasta, CA (916) 926–4511

◐ Schedule:
Open year round, although a caretaker is only on hand at the cabin during the climbing season from May through September. Call the ranger station for snow conditions.

⑤ Fees/Permits:
A free day-use permit is required for anyone entering the wilderness. You can get one at the ranger station, or self-issue one at the trailhead. There is a fee and a separate permit required for overnight use. A summit pass and $15-dollar fee are necessary to climb the mountain.

❓ Local Information:
Mount Shasta websites: *www.shasta-home.com, www.mountshasta.com,* or *www.mtshasta.com*

◉ Local Events/Attractions:
Annual Fourth of July Celebration, Mount Shasta City, CA – *three days of parades and live entertainment* • **Cool Mountain Nights,** Labor Day weekend, Mount Shasta City, CA – *street dance, concerts, and other activities*

● Accommodations:
Alpenrose Cottage Hostel, Mount Shasta, CA (530) 926–6724 • **McBride Springs Campground:** *$10 fee. Closed in winter* • **Panther Meadow Campground:** *No fee. Walk-in sites with no water. Limit three days. Closed in winter* • **Mt. Shasta KOA** (530) 926–4029 or 1–800–736–3617: *RV and tent sites and cabins* • Car camping is allowed at **Bunny Flat trailhead,** but only for one night. No fee.

⋒ Organizations:
The Sierra Club Foundation Shasta Land Operation, San Francisco, CA: *www.kid-sart.com/shasta*

⊕ Local Outdoor Retailers:
Mountain Rising Recreational Equipment Rental & Reservations, Mount Shasta City, CA (530) 926–2809 • **Sportsmen's Den,** Mount Shasta City, CA (530) 926–2295 • **The Fifth Season,** Mount Shasta City, CA (530) 926–3606

ⓝ Maps:
USGS maps: McCloud, CA • **USFS maps:** *A guide to the Mount Shasta Wilderness and Castle Crags Wilderness.* Other maps of Mount Shasta are available at the ranger station and at stores in town.

McCloud River Trail

Hike Specs

Start: From the McCloud River Preserve parking area

Length: 5.8-mile out-and-back

Approximate Hiking Time: 2.5 hours

Difficulty Rating: Easy to Moderate due to little elevation change but occasionally rocky, uneven tread

Terrain: Dirt path through riparian streamside vegetation and mixed forest

Elevation Gain: 297 feet

Land Status: Nature Conservancy land (private)

Nearest Town: McCloud, CA

Other Trail Users: Anglers

Canine Compatibility: Dogs not permitted

Getting There

From Yreka: Drive south 39 miles on I-5, then east 10 miles on CA 89 to the town of McCloud. Turn south on Squaw Valley Road/FS 11 and follow it nine miles to the Lake McCloud reservoir. Continue around the right side of the reservoir for 2.3 miles and turn right onto a dirt road, following the signs for Ah-Di-Na Campground and McCloud Preserve. Follow this road up and over the ridge six miles to the campground, and another mile to the preserve, at the end of the road. **DeLorme: Northern California Atlas & Gazetteer:** Page 37 D5

Note: Smoking, camping, and firearms are not permitted in the McCloud River Preserve.

I t takes just a glance at the McCloud River Preserve's information station to know that this short stretch of river is special. The message board reads like a menu for wildlife viewing. The board also displays the latest details on water temperature, insect developments, and other information dear to the hearts of fly fishermen. In fact, the preserve seems to be a sort of Northern California mecca for those interested in casting a line.

Fishing provided the impetus for the Nature Conservancy to establish the McCloud River Preserve in 1973. And the preserve's chief mission still is monitoring and protecting the fish populations in the river. With that in mind, the reserve operates under a set of strictly enforced rules. All fishing is catch-and-release, and no more than 10 anglers are allowed to fish at any time. A tag system is used to keep track of who is fishing: Five spots are reservable, and five are available on a first-come, first-serve basis. No camping is allowed on the preserve, which is open only from sunrise to sunset. It's not unheard of for exceptionally anxious early-risers to be turned away and told to return when the sun rises.

Spring and fall are probably the best times to visit the preserve, due to the spectacular displays of local flora. From April onwards, wildflowers and flowering shrubs compete for insects' attention. Azaleas, bleeding hearts, delphiniums, Shasta lilies, and various lupines and orchids splash the forest with color, along with clouds of dogwood and redbud blossoms. In the fall, the leaves of the various deciduous trees turn bright colors, contrasting sharply with the evergreen needles of the conifers. But

beware: One of the most colorful of the autumn plants is the one you least want to touch. The dreaded three leaves of poison oak turn wonderful shades of yellow and red before finally falling to the ground late in the season.

The preserve protects some six miles of pristine riparian habitat and mixed forest. These environs are tucked into a secluded mountain vale that runs along the waterfront. As you would expect, there are a lot of other wild things here, both in and out of water. River otters are often seen playing in pools or on the riverbanks, where the endemic Shasta salamander also makes its home. Local bird life includes common mergansers, kingfishers, bald eagles, and the endangered spotted owl (of old-growth

McCloud River.

forest fame). Black bears, mountain lions, ringtails, and bobcats all hide out in the forest, seldom to be seen. Wolverines, extremely rare animals in California, have also been sighted in the preserve.

There are several factors that keep this stretch of river secluded: the deep, steep-sloped valleys, the sparse human population, and the last seven miles of really bad road. The dirt road seems to be paved with medium-sized rocks, which stick up out of the ground and create an exaggerated washboard effect. Perhaps the highest compliment for the preserve is that it's worth the hassle of getting here.

MilesDirections

0.0 START at the end of the road. Cross the little wooden bridge and turn left.

0.2 The trail drops to the river's edge for the first time.

0.5 Reach the McCloud Preserve boundary and entrance station. *[FYI. There's an informative bulletin board here, mostly geared toward the fly fisherman, but also interesting for hikers.]*

0.6 The short Nature Loop goes to the right and left, bisected by the main trail. Continue straight.

0.7 The trail passes the other end of Nature Loop. Continue straight again.

1.0 The trail forks here. To the right is the Saddle Cutoff; to the left, the main trail continues along the river. Take the left fork.

1.2 You're now back on the river's edge at the Rope Swing Pool. *[FYI. This is one of many nice swimming holes (water temperature permitting) on the river.]*

1.3 After a brief climb, the trail levels out high above the river. The Mermaid Pool is visible below to the left.

1.5 Saddle Cutoff rejoins the main trail from the right.

1.6 The trail crosses a small rock slide. Below on the river is a small cove called the Snake Pit. Just beyond this, the trail climbs the rocks a bit and becomes hard to discern. A false trail continues below, but the true trail is the upper route.

1.7 *[Side-trip. A spur trail goes steeply down 30 feet to the left. At the end of this is a good pool for swimming.]*

1.8 At this point, the trail splits again, offering an upper and a lower alternative. Take the left (lower) fork. The split trail segments merge again in 0.2 miles.

2.3 The trail crosses Bald Mountain Creek on a log bridge.

2.8 The trail crosses tiny Boundary Creek.

2.9 Big Bend, a forested flat on a bend in the river, marks the turnaround point for this hike. Return the way you came.

5.8 Arrive back at the parking area.

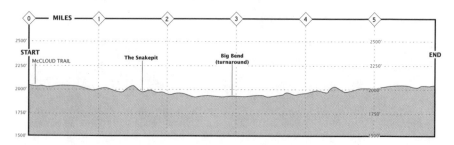

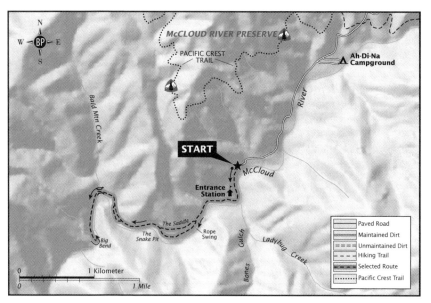

The trail starts at the end of the road, near where you park. You first cross a foot-bridge and hike a third of a mile before coming to the actual preserve entrance. This consists of the caretaker's cabin, a few small outbuildings, and the aforementioned information station. This spot has a wealth of information and will help you get acquainted with the preserve. The message board usually has updated data about fishing conditions and wildlife spottings. And the small kiosk to the left has some photo albums, preserve pamphlets, and tiny vials containing the types of insects that are eaten by the fish in the river.

Continuing past the cabin, the trail wanders through the forest a bit before descending to the river. The path follows the river's course downstream from here—sometimes climbing to bluffs above deep pools, sometimes dropping to the water's edge. In two places along the way, the trail splits into an upper and lower route. In each case, the lower route keeps close to the river and offers more scenic views, while the upper route stays high and is a little shorter. There are several deep pools along the way, most of which are named after obvious geographical features or some early friends of the preserve. In the heat of summer, the Swimming Hole and Rope Swing Pool are particularly inviting, although the glacial runoff from Mount Shasta keeps the water cold year round.

The McCloud River stands as a poignant reminder of the kind of riparian habitat that has disappeared at an alarming rate in the last 100 years or so. Over 90 percent of these riparian areas have been lost in California, making places like the preserve even more important for wildlife. Near the river, the pines and oaks of the forest give way to willows, alders, and an assortment of shrubs and semi-aquatic plants that make up the riparian zone. Roots and dead trees in the water trap sediments and help keep the water clear, while at the same time providing shelter for fish, insects, and mammals.

When you reach the sharp curve in the river called Big Bend, you have reached the turnaround point for this hike. Return the way you came.

A trout fisherman's heaven.

California Indians

The mild climate and natural abundance of California has been attracting people for at least 10,000 years ago. Successive waves of migration from the north, east, and south created a layered population of different cultures and languages. At the time of European contact, there were nearly 40 distinct tribes (each consisting of several smaller groups) living in Northern California alone, speaking hundreds of dialects and languages from six major language families. An abundance of food—especially on the north coast—allowed a relatively high population density. It has been estimated that the California Indian population prior to the Gold Rush was greater than that of Native American populations in all other states combined. European invasion soon changed that, however, decimating the native population with new diseases, destruction of lands used for gathering and hunting, and outright slaughter. From the estimated 300,000 California Indians living here in 1769, only 16,000 were left by the 1900 census. Today, the population has risen to around 320,000—placing one of every six Native Americans in California.

There are roughly 104 federally recognized tribes in the state, and over 30 more who are not recognized, due to scattered members, landlessness, or bureaucratic hurdles. According to some accounts, only one-sixth of the native population in the state is represented by the Bureau of Indian Affairs. Much of this oversight can be traced back to 1851–1852, when the United States reneged on 18 treaties promising California Indians 8.5 million acres in reservation land. Without land, Indians have no tribal base and find it difficult to receive federal recognition.

In spite of continuing difficulties, strong efforts are being made to keep traditional cultures and languages alive, and to teach all Americans about the history and contributions of Native Americans to our society. Several national and state parks in California have included these topics in their interpretive programs, and resources abound on the web for those interested in learning more.

Check out these sites for more information: www.hanksville.org/NAresources/indices/NAhistory.html, www.cimcc.indian.com, or www.californiahistory.org.

Hike Information

◐ Trail Contacts:

The Nature Conservancy, 201 Mission Street, 4th Floor, San Francisco, CA 94105 – *The preserve's staff is unable to handle a large volume of correspondence and has asked that all inquiries be directed to the Nature Conservancy office in San Francisco.*

◑ Schedule:

Open year round, from dawn to dusk. The best hiking is from April to October, as the weather becomes very cold and the road is often snowed in during the winter.

⑤ Fees/Permits:

No fee, but visitors are asked to sign in at the preserve entrance. (Keep in mind, the preserve is supported by individual contributions and Nature Conservancy memberships.) Anglers must pick up a tag at the preserve entrance. No more than 10 people may fish at one time.

❓ Local Information:

McCloud Chamber of Commerce, McCloud, CA (530) 964-3113 or 1-877-464-3113

◐ Accommodations:

Ah-Di-Na Campground: *Located a mile up the road from the preserve and has 16 units. A fee is charged.*

🏬 Local Outdoor Retailers:

Vaughn's Sporting Goods, Burney, CA (530) 335-2381 • **Mac's Liquor and Deli,** McCloud, CA (530) 964-2193 • **In & Out Mart,** Palo Cedro, CA (530) 547-5448 • **Palo Cedro Market,** Palo Cedro, CA (530) 547-3166 • **Palo Cedro True Value,** Palo Cedro, CA (530) 547-5451

Ⓝ Maps:

USGS maps: Shoeinhorse Mountain, CA; Yellowjacket Mountain, CA. A photocopied trail map is available at the information station.

Burney Falls Trail

Hike Specs

Start: From the Burney Falls Overlook
Length: 3.3-mile out-and-back
Approximate Hiking Time: 1.5 hours
Difficulty Rating: Easy due to little elevation change and smooth trails
Terrain: Mostly dirt path, with some gravel and paved walkway, through pine forests and riparian vegetation, and along chalky bluffs
Elevation Gain: 351 feet
Land Status: State park
Nearest Town: Burney, CA
Other Trail Users: Anglers
Canine Compatibility: Dogs not permitted

Getting There

From Redding: Take I-5 north two miles, then head east on CA 299, 56 miles. Turn left onto CA 89 and head north six miles before turning left into the McArthur-Burney Falls State Park entrance. After passing the entrance booth, park in the lot on the left, across from the log cabin visitor center. The trailhead is at the south end of the lot. *DeLorme: Northern California Atlas & Gazetteer:* Page 38 D1

Burney Falls is, without a doubt, the scene that attracts the most attention in McArthur-Burney Falls State Park. And it should be. At 129 feet, it's not the tallest waterfall in California, nor does it push the most water—but it is certainly one of the prettiest falls, with a broad curtain of water cascading over emerald green moss and dark volcanic rock. The waterfall looks much wider than the creek that feeds it, adding to its beauty. The illusion of extra girth is created because the impermeable rock layer that forms the creek bed above the falls forces the ground water to flow directly out of the cliff on both sides of the creek.

The falls have a special surprise for hikers who visit between spring and fall. Black swifts, normally at home on sea cliffs, make an exception and travel 130 miles inland to nest amongst the moss behind the falls. The curtain of water provides excellent protection for the nests and any developing chicks. The birds' migration to the falls is a real departure from their standard behavior. Swifts are insect eaters that spend almost all of their lives in the air. They only bother to land when they're nesting, and then they only rest on the cliffs where their nest is located.

At the base of the cliffs, below the falls, is a pool that has been scooped out by the rushing water, to a depth of some 22 feet. The stream continues from this pool down a narrow canyon to the still waters of Burney Cove on Lake Britton. The waterway is flanked by verdant streamside vegetation that includes vine maple and flowering currant. In the water, trout are plentiful, and it's not uncommon to see fly fishermen trying their luck in the pools along the way to the lake. As you make your way to the lake, the trail sweeps away from the stream and deeper into the forest. Here, the foliage quickly changes to drier, conifer-dominated vegetation. Ponderosa pine and Douglas fir are the most common trees here, but there's also abundant incense cedar

Burney Falls.

and both white and black oak. Along this section of the trail, listen for the sounds of pileated woodpeckers boring holes into infested trees to get to the bugs inside. And look out for several old irrigation ditches that served the settlements in the valley below before the lake was created.

The falls were named for pioneer settler Samuel Burney, who came to this valley in 1859. Burney was eventually killed in his cabin under mysterious circumstances. But he first left his mark—and his name—on the creek, valley, and waterfall. In 1919, plans to develop the falls prompted the McArthur family to buy the land. They gave it to the people of California a year later for the creation of a park.

The trail eventually meanders back to the waterside, where you'll find the edge of Burney Cove. Just around the bend, there is a small white cliff that appears to be

MilesDirections

0.0 START at the upper falls viewpoint, just south of the parking lot. Take the ramp to the right down into the canyon, to the base of Burney Falls.

0.2 The trail reaches Burney Creek, just below the falls.

0.3 A little spur trail leads left 100 feet to the pool below the falls. Continue straight, downstream.

0.5 The trail passes the footbridge and the return loop of Falls Trail on the left. Continue straight along this side of the creek, following Falls Trail toward Lake Britton.

1.0 The trail reaches the upper edge of Burney Cove. Across the water, the private P.S.E.A. camp (Camp Britton) can be seen.

1.1 To the right of the trail is a chalky bluff consisting of white diatomaceous earth. [*Note. Please resist the temptation to carve in it. Help preserve the park for others.*]

1.2 The Rim Trail heads right. Continue straight.

1.5 The trail reaches a picnic area on the shores of Lake Britton. This is the turnaround point. Follow Falls Trail back to the footbridge you passed at mile 0.5.

2.4 Back at the footbridge, turn right and cross it, turning right again on the other side.

2.5 P.S.E.A. Trail continues straight. Turn left instead and follow Falls Trail up the side of the canyon to the top of Burney Falls.

2.8 At this point, the trail is level with the top of the falls, providing an excellent view. Continue up Falls Trail, as it switchbacks up the canyon.

3.0 A connector trail forks up to the right, leading to the Pacific Crest Trail. Keep going straight on Falls Trail, and turn left onto the wooden footbridge shortly thereafter, crossing back over Burney Creek.

3.1 The trail arrives at a small parking lot. Head left, and pick up the trail as it resumes at the north edge of the lot.

3.3 The trail ends back at the trailhead.

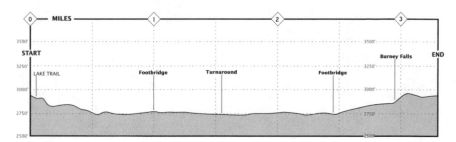

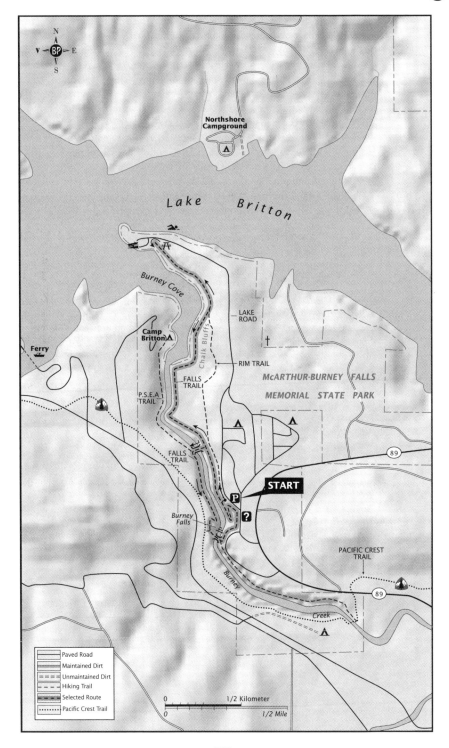

N W BP E S

Northshore
Campground

L a k e   B r i t t o n

Burney Cove

LAKE
ROAD

Camp
Britton

Ferry

Chalk Bluffs

RIM TRAIL

FALLS
TRAIL

P.S.E.A
TRAIL

McARTHUR-BURNEY FALLS
MEMORIAL STATE PARK

FALLS
TRAIL

89

START

P

?

Burney
Falls

PACIFIC CREST
TRAIL

89

Burney

Creek

Paved Road
Maintained Dirt
Unmaintained Dirt
Hiking Trail
Selected Route
Pacific Crest Trail

0   1/2 Kilometer

0   1/2 Mile

made of chalk. Soft and crumbly, the cliff has been an easy target for vandals, who unfortunately have carved names and holes into its surface. But hooligans may not be the only ones interested in the cliff's surface. The cliff is made of diatomaceous earth, a substance prized by gardeners for its pest-combating ability. Diatomaceous earth is made up of diatoms, which are the tiny *shells* of simple, one-celled aquatic organisms. Over the course of billions of years, millions of these diatoms settled at the bottom of a prehistoric ocean that once covered this part of the continent. If you crush a piece between your fingers, you'll see that it's a very fine dust or powder. The substance cuts snails and slugs as they slide over it and dries out insects that try to cross it—thus making it good for pest control. Fortunately, diatomaceous earth is harmless to humans—unless you get it in your lungs.

The turnaround point for this trail is at the picnic area on a narrow peninsula stretching out into Lake Britton. Feel free to go for a swim or rent a canoe for a cruise around the artificial lake, which was created by damming the Pit River in 1923. Several bald eagles and ospreys nest on the lake, surviving on the abundant populations of bass, bluegill, and crappie that thrive in these waters. In addition to the fish, the eagle also feeds on waterfowl and small mammals.

Return on the same trail as far as the wooden footbridge below the falls. Once you cross the bridge and travel up the other side, you're in good position to catch a glimpse of the stream above the falls. Another bridge gives you a vantage point for surveying the wide stream as it rushes toward the falls. It's hard to imagine that this speeding water emerges from the ground just half a mile upstream and has such a short distance to gain momentum. The creek is almost entirely spring-fed, so the flow rate of the falls remains nearly constant year round—at about 100 million gallons per day. Unlike the snow-fed cascades of Yosemite, there's no off-season for Burney Falls.

Lake Britton swimming area.

Hike Information

🌙 Trail Contacts:
McArthur-Burney Falls State Park, Burney, CA (530) 335–2777

🕐 Schedule:
Open year round.

💲 Fees/Permits:
$5 per car entrance fee

❓ Local Information:
Burney Chamber of Commerce, Burney, CA (530) 335–2111

📍 Local Events/Attractions:
Heritage Day, Sunday of Columbus Day weekend, Burney, CA – *19th Century recreations and demonstrations of period crafts and cooking*

🛏 Accommodations:
McArthur-Burney Falls State Park, Burney, CA – *There's a campground in the park, with campsites costing $14 per night. Reservations can be made with DESTINET at 1–800–444–7275.*

🏕 Local Outdoor Retailers:
Vaughn's Sporting Goods, Burney, CA (530) 335–2381 • **Mac's Liquor & Deli,** McCloud, CA (530) 964–2193

🅝 Maps:
USGS maps: Burney Falls, CA

Whitney Butte Trail

Hike Specs

Start: From the Merrill Ice Cave parking lot

Length: 6.5-mile out-and-back

Approximate Hiking Time: 3–3.5 hours

Difficulty Rating: Easy due to good trail and little elevation gain

Terrain: Dirt path, Volcanic highlands and sagebrush steppe

Elevation Gain: 517 feet

Land Status: National monument

Nearest Town: Tulelake, CA

Other Trail Users: Hikers only

Canine Compatibility: Dogs not permitted

Getting There

From Alturas: Take CA 299 west 19 miles. Turn right onto CA 139 just past the town of Canby, and continue 27 miles. Turn left onto CR 97 and drive west three miles, then turn right onto Lava Beds National Monument Road and drive another 18 miles, past the monument entrance station and visitor center. Two miles past the visitor center, turn left at the sign for Merrill Cave, and follow the short road 0.25 miles to the parking lot. The trail starts on the north side of the parking lot. *DeLorme: Northern California Atlas & Gazetteer:* Page 28 C2

The high desert can present an intimidating landscape. For miles in every direction, the surface of the land seems to be laid bare to the brutal sun and parching winds that dominate life here. Aromatic clumps of sagebrush and scraggly juniper trees provide scant protection from the elements. But these features all combine with the strange beauty of dark red, brown, and black volcanic rocks—along with a profusion of peculiar caves and sinkholes—to make this area worthy of national monument status.

The Whitney Butte Trail begins near the Merrill Ice Cave, a notable attraction in its own right. The cave is part of an unusual twist of regional geology. Several caves in the monument support thick deposits of permanent ice that stay frozen year round—yes, even when the surface temperatures exceed 100°F. In order to remain iced-over, the caves must allow snow and water to accumulate and freeze in the winter without letting warm air melt the ice in the summer. What makes this feat possible? First, the caves are made of volcanic stone, which has superb insulating characteristics. Second, ventilation in the caves is fairly limited.

Be aware that the Merrill Ice Cave and parts of other nearby caves were temporarily closed at the time of this writing. Park officials decided to curtail public use of the caverns due to an unexplained partial melting and deterioration of the ice inside. Part of the problem is surely the many visitors who walk on the ice, tracking in dirt and stones from outside. Park scientists are studying these changes in order to develop a plan of action to save and repair the caves. Until more is known, the deeper parts of Merrill Cave are closed, but hikers can still walk down and peer a short way into the icy section through the barricade. Meanwhile, countless other caves in the monument are still open for exploration.

First glimpse of Callahan Lava Flow.

Hike Information

🕐 Trail Contacts:
Lava Beds National Monument, Tulelake, CA (530) 667–2282

⊙ Fees/Permits:
$4 per car entrance fee, and $2 for motorcycle, bicycles, and walk-ins

🄢 Schedule:
Open year round

🝏 Local Events/Attractions:
Modoc Gathering, each July, Lava Beds National Monument, Tulelake, CA (530) 667–2282 – *Held on the monument with elders-panels, dancing, sweats, story-telling, and feasting. Call for more information.*

🛏 Accommodations:
A 40-unit campground is located across the road from the visitor center, charging $10 per night in season, and $6 out of season.

Hike Tours:
Rangers conduct walks and cave trips in summer months. Call (530) 667–2282 for information.

🎒 Local Outdoor Retailers:
Coast to Coast, Alturas, CA (530) 233–4686 • **Sports Hut,** Alturas, CA (530) 233–2423 • **The Belligerent Duck,** Alturas, CA (530) 233–4696 • **All Season's Sports,** Klamath Falls, OR (514) 884–3863

🄽 Maps:
USGS maps: Schonchin Butte, CA. A map of the monument is available at the visitor center.

From the parking lot, the trail heads across the steppe in a northwesterly direction. The sweet scent of sagebrush fills the air, and the soft, sandy ground muffles the sound of your footsteps as you make your way across the landscape. A large part of Lava Beds National Monument is designated official wilderness. And although *wilderness* in Northern California usually means mountains and dense forests, there are no granite peaks or alpine lakes to focus on here—just vast expanses of untouched land and some lonely trails that crisscross it.

This is volcano country, and evidence is everywhere. To the east, a cinder cone called Schonchin Butte rises several hundred feet above the surrounding steppe. Smaller cinder cones are visible dotting the landscape. And volcanic rocks—in several colors, shapes, and types—can be found all around you. Also take note as the trail traverses the northeastern slope of the Medicine Lake volcano that you are walking on the largest volcano (in area) in California. This volcano, known as a shield volcano, formed when thin, smooth-flowing lava sprung from a vent and spread over a wide area before solidifying. The caldera, six miles long and four miles wide, is located some 14 miles south of here at Medicine Lake. The whole monument slopes to the north-

MilesDirections

0.0 START at the north side of the parking lot. The trail enters a wilderness area almost immediately.

0.1 A registration pad is in the box next to the trail. *[Note. Signing in is a good safety precaution, and also helps monument staff determine visitor use.]*

0.8 The hill to your right is Bat Butte.

1.5 The trail crests a low ridge and descends into a shallow valley. Ahead in the distance is Mount Dome.

1.7 *[FYI. There is a good view of Whitney Butte to your left from here.]*

1.8 On the horizon ahead, you can see a series of ridges that ends with Gillem Bluff and Tule Lake.

2.0 An unmarked trail heads right toward Fleener Chimneys. Continue straight.

2.8 The trail passes over the north flank of Whitney Butte.

2.9 As the trail curves left around Whitney Butte, a black wall of rock comes into view ahead. This is the terminal end of the Callahan Lava Flow.

3.1 The trail reaches the edge of the flow and turns right, following the flow's edge.

3.2 The gate marks the end of the hike. Return the way you came.

6.5 Arrive back at the Whitney Butte Trail trailhead.

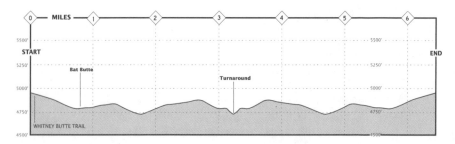

east, but there's no surface drainage because the ground is so porous that any rain or snowmelt immediately sinks into the ground. Since there are no nearby pools, hikers should be sure to bring enough water for the hike.

Bizarre formations—such as underground tube caves, spatter cones, and hornitos—were created as lava spread or erupted from the volcanoes over the surface. The eruptions also left behind vast lava flows that are visible today in the form of wide rivers of stone that drape over the steppe. These lava flows are long since solidified and now sport a sparse population of hardy trees.

As you round the shoulder of Whitney Butte, the *downstream* edge of the Callahan Lava Flow greets you.

A lonely road north of Mt. Shasta.

The flow appears as a 30-foot wall of black rock that's blocking the end of the small valley formed by the butte and a low ridge to the west. The trail ends at the edge of the flow, though the sure-footed may want to climb up onto the flow for a better view. From above, the lava flow looks less like a river than a black glacier—with deep fissures and crevasses formed as the lava cooled irregularly, and jumbles of blocks heaped into great piles. The entire flow spewed out of the ground south of here, marching across the landscape and smothering everything in its path until it finally came to a halt at this spot. **Note:** *Walking on this stuff is treacherous. The lava has nasty jagged edges, so sturdy shoes and caution are recommended.*

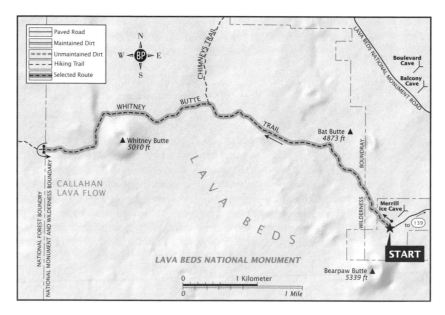

35 Wildlife Viewing Loop

Hike Specs

Start: From the information kiosk at refuge headquarters
Length: 2.7-mile loop
Approximate Hiking Time: 1 hour
Difficulty Rating: Easy due to flat elevation and smooth trails
Terrain: Gravel road and trail through open grassland and marsh, with occasional cottonwoods
Elevation Gain: 47 feet
Land Status: National wildlife refuge
Nearest Town: Alturas, CA
Other Trail Users: Motorists
Canine Compatibility: Dogs not permitted

Getting There

From Alturas: Take Main Street (U.S. 395) south through town, then follow the signs for Modoc National Wildlife Refuge, turning left just before the bridge and driving half a mile on Parker Creek Road before tuning right onto CR 115. Follow this road south 0.8 miles and turn left into the refuge, continuing another mile to the headquarters parking area. **DeLorme: Northern California Atlas & Gazetteer:** Page 40 A3

This trail is one of the shorter day hikes in the book, but it can pack a lot of punch at the right time of year. The best time to explore the wildlife refuge is in spring and fall—from April to May and September to October, to be more precise—when most migratory birds are passing through.

Lying on the Pacific Flyway, one of North America's four principle corridors for migratory bird traffic, the wetlands within the refuge serve as an important link, making this lengthy migration possible. The lakes, marshes, and riparian areas along the Flyway provide food and shelter for transitory populations and serve as wintering, breeding, or mating grounds for other species.

Birds are attracted to water for several reasons. Many eat aquatic plants such as smart weeds, pond weeds, and bulrushes, as well as the abundant mayfly larvae, midges, and snails that thrive in the shallow waters. Different species take advantage of different zones within a wetland area. Shore and wading birds—such as the avocet and black-necked stilt—search for the insects and larvae in the places where land and water meet. Ducks and swans cruise the open water between the cattails and bulrushes, skimming the algae on the water's surface or diving for aquatic plants, snails, and small fish. Predatory birds like red-tailed hawks and bald eagles, in turn, prey on the bounty of waterfowl. Up to six pairs of bald eagles nest on the refuge and can often be seen scouting for their next meal on the highest treetops near open water. Many more pass through during the busier times of year, lured to the area by the abundant prey.

Walking though the broad valley of the refuge, it's obvious that the landscape has been altered. Settlers came here years ago and drained the land to create rich farmlands and pastures for grazing stock. Other pioneers around the state followed suit, thereby destroying most of California's original low-lying wetlands—making refuges like this one all the more important for the birds that depend on the basins for food.

Modoc National Wildlife Refuge was created in 1960 with funds generated from the Migratory Bird Hunting Stamp. Located in high desert country on the western edge of the Great Basin, the refuge covers nearly 7,000 acres and maintains several different habitat types—including sagebrush, farmlands, hay meadows, and riparian areas; in addition to freshwater lakes and ponds. Some of these environs had to be built or rebuilt to make the refuge hospitable for wildlife. Small, artificial islands were created as nesting places for birds whose eggs and chicks would otherwise be easy prey for land predators like skunks and coyotes. Levies were built to keep the water out of surrounding farmlands and to create several independent ponds within the refuge. These ponds allow water levels to be adjusted to benefit the birds' food sources. The result is not necessarily an authentic or strikingly pristine landscape, but it is highly functional. Besides, the birds don't seem to mind. And the wildlife is the star attraction here.

Depending on when you come to the refuge, you're bound to see very different wildlife. Spring and fall generally are considered the best times to visit, because those seasons offer the largest volume of migratory passers-through. Whatever the time of year, morning and evening are the best times to observe the refuge's wildlife.

In the spring, tundra swans, mallards, and pintails join white-fronted geese and several species of wading birds and warblers as they stop over en route to northern habitats. Summer is the season for white pelicans and songbirds like killdeers, marsh wrens, and Western meadowlarks. And fall is when sandhill cranes arrive in large numbers to nest. Winter is less spectacular, but you can still see plenty of ducks—including the American widgeon, common goldeneye, bufflehead, and mallard.

Mule deer and Canada geese.

At any time of the year, mule deer, pronghorn antelope, coyote, raccoon, and black-tailed jackrabbit can be seen prowling the drier parts of the refuge. Northern flicker, black-billed magpie, and great horned owl are also year-round residents.

As you walk through the refuge, move slowly and stay observant. There are opportunities to observe wildlife—some rare and endangered—that you won't find elsewhere. This hike is sort of a Zen-counterpoint to some of the more adventurous hikes in the book. Enjoy it as such.

View from the platform.

MilesDirections

0.0 START at the information kiosk at the refuge headquarters. The trail heads east along Auto-Tour Loop.

0.4 The trail curves to the left. *[**FYI.** To your right is a stand of cattails.]*

0.7 The Auto-Tour Loop continues straight, but we turn right onto Widgeon Pond Nature Trail.

0.8 Widgeon Pond Nature Trail heads left, but first continue straight 0.2 miles to the viewing platform. After you have spent some time there, return to this junction and follow the Widgeon Pond Nature Trail north around Widgeon Pond.

1.4 The trail passes another observation deck on the north side of Widgeon Pond.

1.6 The trail reaches the parking lot for Widgeon Pond. Turn left and follow the Auto-Tour Loop south along the main pond.

2.0 Widgeon Pond Nature Trail heads left. Continue straight, retracing the first leg of the trail to the trailhead.

2.7 Arrive back at the trailhead.

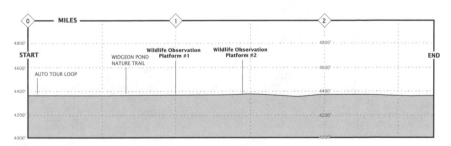

Hike Information

Trail Contacts:
Modoc National Wildlife Refuge, Alturas, CA (530) 233-3572 or www.r1.fws.gov/modocl

Schedule:
Open year round. Office is open from 8 A.M. to 4:30 P.M., Monday–Friday.

Local Information:
Modoc County Chamber of Commerce, Alturas, CA (530) 233-2819

Accommodations:
There are several hotels and four private campgrounds in Alturas, 2.5 miles north of the refuge.

Local Outdoor Retailers:
Coast to Coast, Alturas, CA (530) 233-4686 • Sports Hut, Alturas, CA (530) 233-2423 • The Belligerent Duck, Alturas, CA (530) 233-4696

Maps:
USGS maps: Alturas, CA

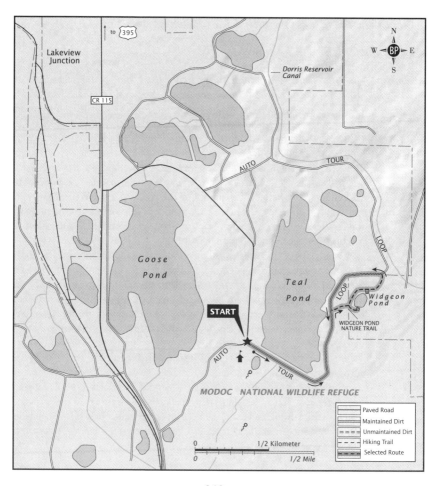

Blue Lake National Recreation Trail

Hike Specs

Start: From the Blue Lake boat ramp
Length: 2.8-mile loop
Approximate Hiking Time: 1–1.5 hours
Difficulty Rating: Easy due to flatness, shortness, and good quality of trail
Terrain: Dirt path through mature ponderosa pine forests and riparian meadows
Elevation Gain: 153 feet
Land Status: National forest
Nearest Town: Likely, CA
Canine Compatibility: Dogs permitted

Getting There

From Alturas: Take U.S. 395 south 18 miles to the tiny town of Likely. Turn left onto Jess Valley Road (FS 64) and drive 13 miles before turning right on Blue Lake Road (FS 39N30) and driving the last two miles to the lake. As you approach the lake, take the spur road to the right, following signs for the boat ramp and the day-use parking lot. The trail starts at the edge of the lake near the boat ramp. *DeLorme: Northern California Atlas & Gazetteer:* Page 41 C5

Leaving the boat dock and fishing pier behind at the trailhead, hikers quickly find themselves alone in their own little chunk of healthy planet. Along with the gorgeous scenery of the wide, blue water and the handsome stands of ponderosa pine, the thriving wildlife here conveys a sense that all is well on Blue Lake. The beavers are a case in point.

Along the northeast side of the lake, several trees appear to be partially cut with an axe, but on closer inspection you can see that the trees were not cut at all; they were chewed. This is the sign of the beaver at work. Weighing up to 66 pounds and reaching four feet in length, beavers are the second-largest rodents in the world—after the South American capybara—and they can gnaw through a five-inch-diameter tree in under half an hour. 1

A mound of sticks in the center of the lake's side arm marks the beavers' lodge. With one or more underwater entrances, a bed of wood chips, and a vent to let in fresh air, the lodge is a well-constructed castle that keeps the beavers warm and safe from predators like coyotes, foxes, bobcats, and otters. From here, these aquatic rodents make frequent forays in search of food and building materials. Hikers tend to see these largely nocturnal creatures in the evening, when human and beaver lifestyles overlap.

Beavers are perfectly adapted to aquatic life, with webbed feet to aid in swimming and a broad, flat tail that works like a rudder. They are protected from the water's cold winter temperatures by a thick layer of fat under their skin, and their oily fur keeps them waterproof. When swimming, clear membranes close over their eyes to protect them from debris, while valves seal off their ears and nostrils. These traits—combined with an impressive breath-holding ability—help beavers stay submerged for up to 15 minutes at a time.

Blue Lake.

As the trail rounds the side arm of the lake and the stream that feeds it, you arrive at the campground—probably as good a place as any to watch the active beavers in the evening. There are some fine specimens of ponderosa pine here, as there are all around the lake. The ponderosa, also known as the Western yellow pine, is the most widely distributed pine in North America. Its golden brown bark, divided into scaly plates surrounded by dark lines, makes it beautiful to look at. And its massive size and straight grain make it one of the most important timber sources in the country.

If you look carefully at some of the tallest ponderosa pines on the lake, you may be lucky enough to spot a bald eagle nest—or you may even see the impressive raptors circling above the water, looking for fish. There are two specific eagles that have

Hike Information

🕐 Trail Contacts:
Warner Mountain Ranger District, Cedarville, CA (530) 279-6116 • **Modoc National Forest,** Alturas, CA (530) 233-5811

🕐 Schedule:
Open year round, but snow may limit access in the winter

💲 Fees/Permits:
Fee for camping, but no day-use fee

🛏 Accommodations:
There is a Forest Service campground on the east side of the lake. There is a fee for campsites.

🎒 Local Outdoor Retailers:
Coast to Coast, Alturas, CA (530) 233-4686 • **Sports Hut,** Alturas, CA (530) 233-2423 • **The Belligerent Duck,** Alturas, CA (530) 233-4696

🅝 Maps:
USGS maps: Jess Valley, CA

been returning to the lake for the past decade. And rangers say the birds have successfully raised young almost every year.

The trail remains close to the water on this side of the lake. Eventually, the path crosses a causeway over the marshy section at the lake's south end. From here, climb a few feet and enter the thicker forest on the west side of the lake. There is little foot traffic over here and not much to break the quiet solitude of the landscape. Humans are not the only creatures who appreciate the quiet—the dense canopy above is a preferred site for eagles' nests.

As the trail nears the boat ramp and the end of the trail, you drop down to the water's edge at a stagnant cove blocked by downed logs and branches. This type of sheltered area is what biologists call the *littoral* zone. It differs greatly from the deeper, still water in the center of the lake, which is known as the *pelagic* zone. The shallow water harbors various nymphs and insect larvae; and surface insects skitter about, supported by water tension. Algae, tadpoles, and small fish are also found here, as well as waterfowl attracted by the abundance of food.

After passing over a wooden footbridge at the lake's overflow, the trail curves around through the pines for the last 100 feet before emerging at the trailhead.

MilesDirections

0.0 START at the Blue Lake National Recreation Trail sign to the right of the boat ramp.

0.1 The trail passes a small wooden fishing dock.

0.3 *[FYI. There are some beaver-chewed trees on both sides of the trail.]*

0.7 The trail joins the campground access road near the fee station. Continue south along the road.

0.8 The trail leaves the road, continuing to the right

1.4 The lake is shallow and marshy here, and full of lily pads.

1.5 A spur trail heads up to a pair of build-

ings. Continue to the right on the main trail, keeping to the edge of the lake.

1.6 The dirt path changes to gravel causeway, crossing the wet meadow at the southern end of the lake. *[FYI. To the right out in the lake, a couple of beaver lodges are visible.]*

1.8 On the edge of a boulder field, some stumps have been conveniently cut as chairs along the trail.

2.4 The trail drops down near the water's edge on a small arm of the lake.

2.5 A wooden bridge spans the lake's outlet.

2.6 A culvert passes under the trail, with a small water gate below to the left.

2.8 Arrive back at the trailhead.

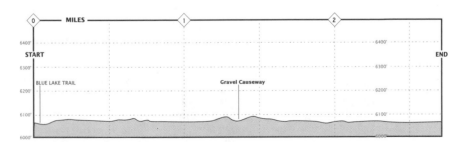

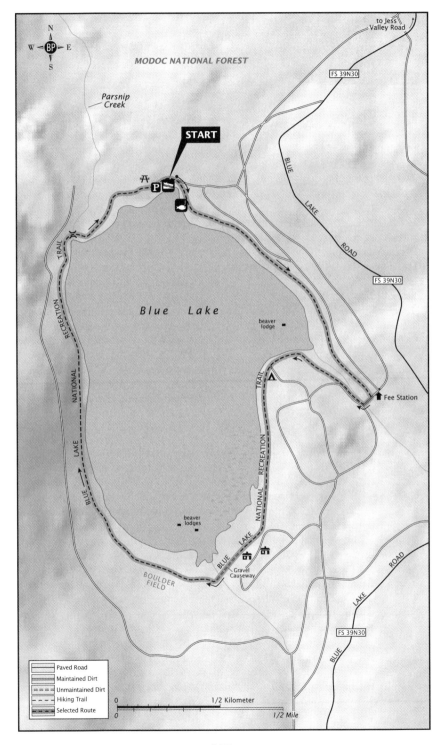

Blue Lake National Recreation Trail

to Jess Valley Road

FS 39N30

MODOC NATIONAL FOREST

Parsnip Creek

N
W · BP · E
S

START

P

Blue Lake

BLUE LAKE ROAD

FS 39N30

beaver lodge

Fee Station

NATIONAL RECREATION TRAIL

BLUE LAKE

BLUE LAKE NATIONAL RECREATION

beaver lodges

Gravel Causeway

BLUE LAKE ROAD

BOULDER FIELD

FS 39N30

	Paved Road
	Maintained Dirt
	Unmaintained Dirt
	Hiking Trail
	Selected Route

1/2 Kilometer

0

0   1/2 Mile

Bizz Johnson Trail

Hike Specs

Start: From the Susanville Depot

Length: 13.4-mile out-and-back

Approximate Hiking Time: 6–8 hours (overnight possible)

Difficulty Rating: Easy due to mild grade and smooth trail

Terrain: Dirt and gravel road through a small but dramatic river canyon

Elevation Gain: 908 feet

Land Status: Bureau of Land Management land

Nearest Town: Susanville, CA

Other Trail Users: Cyclists, equestrians, and anglers

Canine Compatibility: Dogs permitted

Getting There

From Susanville: Turn south onto South Weatherlow Street, from its intersection with CA 36 in the center of town. (South Weatherlow soon becomes Richmond Road.) Continue 0.5 miles to the train tracks. Turn left before the tracks for the Susanville depot visitor center and museum, or right just past the tracks for the trailhead. Start from either place. • **Public Transportation:** Lassen Rural Bus runs three times each weekday along CA 36 between the trailheads in Westwood and Susanville, also stopping at the Devil's Corral Trailhead (the turnaround point for this hike). Weekend shuttles are available once a month. For reservations or more information, call (530) 252-7433. Cab and shuttle service is available through Mt. Lassen Cab & Shuttle Service, (530) 257-5277. *DeLorme: Northern California Atlas & Gazetteer:* Page 60 A2

The Bizz Johnson Trail is a classic example of a good rails-to-trails conversion. The path traverses a rugged natural landscape in a mountainous region while maintaining a wide, smooth trail and a consistent grade of three percent or less—all this and no cars, too! In the spirit of making the best out of a bad situation, rails-to-trails proponents have turned the loss of yet another railroad into a unique recreational opportunity. By creating a park on the site of an old train route, trail designers were able to take advantage of railroad engineering that would be considered more than a little excessive by normal trail construction standards. The trail name honors Harold T. "Bizz" Johnson—a member of the U.S. House of Representatives from 1958 to 1980 who helped push the rails-to-trails conversion through Congress after the old Fernley & Lassen Railroad branch line was abandoned in 1978 by the Southern Pacific Railroad.

The Fernley & Lassen line was active from its construction in 1914 through 1956, when all railroad operations on the line ceased. In its heyday, the railroad linked Susanville to the town of Westwood—then home to the world's largest pine lumber mill, owned by Minnesota lumberman Thomas Barlow Walker's Red River Lumber Company. Walker signed a contract in 1912 with the Southern Pacific Railroad to build a line to his new mill in exchange for exclusive rights to haul the lumber and

raw timber for the next five years. Construction of the line through the rugged Susan River Canyon was difficult, but the route was finished by 1914. Trains then began carrying freight and passengers from Westwood to Fernley, Nevada, and to points north, east, and south of there. For the most part, the line remained busy into the 1950s. But when trucks began to compete with the railroads for freight, the need for the line gradually diminished. And when the No. 2 Bridge in Susanville was damaged by flood in 1955, it was never repaired. The line was dormant for nearly 20 years before being officially abandoned. Then efforts began to convert the old train route into a recreational trail. Clearly, the project was a success, and now hikers, bicyclists, equestrians, and anglers enjoy the trail year round. Come winter, cross-country skiers make use of the trail. Be sure to visit the historic train depot in Susanville, which serves as the trail's official trailhead and museum.

Bridges and basalt.

Heading west from the Susanville Depot, the trail follows a few yards of remaining track through a residential neighborhood before leaving the town and delving into the peaceful haven of the Susan River Canyon. One would expect for both the town and the river that flows through it to be named after a woman called Susan. Surprisingly, however, they are each named for a different Susan. The town of Susanville, previously known by other names, was christened in 1858 for the daughter of town founder Isaac Roop. The Susan River was named six years earlier for Susan Nobles, the wife of Nobles Emigrant Trail-builder William H. Nobles.

MilesDirections

0.0 START at the Susanville Depot. Head west along the railroad tracks, past the caboose.

0.1 The trail leaves the old grade, heading downhill to the right. Turn right onto South Lassen Street, cross the bridge, and turn left onto the next road. The trail passes several houses before returning to the old grade.

0.2 Continue west on the straight gravel path past a car gate. Pedestrians and cyclists may pass.

0.5 At Hobo Camp, the trail crosses a wide wooden bridge.

0.7 There are fine examples of basalt cliffs on the right.

1.0 The trail crosses another bridge. Spur trails access the river on both ends of the bridge.

2.4 Another bridge spans the Susan River.

2.6 There is a large basalt cliff on left, as you cross the next bridge.

4.0 Cross another bridge, continuing west.

4.1 The trail reaches the first big tunnel, passing through a rocky promontory. *[**Option.** There is a narrow, rocky bypass trail on right, for people uncomfortable with the dark tunnel.]*

4.2 The bypass trail rejoins main route at the other end of the tunnel.

4.4 The trail crosses a short bridge as the second tunnel comes into view.

4.5 The second tunnel opens before you. *[**Option.** This tunnel is shorter, but there is also a bypass trail on the right.]*

4.6 The bypass trail rejoins the main route at the other end of the tunnel.

4.7 *[**FYI.** There is an undeveloped camping area on right, near the river.]*

4.8 Cross another bridge.

6.5 Pass through the car gate and continue straight on the Bizz Johnson Trail.

6.7 The trail reaches the Devil's Corral trailhead. This is the turnaround point. Return the way you came.

13.4 Arrive back at the Susanville Depot.

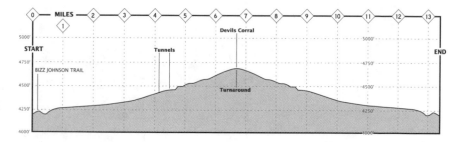

250

The State of Nataqua

In the early days of California's statehood, its eastern border was ill defined and sparsely populated by independence-minded pioneers. Preferring self-rule to the status of a minor county in California, settlers in the Susanville area got together and declared the state of Nataqua (a Paiute name) in 1856. Its borders encompassed Northern California east of the Sierra crest, and much of northwestern and central-western Nevada.

The laws and elected officials of Nataqua effectively governed the area until 1863, when increased gold and silver mining activity prompted a survey of California's eastern boundary. Subsequent attempts at tax collection led to a shoot-out in Susanville between Nataquans and a Plumas County sheriff's posse, who had come to enforce California taxation.

The state of Nataqua is now little more than a memory, but the spirit of independence lives on in this isolated, weather-beaten corner of the Old West.

The canyon is not particularly deep, nor is the river large and raging. But the abundant dark rock of peculiar basalt formations makes for ruggedly handsome scenery, and the remaining railroad structures serve as reminders of the Old West history associated with the trail. In addition to crossing numerous bridges, the trail passes through two railroad tunnels between Susanville and Devil's Corral—providing a real treat for those hikers not afraid of the dark. The longer of the two tunnels is particularly impressive to explore. Both are straight, so there is always light at the other end. But toward the center of the tunnel, that bright spot ahead robs you of

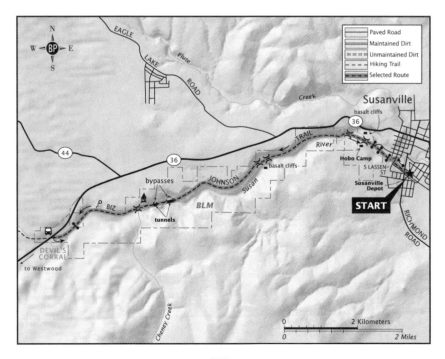

your night vision and leaves the immediate surroundings lost in inky blackness. If this sort of thing is not your cup of tea, there are narrow footpaths that bypass each of the tunnels.

The turnaround point for this hike is Devil's Corral, but the Bizz Johnson Trail continues another 18.7 miles to Mason Station. A longer hike is possible, especially in conjunction with a shuttle (*see Getting There*).

Basalt cliffs.

Hike Information

● Trail Contacts:

U.S. Department of the Interior, Bureau of Land Management, Eagle Lake Field Office, Susanville, CA (530) 257-0456 or *www.ca.blm.gov/eaglelake* • **U.S. Department of Agriculture,** Lassen National Forest, Eagle Lake District Office, Susanville, CA (530) 257-4188 or *www.r5.fs.fed.us/lassen* • **Lassen Land & Trails Trust,** Susanville, CA (530) 257-3235

● Schedule:

Open year round, although snow may hamper walking in winter

● Fees/Permits:

No fees. Permit required only for campfires.

● Local Information:

Lassen County Chamber of Commerce, Susanville, CA (530) 257-4323 • **Local news magazine website:** *www.susanvillenews.com* • **BLM website:** *www.ca.blm.gov/eaglelake/bizzreca.html* • **National Forest website:** *www.r5.pswfs.gov/heritage/051.htm* • **Trail information website:** *www.lassennews.com/lctvg/vg/bizz.htm*

● Local Events/Attractions:

The Bureau of Land Management operates wild horse and burro corrals near the town of Wendel (15 miles east of Susanville) for the purpose of training and coordinating adoption of the animals.

● Organizations:

Rails-to-Trails Conservancy, California Field Office, San Francisco, CA (415) 397-2220

● Public Transportation:

Lassen Rural Bus: (530) 252-7433 – *bus service* • **Mt. Lassen Cab & Shuttle Service:** (530) 257-5277 – *cab and shuttle service*

● Local Outdoor Retailers:

Sports Nut, Chester, CA (530) 258-3327 • **Allen's Enterprises,** Susanville, CA (530) 257-2506

● Maps:

USGS maps: Susanville, Ca; Roop Mountain, CA

Fantastic Lava Beds Loop

Hike Specs

Start: From the Cinder Cone Trail trailhead
Length: 13.0-mile loop
Approximate Hiking Time: 6–7 hours (overnight possible)
Difficulty Rating: Easy to Moderate due to two short, steep sections
Terrain: Dirt path through heavy pine forests, volcanic cinder dunes, and riparian aspen groves
Elevation Gain: 1,944 feet
Land Status: National park
Nearest Town: Old Station, CA
Other Trail Users: Anglers
Canine Compatibility: Dogs not permitted

Getting There

From Susanville: Head west six miles on CA 36 to the junction with CA 44. Turn right onto CA 44 and continue another 35 miles before turning left onto the Butte Lake Access Road. Drive along this gravel road six miles to the entrance station (self-service), and continue another 0.3 miles before turning right into the Cinder Cone trailhead parking lot. The trail starts at the far end of the lot.
DeLorme: Northern California Atlas & Gazetteer: Page 49 D4

History buffs, take note. The Fantastic Lava Beds Loop starts off by following the Nobles Emigrant Trail from the trailhead to Cinder Cone. The path was built around 1851 as an alternative to the Lassen Trail and carried many wagon trains through the area while bringing settlers and miners to California. While the history of the trail is fascinating, the true star of this hike is undeniably the geology. Geologically speaking, volcanic activity in the park is quite recent, and the signs are still fresh on the land.

The first stop on this tour is Cinder Cone, a natural monument in classic volcano form that towers above rolling dunes of volcanic cinder. About half a mile in diameter at its base, this dormant cone stands 750 feet above the surrounding plain and is topped by a 240-foot-deep crater. Called a *tephra* cone by geologists, Cinder Cone was formed when a volcanic vent opened in the earth's surface and began spewing cinder, ash, and lava bombs into the air. Ash covered the surrounding landscape, while the heavier bombs and cinder piled up around the vent. This weightier debris eventually formed a cone with sides sloping at about 30 to 35 degrees, the classic *angle of repose*. Water erosion has not been a factor for Cinder Cone, because the volcano is made of such porous material that water just seeps through it. As a result, the near-perfect cone remains unmarred by gullies. The trail up the side of the cone seems steeper than it really is—mainly because the loose cinder underfoot makes climbing difficult—but the crater and view from the rim are well worth the trouble. The double rim of the crater is evidence that the cone was formed by at least two separate eruptions; though it is likely even more eruptions played a role. (A short spur trail leads down into the crater for those wishing to stand in the maw of a volcano.)

Once you descend the opposite side of Cinder Cone, the trail reaches the Painted Dunes and the source of the lava flows that formed the Fantastic Lava Beds. Scientists think that four lava flows formed the southern side of Cinder Cone's base. They believe the first one erupted around 1567, with subsequent flows in 1666, 1720, and 1785. The 1666 flow is credited with creating the Painted Dunes. The dunes got their vibrant hues from the cinder and ash that fell from the cone onto lava that was still hot. The lava-and-ash combination cemented, oxidized the ash, and created the gray, brown, and red coloration that makes these dunes unforgettable. The third flow, in 1720, formed a natural dam across Butte Creek, thereby creating Snag Lake.

From the Painted Dunes, the trail drops back down to the ash-covered plain and heads south alongside the river of stone. The lava flow is truly impressive, with the twisted and tortured magma creating bizarre shapes—some of which tower 30 feet above the trail. The lava is colorful as well, ranging from pale gray to bright red to nearly black. At the southern edge of this otherworldly landscape, the lava flow ends abruptly in the broad, shallow waters of Snag Lake.

MilesDirections

0.0 START at Cinder Cone Trail trailhead. The trail follows the edge of Fantastic Lava Beds to the base of Cinder Cone.

0.4 Prospect Peak Trail heads right. Continue straight on Cinder Cone Trail.

0.7 The trail enters designated wilderness.

1.0 The Noble Emigrant Trail heads right, bypassing Cinder Cone. Take the left fork, to the base of the volcano.

1.1 Reach Cinder Cone. The trail climbs steeply up the north flank of the volcano.

1.2 Reach Cinder Cone's summit. Circle around to the other side of the rim and follow the trail as it descends the south side of the volcano's base to the Painted Dunes.

1.5 Turn left onto Snag Lake Trail, and head south along the Painted Dunes and Fantastic Lava Beds.

1.9 A trail heads right to Rainbow Lake. Continue straight on Snag Lake Trail.

3.4 Snag Lake comes into view on the left. Continue south along the western shore of the lake.

3.6 Still on the shores of Snag Lake, the trail passes through an old forest fire zone, where most of the standing trees are dead and charred.

5.0 Another trail heads right to Rainbow Lake. Continue straight on Snag Lake Trail.

5.7 Horseshoe Lake Trail continues straight to Horseshoe Lake. Turn a sharp left, and follow Snag Lake Trail around the south end of Snag Lake.

5.9 The trail crosses Grassy Creek via a small footbridge.

6.0 A trail heads right to Juniper Lake. Continue straight.

7.9 The trail leaves the shore of Snag Lake, passing through some beautiful aspen groves and heading north to Butte Lake.

10.3 The trail reaches the south end of Butte Lake.

10.6 A trail heads right to Widow Lake. Continue straight along the lake shore.

12.2 At the north end of Butte Lake, the Horse Trail continues straight, along Butte Creek. Cross the creek on the jammed logs, and follow the trail as it switchbacks up the ridge.

12.5 The trail levels out on the ridge, offering an excellent view south over Butte Lake and the lava beds before heading down the other side to the day-use area.

13.0 Arrive back at the Cinder Cone Trail trailhead.

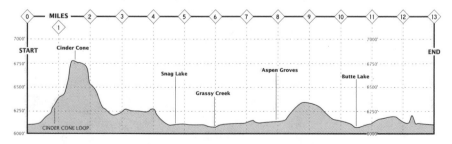

256

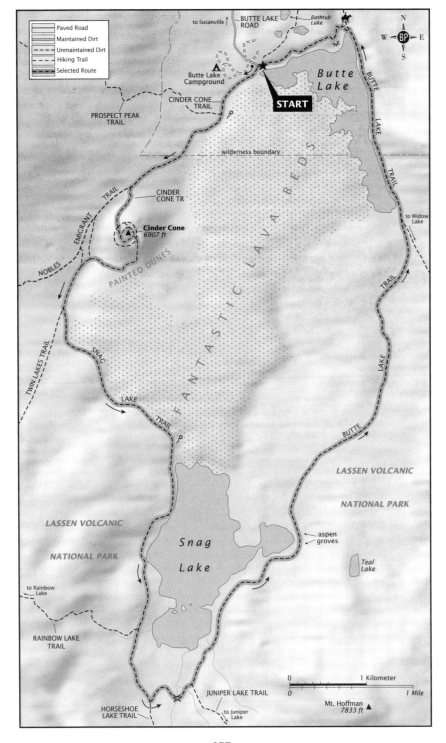

Paved Road
Maintained Dirt
Unmaintained Dirt
Hiking Trail
Selected Route

to Susanville ↑
BUTTE LAKE ROAD
Bathtub Lake

Butte Lake

START

N
W — BP — E
S

Butte Lake Campground

CINDER CONE TRAIL

PROSPECT PEAK TRAIL

wilderness boundary

CINDER CONE TR

EMIGRANT TRAIL

Cinder Cone
6907 ft

PAINTED DUNES

FANTASTIC LAVA BEDS

BUTTE LAKE TRAIL

to Widow Lake

NOBLES

TWIN LAKES TRAIL

SNAG LAKE TRAIL

BUTTE LAKE TRAIL

LASSEN VOLCANIC NATIONAL PARK

aspen groves

Teal Lake

LASSEN VOLCANIC NATIONAL PARK

Snag Lake

to Rainbow Lake

RAINBOW LAKE TRAIL

JUNIPER LAKE TRAIL

to Juniper Lake

HORSESHOE LAKE TRAIL

0   1 Kilometer
0   1 Mile

Mt. Hoffman
7833 ft

The trail continues south, past the charred tree trunks that mark the work of a recent forest fire, and eventually circles the lake to return to the other side. There are several good campsites on Snag Lake. Most of them are on the east side, tucked in among the trees on the level shoreline. From these campsites, the trail heads north toward Butte Lake and passes through groves of quaking aspen, recognizable by their trembling leaves and smooth, cream-colored trunks that brighten the otherwise dark forests. These groves are fabulous in autumn, when the contrast between their newly turned gold leaves and the dark green of the surrounding conifers is truly dazzling.

Butte Lake lies at the northern end of the Fantastic Lava Beds. Like its sister to the south, the lake is bounded on one side by the glacier-like lava flow, which must have made one hell of a steam cloud as it plowed into the cold water. Islands of black lava form a sort of volcanic archipelago and provide plenty of underwater hiding places for the lake's fish, which are sought by anglers from the nearby campground and day-use area.

A Glossary of Volcanic Terms

'A'a. *A very rough, jagged, and irregular type of lava formed when viscous flowing pahoehoe lava loses heat and gases. Pronounced ah-ah, this is an Hawaiian expletive for pain (translation: "Ow!") that was used often when walking barefoot over hardened lava of this type.*

- **Cauliflower.** *'A'a. Lava that hardened in transition from pahoehoe to 'a'a, taking the shape of many small lumps on a solid mass of lava. Often found on the floors of lava tubes.*
- **Hornito.** *A small spatter cone that formed above a lava tube as pressure forced the molten lava out through the roof of the tube.*
- **Lavacicles.** *Small stalactites that often form on the ceiling of lava tubes. Flowing lava below heats the existing rock to the melting point, causing it to drip.*
- **Lava Tube.** *An underground conduit formed when lava flowing through a channel forms a crust on top, while the still-molten rock below continues to flow, eventually draining the tube as the source of the lava ceases.*
- **Pahoehoe.** *Hawaiian for "smooth," pronounced pah-hoy-hoy. Used to denote a free-flowing type of lava that hardens into a smooth, often ropy-looking exterior. This is the only type of lava that forms lava tubes. As it flows and cools, losing gases along the way, pahoehoe can turn into 'a'a lava, but never the other way around.*
- **Rafted Breakdown.** *A formation created when a piece of a tube's lining falls onto a fresh lava flow, and is carried downstream, like a raft, before hardening.*
- **Shield Volcano.** *A low, very broad volcano formed by viscous lava flowing at a steady rate from the source, creating extensive lava flows and often lava tubes.*
- **Spatter Cone.** *A steep-sided mound created by lava erupting from a fissure or vent, with globs of lava gradually building up the cone as they land around the source.*

Before lava flows blocked the stream, Butte Lake was fed by Butte Creek, which now empties into Snag Lake. Instead of backing up and flowing around the lava beds, however, the water percolates down through the porous volcanic rock to keep Butte Lake filled.

The trail leaves the wilderness and circles around the north end of the lake, climbing a steep ridge for one last panorama of this fantastic landscape before returning through the day-use area to the trailhead.

Hike Information

☎ Trail Contacts:
Lassen Volcanic National Park, Mineral, CA (530) 595–4444 or *www.nps.gov/lavo*

⏱ Schedule:
Open year round, but heavy snow can severely limit access from late October through June.

⑤ Fees/Permits:
$10 per car entrance fee at the park gate. ($5 per person on foot, bike, or motorcycle.) Good for seven days (camping not included). If you plan on coming back within a year and/or you live within a reasonable distance, $20 will get you a 12-month pass.

❓ Local Information:
Useful information: *www.gorp.com/gorp.resource/us_national_park/ca_lasse.htm* or *www.lassen.volcanic.national-park.com*

💡 Local Events/Attractions:
The Caribou Wilderness, managed by Lassen National Forest, Susanville, CA (530) 257–2151 – *accessed via CA 44 east of the park*

🍽 Accommodations:
Lassen Volcanic National Park, Mineral, CA – *There are eight campgrounds within the park, not including backcountry spots. All sites (except very large groups) are first-come, first-served.*

🍴 Restaurants:
Within the park, there are concessionaire-run snack bars near the northwest and southwest park entrances, and a cafe at the southwest entrance location.

Hike Tours:
Lassen Volcanic National Park, Mineral, CA (530) 595–4444 ext. 5133 – *Call for information on ranger-led programs for organized groups.*

🎗 Organizations:
Lassen Loomis Museum Association, Mineral, CA (530) 595–3399 • **Lassen Park Foundation,** Chico, CA (530) 898–9309

🅑 Other Resources:
Volcanoe website: *www.volcano.und.nodak.edu/vw.html*

🏪 Local Outdoor Retailers:
Vaughn's Sporting Goods, Burney, CA (530) 335–2381 • **Sports Nut,** Chester, CA (530) 258–3327 • **Koch Brothers Sporting Goods,** Shingletown, CA (530) 474–5335 • **Allen's Enterprises,** Susanville, CA (530) 257–2506

Ⓝ Maps:
USGS maps: Prospect Peak, CA

39

Chaos Crags Trail

Hike Specs

Start: From the Chaos Crags Trail trailhead
Length: 4.6-mile out-and-back
Approximate Hiking Time: 2.5 hours
Difficulty Rating: Moderate due to some steep, rocky trail near the lake
Terrain: Dirt path through mature Jeffrey pine forests and along sparse rocky ridges and a bit of talus
Elevation Gain: 920 feet
Land Status: National park
Nearest Town: Mineral, CA
Other Trail Users: Hikers only
Canine Compatibility: Dogs not permitted

Getting There

From Redding: Head east approximately 48 miles on CA 44. Turn right onto the Lassen Peak Highway (CA 89 South) and drive 0.5 miles to the Lassen Volcanic National Park entrance station. *(Note. This road is closed in winter.)* Continue another 0.6 miles past the entrance station, and turn right at the sign for Manzanita Lake. About 0.1 miles later, the road curves sharply right and there's a turnout on the left side of the road. This is the Chaos Crags Trail trailhead. *DeLorme: Northern California Atlas & Gazetteer:* Page 48 D2

Note: During the winter months, Lassen's roads are buried under 15 to 40 feet of snow!

Lassen Volcanic National Park is one of those places you want to drag everyone you know to see. It's just magical in a way that no photograph can ever capture. Lassen is surprisingly uncrowded for a park of its caliber—even during the peak season—because it's located off the beaten path in the sparsely populated northeastern part of California. The tourists who do make it here almost always stick to the—admittedly impressive—thermal areas and Lassen Peak, leaving the rest of the park open for solitude-lovers to enjoy at their leisure.

The park is named for Danish immigrant, explorer, and would-be developer Peter Lassen, who in the 1840s blazed the Lassen Trail, which passed southeast of here on its way to Lassen's Ranch on the Sacramento River. The path was supposed to provide an alternate route into California for the steady stream of settlers, to whom Lassen was hoping to sell parcels of land he had been granted by the Mexican government. Alas, the route turned out to be a dud. The trail passed over the mountains at Goose Lake—in the extreme northeastern corner of the state—and managed to avoid sky-high mountain passes and the most rugged terrain. But it did so at a cost. The detour added almost a month to the already long, arduous journey emigrants faced, and few weary travelers considered the extra mileage a bargain. Settlers were willing to risk steep canyons and the inclement weather of higher elevations if they could just *get there already!* An additional impediment for the trail was, ironically, Peter Lassen—who guided settlers along his trail and was, according to some sources,

photo by Mirjam Brett

Lichen on Ponderosa Pine.

not the best of guides. He was threatened on at least one occasion by irate settlers fed up with him and his "shortcut." Understandably, the Lassen Trail soon was abandoned. It was replaced in 1851 by a less circuitous route, blazed by William Nobles. The Nobles Emigrant Trail took a more direct east-west approach, passing through the present-day park to within half a mile of the Chaos Crags Trail trailhead.

In spite of his dubious navigational skills, Peter Lassen nevertheless was regarded as something of a founding father in the region. In addition to this national park, a national forest, a county, and a school (among other things) have been named for him.

The trail to Crags Lake gets off to a pleasant start with a leisurely stroll over level ground through a mature stand of Jeffrey pine. If you're new to the species, take a moment to sniff at the flaky bark of these stately trees. The mild, sweetly agreeable odor has been described as reminiscent of everything from butterscotch to vanilla to lemons. It's this smell that helps to distinguish the Jeffrey pine from the similar-looking ponderosa pine, which grows farther up the trail.

The mountains in the park are at the southern end of the Cascade Range—the Sierra Nevada begins just 20 miles south of here. Because Lassen is located at the natural crossroad of these distinct mountain ranges—each with its own unique geology and plant life—Lassen has an abundance of plant species, with representatives from both northern and southern bioregions. There are about 780 plant species within

MilesDirections

0.0 START at the Chaos Crags Trailhead. The trail heads east through an airy stand of ponderosa pine. [**Note.** *If snow still obscures the trail, follow the round yellow plastic blazes on the trees.*]

0.6 The trail goes downhill slightly as it passes over an ancient glacial moraine, then begins to climb again.

0.7 The trail crosses a tiny stream.

1.4 After a brief level period, the trail begins to climb again.

1.9 [**FYI.** *Ahead of you, an excellent view of Chaos Crags opens up.*]

2.1 The trail pops out onto a barren ridge, offering a nice view of Table Mountain to the north.

2.2 As the trail rounds a corner, a huge talus slope can be seen ahead. [**FYI.** *This is the base of Chaos Crags. Crags Lake is at the bottom of the slope.*]

2.3 The trail drops down a short slope to Crags Lake, which is full of large tadpoles in summer. This is the turnaround point for the hike. Return the way you came.

4.6 Arrive back at the trailhead.

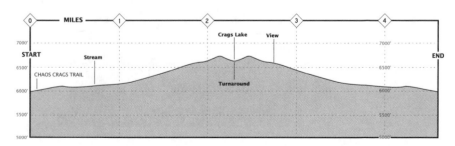

Lassen's boundaries, compared to only 485 species at Mount Shasta. Plants found in the park range from wild iris, spotted coralroot, and pyrola at lower elevations, to the rare golden drabe and smelowskia, which grow only high on Lassen Peak.

As you begin the climb up the northern flank of Chaos Crags, you stand in the path of a series of monumental landslides that came crashing down this slope sometime around 1670. The slides resulted in the formation of the Chaos Jumbles. According to geologists, superheated ground water caused a steam explosion. Enough hot rock came down at once that the whole mass trapped and rode on a layer of compressed air, which acted to lubricate the slide and allowed it to reach very high speeds. The slide traveled so fast that it continued nearly 400 feet up the side of neighboring Table Mountain before finally coming to rest. The same catastrophic event dammed nearby Manzanita Creek with tons of hastily deposited debris, thereby creating the present-day Reflection and Manzanita Lakes. Who says geology is dull?

It's soon obvious that this area has seen some serious volcanic activity. In fact, it's said that virtually every rock in the park originated as liquid magma in an active volcano. Lassen Peak is one of only two recently active volcanoes in the contiguous United States. The other one, Washington's infamous Mount Saint Helens, blew its top in 1980—somewhat eclipsing the notoriety Lassen had enjoyed since its last active period ended around 1921.

Shortly before reaching the lake at the end of the trail, the forest opens to reveal Chaos Crags in its full panoramic majesty. The Crags are the weathered remnants of so-called *plug-dome* volcanoes. These volcanoes are formed when thick, low viscosity (dacite) lava hardens inside volcanic vents rather than flowing out into the sur-

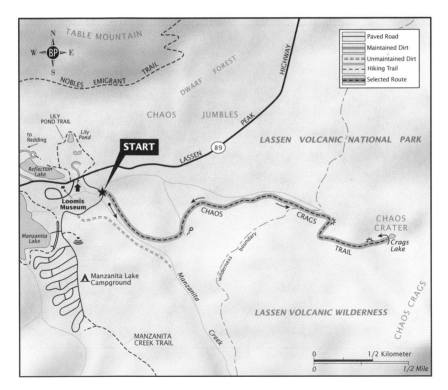

rounding terrain, thereby plugging the volcano's vent. From the summit, steep talus slopes fall to the tiny pool of Crags Lake. The lake, which lies in the path of little, regularly occurring rockfalls, has been growing smaller and smaller as the years go by. Enjoy it while you can!

Choas Crags from the trail.

Hike Information

🕭 Trail Contacts:
Lassen Volcanic National Park, Mineral, CA (530) 595–4444 or *www.nps.gov/lavo*

🕓 Schedule:
Open year round, but heavy snow can severely limit access from late October through June

💲 Fees/Permits:
$10 per car entrance fee at the park gate. ($5 per person on foot, bike, or motorcycle.) Good for seven days (camping not included). If you plan on coming back within a year and/or you live within a reasonable distance, $20 will get you a 12-month pass.

❓ Local Information:
Useful information: *www.gorp.com/gorp. resource/us_national_park/ca_lasse.htm* or *www.lassen. volcanic.national-park.com*

🎯 Local Events/Attractions:
Subway cave, about 10 miles north of the northwest park entrance on CA 89/44 – *A good example of a lava tube cave.*

♿ Accommodations:
Lassen Volcanic National Park, Mineral, CA – *There are eight campgrounds within the park, not including backcountry spots. All sites (except very large groups) are first-come, first-served.*

🍴 Restaurants:
Within the park, there are concessionaire-run snack bars near the northwest and southwest park entrances, and a cafe at the southwest entrance location.

Hike Tours:
Lassen Volcanic National Park, Mineral, CA (530) 595–4444 ext. 5133 – *Call for information on ranger-led programs for organized groups.*

🚶 Organizations:
Lassen Loomis Museum Association, Mineral, CA (530) 595–3399 • **Lassen Park Foundation,** Chico, CA (530) 898–9309

✏ Other Resources:
Volcanoe website: *www.volcano.und. nodak.edu/vw.html*

🏔 Local Outdoor Retailers:
Vaughn's Sporting Goods, Burney, CA (530) 335–2381 • **Sports Nut,** Chester, CA (530) 258–3327 • **Koch Brothers Sporting Goods,** Shingletown, CA (530) 474–5335 • **Allen's Enterprises,** Susanville, CA (530) 257–2506

Ⓝ Maps:
USGS maps: Manzanita Lake, CA; West Prospect Peak, CA

Mill Creek Trail

Hike Specs

Start: From the Mill Creek Trail trailhead in the Black Rock Campground

Length: 10.0-mile out-and-back

Approximate Hiking Time: 4–5 hours (recommended as overnight)

Difficulty Rating: Moderate due to poorly maintained trail and brushy vegetation

Terrain: Dirt path and dirt road through brushy, rugged canyons and oak-shaded grassland

Elevation Gain: 2,253 feet

Land Status: National forest, wilderness area, and private property

Nearest Town: Red Bluff, CA

Other Trail Users: Anglers and equestrians

Canine Compatibility: Dogs permitted

Getting There

From Red Bluff: Drive east some 23 miles on CA 36 to the town of Paynes Creek. Turn right (south) on Plum Creek Road, and follow it eight miles before turning right (south) on the graveled Ponderosa Way. Follow this road south 16 miles to the huge monolith called Black Rock. Below the rock, and just before crossing Mill Creek, turn right into the Black Rock Campground. If you plan on camping in the wilderness, park outside the campground to avoid the fee. The Mill Creek Trail trailhead is at the west end of the campground. *DeLorme: Northern California Atlas & Gazetteer:* Page 58 C1

I t seems almost unbelievable, in this age of sprawl and population growth, that a large area like the Ishi Wilderness can exist in this location and remain relatively unchanged from what it was 200 years ago. And yet here it is. The rugged landscape certainly has something to do with Ishi's perseverance—even today the Mill Creek Trail trailhead is only accessible via 20 miles of steep, winding gravel roads. The place is also dry, and the brutal sun fairly toasts the ground during the long summers. Perhaps it was simply the abundance of good farming and grazing land to the west and the thick mountain timberland to the east that prompted settlers take one look at these desolate canyons and mutter, *Why bother?* In any case, the European-Americans' indifference enabled a small band of Yahi Indians to maintain a traditional life here in the Mill Creek and Deer Creek canyons for nearly 40 years after the tribe was believed to be wiped out.

The Yahi were the southernmost of four Native American tribes, collectively known as the Yana Indians, all of whom lived in neighboring valleys and spoke different dialects of a Hokan tongue. Life changed abruptly for these people when settlers began pouring in to the area in the 1840s. Peter Lassen built his infamous, albeit short-lived, emigrant trail down the ridge between Mill Creek and Deer Creek—right through the middle of the Yahi homeland. The Gold Rush started shortly thereafter and brought waves of miners into the area. Many of these settlers stayed on to populate the productive farmlands of the Sacramento Valley.

The Yahi, known as the *Mill Creeks* to early settlers, were seen by settlers as particularly warlike. From 1850 through 1870, a series of massacres by locally financed

Mill Creek.

"Indian fighters" reduced the Yahi population to what was thought to be extinction. But a band of some 40 Yahi managed to escape the killings. These Yahi lived in fear, and secrecy, for many years. To survive, they hid in thick brushes and caves and smothered the smoke of their cooking fires in order to remain unseen. There were occasionally rumors that *wild* Indians had been spotted in the hills, but townspeople generally scoffed at these stories. Meanwhile, the hardships and constant fear of dis-

MilesDirections

0.0 START at Mill Creek Trail trailhead at the west end of Black Rock Campground. Follow Mill Creek Trail due west.

0.3 The trail joins a dirt road. Turn left onto the road, and continue west.

0.7 A locked gate blocks the road. Mill Creek Trail continues through the pedestrian gate just above the road to the right, passing through a private cattle ranch.

0.9 The trail follows some gravel causeway built at wet spots in the meadow.

1.2 After crossing a small stream, the trail passes a rock wall on the left as it re-enters the oak forest.

1.3 The trail crosses a small stream here.

1.5 Cross another stream.

2.0 An unlocked cattle gate blocks the trail. Open the gate and pass through, continuing straight on Mill Creek Trail

2.1 Ford the small stream and continue straight.

2.3 *[FYI. Off the trail to the left is a good camping spot, and a nice swimming hole to boot.]*

2.5 The trail seems to fork here. Take the upper (right) fork, continuing west on Mill

Creek Trail as it crosses the rock-strewn slopes of the canyon.

2.6 Cross another small stream.

2.7 The trail is high above the valley floor now, offering excellent views of this rugged country.

3.7 A slightly larger stream requires crossing here, but conveniently-placed rocks make it easy.

3.8 The trail crosses yet another small stream then begins to descend, dropping closer to Mill Creek.

3.9 The trail passes below a wispy little waterfall in a cool hollow.

4.1 Once again low, near the banks of the creek, the trail passes through a moist riparian zone. *[**Note.** Beware of poison oak!]*

4.5 After climbing again, the trail crosses a narrow ledge high above Mill Creek, offering a nice view downstream.

5.0 The trail descends again and crosses a wide, grassy meadow to access Mill Creek. This is the turnaround point. Return the way you came.

10.0 Arrive back at the trailhead.

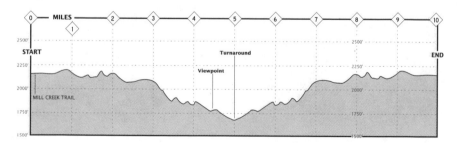

covery took their toll on the Yahi, and their numbers continued to dwindle until only one remained by 1908.

That man was discovered, terrified and half-starved, outside a slaughterhouse on the outskirts of Oroville on August 29, 1911. Local police took the man into protective custody, and soon news stories of the "wild man" were circulating around the state. These tales eventually attracted the attention of two San Francisco anthropologists, Alfred L. Kroeber and Thomas T. Waterman. Kroeber and Waterman identified the "wild man" as a Yahi, took responsibility for him, and offered him a home at the Museum of Art & Anthropology of the University of San Francisco, where they both worked. The scientists soon found they could communicate with the man using word lists from dialects similar to Yahi and other linguistic data.

Kroeber and Waterman's success surely was due in part to their knowledge of Native American cultures. The Yahi, like many other Native people in California, believed that names were powerful and personal things. Out of respect, they generally addressed each other by nicknames or titles. The anthropologists understood these beliefs and did not press the Yahi man for his name, choosing instead to simply refer to him as Ishi, which is the Yahi word for "person."

Ishi remained at the museum, where he quickly learned the ways of the modern world. He also taught the anthropologists a lot about a culture that had remained largely unchanged by American civilization. The scientists observed Ishi and carefully documented every aspect of his being—from his physical form and movements (especially as he practiced archery, hunting, and pressure flaking) to his beliefs and personality. For their part, the anthropologists tried to make Ishi comfortable. They gave him a job as janitor of the museum so he could earn some money, and they accompanied him on extended trips to his former haunts. Sadly, after four years and seven months at the museum, Ishi contracted tuberculosis—one of the diseases imported by Europeans—and the last of the Yahi passed away.

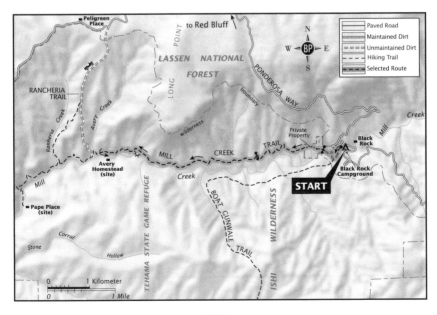

The trail through Ishi's world begins at Black Rock, an intrusive basalt plug that stands like a huge misshapen sentinel towering over the valley below. The plug once was covered by softer rock but has been left exposed by erosion from Mill Creek. The trail climbs up from the Black Rock Campground through a sparse oak woodland and joins an access road that winds toward a locked gate. The trail travels above a small cattle ranch and past some old stone walls before entering the wilderness at a cattle gate. The rest of the hike meanders across the slopes of the canyon, sometimes dropping down through grassy meadows to a swimming hole on Mill Creek and sometimes climbing up to rock knobs high above the valley. The turnaround point for the hike comes as the forest once again gives way to a grassy meadow. Across the creek, an even larger meadow stretches across a wide flat space that was once the site of the Avery Homestead. Although increasingly sketchy, the Mill Creek Trail continues, in theory at least, farther downstream. Enjoy the solitude of this forgotten wilderness, and return the way you came.

Black Rock.

Hike Information

📞 Trail Contacts:
Lassen National Forest, Almanor Ranger Station, Chester, CA (530) 258–2141 or *www.r5.fs.fed.us/lassen*

🕐 Schedule:
Open year round, though spring and fall are the best times to visit

💲 Fees/Permits:
No permits required, except free campfire permit, which is available at Forest Service offices

❓ Local Information:
Chester/Lake Almanor-Chamber of Commerce, Chester, CA (530) 258–2426 or 1–800–350–4838 or *www.plumas.ca.us/visitors_bureau/html/chester.html* • **Tehama County website:** *www.tehamacounty.com* • **Local information website:** *www.discoverredbluff.com*

📍 Local Events/Attractions:
Volunteers willing to donate some time helping archeologists and historians work on special projects should call Passport in Time clearing house at 1–800–281–9176.

🛏 Accommodations:
Black Rock Campground: *located at the trailhead and costs $11* • **McCarthy Point Cabin:** *The Forest Service rents a former fire lookout, perched on nearby*

McCarthy Point. The two-room cabin costs $60/night Friday and Saturday, and $40 Sunday through Thursday. Call (530) 258–2141 for reservations.

📖 Other Resources:
Ishi in Two Worlds: A Biography of the Last Wild Indian in North America by Theodora Kroeber • *Ishi the Last Yahi: A Documentary History,* edited by Robert F. Heizer and Theodora Kroeber • *Ishi the Last of His People* by David R. Collins, Kris Bergren

🛍 Local Outdoor Retailers:
Sports Nut, Chester, CA (530) 258–3327 • **Mountain Impact,** Chico, CA (530) 894–1596 • **Big 5 Sporting Goods,** Chico, CA (530) 891–1545 • **Chico Sports Ltd.,** Chico, CA (530) 894–1110 • **Copeland Sports,** Chico, CA (530) 894–5366 • **K Shot,** Chico, CA (530) 342–1691 • **Mountain Sports,** Chico, CA (530) 345–5011 • **Play It Again Sports,** Chico, CA (530) 345–7427 • **Royal's Team Sports,** Chico, CA (530) 894–8592 • **Paradise Sporting Goods,** Paradise, CA (530) 877–5114 • **Sport Wild Sporting Goods,** Red Bluff, CA (530) 527–3225 • **Tops Mini Mart,** Red Bluff, CA (530) 527–1859

🅝 Maps:
USGS maps: Panther Spring, CA; Barkley Mountain, CA

Honorable Mentions

Lava Land

Compiled here is an index of great hikes in the Lava Land region that didn't make the A-list this time around but deserve recognition. Check them out and let us know what you think. You may decide that one or more of these hikes deserves higher status in future editions or, perhaps, you may have a hike of your own that merits some attention.

(1) Captain Jack's Stronghold

At the north end of Lava Beds National Monument lies a jumble of volcanic ramparts and trenches that were effectively used as a fortress in 1870s by the Modoc Indians during a battle with the U.S. Army. (See *Captain Jack & the Modocs* on page 208.) The trail begins at the Captain Jack's Stronghold parking lot and runs two concentric loops through the historic site. The outer loop is 1.5 miles and the inner, shorter loop is 0.5 miles. For more information contact: Lava Beds National Monument, Tulelake, CA (530) 667–2282. *DeLorme: Northern California Atlas & Gazetteer:* Page 28 B2

(J) Highgrade National Recreation Trail

A six- to eight-mile out-and-back hike, depending on the turnaround point. From the trailhead high above Goose Lake in the Warner Mountains, the trail traverses the wind-blown bald hills that were the scene of a minor gold rush in the late 1880s. Great views of the Goose Lake basin to the west and the Great Basin to the east. From Alturas, head north 32 miles on CA 395. Turn right onto FS 30 and go 2.2 miles, turning left after the third cow gate. Drive north 1.5 miles on this road, and turn right onto the paved FS 9. Drive 0.7 miles until just past Buck Creek Station and turn left onto FS 47N72, following it seven miles to the Highgrade Trail trailhead. The trail starts on the left berm above a bend in the road. For more information contact: Modoc National Forest, Alturas, CA (916) 233-5811. **DeLorme: Northern California Atlas & Gazetteer:** Page 31 A6

(K) Tamarack Trail

An easy 6.0-mile loop through the boggy marshes and scattered lakes of the Thousand Lakes Wilderness. From the Tamarack Trail trailhead, the trail leads to Barrett Lake and several small water bodies, then circles back past larger Lake Eiler and Eiler Butte, before returning to the trailhead. To get to the trailhead from Redding, head east on CA 44 for 46 miles to the junction with CA 89. Continue north on CA 44/89 another 14 miles to the town of Old Station, where CA 44 turns east toward Susanville. Continue north on CA 89 another seven miles and turn left onto the graveled FS 33N25. Follow this road 6.4 miles, following wilderness signs to the trailhead. For more information contact: Hat Creek Ranger District, Fall River Mills, CA (530) 336-5521. **DeLorme: Northern California Atlas & Gazetteer:** Page 48 C2

Sierra Nevada & Gold Country

Sierra Nevada & Gold Country

The Hikes

Monroe Ridge **41.**
Hardrock Trail **42.**
Independence Trail **43.**
Feather Falls **44.**
Mount Judah Loop **45.**
Rubicon Trail **46.**
Mount Tallac **47.**
Woods Lake Loop **48.**
Bull Run Lake **49.**
South Grove Trail **50.**

Honorable Mentions

L. Western States Pioneer Express Trail
M. Waterfall Trail (at Grover Hot Springs)

Sierra Nevada & Gold Country

The high granite peaks of the Sierra Nevada have a reputation as a mecca for hikers—and deservedly so. Here nature has uplifted a block of the earth's crust, carved deep valleys with rivers, polished it into round and pleasing shapes, carpeted it with vast forests and soft meadows, and filled it with all sorts of interesting critters. A large portion of this wonderland is preserved in federally protected wilderness areas, and accessed by roads and highways traversing the range from east to west via major passes. Many of these routes can be traced back to emigrant routes used by European-American settlers in the 19th Century, and to Native American footpaths earlier still. The most-traveled pass in the Sierra Nevada is Donner Pass, near the town of Truckee, traversed by several lanes of Interstate 80 on its way to Sacramento and the Bay Area. The shores of Donner Lake were the scene of the infamous Donner Tragedy of 1846–1847.

This section covers the Sierra Nevada from the Carson-Iceberg Wilderness—just south of California 4—north to where the Sierra Nevada gives way to the volcanic Cascade Range, roughly using the North Fork of the Feather River as a boundary. Near the center of all this, on the eastern side of the range, is Lake Tahoe—itself a mecca for all sorts of outdoor recreation. Desolation Wilderness, west of Lake Tahoe, is one of the most popular wilderness areas in the state. Add to that a patchwork of public lands, like Plumas, Tahoe, Eldorado, Stanislaus, and Toiyabe national forests and several state parks—and you have countless alternatives in this region.

Gold Country is the term generally used to describe the western foothills and low-lands of the Sierra Nevada, characterized by rolling oak-covered hills and broad river valleys. Angel's Camp, Placerville, Auburn, and Grass Valley are some of the Gold Country towns that can trace their history back to the Rush of 1849, following the discovery of gold at Sutter's Mill on the South Fork of the American River. Several state parks highlight this history, as well as that of local Native American tribes.

Overview

Monroe Ridge Trail

Coloma, which now lies mostly within Marshall Gold Discovery State Park, was the epicenter of the California Gold Rush during the mid 1800s. It's clear from the outset of the hike—which starts at a monument to gold-discoverer James Marshall—that this area was not passed over by the Gold Rush. The Monroe Ridge Trail continues on a loop through oak forests and overgrown orchards belonging to the Monroe family, one of California's unsung African-American pioneer families. And at the halfway point, the trail passes through the historic town center. *(See page 280.)*

Hardrock Trail

Over six million ounces of gold were removed from these hills during the 100 years the mines were in operation. A walk through the park along the two-mile Hardrock Trail takes you by mines, machinery, and buildings connected with hard-rock gold mining. The trail also highlights a nice bit of Sierra-foothill scenery. *(See page 286.)*

Independence Trail

This region's South Yuba River Project is a California state park in the making, slowly taking shape out of independently owned public and private lands. The wide trails remain nearly flat, despite the steepness of the surrounding mountains—making this hike perfectly wheelchair accessible. The Independence Trail follows the course of the defunct Excelsior Canal, built in 1859 to carry water to a gold-mining operation 25 miles away.

Old mine artifacts have been impressively rebuilt into trail structures, including several wooden flumes that now serve as pedestrian bridges. Possibilities exist for longer hikes. *(See page 292.)*

Feather Falls

The spectacular Feather Falls is the sixth-tallest waterfall in the United States. The best time to view it is in the springtime, when the water is high due to snowmelt. On the return loop, the trail passes a large, flat rock with several conical depressions in its surface. In by-gone days, Native Americans used these depressions as mortars to grind acorns. *(See page 296.)*

Mount Judah Loop Trail

The Mount Judah Loop follows a section of the Pacific Crest Trail that traverses the Sierra Nevada range north and south of Donner Pass. From the summit, there are excellent views of the mountains and valleys that lie on either side of the pass. The region got its name from the infamous Donner Party, who was trapped by snowstorms while attempting to cross the mountains late in the winter of 1846–1847. *(See page 302.)*

Rubicon Trail

This is an inspiring hike along the tree-and-granite shores of Lake Tahoe, the largest alpine lake in the United States. From D.L. Bliss State Park, the trail heads south to Emerald Bay and Vikingsholm, a summer home built for industry-heiress Lora J. Knight in the style of a Scandinavian chieftain's house. The trail offers a glimpse of Lake Tahoe in its natural state—unfettered by vacation homes and boat docks—and presents hikers with the rare opportunity to be alone on the shores of the Lake of the Sky. *(See page 308.)*

Mount Tallac Trail

This hike is a strenuous jaunt up steep, rocky trails to the ragged peak of Mount Tallac—9,735 feet above sea level and a good 3,500 feet above nearby Lake Tahoe. The summit rewards hikers with a stunning aerial view of the entire Lake Tahoe basin on one side. In the opposite direction, Desolation Wilderness and Sierra Nevada spread out in an amazing panorama. Be sure to come prepared for sudden changes in climate, as weather can be unpredictable at the summit. And if you're coming from lower elevations, consider acclimatizing for a few days before taking this hike to avoid altitude sickness. *(See page 314.)*

Woods Lake Loop

The Woods Lake Loop explores an alpine basin in the High Sierras near Carson Pass, named for famous explorer and scout Kit Carson. From the Woods Lake campground, the trail follows a mild grade up into the Mokelumne Wilderness and stops off at the pristine Winnemucca and Round Top lakes. Observe the wide vistas across the mostly treeless landscape before returning to the campground via a steeper route. *(See page 320.)*

Bull Run Lake Trail

This hike visits the meadows and glacier-polished bedrock of the western Sierra Nevada. The trail ends at the gorgeously situated Bull Run Lake, backed by granite cliffs and complete with a rock island. The trail is short enough to do as a day hike, but the lake is a wonderful place to spend a night. *(See page 326.)*

South Grove Trail

One of only 75 remaining groves of giant sequoia, the South Grove of Calaveras Big Trees State Park is a truly inspiring sight. This loop trail passes through previously logged-over land to reach a stand of the park's largest trees. A side trip will take you to the Agassiz Tree, the largest sequoia in the park and one of the world's top 10 biggest trees. An interpretive guide is available from the visitor center, with names and information about individual trees along the trail. *(See page 332.)*

Monroe Ridge Trail

Hike Specs

Start: From the Marshall Monument parking area
Length: 3.4-mile loop
Approximate Hiking Time: 1.5–2 hours
Difficulty Rating: Easy to Moderate due to some steep sections
Terrain: Dirt path and some paved road through oak forests and over tall, rolling hills
Elevation Gain: 737 feet
Land Status: State park
Nearest Town: Coloma, CA
Other Trail Users: Hikers only
Canine Compatibility: Dogs not permitted

Getting There

From Placerville: Head north about seven miles on CA 49 to the tiny town of Coloma. As the highway enters town, it turns right onto Sacramento Street. At this point, turn left onto Cold Springs Road, then right 0.1 miles later, onto Monument Road (CA 153). Follow Monument Road for 0.4 miles, up to the Marshall Monument parking area. The trail starts just before the parking lot, where a small park road heads up the hill behind a locked gate. *DeLorme: Northern California Atlas & Gazetteer:* Page 87 B7

The obvious purpose of Marshall Gold Discovery State Park is to commemorate James Marshall's fateful gold find in 1848. Marshall, then a carpenter working on John Sutter's new mill, found a few bits of gleaming yellow metal while he was inspecting the construction site. That innocent discovery set off a series of events that changed the course of American history. Marshall's tale has been told often and well. But there is another story in Coloma, and it has even more to do with this hike than does Marshall's famous find.

The story of the Monroe family begins in 1849 with an African-American woman named Nancy Gooch, who was brought to California as a slave. At that time, during the height of the Gold Rush, California was still an unorganized territory, and slavery was neither specifically legal nor illegal. Local sentiment, however, was another matter, and Gooch's master soon was pressured into granting her freedom. She found a job working as a laundress for busy gold miners and eventually scraped together the $700 needed to buy the freedom of her son, Andrew Monroe, and his wife, Sara, who were slaves in Missouri. The Monroes arrived in California via covered wagon with little but their freedom. Andrew soon increased his family's holdings to about 80 acres, which included Sutter's Mill, the site of Marshall's gold discovery. The family stayed on the land until the 1940s, when it was sold to the state for use as a park. Andrew's son, Jim—Nancy's grandson—lived on the land until 1988, when he passed away at the age of 99.

The history of African-Americans in California is a rarely told, but fascinating story. Prior to the Gold Rush and the establishment of California as a state, there were no more than a handful of black Californians. With the onslaught of the Gold

Bedrock mortar, once used by Native Americans to grind acorns.

Rush, however, free African-Americans were drawn to the state along with thousands of people from all over the world. In 1850, a census counted 962 "persons of color" in California. By 1860, there were 4,086. Most of these black pioneers settled in gold country, around the Middle Fork of the American River. Few of these early black settlers became famous, but one exception was mountain man Jim Beckwourth, who pioneered an emigrant trail over one of the Sierra Nevada's lowest passes—near present-day California 70.

In 1850, California was admitted to the union as a free state, but the trials were far from over for the area's black settlers. Nancy Gooch was lucky in that local sentiment in 1849 had been in her favor. But with so many settlers pouring into the state, popular opinion again shifted. In 1852, a version of the Fugitive Slave Law was passed, condemning escaped slaves to prison. And in the previous year, legislation

MilesDirections

0.0 START at Monroe Ridge Trail trailhead, located just before the Marshall Monument parking lot on the uphill side of Monument Road. Head up the road behind the gate.

0.1 The trail passes the old Monroe spring house on the left. At this point, the road turns to dirt path and switchbacks up the hill.

0.9 Reach Monroe Summit. There are great views from here of the surrounding country. Picnic tables provide seating for a leisurely lunch.

1.2 A deep hole has been dug in the ground to the right, now surrounded by a fence to protect hikers. *[FYI. This is an old gold mine test pit, dug by a member of the Monroe family.]*

1.4 Fire Road heads downhill to the right. Continue straight along the ridge.

1.7 Another picnic table offers a chance to rest and enjoy the views from the ridge.

1.9 The trail reaches its northernmost point, offering views of the South Fork American

River valley below, before turning a sharp right and heading downhill through dense forest.

2.2 The trail crosses an old diversion ditch, once used for mining and irrigation purposes.

2.3 The Monroe Ridge Trail joins the gravel Fire Road. Continue downhill on the Fire Road.

2.4 Turn right onto the shoulder of CA 49 and follow the road past a row of houses.

2.6 The trail turns toward the forest again, aiming for the Indian bedrock mortar, visible on the edge of the forest to the right. Turn left behind the rock, and head south.

2.7 Just before the picnic area, turn right onto Monument Trail, and begin climbing uphill via a series of wooden steps and switchbacks.

3.1 The trail crosses the same old diversion ditch as it climbs to the Marshall Monument.

3.4 Arrive back at the Marshall Monument parking area.

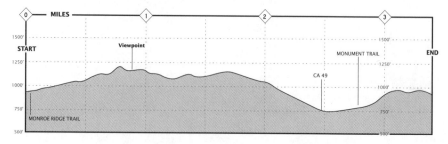

was passed prohibiting people with more than one-half Negro blood from testifying against a white person in court.

The fight for civil rights began almost immediately with the formation of the Franchise League of San Francisco, which petitioned the state assembly to repeal these laws. The league won its battle in 1862—but not before hundreds of black Californians had accepted an invitation from the Canadian government in 1858 and moved to British Columbia.

Until they gained the freedom to testify, African-Americans had to fight their legal battles through white friends. But this did not stop them from fighting. Biddy Mason, a woman enslaved to a visiting Texan was set free in a landmark 1856 trial and lived out her years as a prominent citizen in Los Angeles. In a similar case the following year, Archey Lee won his freedom with a defense that was financed by 4,000 free African-Americans. The freedom movement began in earnest once blacks were allowed to testify in court. During this time, Mary Ellen Pleasant—known as the *mother* of civil rights in California—was one of the most prominent civil rights activists. By the turn of the century, black Californians were doing better than their

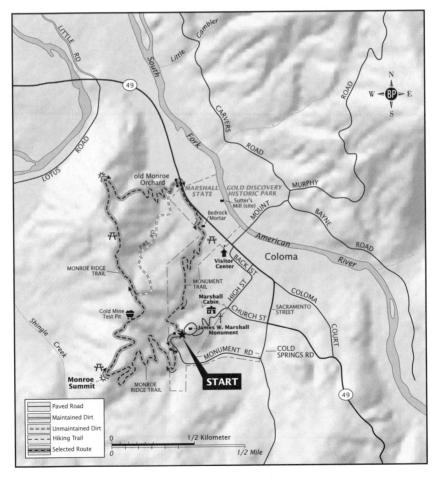

counterparts back East. They could serve as jurors and hold public office, but as in other parts of the country, such victories proved fleeting and difficult to maintain.

The Monroe Ridge Trail encircles the homestead of the Monroe family, passing by several spots where reminders of that era can still be seen. The hike starts on a hill overlooking the town near the James Marshall Monument and gravesite. The path winds down through the dense oak forest past an old irrigation ditch to the center of historic Coloma. Heading north along the road for a short distance, the trail once again climbs into the forest—this time through part of the old Monroe orchard. The path climbs to the ridge, offering an impressive view of the river and the rolling hills of gold country. From here you follow the ridge south to another vista point, returning at last to the parking lot below the monument. A brochure is available from the visitor center that explains some of the historic sites along the trail and tells a little more of the Monroe story.

Hike Information

📞 Trail Contacts:

Marshall Gold Discovery State Historic Park, Coloma, CA (530) 622–3470 or *www.windjammer.net/coloma*

🕐 Schedule:

Open year-round, 8 A.M. to sunset. Museum is open daily, 10 A.M.–5 P.M.

💲 Fees/Permits:

$2 day-use fee, payable at the visitor center

❓ Local Information:

Town of Coloma-Lotus website: *www.coloma.com* • **Town of Placerville,** CA (530) 642–5200 or *www.ci. placerville.ca.us*

❗ Local Events/Attractions:

Gold Discovery Day, in January, Coloma, CA – *Living history, gold panning, food and music. Call park for information* • **Coloma Fest,** in June, Coloma, CA – *Speakers, tours, living history, and music. Call park for information.*

🎒 Organizations:

Gold Discovery Park Association, Coloma, CA (530) 622–6198

🔖 Other Resources:

California African-American Museum website: *www.caam.ca.gov*

🏪 Local Outdoor Retailers:

Auburn Outdoor Sports, Auburn, CA (530) 885–9200 • **Big 5 Sporting Goods** Auburn, CA(530) 887–8326 • **Sierra Mountain Sports,** Auburn, CA (530) 887–8636 • **Adventure Sports,** Carmichael, CA (916) 971–1800 • **Copeland Sports,** Carmichael, CA (916) 971–0802 • **Big 5 Sporting Goods,** North Highlands, CA (916) 332–6511 • **Big 5 Sporting Goods,** Placerville, CA (530) 295–8290 • **Mountain & Surf Pro Shop,** Placerville, CA (530) 622–3034 • **Raymond's Liquor & Sporting,** Placerville, CA (530) 622–3606 • **Adventure Sports,** Sacramento, CA (916) 971–1800 • **All American Sports Fan,** Sacramento, CA (916) 442–5066 • **Athletics Unlimited,** Sacramento, CA (916) 483–2352 • **Big 5 Sporting Goods,** Sacramento, CA (916) 427–0978 or (916) 488–5060 • **Champs Sports,** Sacramento, CA (916) 393–4482 or (916) 921–1139 • **Copeland's Sports,** Sacramento, CA (916) 429–9199 • **Peak Adventures,** Sacramento, CA (916) 278–6321 • **Sierra Outfitters,** Sacramento, CA (916) 922–7500

🗺 Maps:

USGS maps: Coloma, CA

Hardrock Trail

Hike Specs

Start: From the Hardrock Trail trailhead
Length: 2.4-mile loop
Approximate Hiking Time: 1.5 hours
Difficulty Rating: Easy due to low elevation gain and smooth trail
Terrain: Gravel road and dirt path through conifer-forested Sierra Nevada foothills
Elevation Gain: 246 feet
Land Status: State park
Nearest Town: Grass Valley, CA
Other Trail Users: Equestrians and cyclists
Canine Compatibility: Leashed dogs permitted

Getting There

From Sacramento: Drive east about 33 miles on I-80 to the town of Auburn. Turn north onto CA 49 and continue 24 miles before exiting at Empire Street in Grass Valley. Follow Empire Street east 1.8 miles and park at the Empire Mine State Historic Park lot. The trailhead is a few yards inside the massive wooden gate, reached via the visitor center in the low building to the right. *DeLorme: Northern California Atlas & Gazetteer:* Page 79 C6

Tucked into the rough folds of the Sierra Nevada foothills, the Empire Mine represented the most successful chapter of Californian gold mining history. Unlike most of the crusty 49ers who saw the *easy* gold dry up soon after arriving on the scene, miners at the Empire continued to extract the precious metal for more than 100 years. What made the Empire so much more successful? Technique. Most of the 49ers used placer mining in an effort to find *free* gold deposits lying loose in sediments. The stereotypical old geezer in dusty overalls crouching by a stream with a gold-sifting pan is one example of this type of mining, as are more complex sluice-and-rocker and hydraulic techniques. Hardrock deposits—like those found at the Empire—are more extensive and sometimes contain huge amounts of gold. But the metal is mixed in with mineral deposits underground and requires enormous amounts of labor and equipment to remove. Since individuals did not have the resources needed to mine the hard-rock deposits, large mining companies were formed soon after the initial, *easy* gold rush ended.

The hike begins inside the massive wooden gate that marks the entrance to the mine yard, just past the visitor center. The mine yard is full of rusting iron machine-hulks—evidence of the difficulties involved in separating gold from ore after it was brought to the surface. Amidst the battered old buildings of the mine is the remaining lower half of the old headframe. This towering structure was used to house the pulleys and cables that brought ore and miners up from the depths of the mine. Unfortunately, the headframe was deemed a safety hazard and partially torn down in 1969. Heading south, the trail passes by the ruins of several mine facilities. Be sure to check out the foundations on the left; they mark the location of the stamp mills, where ore once was crushed 24 hours a day. During its heyday, the Empire Mine kept

scores of stamps—some weighing 1,750 pounds apiece—running around-the-clock and creating a hellish racket that was audible for miles.

Farther up on the right side of the trail are the remains of the old cyanide plant, which stands as a reminder of gold mining's ecological dark side. In this plant, crushed ore was combined with mercury and the amalgam was put into vats filled with a cyanide solution. The mixture dissolved the gold out of the amalgam, at which point zinc dust was added to the vat to precipitate out the gold. While this method improved production by 40 percent, it also resulted in toxic waste tailings being dumped on the other side of the cyanide plant. Those seven acres of land are now off-limits to visitors, due to high levels of lead, arsenic, and mercury. The park is currently developing plans to clean up the waste and rid the area of these environmental hazards.

Over the years, several surrounding gold mines were bought out and incorporated into the Empire—called the Empire-Star Mines Company after merging with the

Stamps used to crush ore.

North Star Mine—and relics of these smaller mines can be seen along the trail as it continues its loop around the park. Some, like the Orleans and North Star mines, were the Empire's intense rivals before being absorbed. The North Star Mine even tried to sue the Empire for underground trespassing in 1908.

The WYOD Loop Trail, which connects to the Hardrock Trail, leads to one of the least successful mines in the area. Its name stands for "Work Your Own Diggings" Mine. The mine was unique in leasing out mine sections to independent operators, who could work their portions as they saw fit. Unfortunately, the WYOD buildings were plagued by fires and had been abandoned by the time the Empire took control.

All told, the Empire Mine removed an estimated 5.8 million ounces of gold from the cold, hard rock under these hills. And the deepest of its 367 miles of shafts reached down nearly a vertical mile below the surface. At its peak just before World War II, the mines employed over 800 employees, most of them second- and third-generation Cornish emigrants.

MilesDirections

0.0 START at the Hardrock Trail trailhead, just inside the main gate. Head south past the ore stamps on Hardrock Trail.

0.2 Cyanide works (ruins) on the right. *[Note. The tailings below to the right are still toxic, and have yet to be dealt with. This area is obviously off-limits to hikers, so stay on the trail.]*

0.3 The trail passes the site of the Orleans Stamp Mill. Little remains of it now. Just before the locked gate blocking the road, follow Hardrock Trail as it veers right, heading west.

0.4 Osborn Hill Trail heads left. Continue straight.

1.1 An unnamed trail continues straight, toward a residential area. Turn right, still following Hardrock Trail.

1.2 The south end of WYOD Loop heads right. Continue straight.

1.4 Stacey Lane Trail goes left. At this point you can view WYOD mine to the right. Continue straight.

1.5 The north end of WYOD Loop heads back to the right. Continue straight on Hardrock Trail.

1.6 The trail reaches the Penn Gate parking lot. Just before the parking lot, a trail heads right at a sign for the visitor center. Turn right onto that trail, which is named Empire Street Trail.

1.9 WYOD Loop Alternate heads right, connecting Empire Street Trail with WYOD Loop.

2.4 The trail reaches the visitor center and the end of the hike.

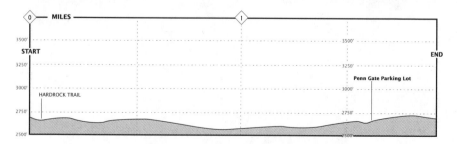

Cornish miners, who were well respected for their experience in the hard-rock tin and copper mines of Britain, began emigrating to California around 1870 when hard-rock gold mining began in earnest. These miners brought special skills and knowledge with them, including the technology to remove ground water from the shafts that allowed deeper mining and exploration. This and other Cornish innovations greatly benefited the mining industry.

As with any group of immigrants, the Cornish brought much of their culture with them—including their traditional miners' lunch pails, which were filled with warm tea, saffron buns, and the indispensable Cornish pasty. The immigration was so thorough that the population in some towns was 75 percent Cornish. Even today, traces of this Cornish past can be seen throughout the region.

The trail ends back at the visitor center, which is housed near the former mine owner's cottage in the carriage house. The "cottage" of the Empire Mine's most prominent owner, William Bourn Jr., has been restored to its 1905 appearance and is now used as a living history museum. The house is surrounded by extensive English-style gardens that are maintained by park staff to be true to the mine's glory days, when Bourn and mine director George Starr used to entertain guests there.

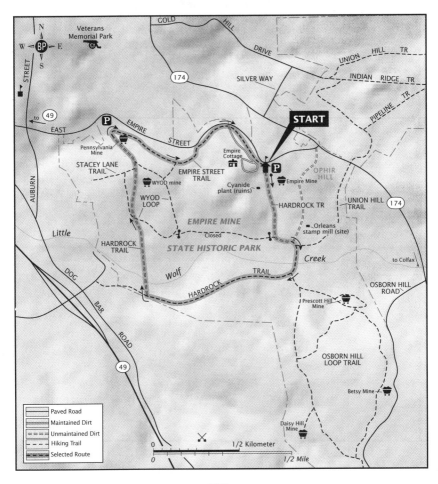

Stamp mill foundations at the Empire Mine.

Ore cars.

Hike Information

Trail Contacts:
Empire Mine State Historic Park, Grass Valley, CA (530) 273–8522 or www.cal-parks.ca.gov

Schedule:
Open year round, but call for seasonal hours

Fees/Permits:
$2 entrance fee

Local Information:
Grass Valley-Nevada County Chamber of Commerce, Grass Valley, CA (530) 273–4667 • **Local websites:** *www.coolspots.com/ca/nev/cool0298. html* or *www.ncgold.com/goldrush-town/empiremine.html*

Local Events/Attractions:
Cornish Christmas Celebration, every Friday for the few weeks before Christmas, Grass Valley, CA – *music and food in historic downtown*

Accommodations:
There are numerous private hotels and campgrounds in Grass Valley and the vicinity.

Hike Tours:
Empire Mine State Historic Park, Grass Valley, CA – *Docent-led tours of the mining facilities and historic buildings are given during the season. See visitor center for more information.*

Local Outdoor Retailers:
Auburn Outdoor Sports, Auburn, CA (530) 885–9200 • **Batter's Box,** Auburn, CA (530) 823–1919 • **Big 5 Sporting Goods,** Auburn, CA (530) 887–8326 • **All American Sporting Goods,** Grass Valley, CA (530) 274–1652 • **Free Flight Sports,** Grass Valley, CA (530) 272–7790 • **Sports Fever,** Grass Valley, CA (530) 477–8006

Maps:
USGS maps: Grass Valley, CA

Independence Trail

Hike Specs

Start: From the Independence Trail trailhead
Length: 4.2-mile out-and-back
Approximate Hiking Time: 2 hours
Difficulty Rating: Easy due to very little elevation gain and a level, well made trail
Terrain: Dirt path and wooden walkway through mixed conifer-oak woodlands and a deep river valley
Elevation Gain: 726 feet
Land Status: State park and national forest
Nearest Town: Nevada City, CA
Other Trail Users: Hiker only
Canine Compatibility: Leashed dogs permitted

Getting There

From Sacramento: Take I-80 east 33 miles to the city of Auburn. Exit onto CA 49 and head north 30 miles to Nevada City. Follow signs for CA 49 through town, and continue on this highway another 5.5 miles north of Nevada City. The Independence Trail trailhead is a long turnout with parking on both sides of the highway, about 0.5 miles before the South Yuba River Bridge. The hike starts on the right (east) side of the highway, at the bulletin board • **Public Transportation:** From Nevada City, take Gold Country Stage bus No.10 to the Independence Trail trailhead. For more information call Gold Country Stage (530) 477–0103 or visit *www.co.nevada.ca.us/ gcstage.* Amtrak train-to-bus connections are available in Nevada City from Sacramento and the Bay Area. *DeLorme: Northern California Atlas & Gazetteer:* Page 79 B6

T he Independence Trail provides something that is in very short supply in the North Sierra—a level hike with practically no elevation change. The trail's builders managed to keep the walk level in spite of a steep, rugged landscape that would normally require a prohibitive amount of labor and expense. But the engineers had help. The trail clings to the side of the steep-walled South Yuba River Valley, perched high above the river and following the path of the historic Excelsior Mining Ditch. Throngs of miners blazed this trail, their labors fueled by the lust for gold and the desire to be filthy rich. In the end they were all filthy, but few ever got rich.

After James Marshall discovered gold in 1848 at Sutter's Mill, miners poured into California to scour the Sierra rivers and tributaries for the precious ore. Almost 90 percent of the gold recovered in California was found quickly using gold-panning and rocker methods. But the as-yet unsuccessful fortune-seekers refused to give up, consolidating claims to form large mining companies and devising new ways to separate

the gold from the ground. At the height of the Gold Rush, ditches like the Excelsior were built all over the Sierra and used for hydraulic mining, which requires a great deal of water under high pressure. Each ditch would divert water from a high source, usually many miles from where it was needed, and bring it as close to the mine as possible. The ditches then fed the water into pipes, called *penstocks*, which dropped rapidly to the active mining sites—known as *diggins*. All the while, this process built pressure in the pipes. The penstocks forced the torrents into water cannons, called *monitors*, which were used to blast away at hillsides—washing rocks, soil, and any-

Hike Information

Trail Contacts:
South Yuba River State Park, Penn Valley, CA (530) 432–2546 or (530) 273–3884 or *www.ncgold.com/Museums_Parks/syrp/htm*

Schedule:
Open year round

Fees/Permits:
No fees or permits required

Local Information:
Grass Valley-Nevada County Chamber of Commerce, Grass Valley, CA (530) 273–4667 • **Local websites:** *www.coolspots.com/ca/nev/cool0298. html* or *www.ncgold.com/goldrushtown/ empiremine.html*

Local Events/Attractions:
Cornish Christmas Celebration, every Friday for the few weeks before Christmas, Grass Valley, CA – *music and food in historic downtown* • **South Yuba River State Park:** *Check out the park's bridges and historical sites.*

Accommodations:
There are numerous private hotels and campgrounds in Grass Valley and the vicinity.

Organizations:
Sequoya Challenge, Grass Valley, CA (916) 265–9398

Public Transportation:
Gold Country Stage: (530) 477–0103 or *www.co.nevada.ca.us/gcstage – bus service*

Local Outdoor Retailers:
Auburn Outdoor Sports, Auburn, CA (530) 885–9200 • **Batter's Box,** Auburn, CA (530) 823–1919 • **Big 5 Sporting Goods,** Auburn, CA (530) 887–8326 • **Sierra Mountain Sports,** Auburn, CA (530) 887–8636 • **All American Sporting Goods,** Grass Valley, CA (530) 274–1652 • **Free Flight Sports,** Grass Valley, CA (530) 272–7790 • **Sports Fever,** Grass Valley, CA (530) 477–8006 • **Wolf Creek Wilderness,** Grass Valley, CA (530) 265–9653

Maps:
USGS maps: Nevada City, CA

thing else in the way out through sluice boxes, where the heavier gold collected in riffles on the bottom.

The method was effective, but it was also very destructive to the environment. Not only were entire hillsides washed away, but the increased sediment in streams and rivers wreaked havoc downstream. Sacramento suffered several major floods, and the San Francisco Bay was partially filled with sediment before hydraulic mining finally was outlawed.

The Excelsior Ditch was long since abandoned when modern day trail planners noticed it was long, flat, and wide enough for wheelchairs. Thus the idea for the Independence Trail was born. Thanks to the recent efforts of South Yuba River Project employees and volunteers, the former mining and irrigation ditch has been transformed into a wheelchair-accessible trail. Several of the timber-framed wooden flumes that once carried water over deep ravines have been rebuilt as pedestrian bridges that are complimented by wooden walkways and viewing platforms spread out along the trail.

The South Yuba River Project is a patchwork of state and federally owned land stretching across a 20-mile span of the South Yuba River. The park encompasses several historic sites and structures, including the Bridgeport Mining Camp, the 600-foot

MilesDirections

0.0 START at the Independence Trail trailhead. At the bulletin board, follow the Independence Trail as it turns left, heading past the restroom along the path of an abandoned mining ditch.

0.1 A trail crosses a reconstructed wooden trestle. The highway is visible below to the left.

0.3 At this point is a wooden-plank observation deck overlooking the South Yuba River Canyon.

0.7 The trail crosses a particularly long and high trestle. This one is about 40 feet up and 100 feet long.

0.8 The trail crosses another trestle and passes under overhanging rocks.

0.9 *[FYI. The picnic table on the right is a good place to have lunch or a snack.]* A little wood-

en sluice carries water under the trail here.

1.3 The trees open up at this point, offering a view of the river, far below. Also visible are the present South Yuba River Bridge and, upriver, the bridge that preceded it (now decommissioned).

1.5 The trail spans another gap via a reconstructed trestle.

1.7 *[FYI. Another picnic table presents itself on the right.]*

2.1 A dirt jeep trail crosses the path. This is the turnaround point for this hike. Return the way you came.

4.2 Arrive back at the trailhead.

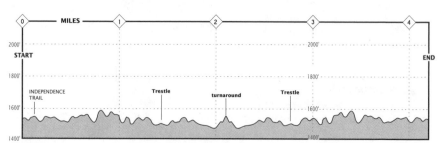

Miner's Tunnel, the 8,000-foot North Bloomfield Drain Tunnel, and the Purdon Crossing Bridge, all of which date to the late 19th Century. One of the highlights of the trail is the venerable Bridgeport Covered Bridge, located about six miles downstream from the trailhead. The 251-foot bridge is thought to be the longest single-span covered bridge in the world—and it was built in 1862, which makes the record even more impressive.

The story of the South Yuba River Project dates back to 1978, when the California Department of Parks & Recreation (DPR) began purchasing property near Jones Bar for a new state park. The DPR acquired the Bridgeport Ranch in 1986 from the non-profit organization Sequoya Challenge, which had purchased it the previous year. Other land for the fledgling state park was supposed to come from the Bureau of Land Management (BLM), but the BLM changed its mind in the mid 1990s. Now there's a complex system of joint management of South Yuba River public lands that involves the DPR, BLM, and Sequoya Challenge.

The hike starts about half a mile south of the South Yuba River Bridge on California 49, where there is a small parking lot and restroom. The profile of the old ditch is still obvious, and the trail follows the canal bed's sweeping curves around the contours of the hillside. At several spots along the trail, the trees open up to reveal excellent views of the valley and the river below. And the reconstructed flumes are now bridges that span rocky gaps. The trail remains easy until it reaches the state park's boundary. That's where the maintained portion of the trail ends. The turn-around point for this hike arrives shortly thereafter, at the junction where a dirt jeep trail intersects the path.

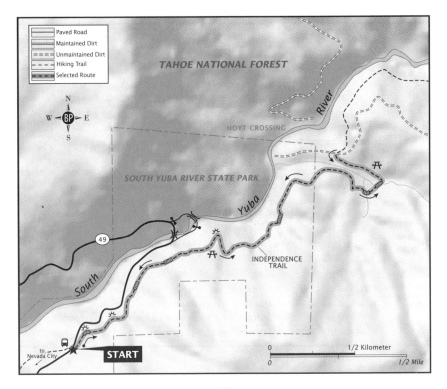

Feather Falls

Hike Specs

Start: From the Feather Falls National Recreation Trail trailhead
Length: 8.4-mile loop
Approximate Hiking Time: 4–5 hours
Difficulty Rating: Easy to Moderate due to steep section near falls
Terrain: Dirt path through deep river canyon with dense forest and huge granite formations
Elevation Gain: 2,622 feet
Land Status: National forest
Nearest Town: Oroville, CA
Other Trail Users: Cyclists and equestrians
Canine Compatibility: Dogs permitted

Getting There

From Oroville: From Oroville Dam Boulevard, turn right onto Olive Highway (CA 162) and head east five miles. Turn right onto Forbestown Road and follow it another seven miles. Turn left onto Lumpkin Road, driving north 11.6 miles before turning left at the sign for the Feather Falls Trail trailhead. Follow this road 1.7 miles to the Feather Falls Parking Area. *DeLorme: Northern California Atlas & Gazetteer:* Page 69 D5

The main attraction of the Feather Falls National Recreation Trail is obviously the waterfall. At 640 feet, Feather Falls is the sixth-highest waterfall in the United States and the fourth-highest in California. The falls are at their most spectacular in the spring, when runoff from the melting winter snow pack is at its greatest. The trail divides into two possible routes shortly past the trailhead and rejoins below the falls, at which point the path becomes steep and rocky as it climbs the last quarter mile to an observation deck. From here—perched on a granite knob jutting out into the valley—you're nearly level with the top of the falls. This vantage point gives you a bird's-eye view of the stream as it plunges hundreds of feet to the base of the falls, which is hidden from view far below. The observation deck also affords an impressive view of the valley you just traversed.

There are at least three reasons, other than the falls, to visit during springtime. First of all, visiting in the spring allows hikers to miss the worst of the heat. Since the falls are relatively low in elevation, temperatures in the area commonly reach 90°F to 100°F on summer days. Coming in autumn would also solve that problem—and the crowds would be smaller—but you'd miss the bright display of regional wildflowers. The color show begins in March, peaks in April and May, and concludes as late as October with a few late-bloomers. Over 180 wildflower species provide splashes of color to the otherwise sedate forest scene along the trail. Some of the more showy species of flowering plants include the purple-pink shooting star, the bright red Indian paintbrush, the orange-yellow bush monkey-flower, and the crimson Clarkia. Less obvious—but still pleasant—are the yellow wood violet and the alum root. Also be on the lookout for wild ginger, a ground-hugging vine that hides its maroon flowers under large leaves.

Feather Falls.

In late spring and early summer, observant hikers can look forward to yet another seasonal spectacle on the Feather Falls Trail. Thousands of ladybugs swarm to the region each year to hibernate near Frey Creek. When the time is right, they all come out to play, filling the air and carpeting the forest floor. Any other insect present in these numbers would likely inspire horror, but the ladybugs create a sense of awe and wonder, especially when the sunlight illuminates their tiny, translucent wings.

If you're seeking a less seasonal point of interest, be sure to look for the outcropping of granite that bulges up from the forest floor beneath a gnarled old oak tree along the eastern branch of the trail. There are several holes in the top of the rock, each about six to eight inches in diameter and six to 10 inches deep. The holes are so random and weathered that they almost appear to be naturally formed. But in fact, they are grinding mortars that were formed over many years by women of the local

MilesDirections

0.0 START at the north end of the parking lot by the bathrooms.

0.4 At this point the Feather Falls National Recreation Trail forks, offering two routes to the falls. Take the right fork. (You'll eventually return to this spot via the left fork.)

1.4 The trail crosses a small creek via a wooden bridge.

1.9 At the next stream crossing (also with a wooden bridge), there is a small waterfall on the right, above the trail.

2.6 From here Bald Rock Dome is visible on the left. *[FYI. This landmark is very important in local native lore.]*

4.4 The return loop of the trail goes straight. Turn right, and follow the trail up several switchbacks to the falls overlook.

4.7 The trail levels out, and the top of Feather Falls can be seen. Turn left onto the Overlook Trail and head down to the viewing platform.

4.8 At viewing platform, all but the lowest reaches of Feather Falls is visible, as well as a spectacular panorama of the valley downstream. Turn around and retrace your path to the junction with the return loop.

5.1 Back at the junction, turn right and continue via the return loop of the Feather Falls Trail.

6.5 At this point to the right, a closer view of Bald Rock Dome can be had.

7.0 The trail crosses Frey Creek via a 20-foot wooden bridge. *[FYI. In summer, ladybugs (a.k.a. ladybird beetles) can be found here in the thousands.]*

7.7 A short spur trail leads right to the grinding rock historic site. *[FYI. The bedrock mortars here were used by local Native Americans to grind acorns into meal.]*

8.0 The return loop returns to the original junction. Continue straight along the first part of the trail to the trailhead.

8.4 Arrive back at the trailhead.

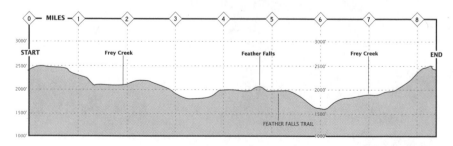

Maidu people, who used the rock to grind acorns into flour for soups and bread. Many sites in the area are still sacred to the Maidu, especially Bald Rock Dome, which is visible from several points along the hike. According to the Maidu, this mountainous area was created by Worldmaker after a great flood. The region was supposed to be perfect, but the malicious Coyote followed Worldmaker around, causing trouble and introducing death and suffering to the world. Another Maidu legend says the monster Uino makes his home here and protects the Middle Fork of the Feather River from his vantage point high atop Bald Rock.

The Maidu were once a very populous group, with a territory ranging over most of the northwestern Sierra Nevada. As with most California Indians, they had a varied diet and subsisted on gathered roots and plants, occasional game, and their dietary staple of acorns. They lived simply, sleeping in modest huts in the winter and preferring to stay outside in the summer. Storytellers were an important part of the culture, in charge of preserving and teaching the tribe's myths of creation and the adventures of gods and spirits that helped explain the world. The story of the Maidu is similar to the tale of most California Indian tribes: Their lives were devastated when waves of settlers flooded into their homeland, bringing potent new diseases, axes to fell the

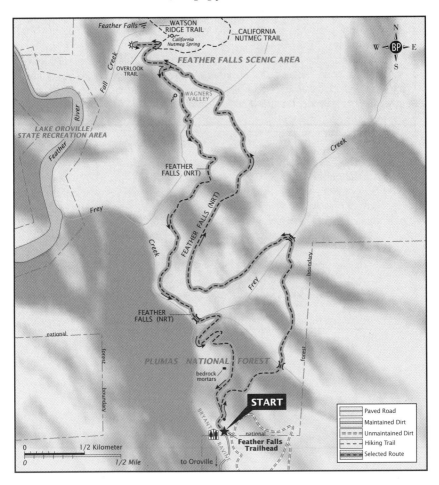

trees, and guns to get rid of the *diggers* (a derogatory nickname used by settlers to describe the local Native Americans, who often dug roots and tubers for food). By 1890, it was estimated that the native population had been reduced by up to 96 percent. Over 100 years later, the Maidu have recovered somewhat and maintain a strong presence in the area.

Cooking with Acorns

The extensive oak woodlands of Northern California have long provided Native Americans with a steady supply of food, and they in turn cared for the oak groves by carefully using fire to keep rival plants down and to control pests that might otherwise be attracted to rotting acorns.

Acorns are produced in staggering numbers every year, and are easily stored for extended periods of time, making them an excellent way to ensure a supply of food year round. Because of the strong tannins in the acorns, they're naturally resistant to rot, but this substance also makes them very bitter and unpalatable. California Indians solved this problem by shelling and pounding the acorns into meal—often in the bedrock mortars still found in rocky areas. They would then repeatedly pour hot water over the meal to leach out the tannins.

Once palatable, the acorn meal is then cooked with water to make a warm mush, combined with chopped meat in a stew, or formed into patties and baked or fried. Acorn meal can also be incorporated into modern recipes for bread, muffins, and pancakes by substituting half of the wheat or corn flour for acorn meal.

Some tips to remember when making acorn meal:

- *California Indians prefer acorns from valley oak, black oak, and tan oak (not a true oak, but close enough).*
- *Gather fallen acorns that still have the caps on (these are truly ripe, and are less likely to have worms).*
- *Discard any acorns with holes in the shell.*
- *After shelling, allow acorns to dry out completely before grinding to a fine meal.*
- *Place meal in a clean cloth and leach it thoroughly by pouring water over it several times. (Incidentally, the cloth will be stained from the tannins.)*

Cook, season to taste, and enjoy this traditional food!

Hike Information

📞 **Trail Contacts:**
Plumas National Forest, Feather River Ranger District, Oroville, CA (530) 534-6500

🕐 **Schedule:**
Open year round, but due to weather spring and fall are best times to visit

💲 **Fees/Permits:**
No fees or permits required

❓ **Local Information:**
Chico Chamber of Commerce, Chico, CA (530) 891-5556 or (800) 852-8570 or *www.chicochamber.com* • **City of Oroville website:** *www.oroville-city.com*

📍 **Local Events/Attractions:**
Salmon Festival, in September, Oroville, CA • **Fourth of July Fireworks,** at Lake Oroville, Oroville, CA

🎒 **Local Outdoor Retailers:**
Big 5 Sporting Goods, Chico, CA (530) 891-1545 • **Chico Sports Ltd,** Chico, CA (530) 894-1110 • **Copeland Sports,** Chico, CA (530) 894-5366 • **Dyer's Athletics,** Oroville, CA (530) 533-5405 • **In Step Shoes,** Chico, CA (530) 345-6311 • **K Shot,** Chico, CA (530) 342-1691 • **Mountain Sports,** Chico, CA (530) 345-5011 • **Play It Again Sports,** Chico, CA (530) 345-7427 • **Powell Fly Shop,** Chico, CA (530) 345-9983 • **Royal's Team Sports,** Chico, CA (530) 894-8592 • **Huntington's Sportsman's Store,** Oroville, CA (530) 534-8000 • **Paradise Sporting Goods,** Paradise, CA (530) 877-5114

🗺 **Maps:**
USGS maps: Brush Creek, CA; Forbestown, CA

Mount Judah Loop Trail

Hike Specs

Start: From the Pacific Crest Trail trailhead off I-80

Length: 12.9-mile out-and-back

Approximate Hiking Time: 6 hours

Difficulty Rating: Moderate due to good trail with some steep sections and high elevation

Terrain: Dirt path and a short stretch of gravel road through a landscape of High Sierra granite and trees

Elevation Gain: 2,745 feet

Land Status: National forest

Nearest Town: Truckee, CA

Other Trail Users: Equestrians

Canine Compatibility: Dogs permitted

Getting There

From Truckee: Head west 8.5 miles on I-80 and take the Castle Peak exit. Turn left, crossing under the two interstate overpasses, and turn left again at the T-intersection. Follow this road 0.25 miles to its end at the Pacific Crest Trailhead. The trail begins at the east end of the parking lot. *DeLorme: Northern California Atlas & Gazetteer:* Page 81 B5

The Sierra Nevada range has long served as the last barrier to the Golden State. For early Spanish missionaries, and later Mexican colonists, the mountains were seen as a wall that would keep land-hungry gringo settlers at bay for centuries. Those predictions underestimated the determination of American settlers, however, and by the 1820s, Anglo fur trappers like Peter Ogden and Jedediah Smith began traversing the range in search of adventure and beaver pelts. It was not long before settlers started making the rigorous journey. In 1841, the Bidwell-Bartleson emigrant party crossed the range at a spot between the Walker and Stanislaus rivers; and 1844 saw the Stephens-Townsend-Murphy party make a successful crossing with their wagons via what would later be known as the Truckee Route, named for the man who had helped them find the path. This pass became the most favored of all the passes and cutoffs used to cross the Sierra, including Carson Pass to the south and the Lassen and Nobles Emigrant trails farther north.

When the Stephens-Townsend-Murphy party arrived at the alkaline flats of Nevada's Humboldt Sink, the group members debated what to do. They wanted to continue on the tough trail toward the Sacramento Valley, but they weren't content to abandon their wagons as previous groups had been forced to do. Also, the group's leaders were convinced that the best way to cross the mountains was to head due west. Luckily, the party found an old Indian who agreed to lead them west to a river that flowed east out of the mountains. The emigrants called the helpful guide Truckee, because he used the word often when answering questions. It later turned out that "truk-ee" was a Paiute word meaning "all right" or "very well." The old man turned out to be chief of the Paiute Indian Nation and father to Winnemucca (who later achieved fame in his own right). The emigrants may have been ignorant, but

they were also very grateful and named the river in the chief's honor. Later, the meadows and the town also were given Truckee's name. The Stephens-Townsend-Murphy party made it safely to the Sacramento Valley and Sutter's New Helvetia settlement, and the group even managed to bring its wagons over—a feat that sometimes involved unloading and hoisting the wagons up vertical rock faces.

Two years later, in the winter of 1846–1847, another wagon train attempted the same route but met with a less pleasant fate. The Donner Party, a group of emigrants from the Midwest, faced a number of unexpected hardships and delays that ultimately led to tragedy. To start with, they were late. A disproportionate number of elderly and young children in the group had slowed progress, and a misguided *shortcut* through the Utah wilderness cost them weeks of time. The quarrelsome group reached the base of the Sierras on October 28 and unwisely decided to rest for five days before attempting the pass. The snow came early that year, and by November 5, the party was stuck at the east end of Donner Lake (then called Truckee Lake). The snowed-in pioneers failed to watch their livestock, and many of the animals wandered off. Without the livestock, the emigrants were missing a key source of food. Several attempts were made to get small rescue parties over the pass, but it was mostly too little, too late. When the ordeal was finally over, only 48 of the original 89 travelers survived. Those still alive had subsisted on the bodies of their dead companions. A state

The trail to the summit of Mt. Judah.

park and monument now mark the spot where the Donner Party constructed make-shift cabins that they stayed in during the winter.

Nowadays, with wide highways and railroad tracks smoothly traversing the summit, it's hard to imagine why the Donner Party had such a hard time passing this obstacle. Interstate 80 sweeps travelers over the summit in a matter of minutes. But

MilesDirections

0.0 START at the Pacific Crest Trail trailhead off I-80. The Pacific Crest Trail (PCT) trailhead spur starts at the east end of the parking lot. Take this trail.

0.1 Glacier Meadow Loop heads left. Continue straight on the PCT trailhead spur.

0.4 The other end of Glacier Meadow Loop heads left. Continue to the right, hiking past a small lake.

0.7 The Pacific Crest Trail heads north to Summit Lake on the left. Continue straight on the south-bound Pacific Crest Trail to Donner Pass.

2.5 The trail rounds a small lake and continues south.

3.0 The trail crests a rocky ridge and begins to descend via several switchbacks toward Donner Pass.

3.5 The sheer rock walls on the right are popular with rock climbers. On good-weather days, you may see some in action.

4.0 Reach Donner Pass. Cross Donner Pass Road (old Highway 40) and follow the gravel road on the other side south past the Alpine Skills Institute.

4.2 At the point where the gravel road curves right, turn left into a gravel turnout. The Pacific Crest Trail continues south behind the bulletin

board. Follow this trail as it climbs up the south side of Donner Pass.

5.2 Turn left off of the Pacific Crest Trail and onto the north end of Mount Judah Loop.

5.4 Several unmarked spur trails head left for views from the prominent rock outcroppings. Continue straight on Mount Judah Loop.

5.7 Donner Peak Trail continues straight. Turn right and follow Mt. Judah Loop uphill to the ridge.

6.0 The trail levels out below a ridge on the exposed slopes of Mount Judah.

6.2 The trail tops the ridge, offering great views to the east and west.

6.3 Arrive at Mount Judah summit. From here, hikers can enjoy 360-degree views of the northern Sierra Nevada. The trail continues south.

6.7 Mount Judah Loop ends at the Pacific Crest Trail. Turn right, and follow the Pacific Crest Trail north through a ski area.

7.7 The north end of Mount Judah Loop heads right. Continue straight, retracing your route back to the trailhead.

12.9 Arrive back at the trailhead.

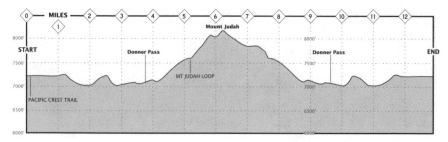

304

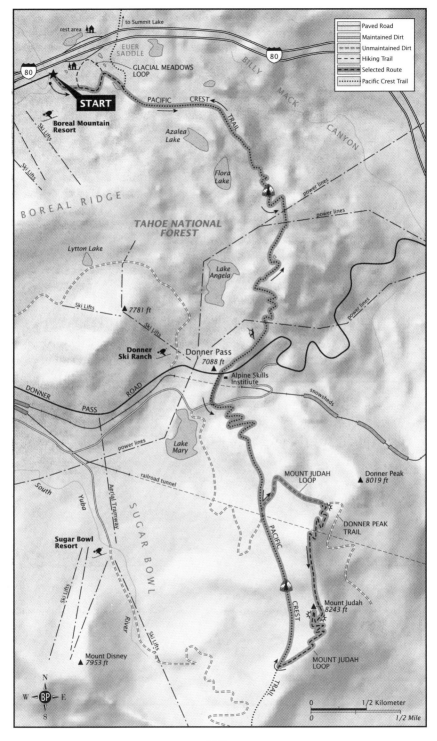

Railroad tunnels and snow sheds on Donner Pass.

don't let the ease of efficient traveling let you overlook the Pacific Crest Trail exit. It's well worth the stop. From the trailhead, the trail winds south through a pale granite landscape swathed in hardy forest growth. The topography gets so convoluted with switchbacks that four miles of trail are needed to reach a point only 1.5 miles away! After passing a few sheer rock walls favored by local climbers, the trail crosses Donner Pass Road (old Highway 40) at Donner Pass and continues south down a gravel road for a few minutes before climbing the slopes of Donner Peak and Mount Judah. The steep-walled valley above Donner Lake is visible from the switchbacks that mark the start of the second leg of the hike, giving a better idea of the challenges those first wagon trains faced.

The Mount Judah Loop climbs up through the recent expansion of a local ski resort (yes, this is public land), before splitting off from the Pacific Crest Trail to circle around and ascend Mount Judah. Hikers will enjoy excellent views from the summit before making the return loop in the Pacific Crest Trail and retracing the first part of the hike to the trailhead.

Donner Lake from the ridge.

Hike Information

Trail Contacts:

Tahoe National Forest, Truckee Ranger Station, Truckee, CA (530) 587–3558 or *www.r5.pswfs.gov/tahoe*

Schedule:

Open year round, but there's heavy snow on the trail in winter

Fees/Permits:

No fees or permits required

Local Information:

City of Truckee Information, Truckee, CA (530) 582–7700 or *www.tahoe.ceres.ca.gov/truckee*

Local Events/Attractions:

Donner Memorial State Park, Truckee, CA (530) 582–7892 or *www.parks.ca.gov*

Organizations:

Pacific Crest Trail Association, 5325 Elkhorn Boulevard #256, Sacramento, CA 95842 or visit *www.pcta.org*

Accommodations:

Clair Tappaan Lodge, Norden, CA (530) 426–3632 or *www.sierraclub.org/outings/lodges/tappaan.asp* – The Sierra Club operates this hostel-style lodge on Donner Summit. It's also open for nonmembers. Reservations are suggested.

Other Resources:

Truckee-Donner Historical Society: *www.tahoenet.com/tdhs/tpnewslt.html*

Local Outdoor Retailers:

Sierra Mountaineer, Truckee, CA (530) 587–2025 • **Bud's Sporting Goods,** Truckee, CA (530) 587–3177 • **Squaw Valley Sport Shop,** Olympic Valley, CA (530) 583–3356 • **Sterling & Co,** Truckee, CA (530) 587–2538 • **The Sports Exchange,** Truckee, CA (530) 582–4510

Maps:

USGS maps: Norden, CA

Rubicon Trail

Hike Specs

Start: From the Calawee Cove Beach Access parking lot
Length: 9.0-mile out-and-back
Approximate Hiking Time: 4.5 hours (does not include time for the Vikingsholm tour)
Difficulty Rating: Moderate due to little elevation gain but rocky, uneven terrain
Terrain: Dirt path along boulder-strewn, forested alpine lakeshore
Elevation Gain: 1,478 feet
Land Status: State park
Nearest Town: South Lake Tahoe, CA
Other Trail Users: Anglers
Canine Compatibility: Dogs not permitted

Getting There

From Truckee: Head south 14 miles on CA 89 to Tahoe City. Continue through town following signs for CA 89, and follow it south along the west shore of Lake Tahoe another 16 miles to the entrance of D.L. Bliss State Park. Turn left into the park and follow the road one mile to the entrance station, continuing straight another 0.5 miles before turning right at the T-intersection and following the road to its dead-end at the Calawee Cove Beach Access parking lot. The trail begins at the south end of the parking lot. • **Public Transportation:** The Tahoe Trolley (coming from the north shore of Lake Tahoe) and the Nifty Fifty Trolley (coming from the south shore of Lake Tahoe) both stop at the Vikingsholm parking lot. A one-mile trail (steep but well-defined) leads from the parking lot down to Vikingsholm (the turnaround point for this hike). For more information, visit *www.laketahoetransit.com*.
DeLorme: Northern California Atlas & Gazetteer: Page 89 A7

The first thing likely to strike new visitors to Lake Tahoe is the curious pairing of pristine alpine landscape with urban development. Coming in from Truckee, California 89 suddenly drops you into the hustle and clutter of Tahoe City. Huge wooden homes, some with high stone walls and iron gates, are packed tightly together along the lakeshore as you head south. Despite the rustic-style architecture, Tahoe is largely the playground of the rich and famous—or at least the rich. All the more refreshing, then, to find that a good portion of the southwest shore has been preserved for the public. The Rubicon Trail follows a 4.5-mile stretch of this densely forested land within the boundaries of the two-for-one D.L. Bliss and Emerald Bay state parks. The trail stays close to the water for the most part, hugging a virtually undisturbed section of shoreline outside the boater's campground and the modest Vikingsholm facilities on Emerald Bay.

Hiking south from Calawee Cove, the trail winds along boulder-strewn cliffs laden with ponderosa, Jeffery, and sugar pines that grow in the thin granitic soil alongside red and white fir and incense cedar. Autumn brings colorful foliage displays as alders, quaking aspen, and sierra maples develop their bright fall leaves. Springtime offers its own show of color from blooming wildflowers—such as leopard lily, columbine, yellow monkey-flower, and bleeding heart—as well as the flowering trees like mountain dogwood and bitter cherry. But at any time of year, it's the lake that provides the main attraction, with its deep, clear blue waters beckoning to be photographed, swum in, boated on, and just plain enjoyed. Mark Twain was not kidding when he declared Tahoe "the fairest picture the whole earth affords."

Native Americans, most notably the Washoe tribe of Western Nevada, have been living near the lake for at least 10,000 years. They'd spend summers on the lake before moving south to the milder climes of the Carson and Eagle valleys for the winter. In 1844, explorer John C. Fremont became one of the first European-Americans to see the lake. He named it Lake Bonpland after a French botanist friend. Luckily, the name didn't stick. In 1870, Placerville city founders renamed it Lake Bigler, after California's third governor. Eventually that name, too, was discarded, and the lake took a name appropriately derived from the Washoe word meaning "big (or high) water"—Lake Tahoe.

Tourism on the lake is nothing new. The first sightseers began trickling in while the California Gold Rush was still a recent memory. At first, the travelers were just passing through on their way from California's dwindling gold fields to the *next big thing* in mining, Nevada's Comstock Lode. By 1870, however, people had heard about Tahoe's natural beauty and began showing up to fish, hike, or just hang out in one of several hotels that had sprung up around the lake. The year before, the Transcontinental Railroad—which passed just north of the lake—was completed,

Fannette Island in Emerald Bay.

making the trip much easier. The lake, previously reachable only by wagon or stage over rough mountain roads, was now connected to the rest of the country by rail. By the turn of the century, upper-class hotels such as the Tallac House, Glenbrook House, and the Grand Central Hotel were catering to the wealthy of the industrial

MilesDirections

0.0 START at the south end of the Calawee Cove Beach Access parking lot. Follow Rubicon Trail south along the shore of Lake Tahoe.

0.1 Lighthouse Trail heads up to the right. Continue straight on Rubicon Trail.

0.2 The trail splits into two branches as it passes a rocky spot, but rejoins a few yards later.

0.3 The trail crosses a small bridge below a rock wall.

0.4 Lighthouse Spur Trail goes off to right, accessing what is left of the tiny old lighthouse. Continue straight on Rubicon Trail.

0.7 A spur trail heads right, connecting with the park entrance road. Continue straight.

0.8 Another spur trail heads right. Continue straight, heading south on Rubicon Trail.

1.0 The trail veers inland and joins a former dirt access road. Turn left and continue south.

1.2 Nature Center Trail heads right. Continue straight.

2.0 The trail drops back down close to the lake, offering gorgeous scenery.

2.4 The trail crosses a small stream.

2.6 A small, hidden beach is on the left next to the trail. This is a good swimming spot in summer.

2.8 Emerald Point Bypass Trail goes right. *[Option. You can use this bypass to cut across Emerald Point.]* Take the left fork to Emerald Point.

3.0 The trail rounds Emerald Point and enters Emerald Bay.

3.2 *[FYI. The small beach and shallow water make this a good swimming spot, complete with views of Emerald Bay.]*

3.3 Emerald Point Bypass Trail heads back to the right. Continue straight to Vikingsholm.

3.9 The trail empties onto a gravel road. Turn left on the road and follow it through Emerald Bay State Park Boat Camp. On the other side of the campground, the trail resumes on the left keeping near to the shoreline.

4.2 The trail crosses small bridge. *[FYI. To the left, Fannette Island can be seen.]*

4.4 The trail crosses four small bridges, then becomes gravel causeway as it enters the day-use area around Vikingsholm. At the fork in the trail, take the left fork to the beach.

4.5 The trail spills out onto the narrow beach in front of Vikingsholm. The house is on the right, and the visitor center is behind and a short walk to the left of the main house. The beach is the turnaround point for trail. Return the way you came.

9.0 Arrive back at the trailhead.

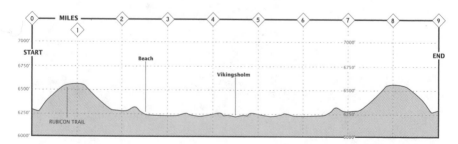

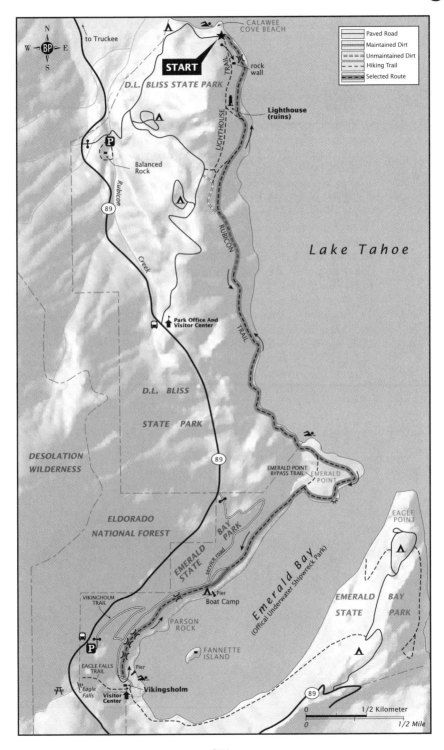

age. And several steamboats plied the waters of the lake, bringing passengers and cargo to various ports along her shores. The largest of these boats, the S.S. *Tahoe*, was launched in 1896 by the very same D.L. Bliss for whom the state park was later named. The boat served without incident for 40 years, but roads and trucks had made utilitarian water transport mostly obsolete by that time. So the Tahoe, along with many other decommissioned vessels, was simply scuttled and left to sink to the bottom of the lake, where it remains today.

Three miles south of Calawee Cove, the Rubicon Trail rounds Emerald Point and offers a view of Emerald Bay's open expanse. Sporting its own share of vintage vessels sunk in relatively shallow waters, the bay was dedicated an official Underwater Shipwreck Park by the state of California in 1994. The site features two large wooden cargo barges from the early 1900s that attract scuba divers, despite the special difficulties involved in high-altitude diving.

But it is the above-water scenery that reminded industry heiress Lora J. Knight of the fjords in Norway, inspiring her to build a Scandinavian-style home here in 1929. It was the fashion at the time to build in period architecture, but Knight went a step further by faithfully recreating a home—right down to the furnishings and interior decorating—in the style of a Viking chieftain. A tour of Knight's Vikingsholm is highly recommended if you're interested in architecture or hand-craftsmanship. And if that's not enough to quench your thirst for interesting older buildings, be sure to look for some of the other mansions still standing around the lake. The most notable are the Ehrman Mansion at Sugar Pine Point State Park and several buildings at the Tallac Historic Site near South Lake Tahoe.

Vikingsholm is the turnaround point for the hike. Enjoy the architecture, and return the way you came. On the way back consider a side trip to the old lighthouse. It's a bit unrewarding since little remains except an outhouse-sized wooden shack.

Viking holm.

Hike Information

Trail Contacts:
D.L. Bliss State Park, Tahoma, CA (530) 525-7277 or *www.parks.ca.gov/ north/sierra/dlbsp303.htm* • **Emerald Bay State Park,** Tahoma, CA (530) 541-3030 (summers only) or *www.parks.ca.gov/north/sierra/ebsp 313.htm* • **Lake Sector Headquarters:** (530) 525-7232

Schedule:
Vikingsholm can be toured daily from mid June through Labor Day, with weekend tours for a few weeks in the fall. Call for more specific park information.

Fees/Permits:
$2 day-use fee. Vikingsholm tours cost $1 for adults.

Local Information:
South Lake Tahoe Chamber of Commerce, South Lake Tahoe, CA (530) 541-5255 • **Tahoe websites:** *www.tahoeinfo.com* or *www.virtual tahoe.com*

Local Events/Attractions:
Valhalla Summer Arts Music Festival, June through August, South Lake Tahoe, CA • **Tallac Historic Site,** South Lake Tahoe, CA – *music, art, dance, food, and activities* • **Tahoe Tallac Association,** South Lake Tahoe, CA (530) 542-4166 (winter) or (530) 541-4975 (summer) or *www.valhalla-tallac.com*

Accommodations:
For state park campground reservations, call 1-800-444-PARK • For national forest campground information, call (530) 573-2674.

Organizations:
Tahoe Heritage Foundation, South Lake Tahoe, CA (530) 544-7383 or *www.tahoeheritage.org* • **League to Save Lake Tahoe,** South Shore Office, South Lake Tahoe, CA (530) 541-5388 or *www.keeptahoeblue.com*

Public Transportation:
Tahoe Area Regional Transit: 1-800-736-6365 or *www.placer.ca. gov/works/tart.htm – summer trolley service for the north shore (Tahoe Trolley)* • **South Tahoe Area Ground Express:** (530) 541-7548 – *summer trolley service for the north shore (Nifty Fifty Trolley)* • **Tahoe transit website:** *www.laketa hoetransit.com*

Local Outdoor Retailers:
Squaw Valley Sport Shop, Olympic Valley, CA (530) 583-335 • **Cathedral Sports Inc,** South Lake Tahoe, CA (530) 542-4722 • **Heavenly Sports,** South Lake Tahoe, CA (530) 544-1921 • **Lake Tahoe Sporting Goods,** South Lake Tahoe, CA (530) 542-2525 • **Sportsman,** South Lake Tahoe, CA (530) 542-3474 • **Tahoe Sports Ltd.,** South Lake Tahoe, CA (530) 542-4000 or (530) 544-2284 • **Village Sports,** Tahoe City, CA (530) 583-3722

Maps:
USGS maps: Emerald Bay, CA

Mount Tallac Trail

Hike Specs

Start: From the Mount Tallac Trail trailhead
Length: 10.2-mile out-and-back
Approximate Hiking Time: 5–6 hours
Difficulty Rating: Difficult due to high elevation and steep trails
Terrain: Dirt path through alpine forests, over meadows, along scree slopes, and up a bare, rocky peak
Elevation Gain: 3,256 feet
Land Status: National forest wilderness
Nearest Town: South Lake Tahoe, CA
Other Trail Users: Anglers and equestrians
Canine Compatibility: Leashed dogs permitted

Getting There

From South Lake Tahoe: Head north on CA 89 approximately 3.5 miles. Turn left onto Forest Road 13N07, at the sign for Mount Tallac Trail trailhead, directly across from the Baldwin Beach entrance. Follow this dirt road as it turns left, then right, continuing another 0.5 miles to the trailhead parking. The trail starts at the large bulletin board and self-registration station • **Public Transportation:** From South Lake Tahoe, take the Nifty Fifty Trolley's Emerald Bay Shuttle to the Mount Tallac Trail trailhead sign. Walk south on FS 13N07 for 0.5 miles to the trailhead at the large bulletin board and self-registration station. For information on schedules, visit *www.laketahoetransit.com.* **DeLorme: Northern California Atlas & Gazetteer:** Page 89 A7

D on't expect to be overwhelmed by the view from below the jagged ridge that rises up to Mount Tallac's peak. True, it is a daunting site when you think that you'll soon be scaling that wall, but with so many mountains ringing Lake Tahoe, Tallac lacks the imposing prominence of a Mount Shasta or even Mount Diablo. That changes when, a little over halfway up the trail, the path starts to zigzag—like a seismograph needle during the big one—right into a massive wall of loose scree.

The Mount Tallac Trail starts not far from California 89 and just a few feet above lake level. It follows a long, low ridge that offers views of Fallen Leaf Lake. Although much smaller than Lake Tahoe, Fallen Leaf Lake is a good-sized recreational lake in its own right. Past the lake, the trail stops off at two smaller bodies of water. These are lakes in the traditional alpine sense of the word—read: *small.* From here, things begin to get serious as the trail becomes less distinct and climbs steeply over the bedrock and boulders of the chaparral- and forest-covered lower slopes. Look out, the scree slope is dead ahead. It's a grueling half mile or so to the ridge, but from there, the trail mellows again as it makes its way along the ridge to the summit.

Due to the trail's high elevation, it's a good idea to acclimatize for a couple of days before attempting the hike—especially if you're coming from a place near sea level. It's also advisable to be prepared for quick changes in weather, as sudden snow and rain showers are possible at almost any time of year. Visibility at the summit varies with the weather, of course, but on a good day, the view is spectacular. Desolation Wilderness is spread out to the west beneath the mountain, and numerous alpine

Lake Tahoe from the summit of Mt. Tallac.

lakes are visible among the glacially polished granite and sparse vegetation. To the north, the eastern edge of the Sierra Nevada range stretches up to Truckee, Donner Pass, and beyond. And to the south, the same range continues peak after peak into what seems like infinity. But the real reason everyone comes up here lies to the east. There, Lake Tahoe rests in all its glory, like some huge, blue swimming pool of the gods. From this elevation, you begin to get a sense of just how big—and unique—this body of water is.

Seen in aerial views from the east, Lake Tahoe looks like a giant bathtub suspended high above the Great Basin of Nevada, with only the thin Carson Range holding back the lake's 39 trillion gallons of water. The lake was created by a combi-

MilesDirections

0.0 START at Mount Tallac Trail trailhead. The trail starts at bulletin board.

0.1 Pass a sign for Desolation Wilderness. *[FYI. This sign does not indicate the actual wilderness boundary. It's simply a reference point.]*

1.0 *[FYI. As the trail climbs along a narrow ridge, there's a nice view to the left of Falling Leaf Lake.]*

1.6 Tallac Springs Trail heads right to a residential area near Lake Tahoe. Go left and follow the sign for Cathedral Lake.

1.7 The trail passes Floating Island Lake. Circle the lake on the left.

2.4 Fallen Leaf Lake Trail heads toward its namesake on the left. Go straight, climbing to Cathedral Lake.

2.5 Reach Cathedral Lake. The trail bends right at the lake, climbing steeply up the rocky slope.

3.0 Leaving the forest cover behind, the trail heads up an open scree slope in a series of switchbacks.

3.5 The trail levels out on the ridge, and curves around to the ridge's north side, heading uphill.

4.5 At this point, there's an excellent view of several Desolation Wilderness lakes to the northwest.

4.8 Gilmore Lake Trail heads left to Gilmore Lake. Turn right, following the Mount Tallac Trail to the summit.

5.0 At a large rocky promontory, there's a great view of Fallen Lake and the south end of Lake Tahoe. The trail becomes a little sketchy here as the ground becomes a jumble of rocks. Follow the path of least resistance to the summit, just a few yards away.

5.1 Reach the summit of Mount Tallac. The 360-degree view from here speaks for itself. This is the turnaround point for the hike. Return the way you came.

10.2 Arrive back at the trailhead.

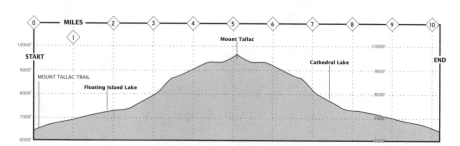

nation of plate tectonics, volcanism, and glaciation beginning some 25 million years ago when the Sierra Nevada block began to rise from the earth. Two parallel faults formed, and as the blocks on either side grew, the valley that would later become the Tahoe Basin sank between them. Later, lava from the volcanic Mount Pluto, on the north shore of the lake, created a natural dam across the basin's outlet and caused the basin to fill with water. At that time, water in the lake was several hundred feet above the present level. This is where glaciation comes into play. Less than a million years ago, glaciers formed in the mountains and carved out the typical U-shaped valleys of Cascade Lake, Fallen Leaf Lake, and Emerald Bay. The glaciers also lowered the level

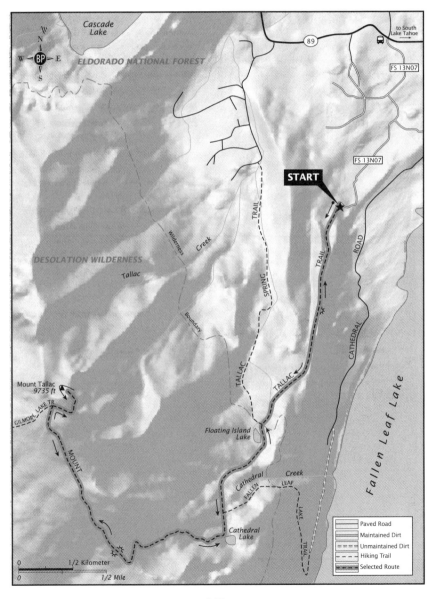

of the lake by carving away at the natural dam holding the water in check. Interestingly enough, end-moraines from the glaciers blocked the original outlet, causing the lake to overflow into what is now the Truckee River Valley. From there, the water from Lake Tahoe flows east, where, rather than emptying into an ocean, it flows into Nevada's Pyramid Lake and evaporates into the hot desert air.

The clarity of Tahoe's water is almost mythical, with average visibility still reaching a depth of 69 feet or so. That level of purity is striking. But it is substantially lower than the lake's historical 100-foot visibility, which has been sullied by the environmental effects of development and overpopulation. Even so, the water here remains unusually clean, mostly because of geography. Up to 40 percent of the precipitation that enters the lake falls directly on the lake's surface, without picking up any sedi-

View of Fallen Leaf Lake from the ridge above a scree slope.

ments. The rest of the precipitation comes mostly from the 63 short streams that flow into the lake from the surrounding mountains. That water is filtered through marshes and meadows, leaving little in the way of nutrients for the algae that thrive and cloud the waters of most lakes.

From Mount Tallac, the return trip is much easier than the ascent. As they say, it's all downhill from here.

Hike Information

○ Trail Contacts:
Lake Tahoe Basin Management Unit, South Lake Tahoe, CA (530) 573–2674

○ Schedule:
Open year round, though access is limited in winter due to snow

$ Fees/Permits:
Free mandatory day-use permits for Desolation Wilderness can be obtained at the trailhead. Permits for overnight use involve fees (varying depending on length of stay), and must be obtained from a Forest Service Office or visitor center, due to quota restrictions.

? Local Information:
South Lake Tahoe Chamber of Commerce, South Lake Tahoe, CA (530) 541–5255 • Tahoe websites: www.tahoeinfo.com or www.virtualtahoe.com

♀ Local Events/Attractions:
Valhalla Summer Arts Music Festival, June through August, South Lake Tahoe, CA • Tallac Historic Site, South Lake Tahoe, CA – music, art, dance, food, and activities • Tahoe Tallac Association, South Lake Tahoe, CA (530) 542–4166 (winter) or (530) 541–4975 (summer) or www.valhalla-tallac.com

● Accommodations:
For state park campground reservations, call 1–800–444–PARK • For national forest campground information, call (530) 573–2674.

● Organizations:
Tahoe Heritage Foundation, South Lake Tahoe, CA (530) 544–7383 or www.tahoeheritage.org • League to Save Lake Tahoe, South Shore Office, South Lake Tahoe, CA (530) 541–5388 or www.keeptahoeblue.com

● Public Transportation:
South Tahoe Area Ground Express: (530) 541–7548 – summer trolley service for the north shore (Nifty Fifty Trolley) • Tahoe transit website: www.laketahoetransit.com

● Local Outdoor Retailers:
Squaw Valley Sport Shop, Olympic Valley, CA (530) 583–335 • Cathedral Sports Inc, South Lake Tahoe, CA (530) 542–4722 • Heavenly Sports, South Lake Tahoe, CA (530) 544–1921 • Lake Tahoe Sporting Goods, South Lake Tahoe, CA (530) 542–2525 • Sportsman, South Lake Tahoe, CA (530) 542–3474 • Tahoe Sports Ltd., South Lake Tahoe, CA (530) 542–4000 or (530) 544–2284 • Village Sports, Tahoe City, CA (530) 583–3722

N Maps:
USGS maps: Emerald Bay, CA

Woods Lake Loop

Hike Specs

Start: From the Winnemucca Lake trailhead
Length: 4.6-mile loop
Approximate Hiking Time: 2–3 hours
Difficulty Rating: Easy to Moderate due to one steep, rocky section
Terrain: Dirt path and some gravel road through sparse upper montane forests, over open meadows, and around alpine lakes
Elevation Gain: 1,236 feet
Land Status: National forest and wilderness area
Nearest Town: South Lake Tahoe, CA
Other Trail Users: Equestrians and anglers
Canine Compatibility: Leashed dogs permitted

Getting There

From South Lake Tahoe: Drive south seven miles on U.S. 50. Turn left onto CA 89 and continue south 11 miles over Luther Pass to Hope Valley, and the junction with CA 88. Turn right onto CA 88 and drive west nine miles to Carson Pass. Another two miles beyond Carson Pass, turn left into the Woods Lake Campground and day-use area. Follow the paved road two miles to the day-use parking. The trailhead is just past the campground entrance on the left. *DeLorme: Northern California Atlas & Gazetteer:* Page 89 C7

This hike is nestled in the Sierra Nevada range just west of Carson Pass, a route named for Kit Carson. The famed explorer and scout found the pass—marking the occasion by carving his name in a nearby tree—while working for John C. Fremont, the man the U.S. government charged with charting the mostly unexplored western territories. In 1843, Freemont completed his mission of mapping out what would later be known as the Oregon Trail. But instead of returning home, he made a somewhat dubious decision to head south. Freemont crossed over the Sierra Nevada somewhere near the present Oregon-California border and took a side trip to Lake Tahoe. He then decided to cross back over the Sierra Nevada—in the middle of winter. The local Washoe Indians advised strongly against the trip, but Fremont persisted and sent Carson ahead to find a route. The group eventually made it to Sutter's Fort, though the effort cost the party the life of one member and the sanity of two others. After recovering from their journey, the surviving group members headed south through the San Joaquin Valley.

Fremont's accounts of these exploits, rewritten by his wife back home, were eagerly consumed by the masses and made both Fremont and Carson national heroes. Of the two, Carson went on to become a legend in his own time, largely because his adventures were embellished and popularized in contemporary *dime novels*. To be fair, though, he really did lead a fascinating life.

Christopher "Kit" Carson was born in Missouri in 1809. He left home when he was 17 years old to become a hunter and trapper in New Mexico. While learning these trades, he made his first trips to California and the Rocky Mountains. The

young Carson later hooked up with Fremont in Colorado, accompanying the elder explorer on expeditions for four years before getting caught up in the Bear Flag rebellion and the Mexican-American War.

After the war, Carson took up ranching and was appointed federal Indian agent in northern New Mexico. He led a campaign there against the Navajos during the Civil War and eventually defeated them—with help from their traditional enemies, the Utes, Pueblos, Hopis, and Zunis. The Navajos were then forcibly relocated from their Arizona home to a reservation at Fort Sumner, New Mexico, where they remained in confinement for four years. Carson later moved to Colorado to expand his ranching business and died there in 1868.

The hike begins at the Woods Lake Campground and day-use area, just past the entrance to the campground. Widely skirting Woods Lake, the path makes its way up a broad basin bordered on all sides by prominent peaks. The trail first passes through dense forest strewn with granite boulders and outcroppings. Just before entering the wilderness, the trees give way to open tundra-like vegetation. From here, the massive dome of Round Top Mountain—the highest point in the Mokelumne Wilderness at

Round Top.

10,381 feet—looms ahead as you make your way up to Winnemucca Lake. To the left, a trail leads over to Carson Pass and the Pacific Crest Trail, past the rounded hump of a mountain known as *the Elephant's Back*. This landform traces its name back to a common expression used during the pioneer days. As the story goes, a rural farmer heard the circus was coming to town, bringing with it an elephant, the likes of which the farmer had never seen. He loaded his produce cart, hitched up his horse, and proceeded to drive to town. When the farmer reached the circus procession, his horse saw the elephant and was terrified. The spooked horse reared, upset the cart, and toppled the produce before running off. In spite of his hardship, the farmer exclaimed, "I don't care, for I have seen the elephant." Often the hardships of the emigrant trail were too much for poor travelers, and they would be forced to return east, where they would also declare "I don't care, for I have seen the elephant." For those settlers who made it this far, the Sierra Nevada must truly have seemed like the last great challenge, and the pass over the summit, the elephant's back.

MilesDirections

0.0 START at Winnemucca Lake trailhead. Cross a small footbridge almost immediately and continue on the Woods Lake Loop.

0.8 *[FYI. A stone arrastra can be seen to the right. This is a structure that was used to crush ore in early gold mining efforts.]*

1.1 The trail enters the Mokelumne Wilderness.

1.6 Reach Winnemucca Lake. Carson Pass Trail heads left at the lake. Turn right following Woods Lake Loop to Round Top Lake.

1.7 Cross a small stream at the lake's outlet via a log bridge.

2.3 The trail tops the low ridge between Winnemucca and Round Top lakes. There are nice views to the east and west from here.

2.6 Reach Round Top Lake. Fourth of July Trail continues straight ahead. Turn right, following Woods Lake Loop downhill.

3.7 The trail passes the ruins of an old mining cabin on the right.

3.8 More historic rubbish is scattered about on the left.

4.0 Newer mine buildings can be seen below on left, and numerous signs make sure you don't go any closer.

4.1 The trail passes an old bulletin board marked Lost Cabin Mine trailhead. Continue down the dirt path.

4.4 Just past a locked gate, the trail becomes a gravel road.

4.5 The trail joins the campground loop road from above. Turn right and follow the paved road to the campground entrance.

4.6 At the campground entrance, turn right onto the main access road for Woods Lake. The trailhead is a few yards up the road on the left.

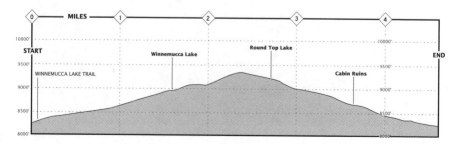

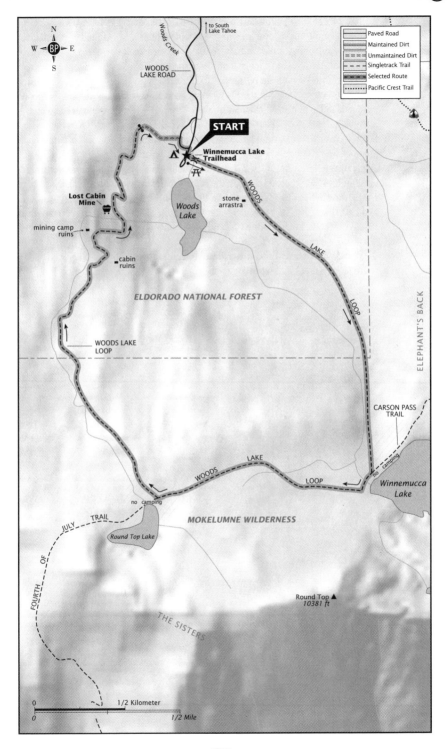

The Mokelumne Wilderness (officially designated in 1984) takes its name from the Mokelumne River, which in turn was named after a Miwok village located far down in the Central Valley in San Joaquin County. Despite its rugged and desolate nature, the area has seen a lot of traffic over the years. The original discoverers were, of course, Native American peoples who visited the upper slopes of the Sierra in summer while looking for game and plants to supplement their diet. In the 1820s, mountain man and explorer Jedediah Smith passed through the area—from west to east—as he wandered the West in search of fur pelts. Four years after Kit Carson led Fremont over the pass, the route was opened to wagons by the Mormon Battalion, a group of 500 Mormon soldiers enlisted by President James K. Polk to assist the U.S. Army in the fight against the Mexicans in California. The battalion set out from a camp in Iowa and traveled through the deserts of the Southwest to San Diego. Once the fighting in Southern California was finished, the battalion headed north to Utah and Salt Lake City. This time, they crossed the Sierra Nevada just south of Carson Pass. Their path, known as the Carson Route, was one of the most heavily used emigrant trails during the Gold Rush.

From Winnemucca Lake, the trail heads west to Round Top Lake before heading north along a creek and returning to the trailhead through the campground.

Hike Information

Trail Contacts:

Eldorado National Forest, Amador Ranger District, Pioneer, CA (209) 295–5900 or *www.r5.fs.fed.us/eldorado/*

Schedule:

Open year round, though access is limited in winter due to snow

Fees/Permits:

Wilderness permits are required for overnight use between April 1 and November 30. Permits are not required for day-use.

Local Information:

Alpine County Chamber of Commerce, Markleeville, CA (530) 694–2475 or *www.alpinecounty.com* • **South Lake Tahoe Chamber of Commerce,** South Lake Tahoe, CA (530) 541–5255 • **Tahoe websites:** *www.tahoeinfo.com* or *www.virtualtahoe.com*

Local Events/Attractions:

Valhalla Summer Arts Music Festival, June through August, South Lake Tahoe, CA • **Tallac Historic Site,** South Lake Tahoe, CA – *music, art, dance, food, and activities* • **Tahoe Tallac Association,** South Lake Tahoe, CA (530) 542–4166 (winter) or (530) 541–4975 (summer) or *www.valhalla-tallac.com*

Accommodations:

Woods Lake Campground: *Located at the trailhead. Call 1–877–444–6777 for reservations.*

Local Outdoor Retailers:

Ken's Sports & Equipment, Camino, CA (530) 644–3181 • **Instant Replay,** Diamond Springs, CA (530) 642–9077 • **Victory Sporting Goods,** Jackson, CA (209) 257–1630 • **Play It Again Sports,** Jackson, CA (209) 223–1223 • **Big 5 Sporting Goods,** Placerville, CA (530) 295–8290 • **Mountain & Surf Pro Shop,** Placerville, CA (530) 622–3034 • **Raymond's Liquor & Sporting,** Placerville, CA (530) 622–3606 • **Cathedral Sports Inc,** South Lake Tahoe, CA (530) 542–4722 • **Heavenly Sports,** South Lake Tahoe, CA (530) 544–1921 • **Lake Tahoe Sporting Goods,** South Lake Tahoe, CA (530) 542–2525 • **Sportsman,** South Lake Tahoe, CA (530) 542–3474 • **Tahoe Sports Ltd.,** South Lake Tahoe, CA (530) 542–4000 or (530) 544–2284 • **Village Sports,** Tahoe City, CA (530) 583–3722

Maps:

USGS maps: Caples Lake, CA; Carson Pass, CA

Bull Run Lake Trail

Hike Specs

Start: From the Stanislaus Meadows trailhead

Length: 7.6-mile out-and-back

Approximate Hiking Time: 4–5 hours

Difficulty Rating: Moderate due to some steep, rocky sections

Terrain: Dirt path and road through alpine meadows and forest, and along glacier-polished granite

Elevation Gain: 1,694 feet

Land Status: National forest and wilderness area

Nearest Town: Bear Valley, CA

Other Trail Users: Anglers, equestrians, and hunters (in season)

Canine Compatibility: Dogs permitted

Getting There

From Stockton: Drive east about 55 miles on CA 4 to the town of Angels Camp. Continue up CA 4 as it climbs the western slope of the Sierra Nevada. The Stanislaus Meadows trailhead parking lot is on the right (south) side of CA 4, 50 miles east of Angels Camp, and two miles east of Lake Alpine. *DeLorme: Northern California Atlas & Gazetteer:* Page 90 D1

For those who've seen the human vacuum of California's extreme northeast, it may come as a surprise to learn that Alpine County is the state's least populous county. In the entire 726 square miles of the county, there are a only about 1,100 residents—and no traffic lights, no high schools, no dentists, no banks, and no supermarkets. Roughly 96 percent of the land is in public ownership, so there is precious little room for more development. But things weren't always so.

In 1859—after thousands of immigrants had poured over Ebbet's Pass looking for gold in California—silver was discovered on the east side of the range near present-day Silver Mountain City. That find brought the mining hopefuls pouring back over the pass, certain that *this* was going to be their lucky break. The miners quickly set up camp and began mining the mountain, founding towns like Markleeville, and establishing Alpine County (population 11,000). Reality soon reared its ugly head, and the miners began to realize they weren't making any money on the meager ore they found. In 1873, the U.S. government dealt the region another blow by deciding the dollar would no longer be backed by silver. With a collective throwing up of hands, most of the miners left. By the 1920s, the region's population had reached an all-time low of 200 people.

The county got its name for obvious reasons. Starting at an elevation of 4,800 feet and rising from there, Alpine County lies, for the most part, astride the rolling foothills and soaring summits of the central Sierra Nevada. The Sierra were created when a giant block of the earth's crust tilted up. The fracture point for this block was on the east side, where the steepest rise currently stands. The mountains seem to rise

up out of the Great Basin like a sheer rock wall, creating a considerable obstacle to early wagon trains. The west side of the Sierras, by contrast, descends rather slowly in a series of peaks and ridges to the wide, flat plains of the Central Valley. Glaciers have scoured the upper slopes into smoothly polished expanses of granite bedrock, cluttered with boulders and lightly covered in brushy coniferous forests. This is the landscape that the Bull Run Lake Trail explores.

The trail starts out at the Stanislaus Meadows parking area, on the south side of California 4, and follows a jeep trail south through broad, flat meadows to the wilderness boundary. These meadows once contained the original emigrant road that came down from Ebbett's Pass. The route was improved in the 1860s when it became Big Trees-Carson Valley Turnpike. At that time, Harvey S. Blood obtained a contract whereby he operated and maintained the road in exchange for permission to collect tolls. He operated the toll station out of Bear Valley from 1864 until 1910. As one would expect in the Wild West, a steady stream of colorful characters passed through over the years. The title of *most exotic* probably goes to the string of nine Bactrian

FYI

The last period of glaciation in the Sierra Nevada ended about 10,000 years ago.

Bull Run Lake.

camels imported in 1861 by merchant Julius Bandmann. The idea was simple: Bandmann planned to use the camels to ship freight across the Nevada desert. But like oil and water, the camels did not mix with the animals already employed in the shipping industry. In fact, the new hump-backed arrivals terrified the horses and oxen. They received a decidedly cool reception from the public, too, and Bandmann's idea was declared a dismal failure. The whole episode was commemorated by artist Edward Vischer, who accompanied the caravan and made several memorable sketches for posterity.

MilesDirections

0.0 START at the Stanislaus Meadow parking area, just off of CA 4. *[Note. The road may be closed in winter due to snow.]*

0.1 The Emigrant Trail (very faint) crosses Bull Run Lake Trail. Continue straight on the dirt road.

0.2 The trail turns right at a barbwire fence, skirting the edge of a large meadow.

0.3 A footpath breaks off from the road and hugs the fence parallel to road, but rejoins it a few yards later.

0.4 The dirt road ends at an old bulletin board marked Stanislaus Meadow Trailhead. The trail continues as a dirt path beyond the sign.

0.6 Following along a barbwire fence, the trail skirts Stanislaus Meadow.

1.5 The trail enters the Carson-Iceberg Wilderness.

2.0 At the confluence of several streams with the North Fork Stanislaus River, the trail makes three rocky stream crossings in quick succession. The trail becomes a little sketchy, but continues in a general east-by-southeast direction, heading upstream on the right bank of the third crossed stream.

2.3 The trail crosses back to the north side of the stream.

2.5 At this point, the trail begins a steep, rocky climb. As it levels out again, the trail curves left across a patch of bedrock. *[Note. When in doubt as to the exact path of the trail, follow the rock cairns spread out along the trail.]*

2.8 Mosquito Lakes Trail goes straight. Turn right, continuing on Bull Run Lake Trail.

3.0 The trail crosses a small stream, and heads left up a patch of slickrock. Follow the rock cairns. Toward the top of the slope, the trail curves right again.

3.5 A small pond is tucked into a pocket of rock on the right side of the trail.

3.6 Just before a tiny stream, the trail turns left and heads uphill. Pay attention to the cairns.

3.8 Reach Bull Run Lake. This is the turn-around point. Return the way you came.

7.6 Arrive back at the trailhead.

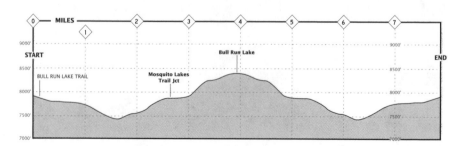

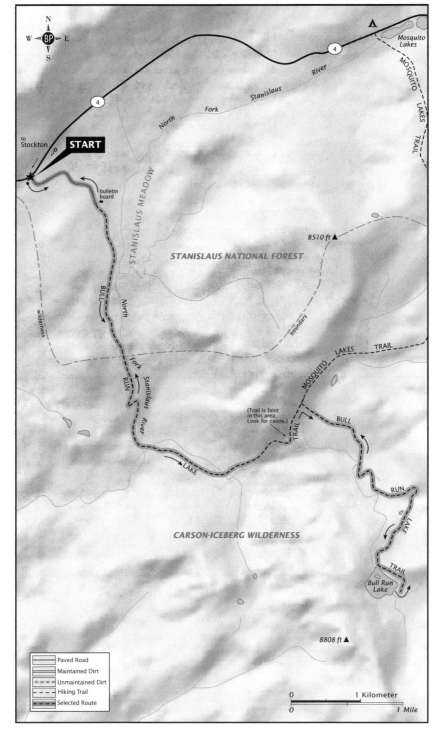

N
W — BP — E
S

4

to Stockton

START

bulletin board

STANISLAUS MEADOW

STANISLAUS NATIONAL FOREST

4

North Fork Stanislaus River

Mosquito Lakes

MOSQUITO LAKES TRAIL

8510 ft ▲

boundary

BULL

North

Fork

RUN

Stanislaus River

wilderness

MOSQUITO   LAKES   TRAIL

(Trail is faint in this area. Look for cairns.)

TRAIL

BULL

LAKE

RUN

CARSON-ICEBERG WILDERNESS

LAKE

TRAIL

Bull Run Lake

8808 ft ▲

Paved Road
Maintained Dirt
Unmaintained Dirt
Hiking Trail
Selected Route

0   1 Kilometer
0   1 Mile

Another local legend is John A. "Snow-Shoe" Thompson, who braved the pass in winter to deliver the U.S. mail. As a boy in Norway, Thompson had learned the art of traveling on homemade *snow skattes*, or skis, which were still a novelty in this country. He used the technique to cross 90 miles of snow-covered ridges with a mailbag on his back. Thompson carried the mail for 20 years, but he never received any payment for his services. He began working for the postal service in 1856 on the promise that he would eventually be paid. When he died in 1876, however, his request for payment was still stuck in U.S. governmental red tape.

En route to Bear Lake, this trail crosses the branching headwaters of the Stanislaus River's North Fork before beginning to climb, gently at first, then in earnest. This is where the classic western Sierra landscape begins. Boulders, manzanita, and slickrock join to create a lumpy wonderland that culminates at Bull Run Lake. A picturesque granite island rests serenely in the lake, which is larger than expected. There are several good camping spots in the vicinity, making this trail a good candidate for an overnight. When you're ready, return the way you came.

Hike Information

📞 Trail Contacts:
Stanislaus National Forest, Calaveras Ranger District, Hathaway Pines, CA (209) 795-1381 or *www.r5.fs.fed.us/ stanislaus*

🕐 Schedule:
Open year round, though access is limited by snow in winter

💲 Fees/Permits:
Wilderness permit required for overnight stays, but not for day-use

❓ Local Information:
Alpine County Chamber of Commerce, Markleeville, CA (530) 694-2475 or *www.alpinecounty.com* • **Calaveras County Chamber of Commerce,** Angels Camp, CA (209) 736-2580 or *www.calaveras.org*

📍 Local Events/Attractions:
Bear Valley Music Festival, late July and early August, Bear Valley, CA (209) 753-2574 or 1-800-458-1618

🛏 Accommodations:
Stanislaus National Forest, Hathaway Pines, CA (209) 795-1381 – *There are numerous campgrounds in the area, including well-developed fee-charging campgrounds at Mosquito and Alpine lakes, and several undeveloped, free camping spots in between. Contact the Forest Service for more information.* • **Lake Alpine Lodge:** (209) 753-6358

🏪 Local Outdoor Retailers:
Big 5 Sporting Goods, Placerville, CA (530) 295-8290 • **Instant Replay,** Diamond Springs, CA (530) 642-9077 • **Ken's Sports & Equipment,** Camino, CA (530) 644-3181 • **Mountain & Surf Pro Shop,** Placerville, CA (530) 622-3034 • **Play It Again Sports,** Jackson, CA (209) 223-1223 • **Raymond's Liquor & Sporting,** Placerville, CA 95667 (530) 622-3606 • **Victory Sporting Goods,** Jackson, CA (209) 257-1630

Ⓝ Maps:
USGS maps: Pacific Valley, CA; Spicer Meadow Reservoir, CA

50

South Grove Trail

Hike Specs

Start: From the South Grove Trail trailhead
Length: 4.8-mile loop
Approximate Hiking Time: 2.5–3 hours
Difficulty Rating: Easy due to little elevation change and good trail
Terrain: Dirt path through an old-growth giant sequoia and second-growth pine forest
Elevation Gain: 834 feet
Land Status: State park
Nearest Town: Arnold, CA
Other Trail Users: Hikers only
Canine Compatibility: Dogs not permitted

Getting There

From Stockton: Drive east about 55 miles to Angels Camp on CA 4, and continue another 23 miles on the same highway to Calaveras Big Trees State Park. The park entrance is on the right (south) side of the road. From the park entrance station, drive straight 8.3 miles to the South Grove parking area. The trail starts on the south side of the lot.
DeLorme: Northern California Atlas & Gazetteer: Page 99 B5

There is something about California and record-breaking trees. Not only does the state have the world's oldest living trees (the Bristlecone pines in the White Mountains of the Inyo National Forest), but it also has the tallest (the coast redwoods) and the biggest in sheer volume (the giant sequoias). Also known as Sierra redwoods or simply *big trees*, these are the trees that put the "big" in Calaveras Big Trees State Park. The giant sequoias (*Sequoiadendron giganteum*) are the largest living things on earth, weighing as much as 4,000 pounds. Although giant sequoias can reach 300-plus feet in height, they are on average slightly shorter than their North Coast cousins, the coast redwoods. It's the sequoias' greater circumference and more massive build that give them their weight advantage. Base diameters of 20 feet are common, and the Agassiz Tree—the largest in the park—is 25 feet in diameter.

As far back as 10,000 years ago, the area in and around the park was home to a Native American tribe of northern Sierra Miwok. European-American settlers who arrived en masse in the 19th Century found that the Miwok were already using the area seasonally for the gathering of food. The Miwok were obviously aware of the huge trees that grew here, but the sequoia did not figure heavily in their culture. When European explorers first stumbled across the trees, they were considerably more impressed.

Names found carved in one of the trees indicate that white men visited the North Grove as early as 1850. But the amazing trees were still relatively unknown until 1852, when Augustus T. Dowd called outside attention to them. In any case, it didn't take long for the sequoias' existence to put the nearby town of Murphys on the map. An improved stage road and hotel were built by the mid 1850s, allowing tourists to access what is now the park's North Grove. The grove soon was acquired and developed by James Sperry and John Perry, who turned it into a thriving tourist

attraction—complete with a "drive-through-tree." The area gained further prominence when humorist Samuel Langhorne Clemens, better known as Mark Twain, wrote about the time he spent here during the 1860s in his famous short story "The Celebrated Jumping Frog of Calaveras County." The North Grove finally was added to the state park system in 1931 as Calaveras Big Trees State Park. Later additions brought the South Grove under park protection.

Hike Information

Trail Contacts:
Calaveras Big Trees State Park, Arnold, CA (209) 795-2334

Schedule:
Open year round, sunrise to sunset. Road from main park buildings to South Grove is closed from mid November to mid April, depending on snow.

Fees/Permits:
$2 entrance fee for day-use

Local Information:
Calaveras County Chamber of Commerce, Angels Camp, CA (209) 736-2580 or www.calaveras.org • Angels Camp Business Association, Angels Camp, CA (209) 736-0049 or www.angelscamp.net

Local Events/Attractions:
Bear Valley Music Festival, late July and early August, Bear Valley, CA (209) 753-2574 or 1-800-458-1618 • Living History Days in Angels Camp, in mid May, Angels Camp, CA (209) 736-0049 • Calaveras County Fair and Jumping Frog Jubilee, in May, Frogtown, CA: www.frogtown.org

Accommodations:
Calaveras Big Trees State Park, Arnold, CA – There is plenty of camping in the state park, as well as in the surrounding national forest. Call 1-800-444-7275 to reserve state park campsites.

Organizations:
Calaveras Big Trees Association, Arnold, CA (209) 795-3840 or www.bigtrees.org

Local Outdoor Retailers:
Ebbetts Pass Sporting Goods, Arnold, CA (209) 795-1686 • Sierra Nevada Adventure Co, Arnold, CA (209) 795-9310 • White Pines Outdoors, Arnold, CA (209) 795-1054 • Pinecrest Sports Shop, Pinecrest, CA (209) 965-3637 • Big 5 Sporting Goods, Sonora, CA (209) 536-9257 • SNAC New & Used Gear, Sonora, CA (209) 532-7365 • Sports Connection, Sonora, CA (209) 533-4949 • Sportsman, Sonora, CA (209) 532-1716 • S & S Gear, Twain Harte, CA (209) 586-6500

Maps:
USGS maps: Boards Crossing, CA; Stanislaus, CA; Crandall Peak, CA

The trail explores this area in an oblong loop that heads up the south side of South Grove Creek and returns along the other side. A spur trail leads farther upstream to some of the more impressive sequoias, including the park's reigning king, the Agassiz Tree. The area has been the scene of past logging, which spared the sequoias but removed most of the other species' old-growth specimens. Fortunately for present and future generations, the giant sequoias had a tendency to shatter when felled and were never considered a profitable lumber tree. The sequoias in the South Grove look somewhat out of place, and all the more immense, without other tall trees around them: They often grow far apart and are separated only by patches of second-growth mixed forest. The giants dwarf these smaller trees, but it takes a human form standing at the base to give a true sense of scale.

Ancestors of the giant sequoia—which were remarkably similar to the present population—grew seven million years ago in the warm, humid Pliocene forests of western Nevada and eastern California. They were plentiful then, but weather changes over the years made life increasingly difficult for the sequoias. As the climate grew drier, the trees began to *migrate*, growing farther westward and disappearing from

MilesDirections

0.0 START at the South Grove Trail trailhead. The trail heads downhill past a large sign and across a small meadow.

0.3 The trail crosses Beaver Creek on an arched footbridge. Just past the bridge, Bradley Grove Trail heads left. Continue straight on South Grove Trail.

1.0 The trail crosses a dirt road and continues up the bank on the other side.

1.3 This point marks the start of the loop portion of the trail. Take the right fork, up the south side of the grove.

1.4 The trail crosses a small wooden footbridge.

1.5 The first giant sequoias appear along the trail. They're hard to miss.

2.1 At the hollow log, the trail turns left and crosses Big Trees Creek via another footbridge.

2.2 To the left is the return loop to the trailhead. Turn right onto the Agassiz Spur to see the park's record holding giant sequoia.

2.6 The Agassiz Tree is on the right. This is the largest tree in the park. *[FYI. The largest tree in the world—also a giant sequoia—is in Sequoia-Kings Canyon National Park.]* Turn around and return to the last junction.

3.0 Back at the junction, continue straight for the return loop through the north side of the grove.

3.5 Reach the end of the loop. Retrace the first part of the trail to the trailhead and parking lot.

4.8 Arrive back at the trailhead.

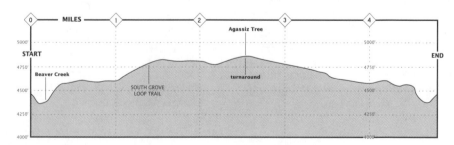

their former home range. At the same time, the land that would become the Sierra Nevada range was rising. The sequoias managed to make it over the Sierra while the mountains were still less than 3,000 feet tall. Then came the onset of glaciation. As glaciers plowed down through the larger river valleys, they subdivided the giant sequoia forest into isolated groves. The sequoias never reestablished themselves—even long after the glaciers melted—largely because of cold air drainage in those deep valleys. Over time, the trees have adapted to the dry summers and cold winters of the western Sierra. They really had no choice but to evolve, because the trees are more or less trapped here. They cannot grow higher, because it is too cold. And they cannot go lower, because it is too dry. So the giant sequoias cling to flats and mild grades on the middle slopes of the Sierra Nevada, where there is just enough water and just enough warmth. Like sharks, horseshoe crabs, and Dick Clark, they are truly ambassadors from another age.

The Agassiz Tree.

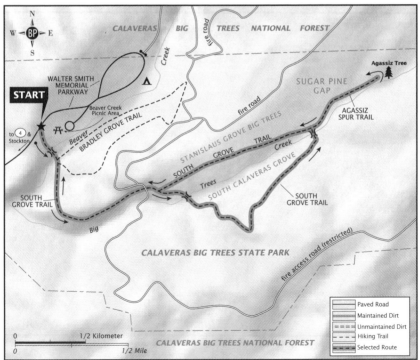

Honorable Mentions

Sierra Nevada & Gold Country

Compiled here is an index of great hikes in the Sierra Nevada and Gold Country region that didn't make the A-list this time around but deserve recognition. Check them out and let us know what you think. You may decide that one or more of these hikes deserves higher status in future editions or, perhaps, you may have a hike of your own that merits some attention.

(L) Western States Pioneer Express Trail

An easy 3.0-mile out-and-back along the wild banks of the Middle Fork of the American River. From Ruck-A-Chucky Campground, the trail follows the north bank of the river, past Ruck-A-Chucky Falls, one of the most dangerous stretches of whitewater on the river. From Sacramento, head east on I-80, exiting at the Auburn-Forest Hill Road, just east of Auburn. Continue east on this road eight miles, and turn right on Drivers Flat Road and follow it down 2.5 miles to the Ruck-A-Chucky Campground. For more information contact: Auburn State Recreation Area, Auburn, CA (530) 885–4527. *DeLorme: Northern California Atlas & Gazetteer:* Page 87 A7

(M) Waterfall Trail (at Grover Hot Springs)

A short 1.5-mile out-and-back hike from the campground to a scenic waterfall. From South Lake Tahoe, head south on CA 50 to CA 89 and south 24 miles to Markleeville. In town, turn right on Hot Springs Road and drive four miles to the park. Turn right into the campground and follow the road along the meadow to a small parking lot and trailhead. The trail heads up-valley, then follows the left fork of the trail up to the waterfall. Check out the hot springs while you're here. For more information contact: Grover Hot Springs State Park, Markleeville, CA (530) 694–2248. *DeLorme: Northern California Atlas & Gazetteer:* Page 90 C2

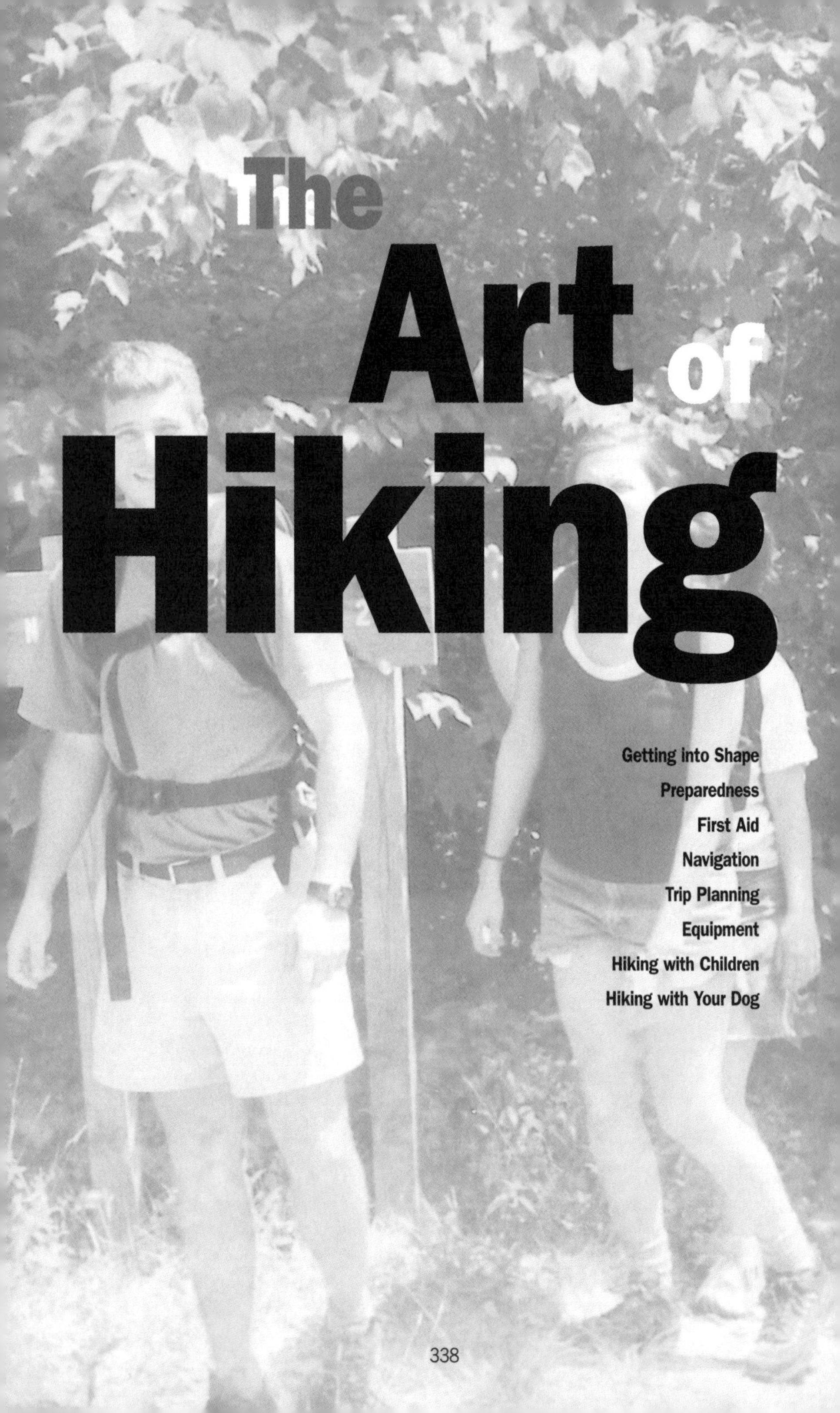

The Art of Hiking

Getting into Shape
Preparedness
First Aid
Navigation
Trip Planning
Equipment
Hiking with Children
Hiking with Your Dog

The Art of Hiking

When standing nose to snout with a grizzly, you're probably not too concerned with the issue of ethical behavior in the wild. No doubt you're just wetting yourself. But let's be honest. How often are you nose to snout with a grizzly? For most of us, a hike into the "wild" means loading up the 4-Runner with everything North Face® and driving to a toileted trailhead. Sure, you can mourn how civilized we've become—how GPS units have replaced natural instinct and Gore-Tex®, true-grit—but the silly gadgets of civilization aside, we have plenty of reason to take pride in how we've matured. With survival now on the back-burner, we've begun to reason—and it's about time—that we have a responsibility to protect, no longer just conquer, our wild places; that *they*, not *we*, are at risk. So please, do what you can. Now, in keeping with our chronic tendency to reduce everything to a list, here are some rules to remember.

Zero impact. Always leave an area just like you found it—if not better than you found it. Avoid camping in fragile, alpine meadows and along the banks of streams and lakes. Use a camp stove versus building a wood fire. Pack up all of your trash and extra food. Bury human waste at least 100 feet from water sources under six to eight inches of topsoil. Don't bathe with soap in a lake or stream—use prepackaged moistened towels to wipe off sweat and dirt or bathe in the water without soap.

Stay on the trail. It's true, a path anywhere leads nowhere new, but purists will just have to get over it. Paths serve an important purpose; they limit our impact on natural areas. Straying from a designated trail may seem innocent but it can cause damage to sensitive areas—damage that may take years to recover, if it can recover at all. Even simple shortcuts can be destructive. So, please, stay on the trail.

Keep your dog under control. You can buy a flexi-lead that allows your dog to go exploring along the trail, while allowing you the ability to reel him in should another hiker approach or should he decide to chase a rabbit. Always obey leash laws and be sure to bury your dog's waste or pack it in resealable plastic bags.

Yield to horses. When you approach these animals on the trail, always step quietly off the trail and let them pass. If you are wearing a large backpack, it's a good idea to sit down. From a horse's perspective, a hiker wearing a large backpack is a scary trail monster and these sensitive animals can be spooked easily.

GETTING INTO SHAPE

Unless you want to be sore—and possibly have to shorten your trip or vacation—be sure to get in shape before a big hike. If you're terribly out of shape, start a walking program early, preferably eight weeks in advance. Start with a 15-minute walk during your lunch hour or after work and gradually increase your walking time to an hour. You should also increase your elevation gain. Walking briskly up hills really strengthens your leg muscles and gets your heart rate up. If you work in a storied office building, take the stairs instead of the elevator. If you prefer going to a gym, walk the treadmill or use a stair-master. You can further increase your strength and endurance by walking with a loaded backpack. Stationary exercises you might consider are squats, leg lifts, sit-ups, and push-ups. Other good ways to get in shape include biking, running, aerobics, and, of course, short hikes.

PREPAREDNESS

It's been said that failing to plan means planning to fail. So do take the necessary time to plan your trip. Whether going on a short day hike or an extended backpack trip, always prepare for the worst. Simply remembering to pack a copy of the *U.S. Army Survival Manual* is not preparedness. Although it's not a bad idea if you plan on entering truly wild places, it's merely the tourniquet answer to a problem. You need to do your best to prevent the problem from arising in the first place. These days the word "survival" is often replaced with the pathetically feeble term "comfort." In order to remain comfortable (and to survive if you really want to push it), you need to concern yourself with the basics: water, food, and shelter. Don't go on a hike without having these bases covered. And don't go on a hike expecting to find these items in the woods.

Water. Even in frigid conditions, you need at least two quarts of water a day to function efficiently. Add heat and taxing terrain and you can bump that figure up to one gallon. That's simply a base to work from—your metabolism and your level of conditioning can raise or lower that amount. Unless you know your level, assume that you need one gallon of water a day. Now, where do you plan on getting the water?

Preferably not from natural water sources. These sources can be loaded with intestinal disturbers, such as bacteria, viruses, and fertilizers. *Giardia lamblia*, the most common of these disturbers, is a protozoan parasite that lives part of its lifecycle as a cyst in water sources. The parasite spreads when mammals defecate in water sources. Once ingested, Giardia can induce cramping, diarrhea, vomiting, and fatigue within two days to two weeks after ingestion. Giarda is treatable with the prescription drug Flagyl. If you believe you've contracted Giardia, see a doctor immediately.

Treating Water. The best and easiest solution to avoid polluted water is to carry your water with you. Yet, depending on the nature of your hike and the duration, this may not be an option—seeing as one gallon of water weighs 8.5 pounds. In that case,

you'll need to look into treating water. Regardless of which method you choose, you should always carry *some* water with you, in case of an emergency. Save this reserve until you absolutely need it.

There are three methods of treating water: boiling, chemical treatment, and filtering. If you boil water, it's recommended that you do so for 10 to 15 minutes. This is often impractical because you're forced to exhaust a great deal of your fuel supply. You can opt for chemical treatment (e.g. Potable Aqua) which will kill Giardia but will not take care of other chemical pollutants. Another drawback to chemical treatments is the unpleasant taste of the water after it's treated. You can remedy this by adding powdered drink mix to the water. Filters are the preferred method for treating water. Filters remove Giardia, organic and inorganic contaminants, and don't leave an aftertaste. Water filters are far from perfect as they can easily become clogged or leak if a gasket wears out. It's always a good idea to carry a backup supply of chemical treatment tablets in case your filter decides to quit on you.

Food. If we're talking about "survival," you can go days without food, as long as you have water. But we're talking about "comfort" here. Try to avoid foods that are high in sugar and fat like candy bars and potato chips. These food types are harder to digest and are low in nutritional value. Instead, bring along foods that are easy to pack, nutritious, and high in energy (e.g. bagels, nutrition bars, dehydrated fruit, gorp, and jerky). If you are on an overnight trip, easy-to-fix dinners include rice mixes with dehydrated potatoes, corn pasta with cheese sauce, and soup mixes. For a tasty breakfast, you can fix hot oatmeal with brown sugar and reconstituted milk powder topped off with banana chips. If you like a hot drink in the morning, bring along herbal tea bags or hot chocolate. If you are a coffee junkie, you can purchase coffee that is packaged like tea bags. You can pre-package all of your meals in heavy-duty resealable plastic bags to keep food from spilling in your pack. These bags can be reused to pack out trash.

Shelter. The type of shelter you choose depends less on the conditions than on your tolerance for discomfort. Shelter comes in many forms—tent, tarp, lean to, bivy sack, cabin, cave, etc. If you're camping in the desert, a bivy sack may suffice, but if you're above the treeline and a storm is approaching, a better choice is a three or four season tent. Tents are the logical and most popular choice for most backpackers as they're lightweight and packable—and you can rest assured that you always have shelter from the elements. *[See Equipment: Tents on page 337]* Before you leave on your trip, anticipate what the weather and terrain will be like and plan for the type of shelter that will work best for your comfort level.

Finding a campsite. If there are established campsites, stick to those. If not, start looking for a campsite early—like around 3:30 or 4:00 pm. Stop at the first decent site you see. Depending on the area, it could be a long time before you find another suitable location. Pitch your camp in an area that's level. Make sure the area is at least 200 feet from fragile areas like lakeshores, meadows, and stream banks. And try to avoid areas thick in underbrush, as they can harbor insects and provide cover for approaching animals.

If you are camping in stormy, rainy weather, look for a rock outcrop or a shelter in the trees to keep the wind from blowing your tent all night. Be sure that you don't camp under trees with dead limbs that might break off on top of you. Also, try to find an area that has an absorbent surface, such as sandy soil or for-

est duff. This, in addition to camping on a surface with a slight angle, will provide better drainage. By all means, don't dig trenches to provide drainage around your tent—remember you're practicing minimum-impact camping.

If you're in bear country, steer clear of creekbeds or animal paths. If you see any signs of a bear's presence (i.e. scat, footprints), relocate. You'll need to find a campsite near a tall tree where you can hang your food and other items that may attract bears such as deodorant, toothpaste, or soap. Carry a lightweight nylon rope with which to hang your food. As a rule, you should hang your food at least 20 feet from the ground and five feet away from the tree trunk. You can put food and other items in a waterproof stuff sack and tie one end of the rope to the stuff sack. To get the other end of the rope over the tree branch, tie a good size rock to it and gently toss the rock over the tree branch. Pull the stuff sack up until it reaches the top of the branch and tie it off securely. Don't hang your food near your tent! If possible, hang your food at least 100 feet away from your campsite. Alternatives to hanging your food are bear-proof plastic tubes and metal bear boxes.

Lastly, think of comfort. Lie down on the ground where you intend to sleep and see if it's a good fit. For morning warmth (and a nice view to wake up to), have your tent face east.

FIRST AID

I know you're tough, but get 10 miles into the woods and develop a blister and you'll wish you had carried that first aid kit. Face it, it's just plain good sense. Many companies produce light-weight, compact first aid kits, just make sure yours contains at least the following:

First Aid

- band aids
- mole skin
- various sterile gauze and dressings
- white surgical tape
- an Ace bandage
- an antihistamine
- aspirin
- Betadine® solution
- a first-aid book
- Tums®
- tweezers
- scissors
- anti-bacterial wipes
- triple-antibiotic ointment
- plastic gloves
- sterile cotton tip applicators
- syrup of ipecac (to induce vomiting)
- a thermometer
- a wire splint

Here are a few tips to dealing with and hopefully preventing certain ailments.

Sunburn. Sunburn: In most parts of Northern California, summer sun can be an intense and constant companion on hikes. If you burn, it is a good idea to take along sunscreen or sun block, protective clothing, and a wide-brimmed hat. If you do get a sunburn, treat the area with aloe vera gel and protect the area from further sun exposure. At higher elevations, the sun's radiation can be particularly damaging to skin, as it is filtered by less of the earth's atmosphere before it reaches you. Remember your eyes are vulnerable to this radiation as well. Sunglasses can be a good way to prevent headaches and permanent eye damage from the sun, especially in places where light-colored rock or patches of snow reflect light up in your face.

Blisters. Be prepared to take care of these hike-spoilers by carrying moleskin (a lightly padded adhesive), gauze and tape, or Band-Aids. An effective way to apply moleskin is to cut out a circle of moleskin and remove the center—like a donut—and place it over the blistered area. Cutting the center out will reduce the pressure applied to the sensitive skin. Other products that can help you combat blisters are Bodyglide® and Second Skin®. Bodyglide® (1–888–263–9454) is applied to suspicious hot spots before a blister forms to help decrease friction to that area. Second Skin® (made by Spenco) is applied to the blister after it has popped and acts as a "second skin" to help prevent further irritation.

Insect bites and stings. You can treat most insect bites and stings by applying hydrocortisone 1% cream topically and taking a pain medication such as ibuprofen or acetaminophen to reduce swelling. If you forgot to pack these items, a cold compress or a paste of mud and ashes can sometimes assuage the itching and discomfort. Remove any stingers by using tweezers or scraping the area with your fingernail or a knife blade. Don't pinch the area as you'll only spread the venom.

Some hikers are highly sensitive to bites and stings and may have a serious allergic reaction that can be life threatening. Symptoms of a serious allergic reaction can include wheezing, an asthmatic attack, and shock. The treatment for this severe type of reaction is epinephrine (Adrenaline). If you know that you are sensitive to bites and stings, carry a pre-packaged kit of epinephrine (e.g., Anakit®), which can be obtained only by prescription from your doctor.

Ticks. As you well know, ticks can carry disease, such as Rocky Mountain Spotted Fever and Lyme disease. The best defense is, of course, prevention. If you know you're going to be hiking through an area littered with ticks, wear long pants and a long sleeved shirt. You can apply a permethrin repellent to your clothing and a DEET repellent to exposed skin. At the end of your hike, do a spot check for ticks (and insects in general). If you do find a tick, coat the insect with Vaseline® or tree sap to cut off its air supply. The tick should release its hold, but if it doesn't, grab the head of the tick firmly—with a pair of tweezers if you have them—and gently pull it away from the skin with a twisting motion. Sometimes the mouthparts linger, embedded in your skin. If this happens, try to remove them with a disinfected needle. Clean the affected area with an anti-bacterial cleanser and then apply triple antibiotic ointment. Monitor the area for a few days. If irritation persists or a white spot develops, see a doctor for possible infection.

Poison ivy, oak, and sumac. These skin irritants can be found most anywhere in North America and come in the form of a bush or a vine, having leaflets in groups of three, five, seven, or nine. Learn how to spot the plants. The oil they secrete can cause an allergic reaction in the form of blisters, usually about 12 hours after exposure. The itchy rash can last from ten days to several weeks. The best defense against these irritants is to wear protective clothing and to apply a non-prescription product called IvyBlock® to exposed skin. This lotion is meant to guard against the affects of poison ivy/oak/sumac and can be washed off with soap and water. Taking a hot shower after you return home from your hike will also help to remove any lin-

poison oak

poison ivy

gering oil from your skin. Should you contract a rash from any of these plants, use Benadryl® or a similar product to reduce the itching. If the rash is localized, create a light Clorox®/water wash to dry up the area. If the rash has spread, either tough it out or see your doctor about getting a dose of Cortisone® (available both orally and by injection).

poison sumac

Snakebites. First off, snakebites are rare in North America. Unless startled or provoked, the majority of snakes will not bite. If you are wise to their habitats and keep a careful eye on the trail, you should be just fine. Though your chances of being struck are slim, it's wise to know what to do in the event you are.

If a *non-poisonous* snake bites you, allow the wound to bleed a small amount and then cleanse the wounded area with a Betadine® solution (10% povidone iodine). Rinse the wound with clean water (preferably) or fresh urine (it might sound ugly, but it's sterile). Once the area is clean, cover it with triple antibiotic ointment and a clean bandage. Remember, most residual damage from snakebites, poisonous or otherwise, comes from infection, not the snake's venom. Keep the area as clean as possible and get medical attention immediately.

If you are bitten by a *poisonous* snake, remove the toxin with a suctioning device, found in a snakebite kit. If you do not have such a device, squeeze the wound—do NOT use your mouth for suction as the venom will enter your bloodstream through the vessels under the tongue and head straight for your heart. Then, clean the wound just as you would a non-poisonous bite. Tie a clean band of cloth snuggly around the afflicted appendage, about an inch or so above the bite (or the rim of the swelling). This is NOT a tourniquet—you want to simply slow the blood flow, not cut it off. Loosen the band if numbness ensues. Remove the band for a minute and re-apply a little higher every ten minutes

If it is your friend who's been bitten, treat him or her for shock—make him comfortable, have him lie down, elevate the legs, and keep him warm. Avoid applying anything cold to the bite wound. Immobilize the affected area and remove any constricting items such as rings, watches, or restrictive clothing—swelling may occur. Once your friend is stable and relatively calm, hike out to get help. The victim should get treatment within 12 hours, ideally, which usually consists of a tetanus shot, antivenin, and antibiotics.

Now, if you are alone and struck by a poisonous snake, stay calm. Hysteria will only quicken the venom's spread. Follow the procedure above and do your best to reach help. When hiking out, don't run—you'll only increase the flow of blood throughout your system. Instead, walk calmly.

California has six poisonous snakes—all of them rattlesnakes. Of these, only the Western rattlesnake is common to Northern California. Although occasionally found as high as 11,000 feet above sea level, rattlesnakes are rare above 5,000 feet. Snakes generally leave the area when they feel the ground vibrations of approaching hikers, but care should be taken when in rattlesnake country. Rattlesnakes will not usually bite unless provoked or surprised. Pay particular attention in areas of dense brush and jumbled rocks, and watch where you put your hands and feet. When stepping over logs, first step on the log, making sure you can see what's on the other side before stepping down.

Scorpions and Spiders: Other creepy-crawlies exist in Northern California which hikers should be aware of. Black widow spiders are found in woodpiles and debris, as well as sheltered locations in buildings. Only the female of the species bites, and the bite can be very painful, and in rare cases fatal. Black widows are about ½ inch, and shiny black with a red hourglass mark on the underside of the abdomen. Small scorpions, up to 1½ inches long are occasionally found here also. The sting of these animals is very painful, but not especially dangerous. Take care when picking up rocks, and when sitting or sleeping on loose stone debris.

Dehydration. Have you ever hiked in hot weather and had a roaring headache and felt fatigued after only a few miles? More than likely you were dehydrated. Symptoms of dehydration include fatigue, headache, and decreased coordination and judgment. When you are hiking, your body's rate of fluid loss depends on the outside temperature, humidity, altitude, and your activity level. On average, a hiker walking in warm weather will lose four liters of fluid a day. That fluid loss is easily replaced by normal consumption of liquids and food. However, if a hiker is walking briskly in hot, dry weather and hauling a heavy pack, he can lose one to three liters of water an hour. It's important to always carry plenty of water and to stop often and drink fluids regularly, even if you aren't thirsty.

Heat exhaustion is the result of a loss of large amounts of electrolytes and often occurs if a hiker is dehydrated and has been under heavy exertion. Common symptoms of heat exhaustion include cramping, exhaustion, fatigue, lightheadedness, and nausea. You can treat heat exhaustion by getting out of the sun and drinking an electrolyte solution made up of one teaspoon of salt and one tablespoon of sugar dissolved in a liter of water. Drink this solution slowly over a period of one hour. Drinking plenty of fluids (preferably an electrolyte solution like Gatorade®) can prevent heat exhaustion. Avoid hiking during the hottest parts of the day and wear breathable clothing, a wide brimmed hat, and sunglasses.

Hypothermia is one of the biggest dangers in the backcountry—especially for day hikers in the summertime. That may sound strange, but imagine starting out on a hike in mid-summer when it's sunny and 80 degrees out. You're clad in nylon shorts and a cotton T-shirt. About halfway through your hike, the sky begins to cloud up and in the next hour a light drizzle begins to fall and the wind starts to pick up. Before you know it, you are soaking wet and shivering—the perfect recipe for hypothermia. More advanced signs include decreased coordination, slurred speech, and blurred vision. When a victim's temperature falls below 92 degrees Fahrenheit, the blood pressure and pulse plummet, possibly leading to coma and death.

To avoid hypothermia, always bring a windproof/rainproof shell, a fleece jacket, Capilene® tights, gloves, and hat when you are hiking in the mountains. Learn to adjust your clothing layers based on the temperature. If you are climbing uphill at a moderate pace you will stay warm, but when you stop for a break you'll become cold quickly, unless you add more layers of clothing.

If a hiker is showing advanced signs of hypothermia, dress him in dry clothes and make sure he is wearing a hat and gloves. Place him in a sleeping bag in a tent or shelter that will protect him from the wind and other elements. Give him warm fluids to drink and keep him awake.

Frostbite. When the mercury dips below 32 degrees Fahrenheit, your extremities begin to chill. If a persistent chill attacks a localized area, say your hands or your toes, the circulatory system reacts by cutting off blood flow to the affected area—the idea being to protect and preserve the body's overall temperature. And so it's death by attrition for the affected area. Ice crystals start to form from the water in the cells of the neglected tissue. Deprived of heat, nourishment, and now water, the tissue literally starves. This is frostbite.

Prevention is your best defense against this situation. Most prone to frostbite are your face, hands, and feet—so protect these areas well. Wool is the material of choice because it provides ample air space for insulation and draws moisture away from the skin. However, synthetic fabrics have recently made great strides in the cold weather clothing market. Do your research. A pair of light silk liners under your regular gloves is a good trick to keeping warm. They afford some additional warmth, but more importantly they'll allow you to remove your mitts for tedious work without exposing the skin.

Now, if your feet or hands start to feel cold or numb due to the elements, warm them as quickly as possible. Place cold hands under your armpits or bury them in your crotch. If your feet are cold, change your socks. If there's plenty of room in your boots, add another pair of socks. Do remember though that constricting your feet in tight boots can restrict blood flow and actually make your feet colder more quickly. Your socks need to have breathing room if they're going to be effective. Dead air provides insulation. If your face is cold, place your warm hands over your face or simply wear a head stocking (called a balaclava).

Should your skin go numb and start to appear white and waxy, chances are you've got or are developing frostbite. Don't try to thaw the area unless you can maintain the warmth. In other words, don't stop to warm up your frostbitten feet only to head back on the trail. You'll do more damage than good. Tests have shown that hikers who walked on thawed feet did more harm, and endured more pain, than hikers who left the affected areas alone. Do your best to get out of the cold entirely and seek medical attention—which usually consists of performing a rapid rewarming in water for 20 to 30 minutes.

The overall objective in preventing both hypothermia and frostbite is to keep the body's core warm. Protect key areas where heat escapes, like the top of the head, and maintain the proper nutrition level. Foods that are high in calories aid the body in producing heat. Never smoke or drink when you're in situations where the cold is threatening. By affecting blood flow, these activities ultimately cool the body's core temperature.

Altitude sickness (AMS). The high lofty peaks, clear alpine lakes, and vast mountain views beckon hikers to the high country. Those who like to venture high may become victims of altitude sickness (also known as Acute Mountain Sickness—AMS). Altitude sickness is your body's reaction to the sudden decline of oxygen levels. While some hikers may feel lightheaded, nauseous, and experience shortness of breath at 7,000 feet, others may not experience these symptoms until they reach 10,000 feet or higher.

Slowing your ascent to high places and giving your body a chance to acclimatize to the higher elevations can prevent altitude sickness. For example, if you live at sea level and are planning a weeklong backpacking trip to elevations between 7,000 and 10,000 feet, be sure to camp a few days above 7,000 feet to give your body a chance to adjust to the new altitude. The prescription drug Diamox can help to prevent altitude sickness, but keep in mind that this drug does nothing to relieve the symptoms of AMS once you get it.

Most hikers who experience AMS develop a headache and nausea and grow lethargic. Advanced signs include slurred speech, severe incoordination, a rapid pulse, and pulmonary edema—fluid in the lungs. The treatment for AMS is simple; descend to lower elevations. Once a victim descends about 1,000 feet, his signs will usually begin to diminish.

NAVIGATION

Whether you are going on a short hike in a familiar area or planning a weeklong backpack trip, you should always be equipped with the proper navigational equipment—at the very least a detailed map and a sturdy compass.

Maps. There are many different types of maps available to help you find your way on the trail. Easiest to find are Forest Service maps and BLM (Bureau of Land Management) maps. These maps tend to cover large areas, so be sure they are detailed enough for your particular trip. You can also obtain National Park maps as well as high quality maps from private companies and trail groups. These maps can be obtained either from outdoor stores or ranger stations.

U.S. Geological Survey topographic maps are particularly popular with hikers—especially serious backcountry hikers. These maps contain the standard map symbols such as roads, lakes, and rivers, as well as contour lines that show the details of the trail terrain like ridges, valleys, passes, and mountain peaks. The 7.5-minute series (1 inch on the map equals approximately two-fifths of a mile on the ground) provides the closest inspection available. USGS maps are available by mail (U.S. Geological Survey, Map Distribution Branch, PO Box 25286, Denver, Colorado 80225) or you can visit them online at *http://mapping.usgs.gov/esic/to_order.html.*

If you want to check out the high tech world of maps, you can purchase topographic maps on CD-ROM. These software-mapping programs let you select a route on your computer, print it out, and then take it with you on the trail. Some software mapping programs let you insert symbols and labels, download waypoints from a GPS unit, and export the maps to other software programs. Mapping software programs such as DeLorme's TopoUSA™ (*www.delorme.com*) and MAPTECH's Terrain Navigator™ (*www.maptech.com*) let you do all of these things and more.

The art of map reading is a skill that you can develop by first practicing in an area you are familiar with. To begin, orient the map so the map is lined up in the correct direction (i.e. north on the map is lined up with true north). Next, familiarize yourself with the map symbols and try and match them up with terrain features around you such

347

as a high ridge, mountain peak, river, or lake. If you are practicing with an USGS map notice the contour lines. On gentler terrain these contour lines are spaced further apart, and on steeper terrain they are closer together. Pick a short loop trail and stop frequently to check your position on the map. As you practice map reading, you'll learn how to anticipate a steep section on the trail or a good place to take a rest break, etc.

The Compass. First off, the sun is not a substitute for a compass. So, what kind of compass should you have? Here are some characteristics you should look for: a rectangular base with detailed scales, a liquid-filled housing, protective housing, a sighting line on the mirror, luminous alignment and back-bearing arrows, a luminous north-seeking arrow, and a well-defined bezel ring.

You can learn compass basics by reading the detailed instructions included with your compass. If you want to fine-tune your compass skills, sign up for an orienteering class or purchase a book on compass reading. Once you've learned the basic skills on using a compass, remember to practice these skills before you head into the backcountry.

If you are a klutz at using a compass, you may be interested in checking out the technical wizardry of the **GPS (Global Positioning System)** device. The GPS was developed by the Pentagon and works off 24 NAVSTAR satellites, which were designed to guide missiles to their targets. A GPS device is a handheld unit that calculates your latitude and longitude with the easy press of a button. The Department of Defense used to scramble the satellite signals a bit to prevent civilians (and spies!) from getting extremely accurate readings, but that practice was discontinued in 2000 and GPS units now provide nearly pinpoint accuracy.

There are many different types of GPS units available and they range in price from $100 to $400. In general, all GPS units have a display screen and keypad where you input information. In addition to acting as a compass, the unit allows you to plot your route, easily retrace your path, track your travelling speed, find the mileage between waypoints, and calculate the total mileage of your route.

Before you purchase a GPS unit, keep in mind that these devices don't pick up signals indoors, in heavily wooded areas, on mountain peaks, or in deep valleys.

A **pedometer** is a handy device that can track your mileage as you hike. This device is a small, clip-on unit with a digital display that calculates your hiking dis-

Magellan GPS unit.

tance in miles or kilometers based on your walking stride. Some units also calculate the calories you burn and your total hiking time. Pedometers are available at most large outdoor stores and range in price from $20 to $40.

TRIP PLANNING

Planning your hiking adventure begins with letting a friend or relative know your trip itinerary so they can call for help if you don't return at your scheduled time. Your next task is to make sure you are outfitted to experience the risks and rewards of the trail. This section highlights gear and clothing you may want to take with you to get the most out of your hike.

Day Hikes

- camera/film
- compass/GPS unit
- pedometer
- daypack
- first-aid kit
- food
- guidebook
- headlamp/flashlight with extra batteries and bulbs
- hat
- insect repellant
- knife/multi-purpose tool
- map
- matches in waterproof container and fire starter
- polar fleece jacket
- raingear
- space blanket
- sunglasses
- sunscreen
- swim suit
- watch
- water
- water bottles/water hydration system

EQUIPMENT

With the outdoor market currently flooded with products, many of which are pure gimmickry, it seems impossible to both differentiate and choose. Do I really need a tropical-fish-lined collapsible shower? (No, you don't.) The only defense against the maddening quantity of items thrust in your face is to think practically— and to do so *before* you go shopping. The worst buys are impulsive buys. Since most of your name brands will differ only slightly in quality, it's best to know what you're looking for in terms of function. Buy only what you need. You will, don't forget, be carrying what you've bought on your back. Here are some things to keep in mind before you go shopping.

Clothes. Clothing is your armor against Mother Nature's little surprises. Weather in Northern California can range from blistering heat to brutal cold, and hikers should be prepared for any possibility, especially when hiking in mountainous areas. Adequate rain protection and extra layers of clothing are a good idea. In summer, a wide-brimmed hat can help keep the sun at bay. In the winter months the first layer you'll want to wear is a "wicking" layer of long underwear that keeps perspiration away from your skin. Wearing long underwear made from synthetic fibers such as Capilene®, CoolMax®, or Thermax is an excellent choice. These fabrics wick moisture away from the skin and draw it toward the next layer of clothing where it then evaporates. Avoid wearing long underwear made of cotton as it is slow to dry and keeps moisture next to your skin.

The second layer you'll wear is the "insulating" layer. Aside from keeping you warm, this layer needs to "breathe" so you stay dry while hiking. A fabric that provides insulation and dries quickly is fleece. It's interesting to note that this one-of-a-kind fabric is made out of recycled plastic. Purchasing a zip-up jacket made of this material is highly recommended.

The last line of layering defense is the "shell" layer. You'll need some type of waterproof, windproof, breathable jacket that'll fit over all of your other layers. It should have a large hood that fits over a hat. You'll also need a good pair of

Overnight Trips

- backpack and waterproof rain cover
- backpacker's trowel
- bandanna
- bear repellant spray
- bear bell
- biodegradable soap
- pot scrubber
- collapsible water container (2-3 gallon capacity)
- clothing—extra wool socks, shirt and shorts
- cook set/utensils
- ditty bags to store gear
- extra plastic resealable bags
- gaiters
- garbage bag
- ground cloth
- journal/pen
- nylon rope to hang food
- long underwear
- permit (if required)
- rain jacket and pants
- sandals to wear around camp and to ford streams
- sleeping bag
- waterproof stuff sack
- sleeping pad
- small bath towel
- stove and fuel
- tent
- toiletry items
- water filter
- whistle

rain pants made from a similar waterproof, breathable fabric. A fabric that easily fits the bill is Gore-Tex®. However, while a quality Gore-Tex® jacket can range in price from $100 to $450, you should know that there are more affordable fabrics out there that work just as well.

Now that you've learned the basics of layering, you can't forget to protect your hands and face. In cold, windy, or rainy weather you'll need a hat made of wool or fleece and insulated, waterproof gloves that will keep your hands warm and toasty. As mentioned earlier, buying an additional pair of light silk liners to wear under your regular gloves is a good idea. They'll allow you to remove your outer-gloves for tedious work without exposing the skin.

During the summer, your main consideration is protecting your skin from sunburn and poison oak that can be found in many parts of Northern California. Wearing long pants and a long sleeve shirt made out of materials such as Supplex® nylon will protect your skin from the damaging rays of the sun and from any poison oak that may be lurking along the trail.

Footwear. If you have any extra money to spend on your trip, put that money into boots or trail shoes. Poor shoes will bring a hike to a halt faster than anything else. To avoid this annoyance, buy shoes that provide support and are lightweight and flexible. A lightweight hiking boot is better than a heavy, leather mountaineering boot for most day hikes and backpacking. Trail running shoes provide a little extra cushion and are made in a high-top style that many people wear for hiking. These running shoes are lighter, more flexible, and more breathable than hiking boots. If you know you'll be hiking in wet weather often, purchase boots or shoes with a Gore-Tex® liner, which will help keep your feet dry.

When buying your boots, be sure to wear the same type of socks you'll be wearing on the trail. If the boots you're buying are for cold weather hiking, try the boots on while wearing two pairs of socks. Speaking of socks, a good cold weather sock combination is to wear a thinner sock made of wool or polypropylene covered by a heavier outer sock made of wool. The inner sock protects the foot from the rubbing effects of the outer sock and prevents blisters.

Once you've purchased your footwear, be sure to break them in before you hit the trail. New footwear is often stiff and needs to be stretched and molded to your foot.

Backpacks. No matter what type of hiking you do you'll need a pack of some sort to carry the basic trail essentials. There are a variety of backpacks on the market, but let's first discuss what you intend to use it for. Day hikes or overnight trips?

If you plan on doing a day hike, a daypack should have some of the following characteristics: a padded hip belt that's at least two inches in diameter (avoid packs with only a small nylon piece of webbing for a hip belt); a chest strap (the chest strap helps stabilize the pack against your body); external pockets to carry water and other items that you want easy access to; an internal pocket to hold keys, a knife, a wallet, and other miscellaneous items; an external lashing system to hold a jacket; and a hydration pocket for carrying a hydration system (which consists of a water bladder with an attachable drinking hose).

For short hikes, some hikers like to use a fanny pack to store just a camera, food, a compass, a map, and other trail essentials. Most fanny packs have pockets for two water bottles and a padded hip belt.

courtesy Johnson Coleman

If you intend to do an extended, overnight trip, there are multiple considerations. First off, you need to decide what kind of framed pack you want. There are two backpack types for backpacking: the internal frame and the external frame. An internal frame pack rests closer to your body, making it more stable and easier to balance when hiking over rough terrain. An external frame pack is just that, an aluminum frame attached to the exterior of the pack. An external frame pack is better for long backpack trips because it distributes the pack weight better and you can carry heavier loads. It's easier to pack, and your gear is more accessible. It also offers better back ventilation in hot weather.

The most critical measurement for fitting a pack is torso length. The pack needs to rest evenly on your hips without sagging. A good pack will come in two or three sizes and have straps and hip belts that are adjustable according to your body size and characteristics.

When you purchase a backpack, go to an outdoor store with salespeople who are knowledgeable in how to properly fit a pack. Once the pack is fitted for you, load the pack with the amount of weight you plan on taking on the trail. The weight of the pack should be distributed evenly and you should be able to swing your arms and walk briskly without feeling out of balance. Another good technique for evaluating a pack is to walk up and down stairs and make quick turns to the right and to the left to be sure the pack doesn't feel out of balance.

Other features that are nice to have on a backpack include a removable day pack or fanny pack, external pockets for extra water, and extra lash points to attach a jacket or other items.

Sleeping bags and pads. Sleeping bags are rated by temperature. You can purchase a bag made of synthetic fiber such as Polarguard® HV or DuPont Hollofil® II, or you can buy a goose down bag. Goose down bags are more expensive, but they have a higher insulating capacity by weight and will keep their loft longer. You'll want to purchase a bag with a temperature rating that fits the time of year and conditions you are most likely to camp in. One caveat: the techno-standard for temperature ratings is far from perfect. Ratings vary from manufacturer to manufacturer, so to protect yourself you should purchase a bag rated 10 to 15 degrees below the temperature you expect to be camping in. Synthetic bags are more resistant to water than down bags, but many down bags are now made with a Gore-Tex® shell that helps to repel water. Down bags are also more compressible than synthetic bags and take up less room in your pack, which is an important consideration if you are planning a multi-day backpack trip. Features to look for in a sleeping bag include: a mummy style bag, a hood you can cinch down around your head in cold weather, and draft tubes along the zippers that help keep heat in and drafts out.

You'll also want a sleeping pad to provide insulation and padding from the cold ground. There are different types of sleeping pads available, from the more expensive self-inflating air mattresses to the less expensive closed-cell foam pads (e.g., Ridge Rest®). Self-inflating air mattresses are usually heavier than closed-cell foam mattresses and are prone to punctures.

courtesy Eureka

Tents. The tent is your home away from home while on the trail. It provides protection from wind, snow, rain, and insects. A three-season tent is a good choice for backpacking and can range in price from $100 to $500. These lightweight and versatile tents provide protection in all types of weather, except heavy snowstorms or high winds, and range in weight from four to eight pounds. Look for a tent that's easy to set up and will easily fit two people with gear. Dome type tents usually offer more headroom and places to store gear. Other tent designs include a vestibule where you can store wet boots and backpacks. Some nice-to-have items in a tent include interior pockets to store small items and lashing points to hang a clothesline. Most three-season tents also come with stakes so you can secure the tent in high winds. Before you purchase a tent, set it up and take it down a few times to be sure it is easy to handle. Also, sit inside the tent and make sure it has enough room for you and your gear.

HIKING WITH CHILDREN

Hiking with children isn't a matter of how many miles you can cover or how much elevation gain you make in a day, it's about seeing and experiencing nature through their eyes.

Kids like to explore and have fun. They like to stop and point out bugs and plants, look under rocks, jump in puddles, and throw sticks. If you're taking a toddler or young child on a hike, start with a trail that you're familiar with. Trails that have interesting things for kids, like piles of leaves to play in or a small stream to wade through during the summer, will make the hike much more enjoyable for them and will keep them from getting bored.

You can keep your child's attention if you have a strategy before starting on the trail. Using games is not only an effective way to keep a child's attention, it's also a great way to teach him or her about nature. Play hide and seek, where your child is the mouse and you are the hawk. Quiz children on the names of plants and animals. If your children are old enough, let them carry their own daypack filled with snacks and water. So that you are sure to go at their pace and not yours, let them lead the way. Playing follow the leader works particularly well when you have a group of children. Have each child take a turn at being the leader.

With children, a lot of clothing is key. The only thing predictable about weather is that it will change. Especially in mountainous areas, weather can change dramatically in a very short time. Always bring extra clothing for children, regardless of the season. In the winter, have your children wear wool socks, and warm layers such as long underwear, a polar fleece jacket and hat, wool mittens, and good rain gear. It's not a bad idea to have these along in late fall and early spring as well. Good footwear is also

important. A sturdy pair of high top tennis shoes or lightweight hiking boots are the best bet for little ones. If you're hiking in the summer near a lake or stream, bring along a pair of old sneakers that your child can put on when he wants to go exploring in the water. Remember when you're near any type of water, always watch your child at all times. Also, keep a close eye on teething toddlers who may decide a rock or leaf of poison oak is an interesting item to put in their mouth.

courtesy Johnson Outdoors

From spring through fall, you'll want your kids to wear a wide brimmed hat to keep their face, head, and ears protected from the hot sun. Also, make sure your children wear sunscreen at all times. Choose a brand without Paba—children have sensitive skin and may have an allergic reaction to sunscreen that contains Paba. If you are hiking with a child younger than six months, don't use sunscreen or insect repellant. Instead, be sure that their head, face, neck, and ears are protected from the sun with a wide brimmed hat, and that all other skin exposed to the sun is protected with the appropriate clothing.

Remember that food is fun. Kids like snacks so it's important to bring a lot of munchies for the trail. Stopping often for snack breaks is a fun way to keep the trail interesting. Raisins, apples, granola bars, crackers and cheese, Cheerios, and trail mix all make great snacks. If your child is old enough to carry his/her own backpack, fill it with treats before you leave. If your kids don't like drinking water, you can bring boxes of fruit juice.

Avoid poorly designed child-carrying packs—you don't want to break your back carrying your child. Most child-carrying backpacks designed to hold a 40-pound child will contain a large carrying pocket to hold diapers and other items. Some have an optional rain/sun hood. Tough Traveler® (1–800–GO–TOUGH or *www.toughtraveler.com*) is a company that specializes in making backpacks for carrying children and other outdoor gear for children.

HIKING WITH YOUR DOG

Bringing your furry friend with you is always more fun than leaving him behind. Our canine pals make great trail buddies because they never complain and always make good company. Hiking with your dog can be a rewarding experience, especially if you plan ahead.

Getting your dog in shape. Before you plan outdoor adventures with your dog, make sure he's in shape for the trail. Getting your dog into shape takes the same discipline as getting yourself into shape, but luckily, your dog can get in shape with you. Take your dog with you on your daily runs or walks. If there is a park near your house, hit a tennis ball or play Frisbee with your dog.

Swimming is also an excellent way to get your dog into shape. If there is a lake or river near where you live and your dog likes the water, have him retrieve a tennis ball or stick. Gradually build your dog's stamina up over a two to three month period. A good rule of thumb is to assume that your dog will travel twice as far as you will on the trail. If you plan on doing a five-mile hike, be sure your dog is in shape for a ten-mile hike.

Training your dog for the trail. Before you go on your first hiking adventure with your dog, be sure he has a firm grasp on the basics of canine etiquette and behavior. Make sure he can sit, lay down, stay, and come. One of the most important commands you can teach your canine pal is to "come" under any situation. It's easy for your friend's nose to lead him astray or possibly get lost. Another helpful command is the "get behind" command. When you're on a hiking trail that's narrow, you can have your dog follow behind you when other trail users approach. Nothing is more bothersome than an enthusiastic dog that runs back and forth on the trail and disrupts the peace of the trail for others. When you see other trail users approaching you on the trail, give them the right of way by quietly stepping off the trail and making your dog lie down and stay until they pass.

Equipment. The most critical pieces of equipment you can invest in for your dog are proper identification and a sturdy leash. Flexi-leads work well for hiking because they give your dog more freedom to explore but still leave you in control. Make sure your dog has identification that includes your name and address and a number for your veterinarian. Other forms of identification for your dog include a tattoo or a microchip. You should consult your veterinarian for more information on these last two options.

The next piece of equipment you'll want to consider is a pack for your dog. By no means should you hold all of your dog's essentials in your pack—let him carry his own gear! Dogs that are in good shape can carry up to 30 percent to 40 percent of their own weight.

Companies that make good quality packs include RuffWear™ (1–888–RUFF–WEAR; *www.ruffwear.com*) and Wolf Packs® (1–541–482–7669; *www.wolfpacks.com*). Most packs are fitted by a dog's weight and girth measurement. Companies that make dog packs generally include guidelines to help you pick out the size that's right for your dog. Some characteristics to look for when purchasing a pack for your dog include: a harness that contains two padded girth straps, a padded chest strap, leash attachments, removable saddle bags, internal water bladders, and external gear cords.

You can introduce your dog to the pack by first placing the empty pack on his back and letting him wear it around the yard. Keep an eye on him during this first introduction. He may decide to chew through the straps if you aren't watching him closely. Once he learns to treat the pack as an object of fun and not a foreign enemy, fill the pack evenly on both sides with a few ounces of dog food in resealable plastic bags. Have your dog wear his pack on your daily walks for a period of two to three weeks. Each week add a little more weight to the pack until your dog will accept carrying the maximum amount of weight he can carry.

You can also purchase collapsible water and dog food bowls for your dog. These bowls are lightweight and can easily be stashed into your pack or your dog's. If you are hiking on rocky terrain or in the snow, you can purchase footwear for your dog that will protect his feet from cuts and bruises. All of these products can be purchased from RuffWear™ (1–888–RUFF–WEAR; *www.ruffwear.com*).

The following is a checklist of items to bring when you take your dog hiking: collapsible water bowls, a comb, a collar and a leash, dog food, a dog pack, flea/tick powder, paw protection, water, and a First Aid kit that contains eye ointment, tweezers, scissors, stretchy foot wrap, gauze, antibacterial wash, sterile cotton tip applicators, antibiotic ointment, and cotton wrap.

First aid for your dog. Your dog is just as prone—if not more prone—to getting in trouble on the trail as you are, so be prepared. Here's a run down of the more likely misfortunes that might befall your little friend.

Bees and wasps. If a bee or wasp stings your dog, remove the stinger with a pair of tweezers and place a mudpack or a cloth dipped in cold water over the affected area.

Heat stroke. Avoid hiking with your dog in really hot weather. Dogs with heat stroke will pant excessively, lie down and refuse to get up, and become lethargic and disoriented. If your dog shows any of these signs on the trail, have him lie down in the shade. If you are near a stream, pour cool water over your dog's entire body to help bring his body temperature back to normal.

Heartworm. Dogs get heartworms from mosquitoes which carry the disease in the prime mosquito months of July and August. Giving your dog a monthly pill prescribed by your veterinarian easily prevents this condition.

Plant pitfalls. One of the biggest plant hazards for dogs on the trail are foxtails. Foxtails are pointed grass seed heads that bury themselves in your friend's fur, between his toes, and even get in his ear canal. If left unattended, these nasty seeds can work their way under the skin and cause abscesses and other problems. If you have a long-haired dog, consider trimming the hair between his toes and giving him a summer haircut to help prevent foxtails from attaching to his fur. After every hike, always look over your dog for these seeds—especially between his toes and his ears.

Other plant hazards include burrs, thorns, thistles, and poison oak. If you find any burrs or thistles on your dog, remove them as soon as possible before they become an unmanageable mat. Thorns can pierce a dog's foot and cause a great deal of pain. If you see that your dog is lame, stop and check his feet for thorns. Dogs are immune to poison oak but they can pick up the sticky, oily substance from the plant and transfer it to you.

Protect those paws. Be sure to keep your dog's nails trimmed so he avoids getting soft tissue or joint injuries. If your dog slows and refuses to go on, check to see that his paws aren't torn or worn. You can protect your dog's paws from trail hazards such as sharp gravel, foxtails, lava scree, and thorns by purchasing dog boots.

Sunburn. If your dog has light skin he is an easy target for sunburn on his nose and other exposed skin areas. You can apply a non-toxic sunscreen to exposed skin areas that will help protect him from over-exposure to the sun.

Ticks and fleas. Ticks can easily give your dog Lyme disease, as well as other diseases. Before you hit the trail, treat your dog with a flea and tick spray or powder. You can also ask your veterinarian about a once-a-month pour-on treatment that repels fleas and ticks.

When you are finally ready to hit the trail with your dog, keep in mind that National Parks and many wilderness areas do not allow dogs on trails. Your best bet is to hike in National forests, BLM lands, and state parks.

Web Sites and Useful Contact Info

National Forests in California (Pacific Southwest Region, Region 5)
www.r5.fs.fed.us
This is the Region 5 home page, with general Forest Service information, and links to the individual National Forests in California. Some permits are available through the internet.

National Park Service
www.nps.gov
General Park Service information, and links to individual National Park web sites. It is possible in some cases to make campground and backcountry permit reservations through the internet.

California State Parks
cal-parks.ca.gov

Bureau of Land Management
www.ca.blm.gov/caso/recreation.html

GORP- Get Outdoor Recreation Pages
www.gorp.com/gorp/activity/hiking/hik_guid.htm
An excellent source of information about recreation opportunities. Although far from complete, there is often more detailed information here than in the government sites.

State of California Resources Agency
ceres.ca.gov/cra/
Links to conservancies, committees, programs and initiatives, and various state agencies that might be of interest to visitors.

California Office of Historic Preservation
ohp.cal-parks.ca.gov
Here is more detailed information about historic buildings and structures in California's State Parks.

California Office of Tourism
gocalif.ca.gov/index2.html
Typical tourist hype, but sometimes useful.

California Snow Conditions
cdec.water.ca.gov/snow/
This site can be helpful when heading for late snow areas. Call the park or forest itself for the most accurate information.

Caltrans
www.dot.ca.gov/
The best source for information on current road conditions.

AAA of Northern CA, Nevada, and Utah
www.csaa.com

The Nature Conservancy
www.tnc.org/

Sierra Club
www.sierraclub.org/

Sempervirens Fund
www.sempervirens.org/

Save-the-redwoods League
www.savetheredwoods.org/

Planning and Conservation League
www.pcl.org/pcl/
"Working to maintain and strengthen environmental laws in California"

Envirolink
www.envirolink.org

American Hiking Society
www.americanhiking.org

Tahoe Rim Trail
www.tahoesbest.com/hiking/trailsbyregion.htm

L

M

N

O

Meet the Author

Dan Brett is a certified wilderness fool. Originally from the Midwest, he was drawn west by the high, lonely call of mountain passes and untamed places. He has worked as a trail crew volunteer in Grand Canyon National Park and Redwood National Park (where he met his wife) and actually got paid to hike around and fix trails in Idaho Panhandle, Inyo, Six Rivers, and Klamath National Forests. When not hiking or writing, he makes music, works wood, builds things, is active politically and environmentally, reads a lot, and generally wishes there were more hours in the day. Dan lives in Arcata with his wife, Mirjam.

Author